Shojo Beat

ORESAMA TEACHER

MIYABI-LOVING STUDENT COUNCIL MEMBERS

ON LEAVE.

Vol. 8

Story & Art by
Izumi Tsubaki

ORESAMA TEACHER

Volume 8
CONTENTS

Chapter 40----------------------3

Chapter 41 -------------------35

Chapter 42-------------------65

Chapter 43-------------------96

Chapter 44------------------129

Chapter 45------------------159

End Notes-------------------191

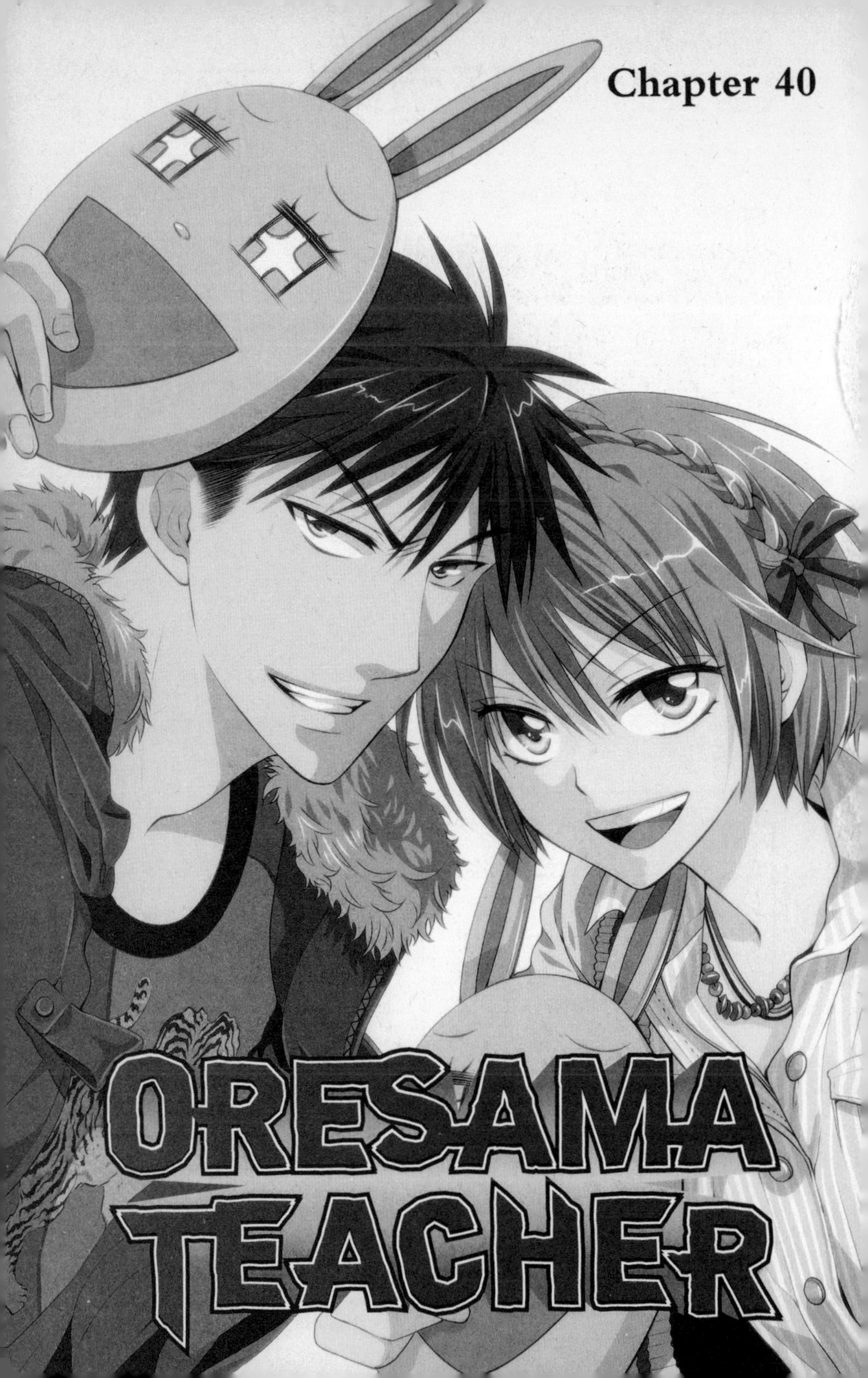
Chapter 40
ORESAMA
TEACHER

THEY REALLY EXIST!

SIDE CHARACTER INTRODUCTION Part 1

WE'RE TAKING A LOOK AT CHARACTERS WHO DIDN'T HAVE NAMES WHEN THEY FIRST APPEARED.

Part 2 is on page 98.

Kohei Kangawa

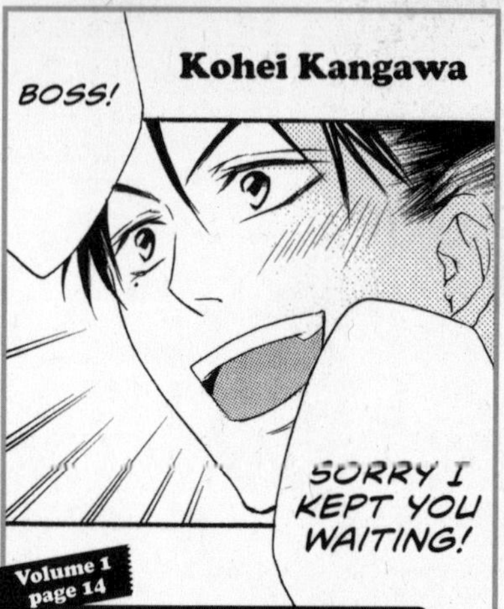
BOSS!
SORRY I KEPT YOU WAITING!

Volume 1 page 14

I WANTED HIM TO APPEAR AGAIN, SO I DREW HIM BETTER THAN THE OTHER THUGS. HE'S IDENTIFIABLE BY THE MOLE UNDER HIS EYE AND HIS DROOPING EYES.

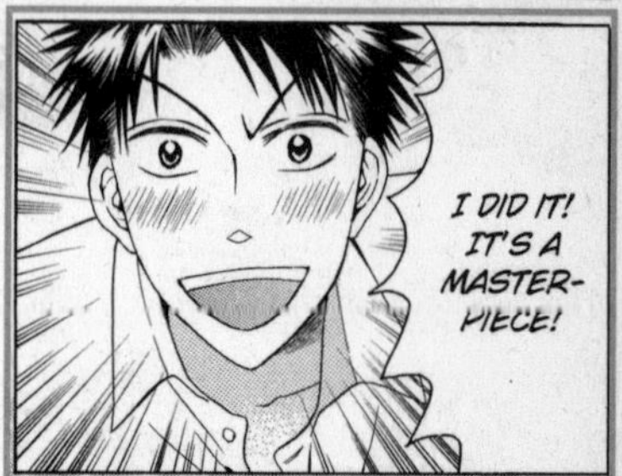
I DID IT! IT'S A MASTER-PIECE!

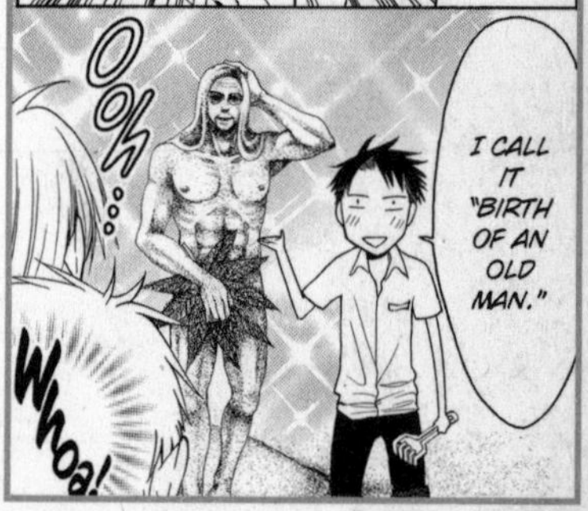
I CALL IT "BIRTH OF AN OLD MAN."
Oooh...
Whoa!

Takumi Yamashita

Volume 4 page 173

HE LOOKS A LOT YOUNGER WHEN HE REAPPEARS IN VOLUME 7. HE'S VERY DEXTEROUS. HE'S IN THE SAME CLASS AS MAIZONO AND OKUBO. THE THREE OF THEM ARE GOOD FRIENDS.

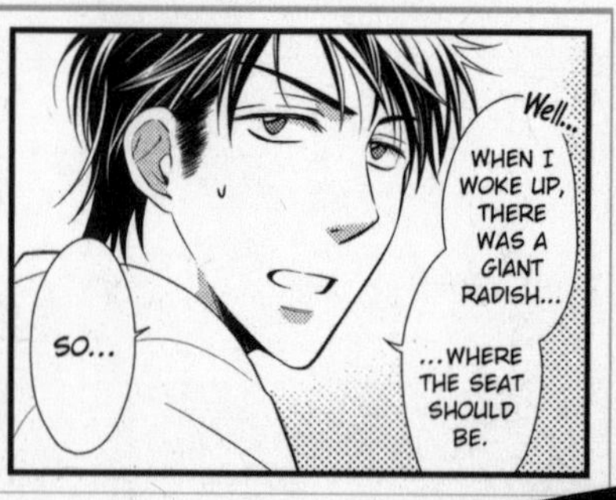
Well...
WHEN I WOKE UP, THERE WAS A GIANT RADISH...
...WHERE THE SEAT SHOULD BE.
SO...

Kotobuki Okubo

Volume 5 page 160

HE FIRST APPEARED IN A FOUR-PANEL STRIP. IN FACT, HE ALMOST EXCLUSIVELY APPEARS IN FOUR-PANEL STRIPS. HE'S AN UNLUCKY BOY. HE'S ALSO AN UNWITTING CHARMER.

ON A SIDE NOTE, OKUBO AND YAMASHITA'S NAMES WERE MENTIONED BEFORE THEY PHYSICALLY APPEARED.

Volume 4 page 143

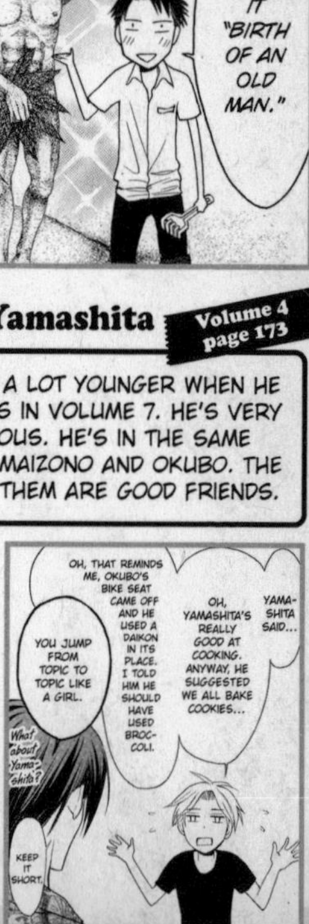
YAMASHITA SAID...
OH, YAMASHITA'S REALLY GOOD AT COOKING. ANYWAY, HE SUGGESTED WE ALL BAKE COOKIES...
OH, THAT REMINDS ME, OKUBO'S BIKE SEAT CAME OFF AND HE USED A DAIKON IN ITS PLACE. I TOLD HIM HE SHOULD HAVE USED BROCCOLI.
YOU JUMP FROM TOPIC TO TOPIC LIKE A GIRL.
What about Yamashita?
KEEP IT SHORT.

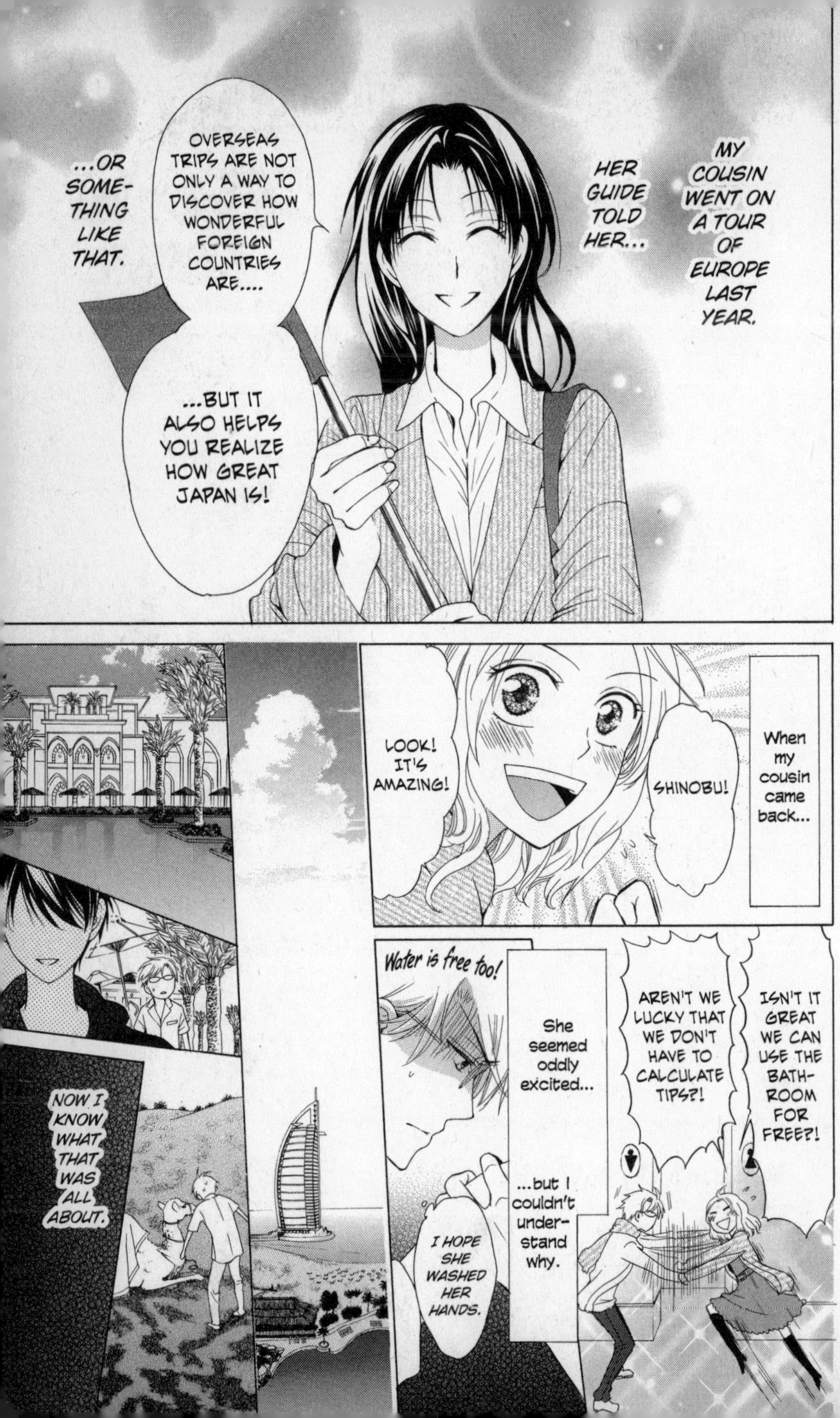
MY COUSIN WENT ON A TOUR OF EUROPE LAST YEAR.
HER GUIDE TOLD HER...
OVERSEAS TRIPS ARE NOT ONLY A WAY TO DISCOVER HOW WONDERFUL FOREIGN COUNTRIES ARE....
...BUT IT ALSO HELPS YOU REALIZE HOW GREAT JAPAN IS!
...OR SOMETHING LIKE THAT.
When my cousin came back...
SHINOBU!
LOOK! IT'S AMAZING!
ISN'T IT GREAT WE CAN USE THE BATH-ROOM FOR FREE?!
AREN'T WE LUCKY THAT WE DON'T HAVE TO CALCULATE TIPS?!
She seemed oddly excited...
...but I couldn't under-stand why.
Water is free too!
I HOPE SHE WASHED HER HANDS.
NOW I KNOW WHAT THAT WAS ALL ABOUT.

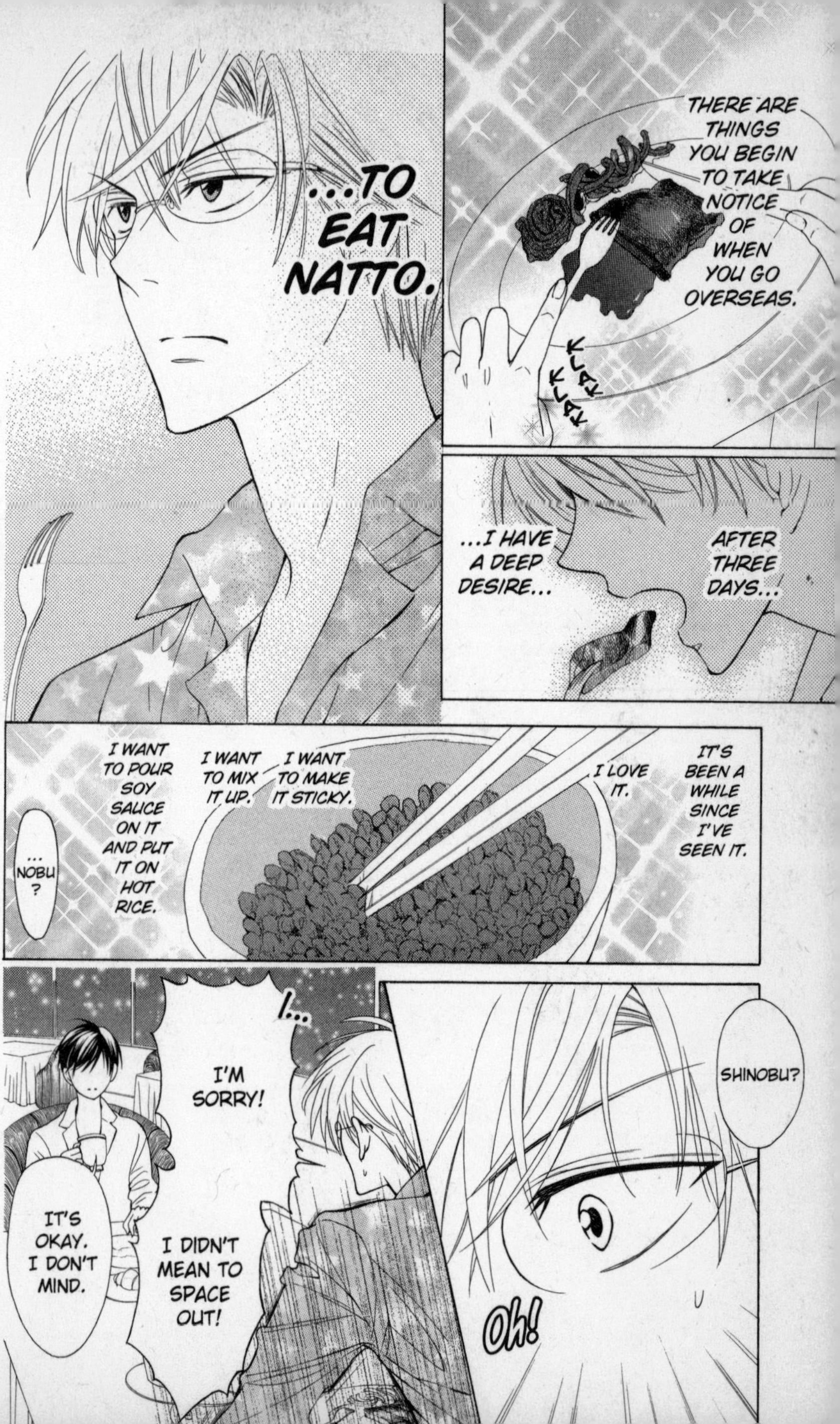
THERE ARE THINGS YOU BEGIN TO TAKE NOTICE OF WHEN YOU GO OVERSEAS.
KLAK KLAK KLAK
AFTER THREE DAYS...
...I HAVE A DEEP DESIRE...
...TO EAT NATTO.
IT'S BEEN A WHILE SINCE I'VE SEEN IT.
I LOVE IT.
I WANT TO MAKE IT STICKY.
I WANT TO MIX IT UP.
I WANT TO POUR SOY SAUCE ON IT AND PUT IT ON HOT RICE.
...NOBU?
SHINOBU?
Oh!
I...
I'M SORRY!
I DIDN'T MEAN TO SPACE OUT!
IT'S OKAY. I DON'T MIND.

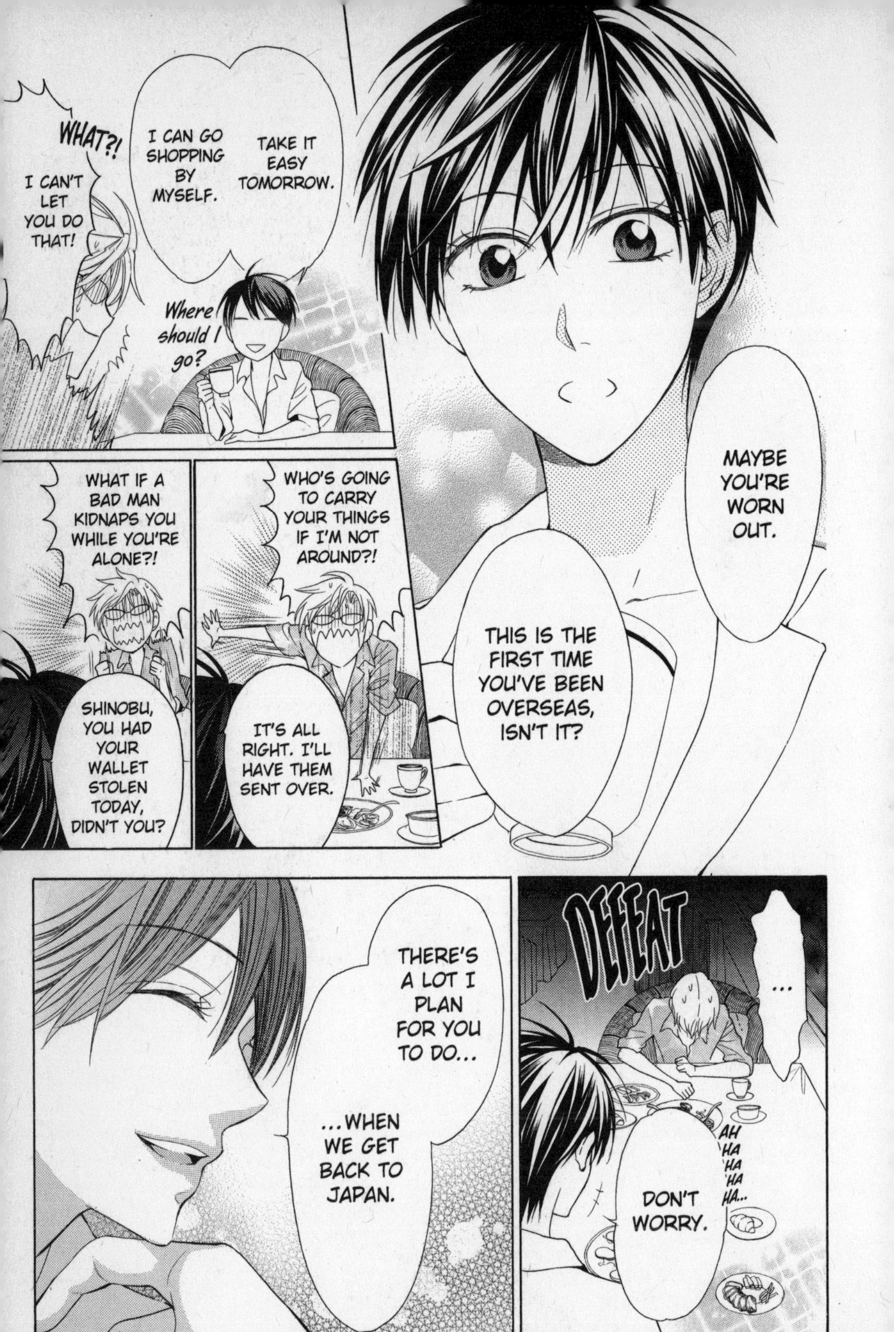
MAYBE YOU'RE WORN OUT.
THIS IS THE FIRST TIME YOU'VE BEEN OVERSEAS, ISN'T IT?
TAKE IT EASY TOMORROW.
I CAN GO SHOPPING BY MYSELF.
Where should I go?
WHAT?!
I CAN'T LET YOU DO THAT!
WHO'S GOING TO CARRY YOUR THINGS IF I'M NOT AROUND?!
IT'S ALL RIGHT. I'LL HAVE THEM SENT OVER.
WHAT IF A BAD MAN KIDNAPS YOU WHILE YOU'RE ALONE?!
SHINOBU, YOU HAD YOUR WALLET STOLEN TODAY, DIDN'T YOU?
DEFEAT
...
AH HA HA HA HA...
DON'T WORRY.
THERE'S A LOT I PLAN FOR YOU TO DO...
...WHEN WE GET BACK TO JAPAN.

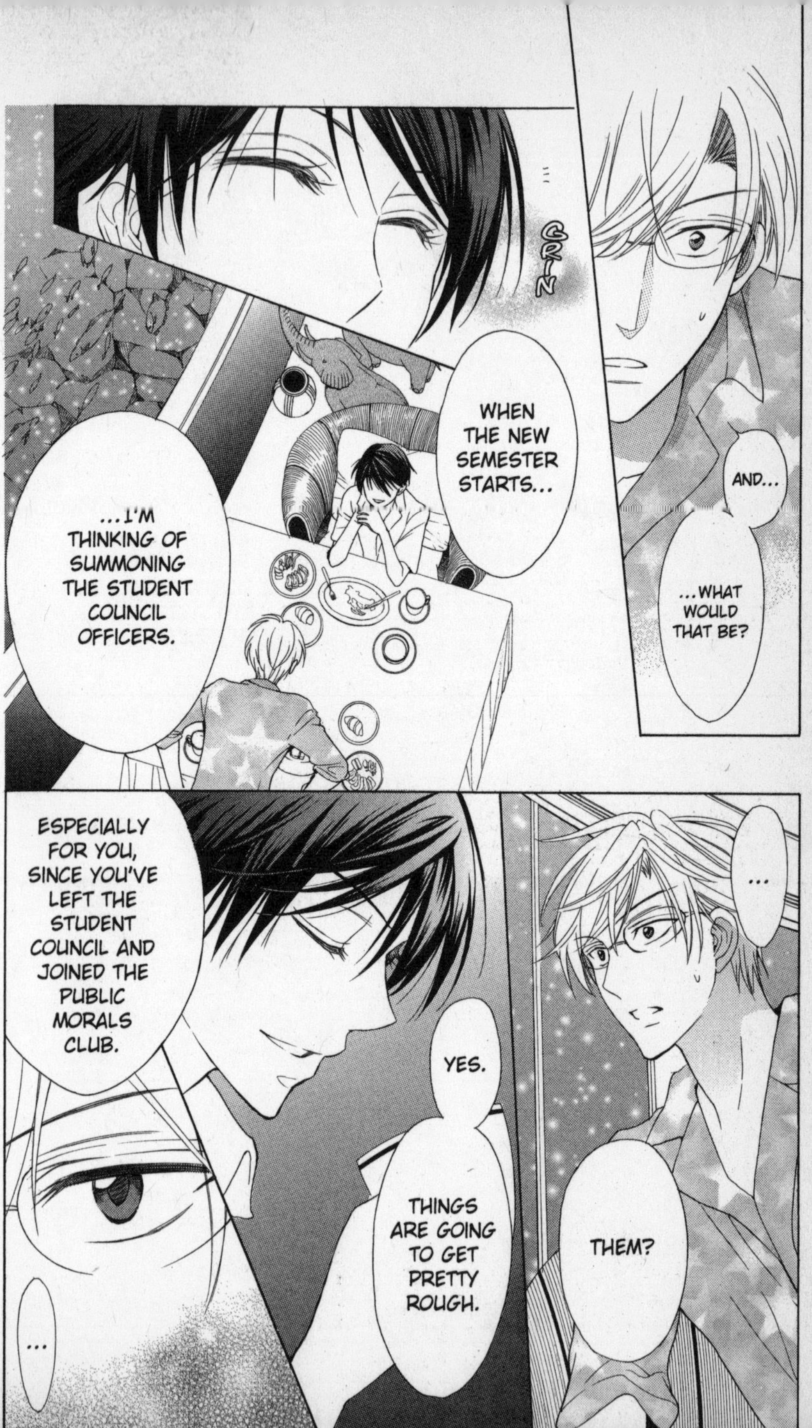
AND...
...WHAT WOULD THAT BE?
GRIN
WHEN THE NEW SEMESTER STARTS...
...I'M THINKING OF SUMMONING THE STUDENT COUNCIL OFFICERS.
...
THEM?
YES.
THINGS ARE GOING TO GET PRETTY ROUGH.
ESPECIALLY FOR YOU, SINCE YOU'VE LEFT THE STUDENT COUNCIL AND JOINED THE PUBLIC MORALS CLUB.
...

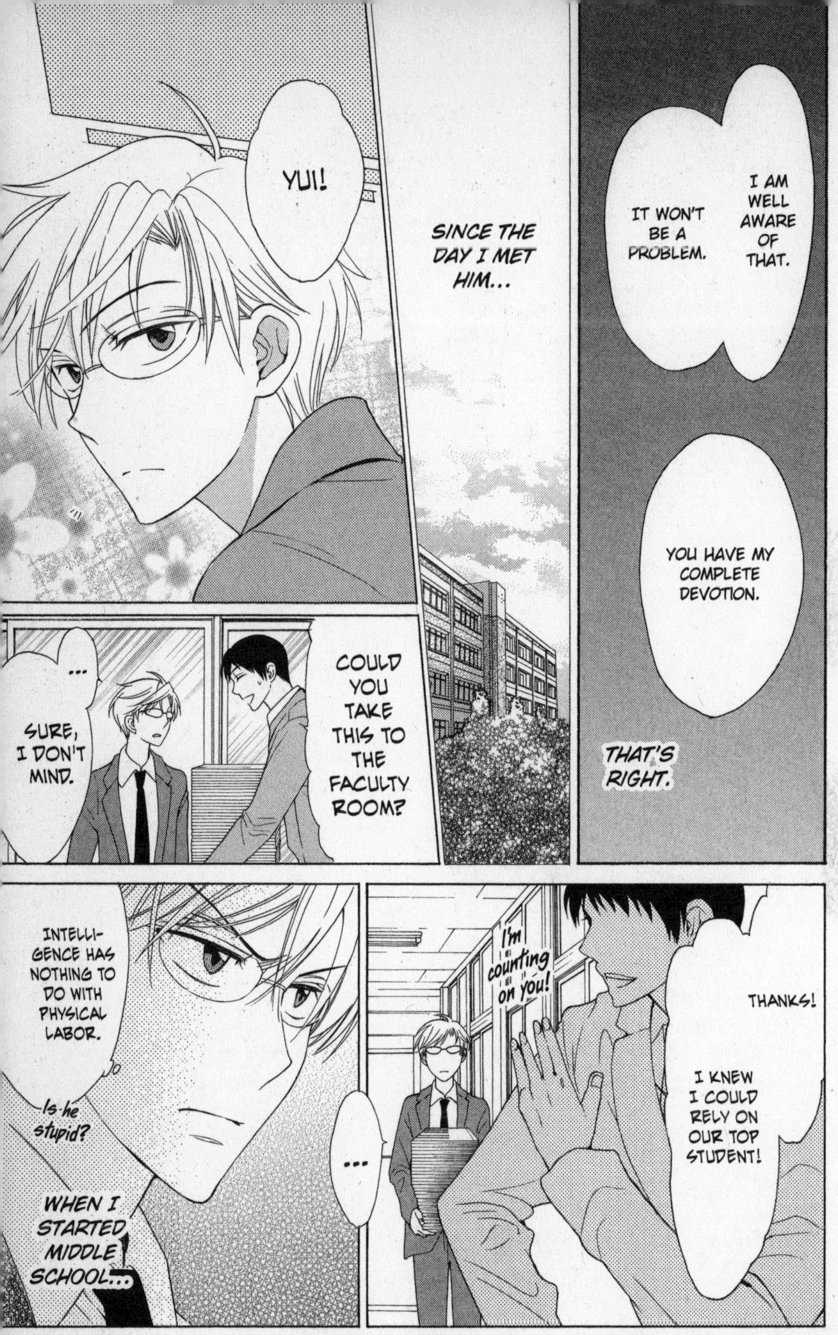
I AM WELL AWARE OF THAT.
IT WON'T BE A PROBLEM.
YOU HAVE MY COMPLETE DEVOTION.
THAT'S RIGHT.
SINCE THE DAY I MET HIM...
YUI!
COULD YOU TAKE THIS TO THE FACULTY ROOM?
...
SURE, I DON'T MIND.
THANKS!
I KNEW I COULD RELY ON OUR TOP STUDENT!
I'm counting on you!
...
INTELLI-GENCE HAS NOTHING TO DO WITH PHYSICAL LABOR.
Is he stupid?
WHEN I STARTED MIDDLE SCHOOL...

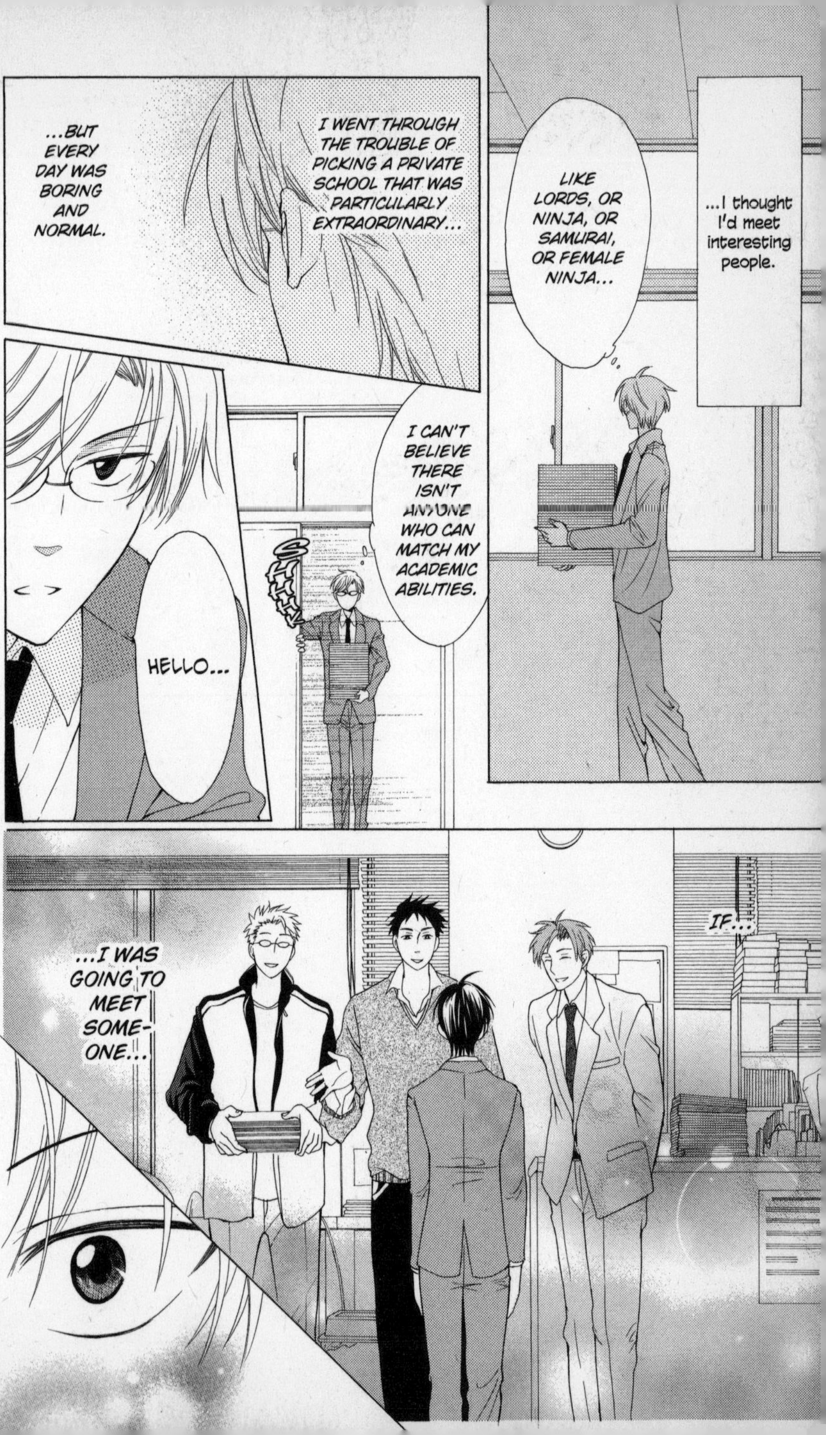
...I thought I'd meet interesting people.
LIKE LORDS, OR NINJA, OR SAMURAI, OR FEMALE NINJA...
I WENT THROUGH THE TROUBLE OF PICKING A PRIVATE SCHOOL THAT WAS PARTICULARLY EXTRAORDINARY...
...BUT EVERY DAY WAS BORING AND NORMAL.
I CAN'T BELIEVE THERE ISN'T ANYONE WHO CAN MATCH MY ACADEMIC ABILITIES.
HELLO...
IF...
...I WAS GOING TO MEET SOME-ONE...

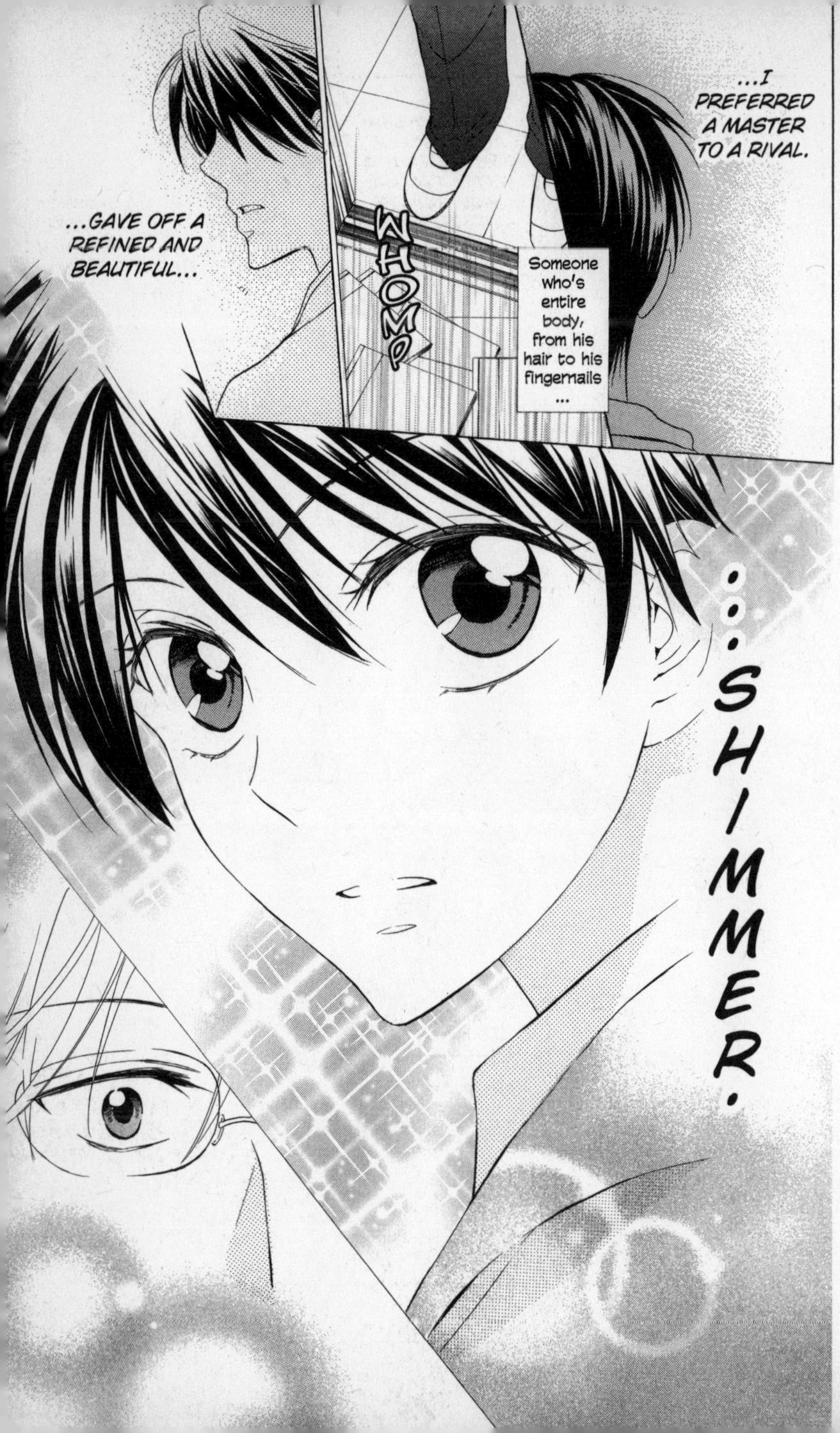
...I PREFERRED A MASTER TO A RIVAL.
Someone who's entire body, from his hair to his fingernails ...
WHOMP
...GAVE OFF A REFINED AND BEAUTIFUL...
...SHIMMER.

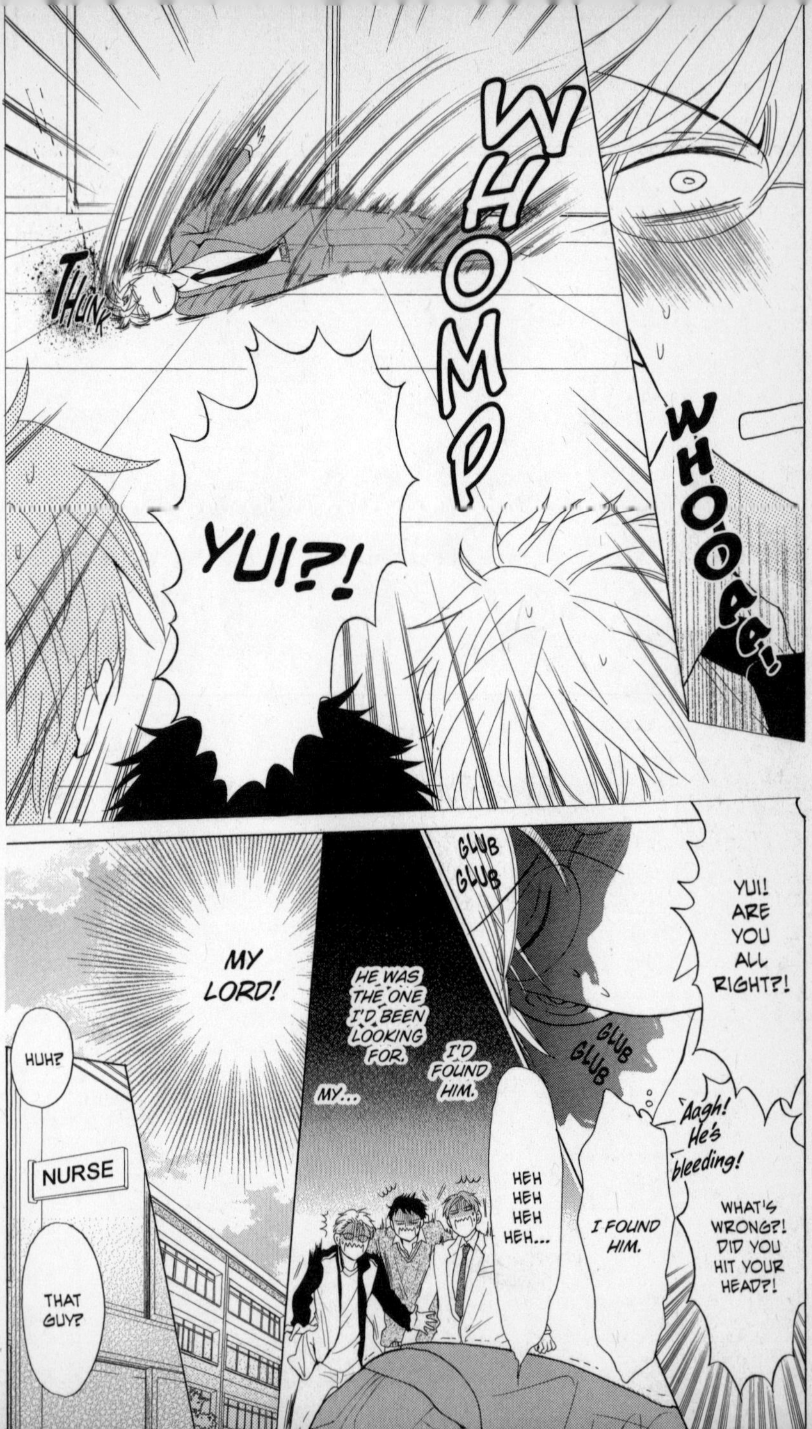
WHOOOAA!
WHOMP
THUNK
YUI?!
GLUB GLUB
YUI! ARE YOU ALL RIGHT?!
GLUB GLUB
Aagh! He's bleeding!
WHAT'S WRONG?! DID YOU HIT YOUR HEAD?!
I FOUND HIM.
HEH HEH HEH HEH...
HE WAS THE ONE I'D BEEN LOOKING FOR.
I'D FOUND HIM.
MY...
MY LORD!
HUH?
NURSE
THAT GUY?

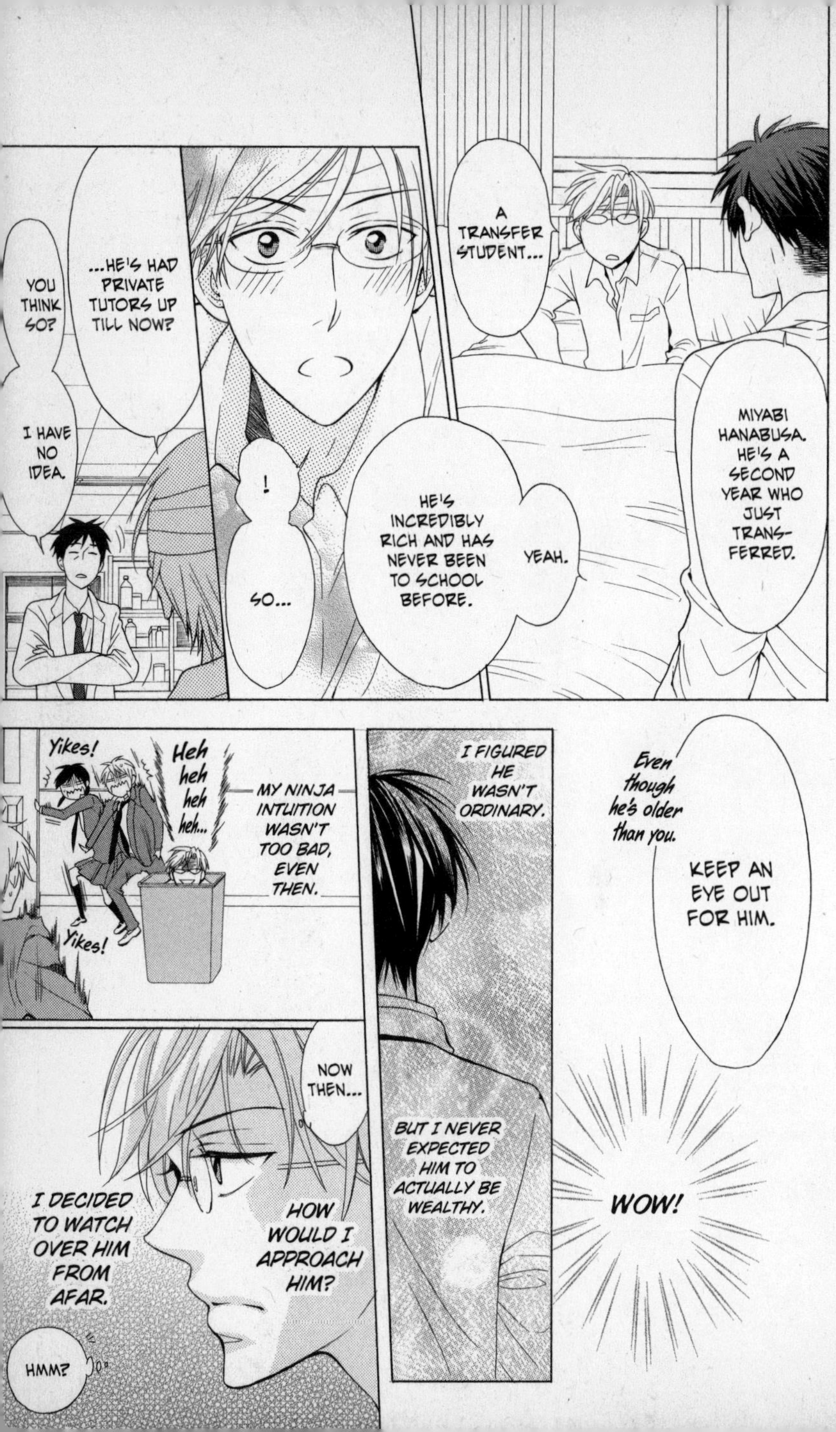
A TRANSFER STUDENT...
MIYABI HANABUSA. HE'S A SECOND YEAR WHO JUST TRANSFERRED.
YEAH.
HE'S INCREDIBLY RICH AND HAS NEVER BEEN TO SCHOOL BEFORE.
!
SO...
...HE'S HAD PRIVATE TUTORS UP TILL NOW?
YOU THINK SO?
I HAVE NO IDEA.
Even though he's older than you.
KEEP AN EYE OUT FOR HIM.
WOW!
I FIGURED HE WASN'T ORDINARY.
BUT I NEVER EXPECTED HIM TO ACTUALLY BE WEALTHY.
MY NINJA INTUITION WASN'T TOO BAD, EVEN THEN.
Heh heh heh heh...
Yikes!
Yikes!
NOW THEN...
HOW WOULD I APPROACH HIM?
I DECIDED TO WATCH OVER HIM FROM AFAR.
HMM?

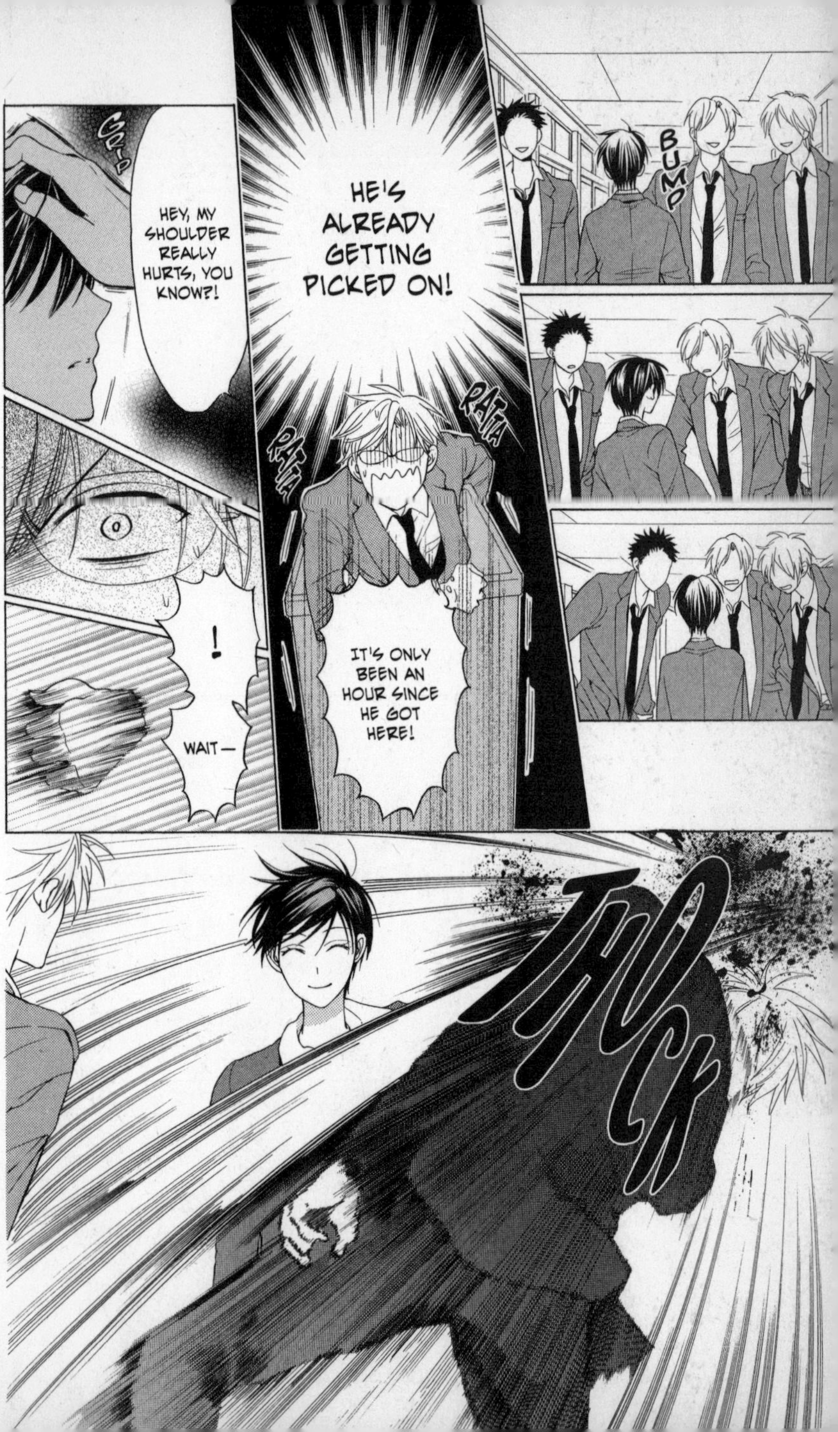
BUMP
HE'S ALREADY GETTING PICKED ON!
RATTA
RATTA
IT'S ONLY BEEN AN HOUR SINCE HE GOT HERE!
GRIP
HEY, MY SHOULDER REALLY HURTS, YOU KNOW?!
!
WAIT—
THUCK

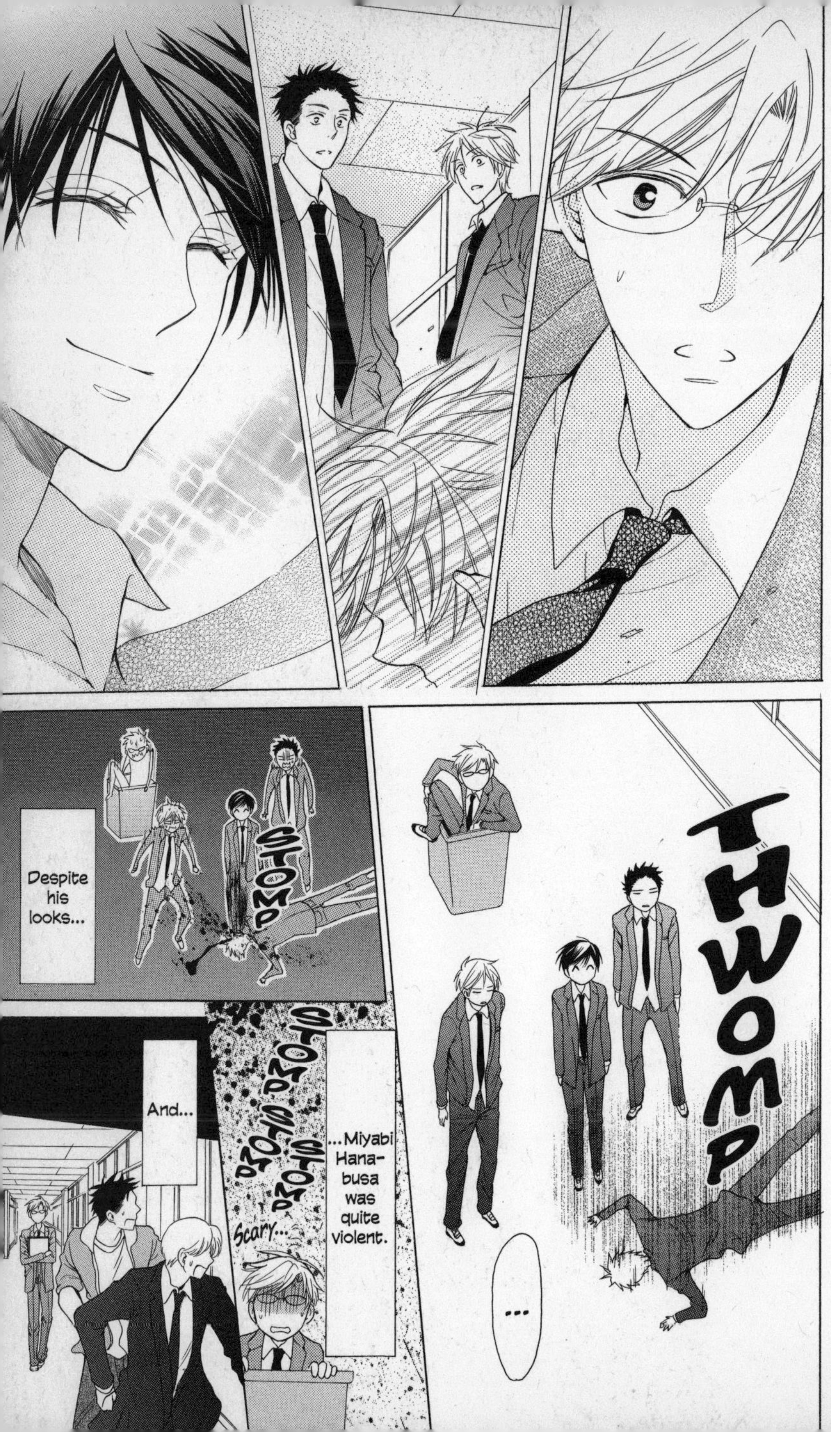
THWOMP
...
Despite his looks...
STOMP
...Miyabi Hanabusa was quite violent.
STOMP STOMP STOMP STOMP
Scary...
And...

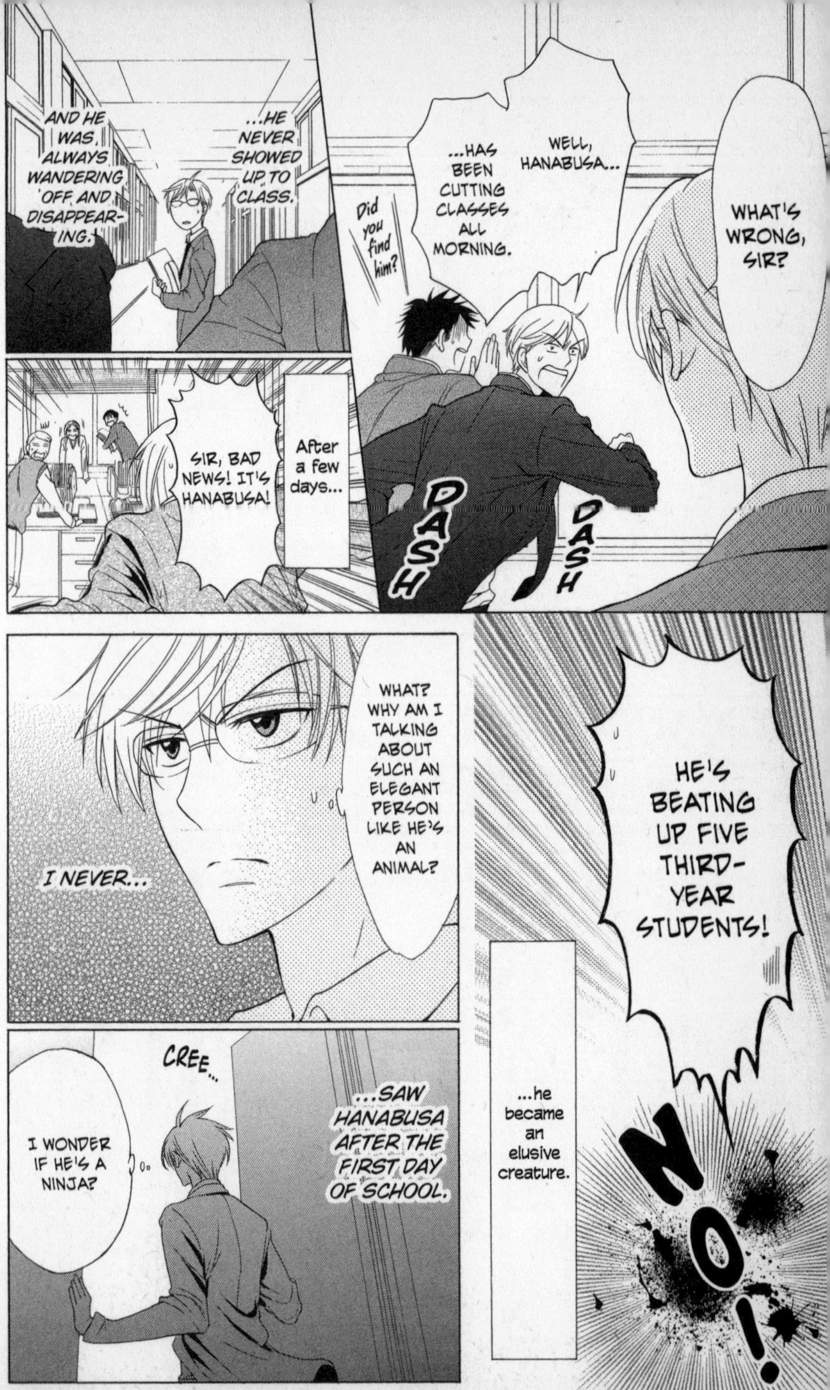
WHAT'S WRONG, SIR?
WELL, HANABUSA...
...HAS BEEN CUTTING CLASSES ALL MORNING.
Did you find him?
DASH
DASH
...HE NEVER SHOWED UP TO CLASS.
AND HE WAS ALWAYS WANDERING OFF AND DISAPPEARING.
After a few days...
SIR, BAD NEWS! IT'S HANABUSA!
HE'S BEATING UP FIVE THIRD-YEAR STUDENTS!
NO!
...he became an elusive creature.
WHAT? WHY AM I TALKING ABOUT SUCH AN ELEGANT PERSON LIKE HE'S AN ANIMAL?
I NEVER...
CREE...
...SAW HANABUSA AFTER THE FIRST DAY OF SCHOOL.
I WONDER IF HE'S A NINJA?

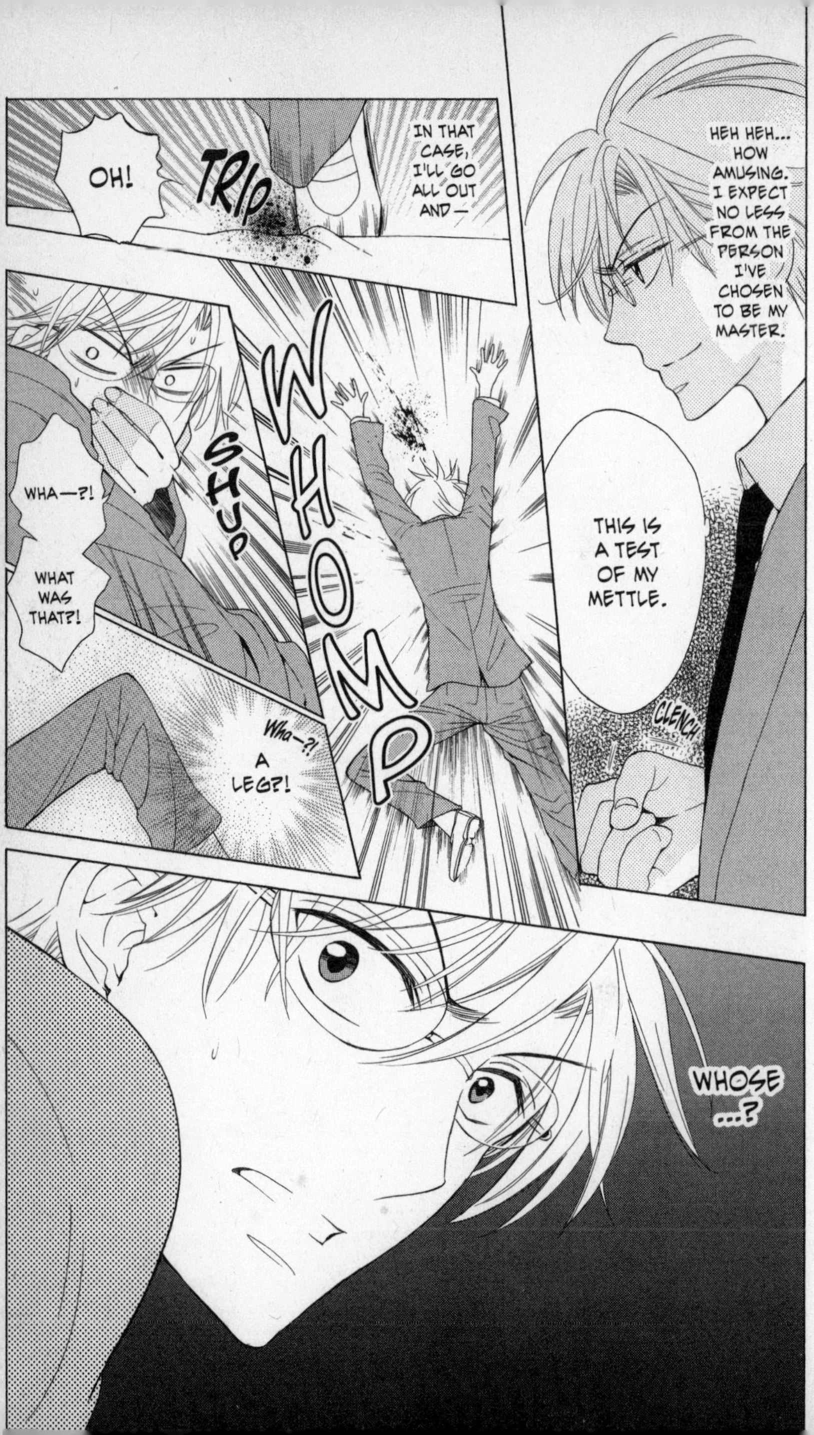
HEH HEH... HOW AMUSING. I EXPECT NO LESS FROM THE PERSON I'VE CHOSEN TO BE MY MASTER.
THIS IS A TEST OF MY METTLE.
CLENCH
IN THAT CASE, I'LL GO ALL OUT AND—
TRIP
OH!
WHOMP
SHUP
WHA—?!
WHAT WAS THAT?!
Wha—?!
A LEG?!
WHOSE ...?

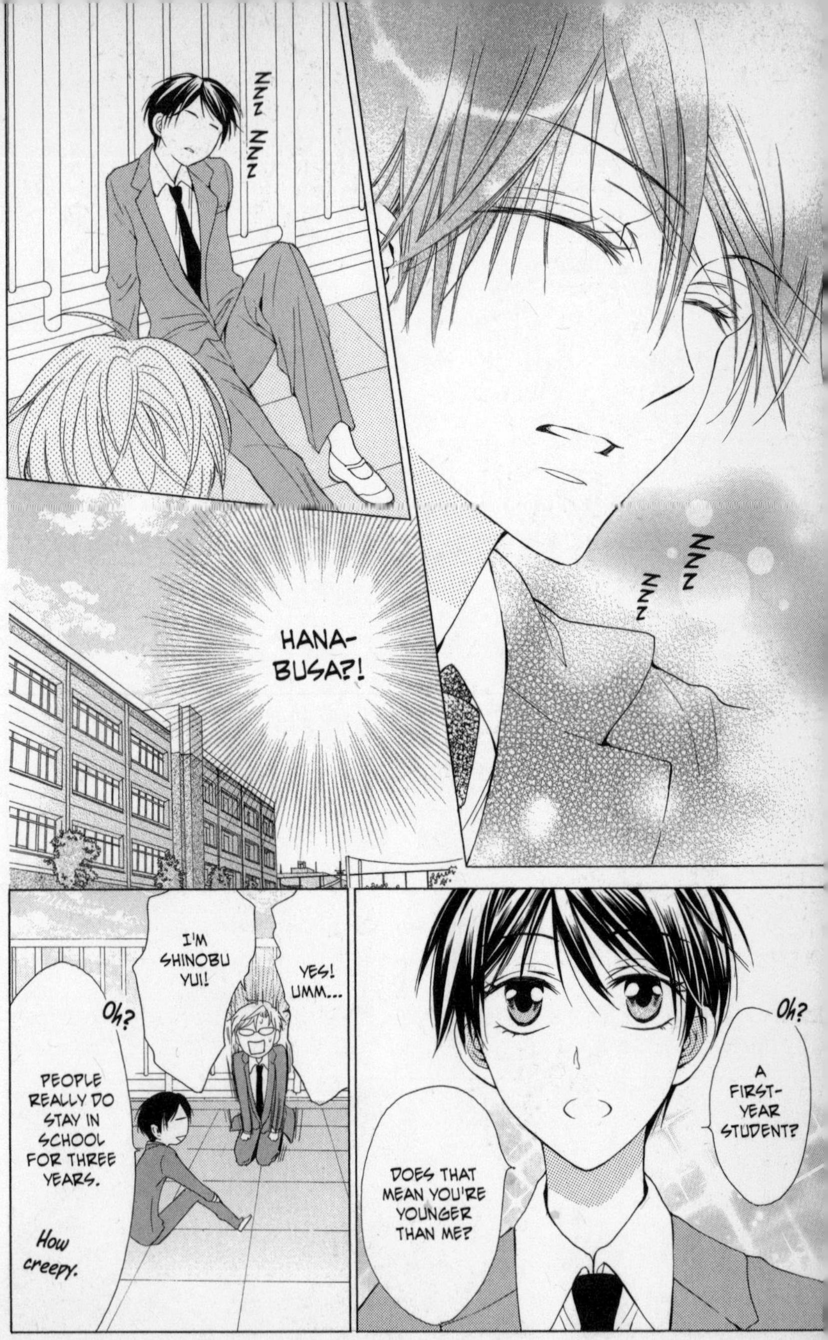

ZZZ
ZZZ
ZZZ ZZZ
HANA-BUSA?!
Oh?
A FIRST-YEAR STUDENT?
DOES THAT MEAN YOU'RE YOUNGER THAN ME?
YES! UMM...
I'M SHINOBU YUI!
Oh?
PEOPLE REALLY DO STAY IN SCHOOL FOR THREE YEARS.
How creepy.

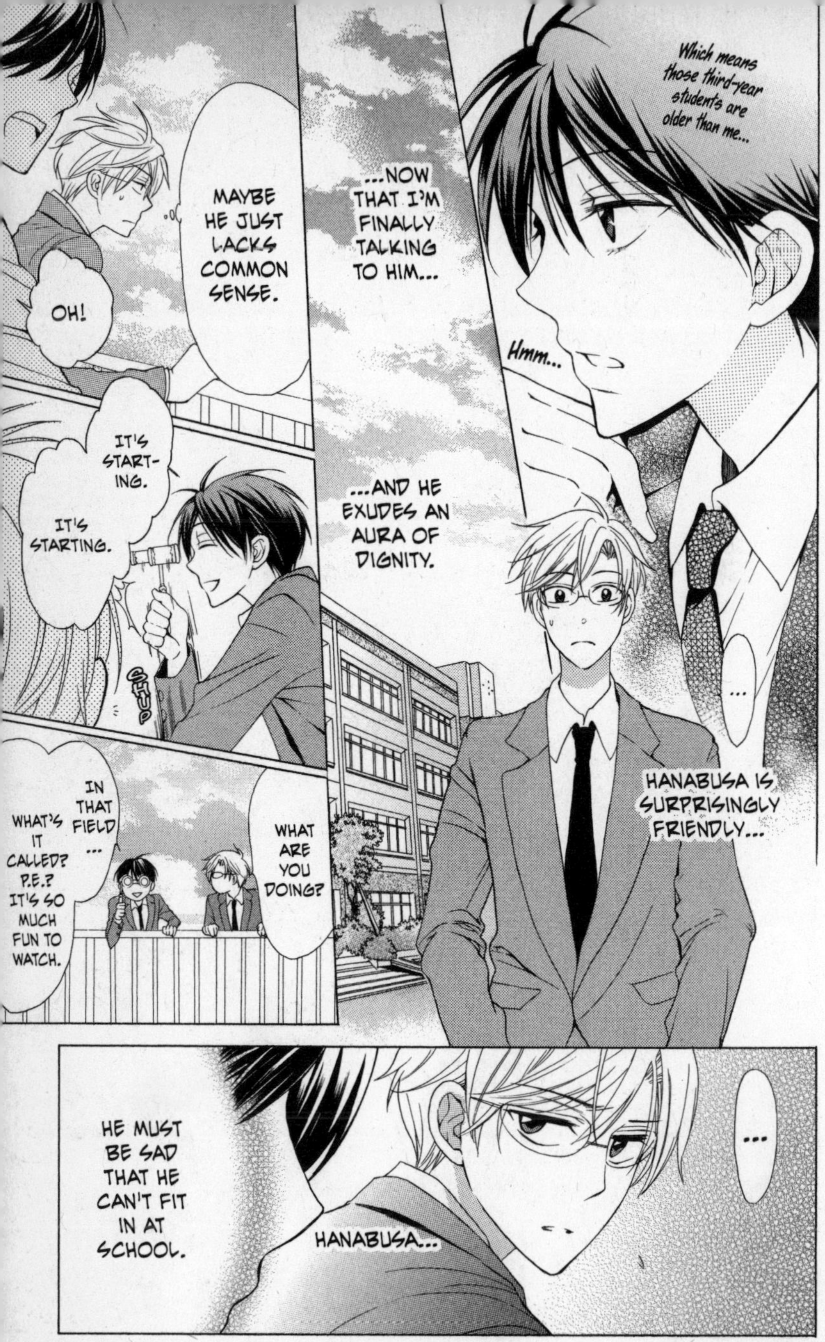
Which means those third-year students are older than me...
Hmm...
...
HANABUSA IS SURPRISINGLY FRIENDLY...
...NOW THAT I'M FINALLY TALKING TO HIM...
...AND HE EXUDES AN AURA OF DIGNITY.
MAYBE HE JUST LACKS COMMON SENSE.
OH!
IT'S STARTING.
IT'S STARTING.
SHUP
WHAT ARE YOU DOING?
IN THAT FIELD...
WHAT'S IT CALLED? P.E.? IT'S SO MUCH FUN TO WATCH.
...
HANABUSA...
HE MUST BE SAD THAT HE CAN'T FIT IN AT SCHOOL.

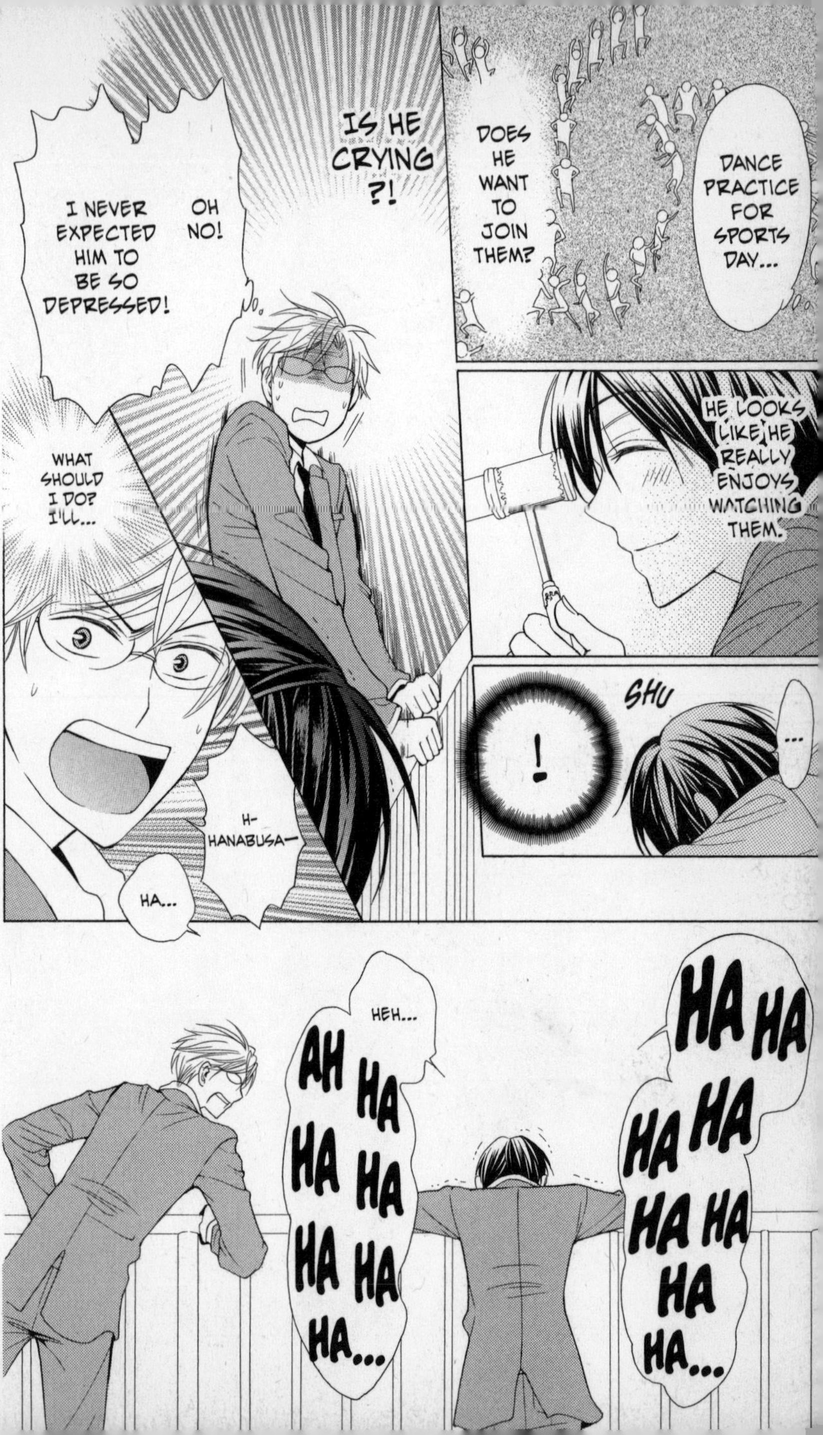
DANCE PRACTICE FOR SPORTS DAY...
DOES HE WANT TO JOIN THEM?
HE LOOKS LIKE HE REALLY ENJOYS WATCHING THEM.
SHU
...
!
IS HE CRYING?!
OH NO!
I NEVER EXPECTED HIM TO BE SO DEPRESSED!
WHAT SHOULD I DO? I'LL...
H-HANABUSA—
HA...
HA HA HA HA HA HA HA HA HA HA HA...
HEH...
AH HA HA HA HA HA HA HA HA HA...

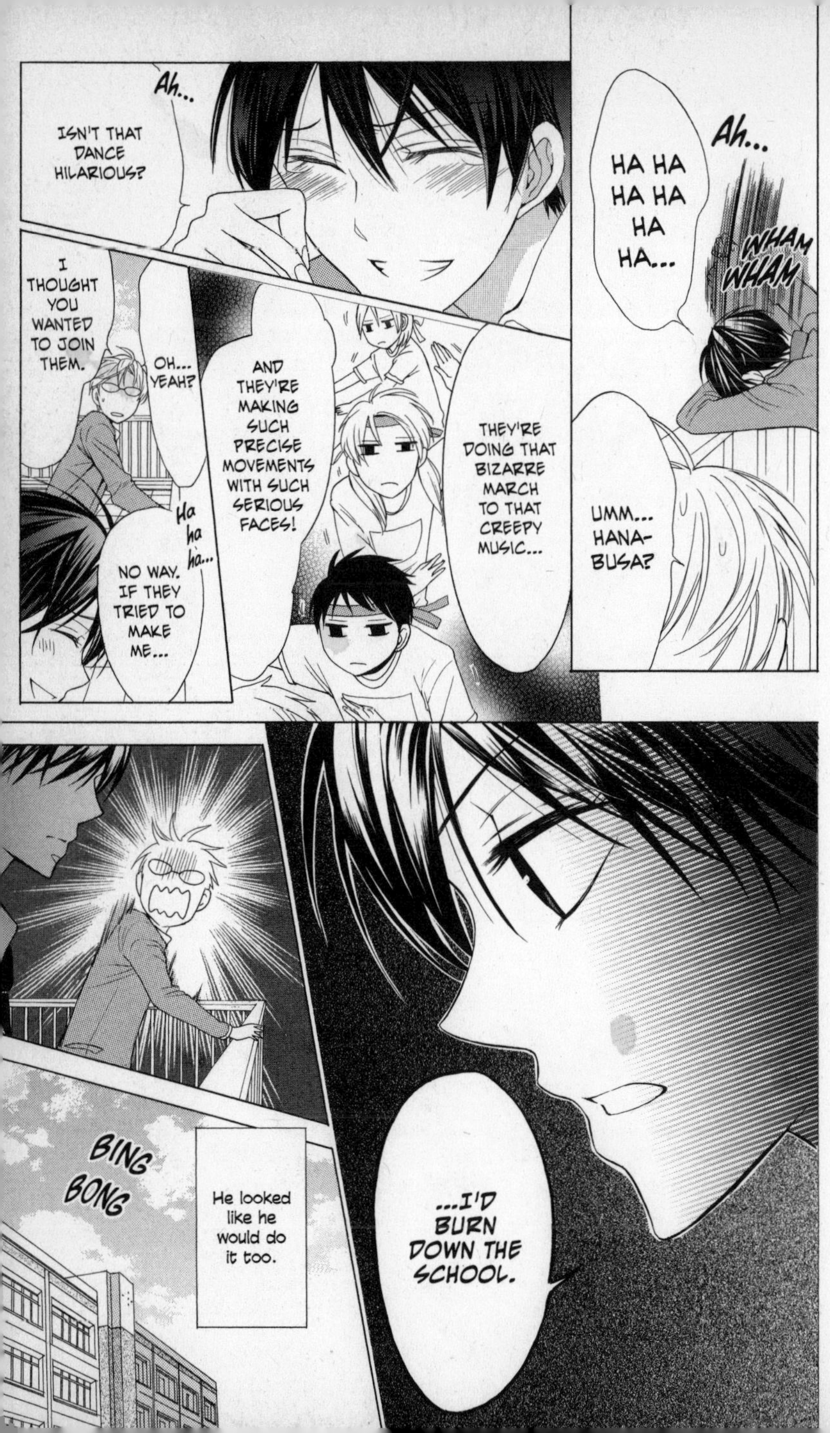
Ah...
HA HA HA HA HA HA...
WHAM WHAM
UMM... HANA-BUSA?
Ah...
ISN'T THAT DANCE HILARIOUS?
THEY'RE DOING THAT BIZARRE MARCH TO THAT CREEPY MUSIC...
AND THEY'RE MAKING SUCH PRECISE MOVEMENTS WITH SUCH SERIOUS FACES!
OH... YEAH?
I THOUGHT YOU WANTED TO JOIN THEM.
Ha ha ha...
NO WAY. IF THEY TRIED TO MAKE ME...
...I'D BURN DOWN THE SCHOOL.
He looked like he would do it too.
BING BONG

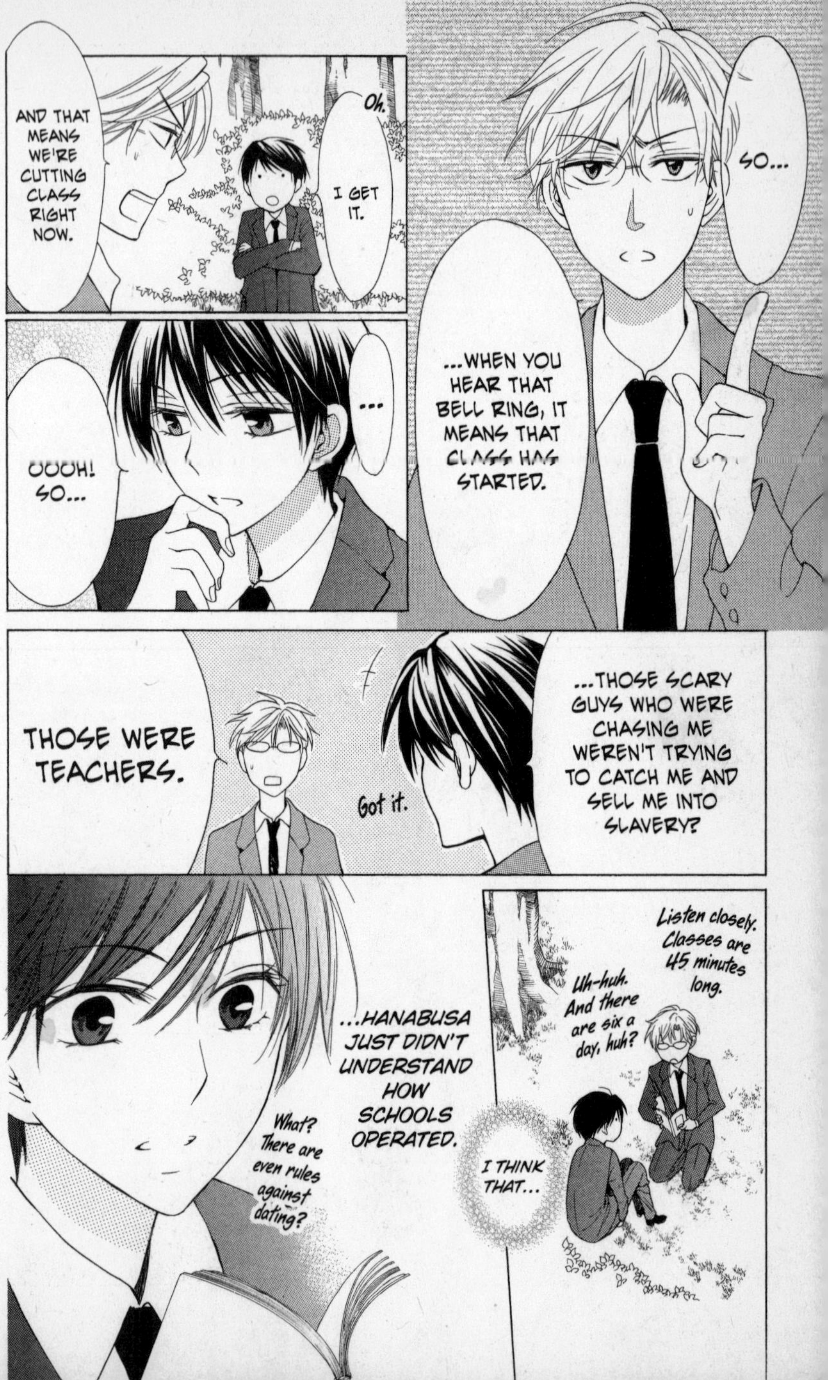
SO...
...WHEN YOU HEAR THAT BELL RING, IT MEANS THAT CLASS HAS STARTED.
Oh.
I GET IT.
AND THAT MEANS WE'RE CUTTING CLASS RIGHT NOW.
...
OOOH! SO...
...THOSE SCARY GUYS WHO WERE CHASING ME WEREN'T TRYING TO CATCH ME AND SELL ME INTO SLAVERY?
Got it.
THOSE WERE TEACHERS.
Listen closely. Classes are 45 minutes long.
Uh-huh. And there are six a day, huh?
I THINK THAT...
...HANABUSA JUST DIDN'T UNDERSTAND HOW SCHOOLS OPERATED.
What? There are even rules against dating?

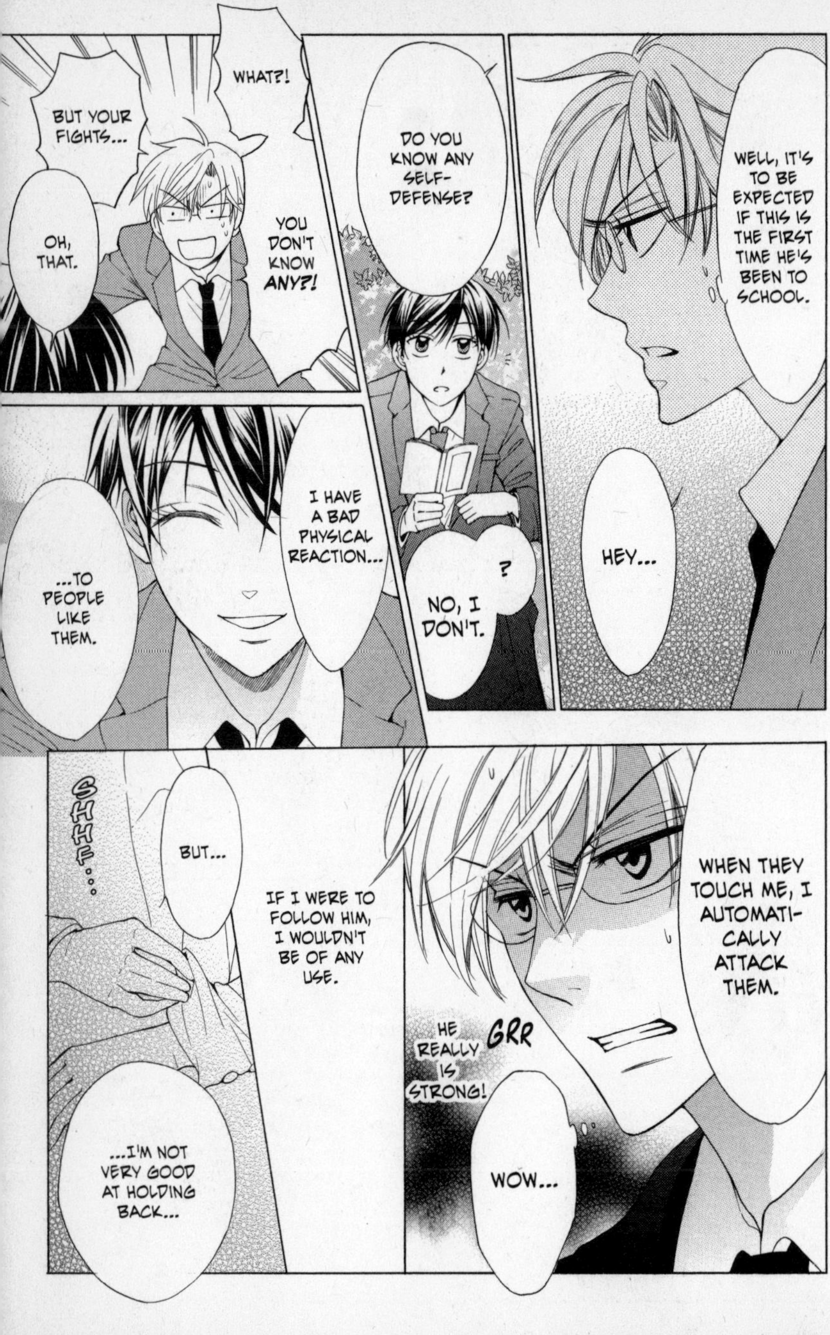
WELL, IT'S TO BE EXPECTED IF THIS IS THE FIRST TIME HE'S BEEN TO SCHOOL.
HEY...
DO YOU KNOW ANY SELF-DEFENSE?
?
NO, I DON'T.
WHAT?!
YOU DON'T KNOW ANY?!
BUT YOUR FIGHTS...
OH, THAT.
I HAVE A BAD PHYSICAL REACTION...
...TO PEOPLE LIKE THEM.
WHEN THEY TOUCH ME, I AUTOMATI-CALLY ATTACK THEM.
GRR
HE REALLY IS STRONG!
WOW...
IF I WERE TO FOLLOW HIM, I WOULDN'T BE OF ANY USE.
SHHF...
BUT...
...I'M NOT VERY GOOD AT HOLDING BACK...

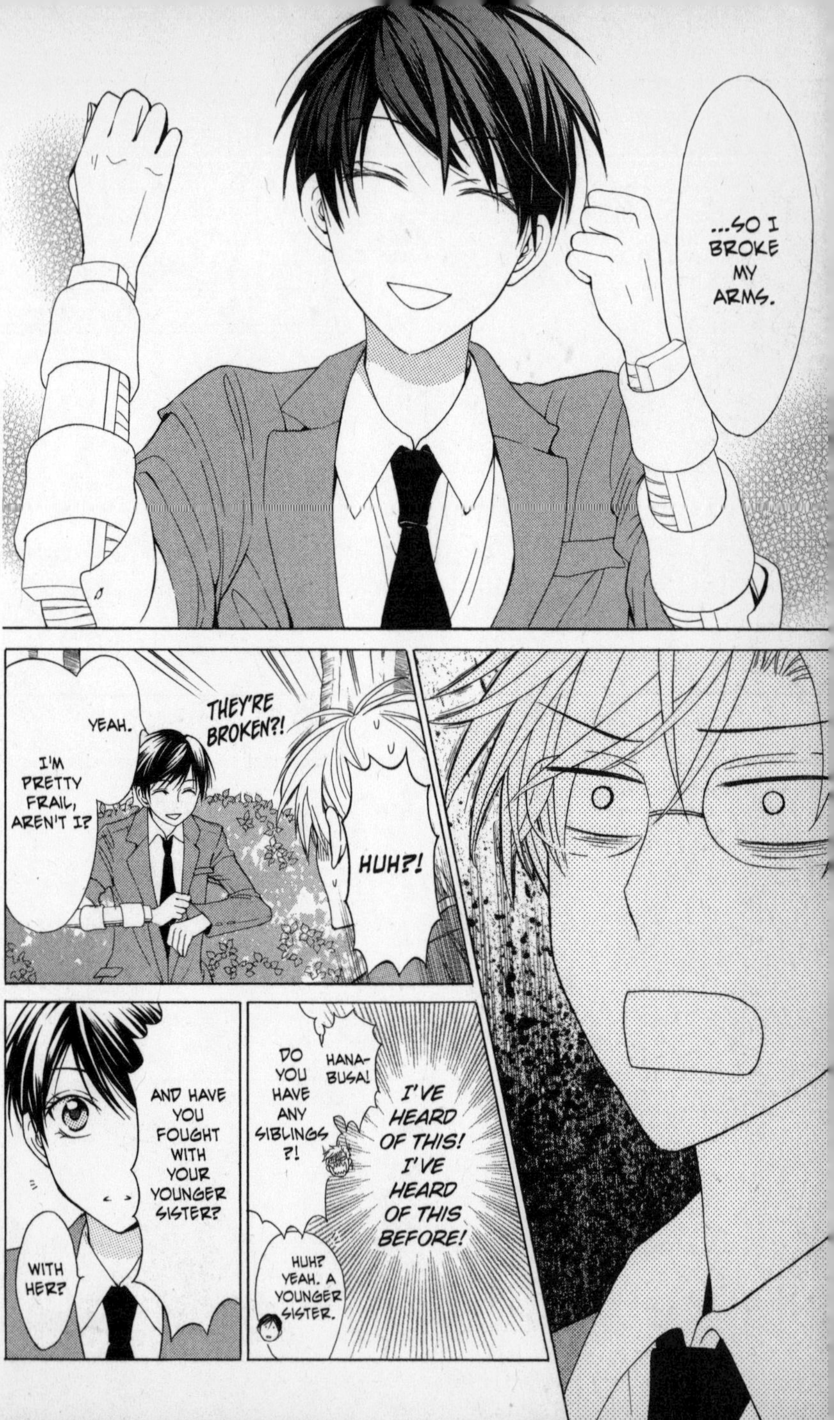
...SO I BROKE MY ARMS.
THEY'RE BROKEN?!
HUH?!
YEAH.
I'M PRETTY FRAIL, AREN'T I?
I'VE HEARD OF THIS! I'VE HEARD OF THIS BEFORE!
HANA-BUSA!
DO YOU HAVE ANY SIBLINGS?!
HUH? YEAH. A YOUNGER SISTER.
AND HAVE YOU FOUGHT WITH YOUR YOUNGER SISTER?
WITH HER?

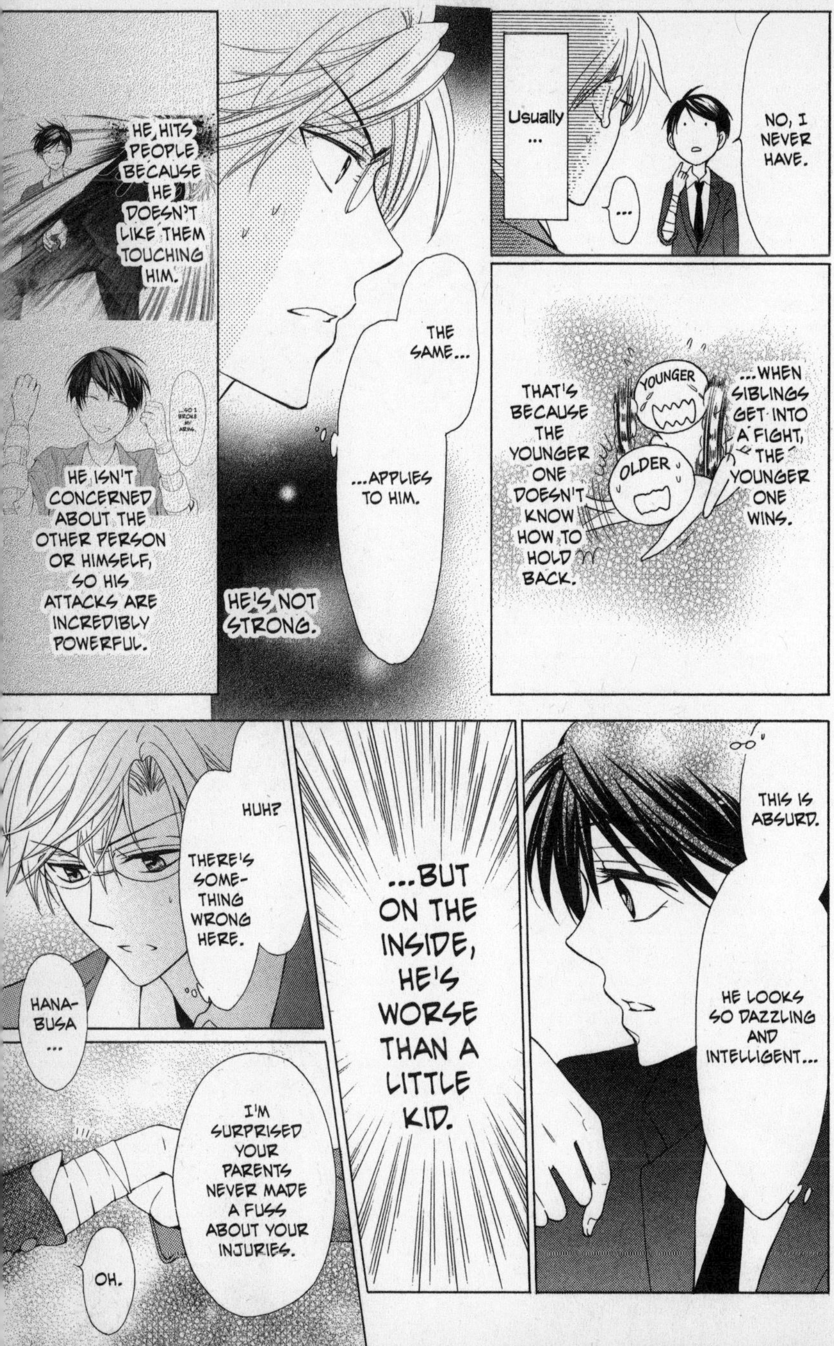
NO, I NEVER HAVE.
...
Usually...
...WHEN SIBLINGS GET INTO A FIGHT, THE YOUNGER ONE WINS.
YOUNGER
OLDER
THAT'S BECAUSE THE YOUNGER ONE DOESN'T KNOW HOW TO HOLD BACK.
THE SAME...
...APPLIES TO HIM.
HE'S NOT STRONG.
HE HITS PEOPLE BECAUSE HE DOESN'T LIKE THEM TOUCHING HIM.
...SO I BROKE MY ARM.
HE ISN'T CONCERNED ABOUT THE OTHER PERSON OR HIMSELF, SO HIS ATTACKS ARE INCREDIBLY POWERFUL.
THIS IS ABSURD.
HE LOOKS SO DAZZLING AND INTELLIGENT...
...BUT ON THE INSIDE, HE'S WORSE THAN A LITTLE KID.
HUH?
THERE'S SOME-THING WRONG HERE.
HANA-BUSA...
I'M SURPRISED YOUR PARENTS NEVER MADE A FUSS ABOUT YOUR INJURIES.
OH.

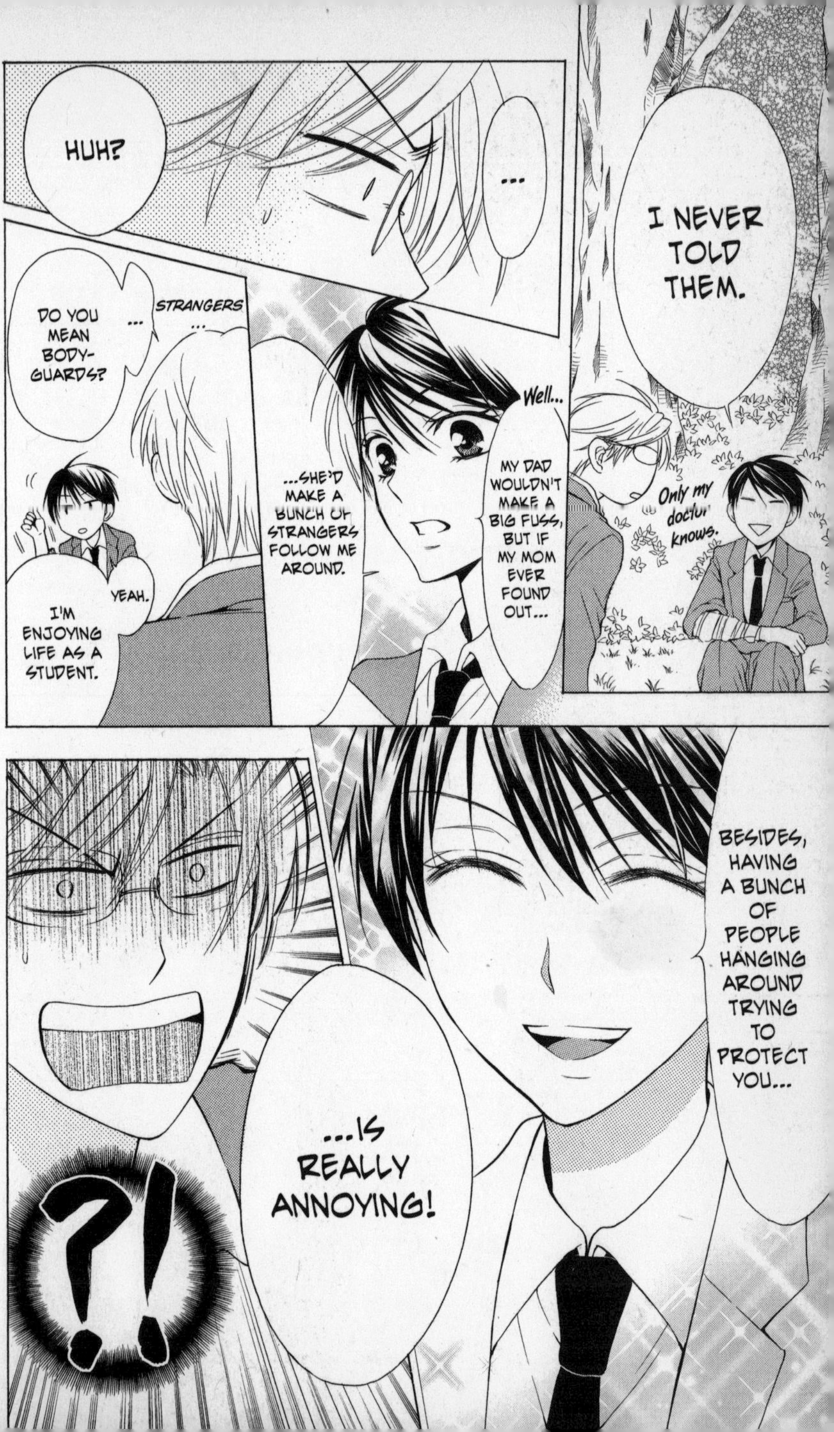
I NEVER TOLD THEM.
Only my doctor knows.
...
HUH?
Well...
MY DAD WOULDN'T MAKE A BIG FUSS, BUT IF MY MOM EVER FOUND OUT...
...SHE'D MAKE A BUNCH OF STRANGERS FOLLOW ME AROUND.
... STRANGERS ...
DO YOU MEAN BODY-GUARDS?
YEAH.
I'M ENJOYING LIFE AS A STUDENT.
BESIDES, HAVING A BUNCH OF PEOPLE HANGING AROUND TRYING TO PROTECT YOU...
...IS REALLY ANNOYING!
?!

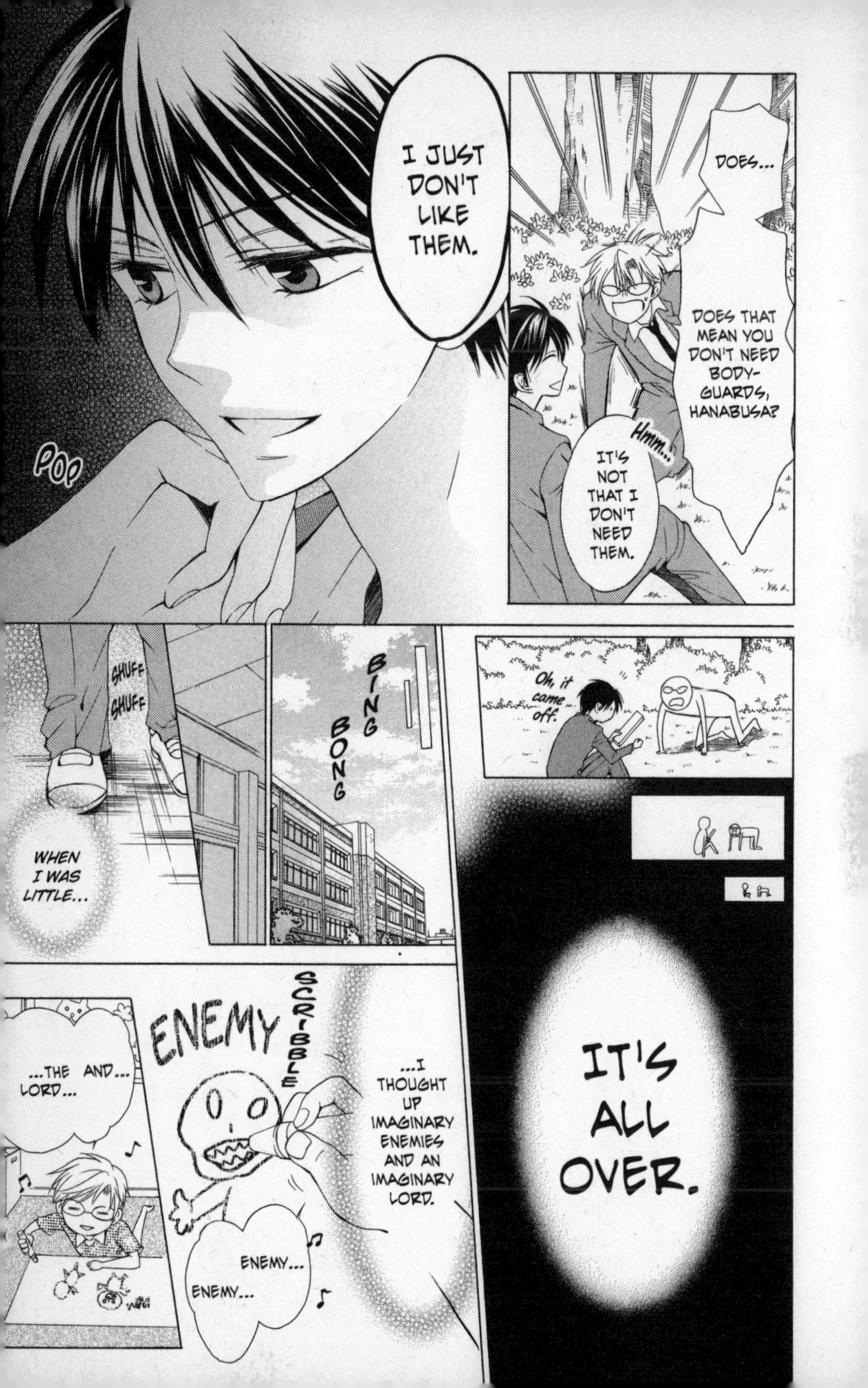
DOES...
DOES THAT MEAN YOU DON'T NEED BODY-GUARDS, HANABUSA?
Hmm...
IT'S NOT THAT I DON'T NEED THEM.
I JUST DON'T LIKE THEM.
POP
Oh, it came off.
IT'S ALL OVER.
BING BONG
SHUFF SHUFF
WHEN I WAS LITTLE...
...I THOUGHT UP IMAGINARY ENEMIES AND AN IMAGINARY LORD.
SCRIBBLE
ENEMY
AND...
...THE LORD...
ENEMY...
ENEMY...

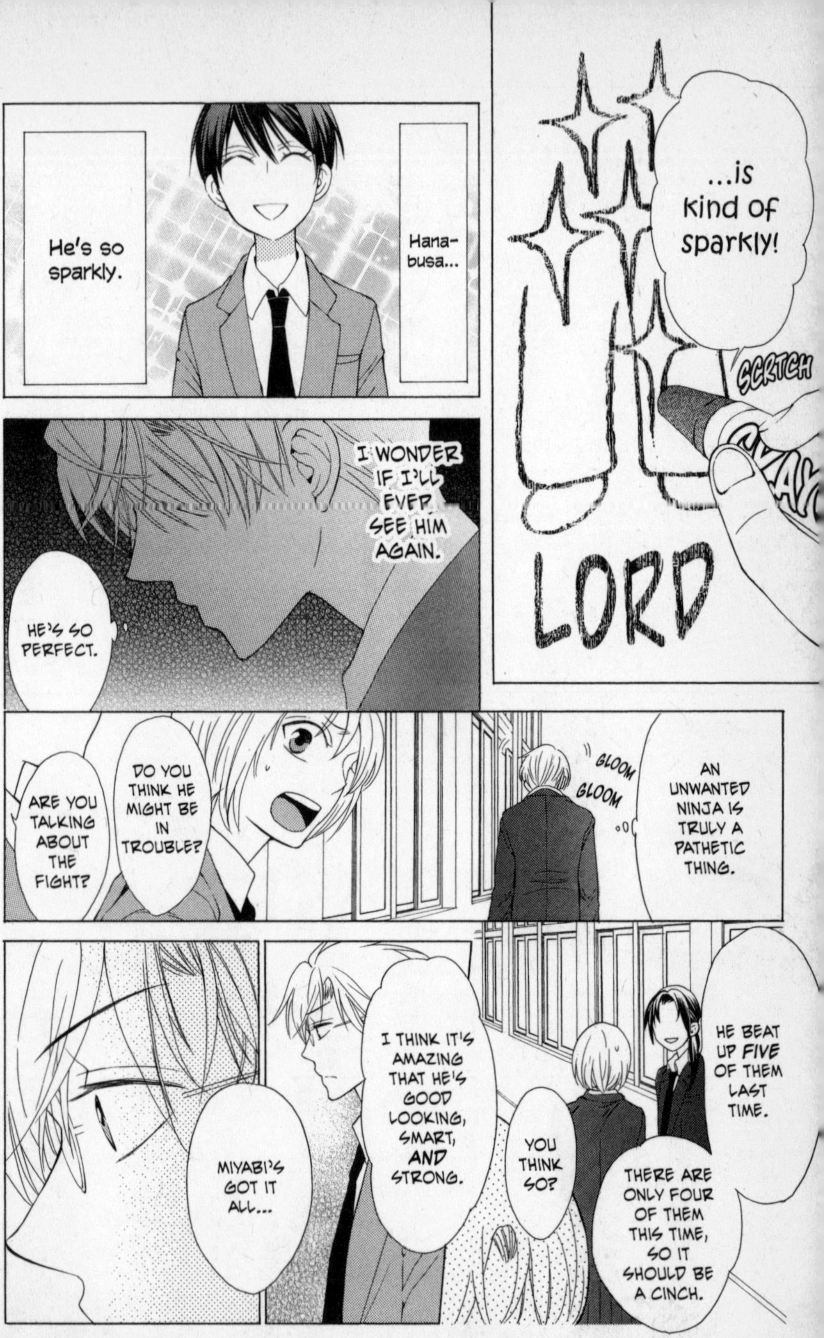
...is kind of sparkly!
SCRTCH
LORD
Hana-busa...
He's so sparkly.
I WONDER IF I'LL EVER SEE HIM AGAIN.
HE'S SO PERFECT.
AN UNWANTED NINJA IS TRULY A PATHETIC THING.
GLOOM
GLOOM
DO YOU THINK HE MIGHT BE IN TROUBLE?
ARE YOU TALKING ABOUT THE FIGHT?
HE BEAT UP FIVE OF THEM LAST TIME.
THERE ARE ONLY FOUR OF THEM THIS TIME, SO IT SHOULD BE A CINCH.
YOU THINK SO?
I THINK IT'S AMAZING THAT HE'S GOOD LOOKING, SMART, AND STRONG.
MIYABI'S GOT IT ALL...

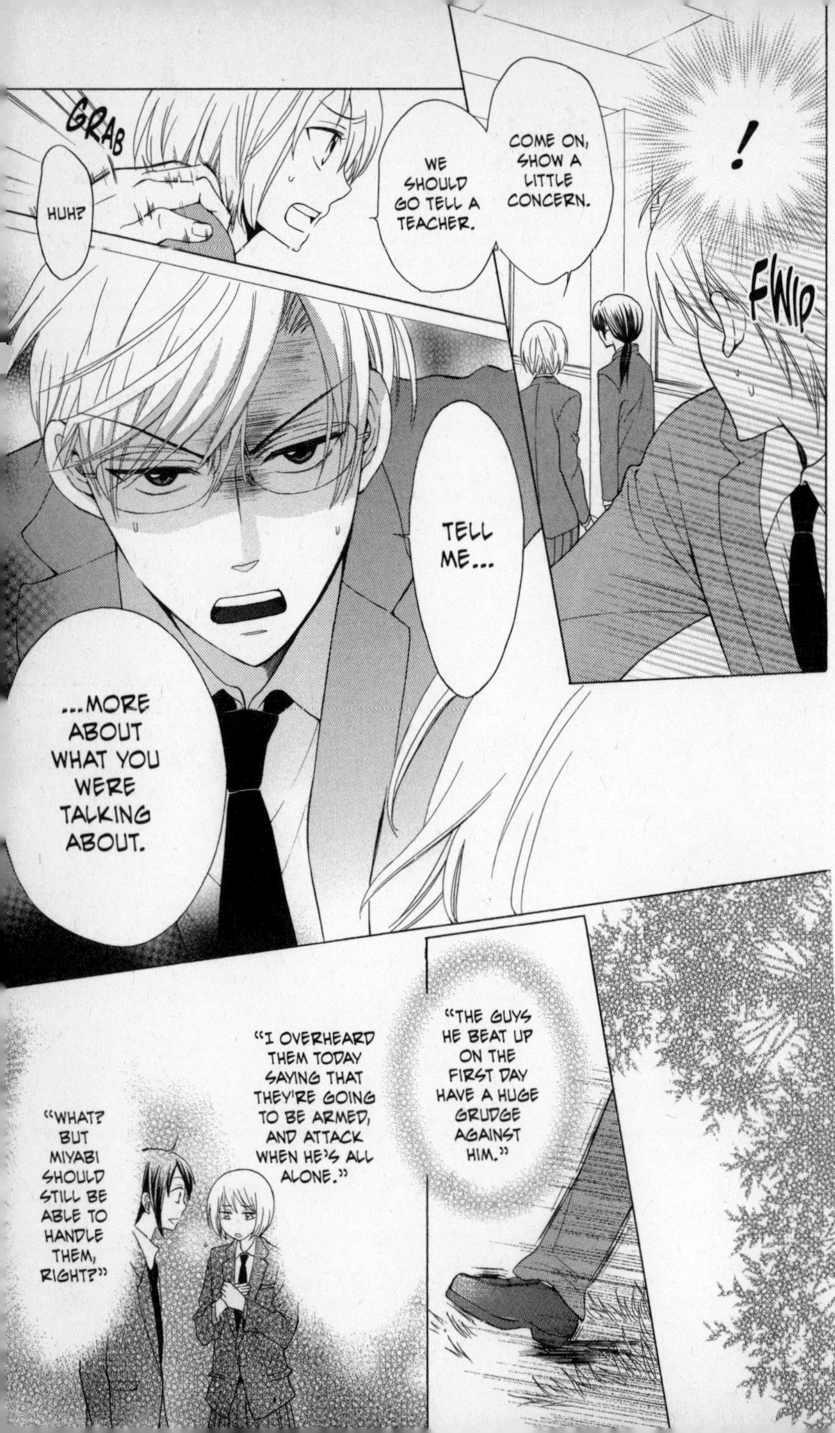
COME ON, SHOW A LITTLE CONCERN.
WE SHOULD GO TELL A TEACHER.
!
FWIP
GRAB
HUH?
TELL ME...
...MORE ABOUT WHAT YOU WERE TALKING ABOUT.
"THE GUYS HE BEAT UP ON THE FIRST DAY HAVE A HUGE GRUDGE AGAINST HIM."
"I OVERHEARD THEM TODAY SAYING THAT THEY'RE GOING TO BE ARMED, AND ATTACK WHEN HE'S ALL ALONE."
"WHAT? BUT MIYABI SHOULD STILL BE ABLE TO HANDLE THEM, RIGHT?"

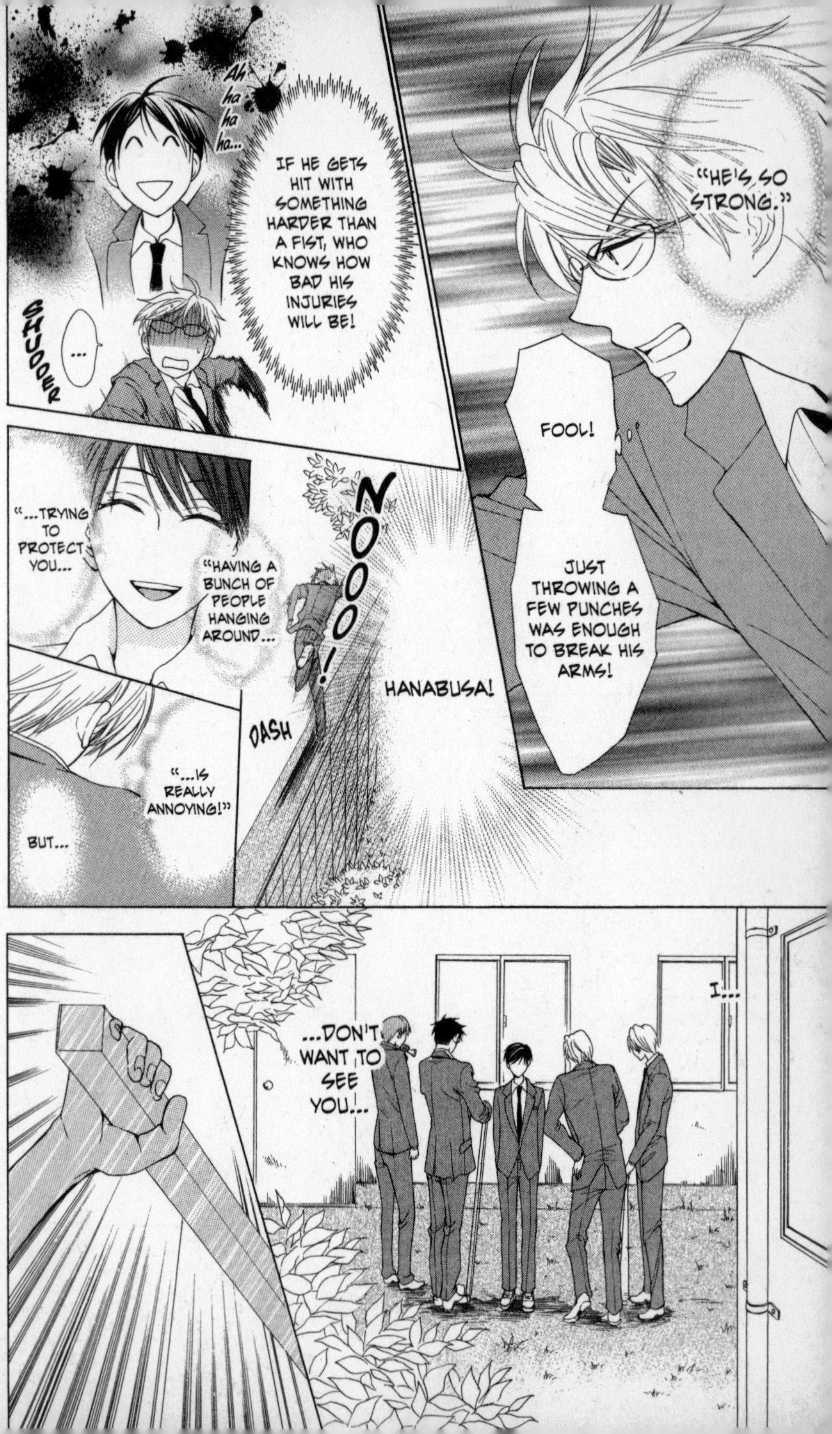
"HE'S SO STRONG."
FOOL!
JUST THROWING A FEW PUNCHES WAS ENOUGH TO BREAK HIS ARMS!
Ah ha ha ha...
IF HE GETS HIT WITH SOMETHING HARDER THAN A FIST, WHO KNOWS HOW BAD HIS INJURIES WILL BE!
...
SHUDDER
HANABUSA!
NOOOO!
DASH
"HAVING A BUNCH OF PEOPLE HANGING AROUND...
"...TRYING TO PROTECT YOU...
"...IS REALLY ANNOYING!"
BUT...
I...
...DON'T WANT TO SEE YOU!...

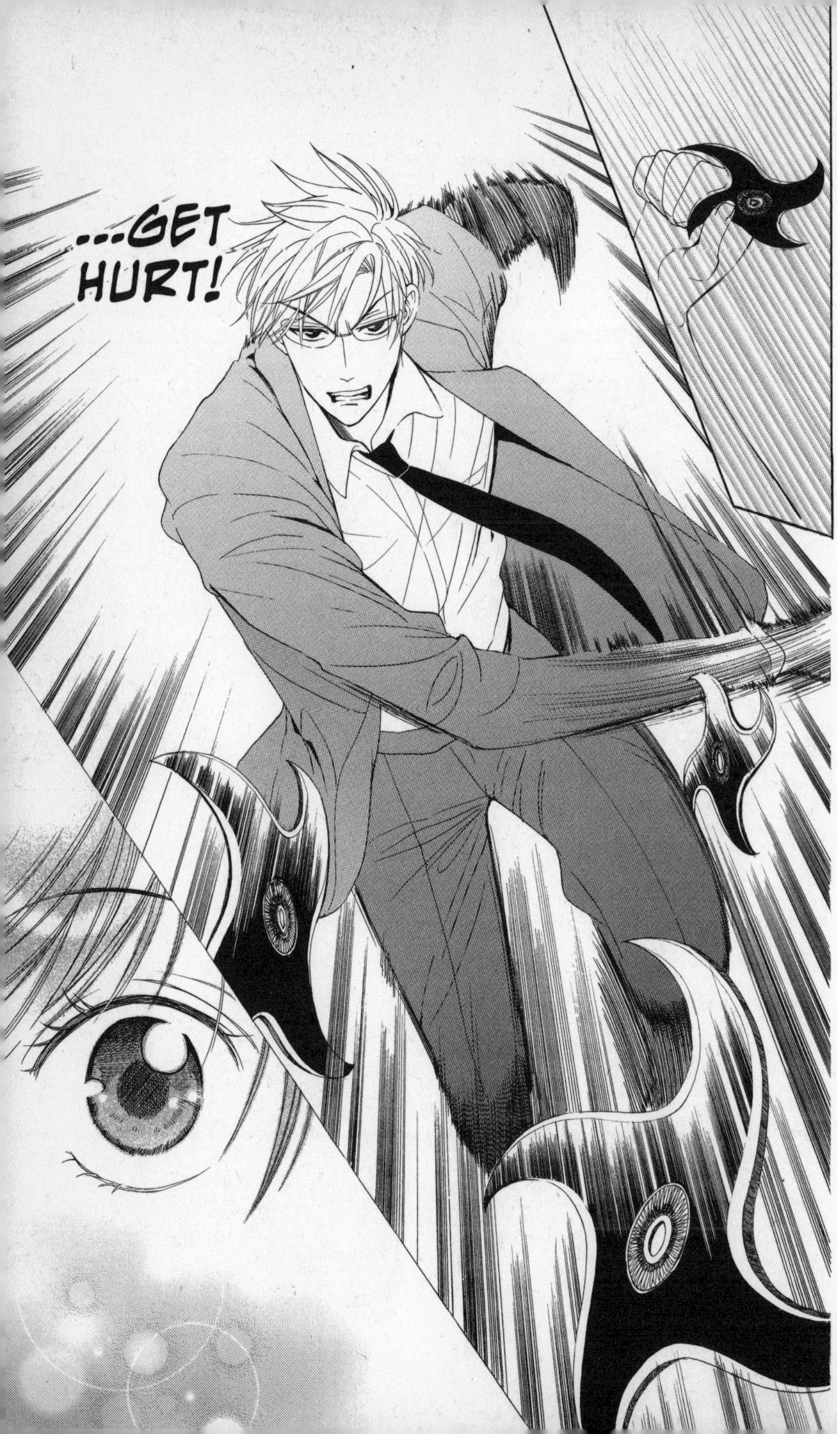
...GET HURT!

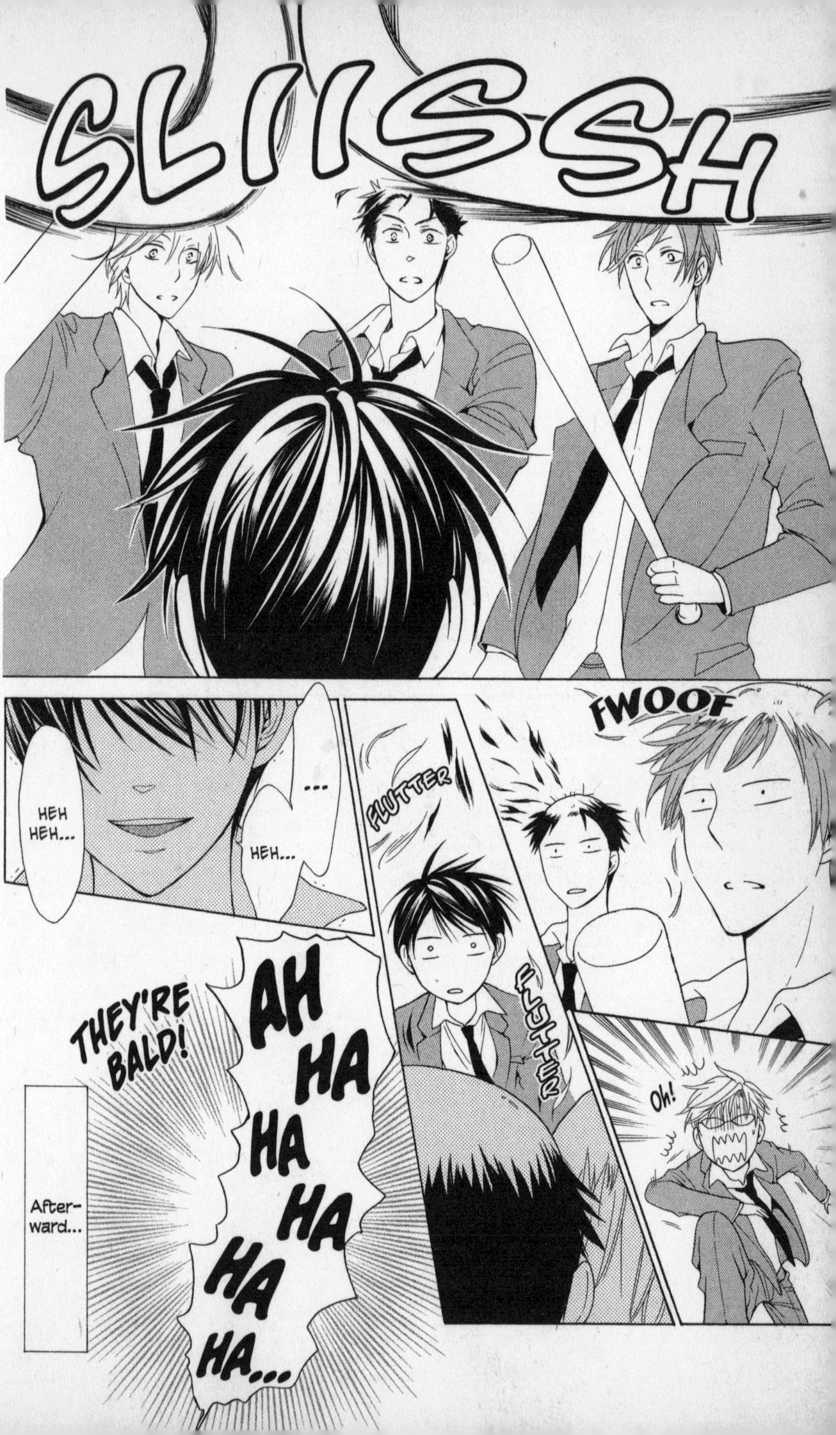
SLIISSH
FWOOF
FLUTTER
...
HEH...
HEH
HEH...
FLUTTER
Oh!
AH HA HA HA HA HA HA HA...
THEY'RE BALD!
After-ward...

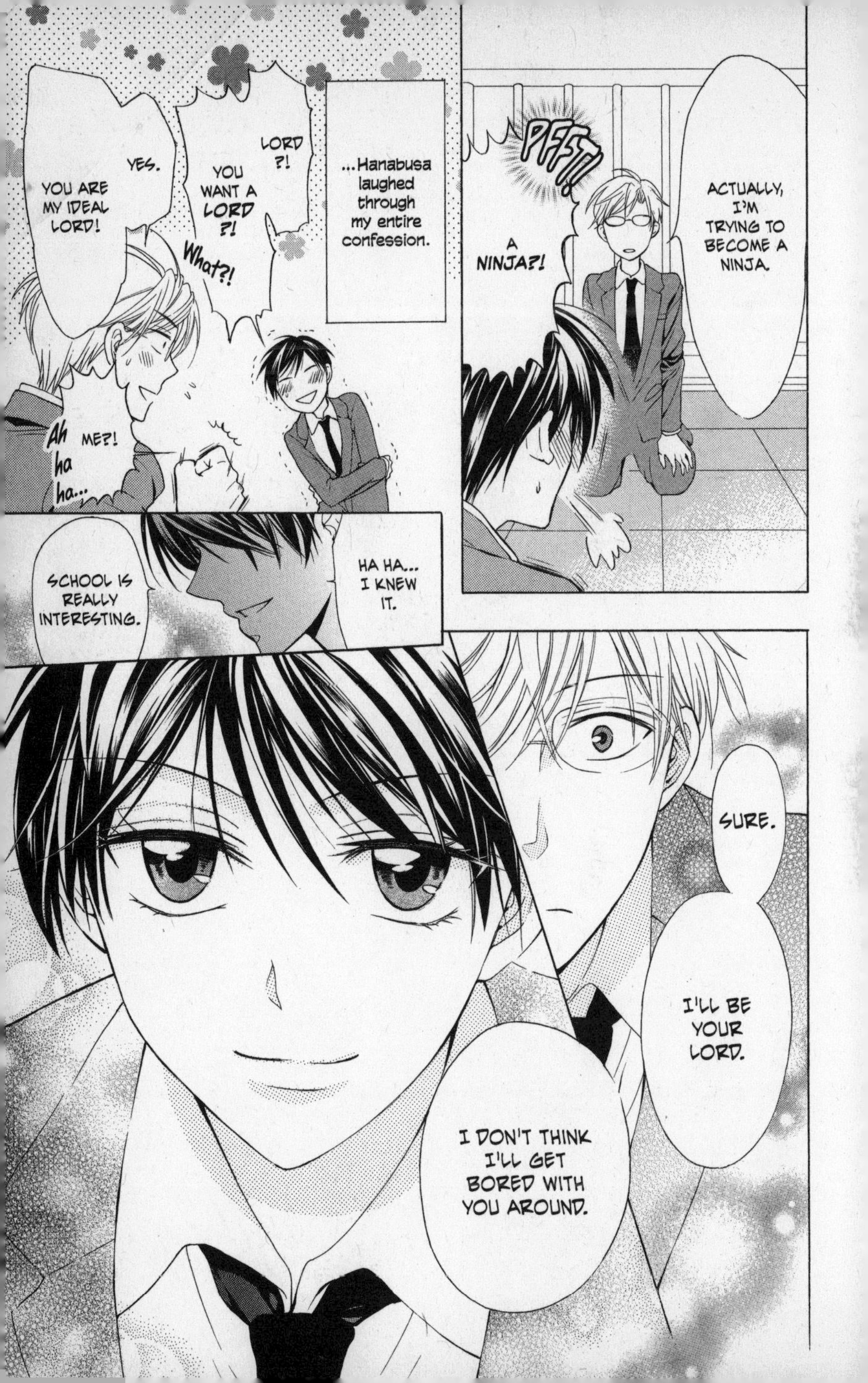
ACTUALLY, I'M TRYING TO BECOME A NINJA.
PFFT!!
A NINJA?!
...Hanabusa laughed through my entire confession.
LORD?!
YOU WANT A LORD?!
What?!
YES.
YOU ARE MY IDEAL LORD!
ME?!
Ah ha ha...
HA HA... I KNEW IT.
SCHOOL IS REALLY INTERESTING.
SURE.
I'LL BE YOUR LORD.
I DON'T THINK I'LL GET BORED WITH YOU AROUND.

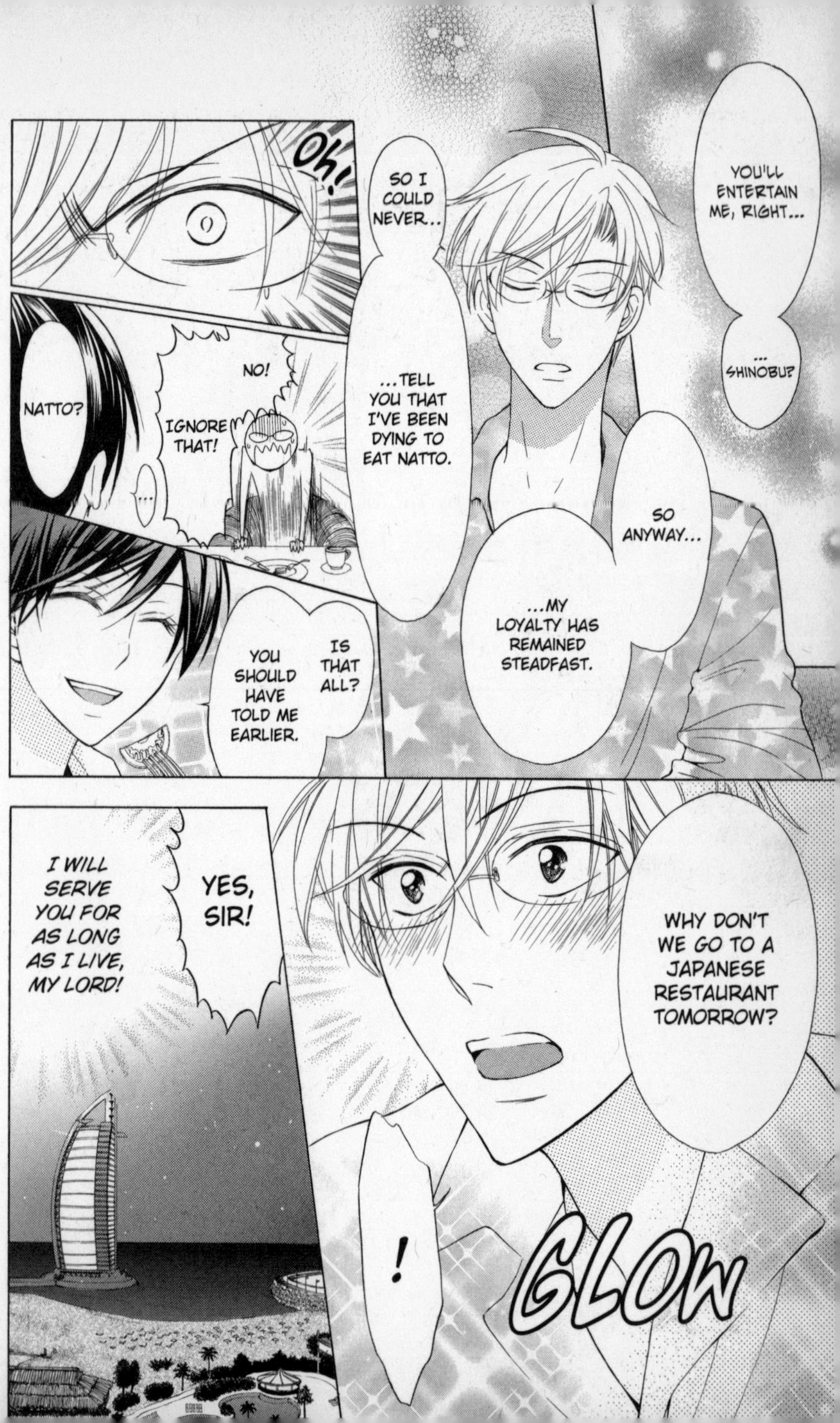
YOU'LL ENTERTAIN ME, RIGHT...
...SHINOBU?
SO I COULD NEVER...
...TELL YOU THAT I'VE BEEN DYING TO EAT NATTO.
SO ANYWAY...
...MY LOYALTY HAS REMAINED STEADFAST.
OH!
NATTO?
NO!
IGNORE THAT!
...
IS THAT ALL?
YOU SHOULD HAVE TOLD ME EARLIER.
WHY DON'T WE GO TO A JAPANESE RESTAURANT TOMORROW?
!
GLOW
YES, SIR!
I WILL SERVE YOU FOR AS LONG AS I LIVE, MY LORD!

Chapter 41

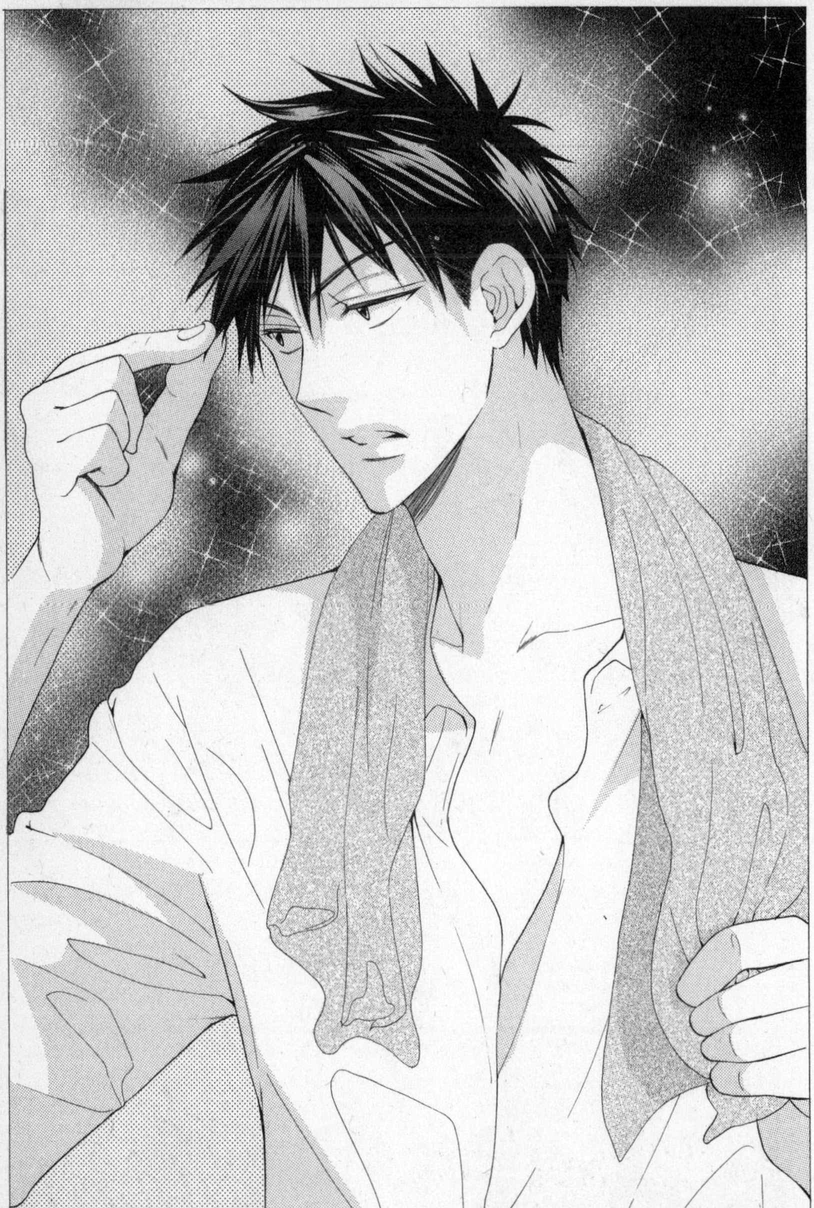

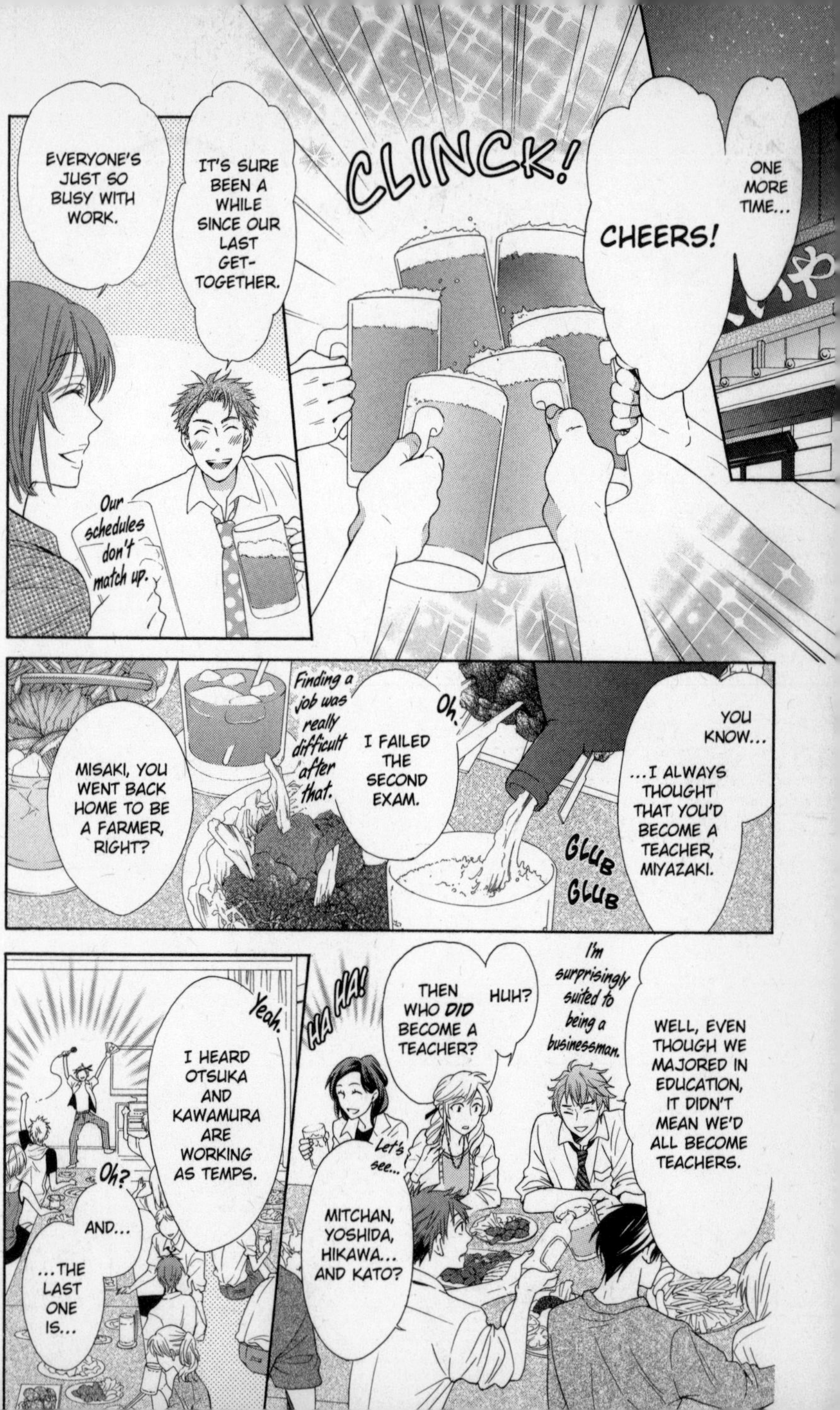
ONE MORE TIME...
CHEERS!
CLINCK!
IT'S SURE BEEN A WHILE SINCE OUR LAST GET-TOGETHER.
EVERYONE'S JUST SO BUSY WITH WORK.
Our schedules don't match up.
YOU KNOW...
...I ALWAYS THOUGHT THAT YOU'D BECOME A TEACHER, MIYAZAKI.
GLUB GLUB
Oh.
I FAILED THE SECOND EXAM.
Finding a job was really difficult after that.
MISAKI, YOU WENT BACK HOME TO BE A FARMER, RIGHT?
WELL, EVEN THOUGH WE MAJORED IN EDUCATION, IT DIDN'T MEAN WE'D ALL BECOME TEACHERS.
I'm surprisingly suited to being a businessman.
HUH?
THEN WHO *DID* BECOME A TEACHER?
HA HA!
Let's see...
MITCHAN, YOSHIDA, HIKAWA... AND KATO?
Yeah.
I HEARD OTSUKA AND KAWAMURA ARE WORKING AS TEMPS.
Oh?
AND...
...THE LAST ONE IS...

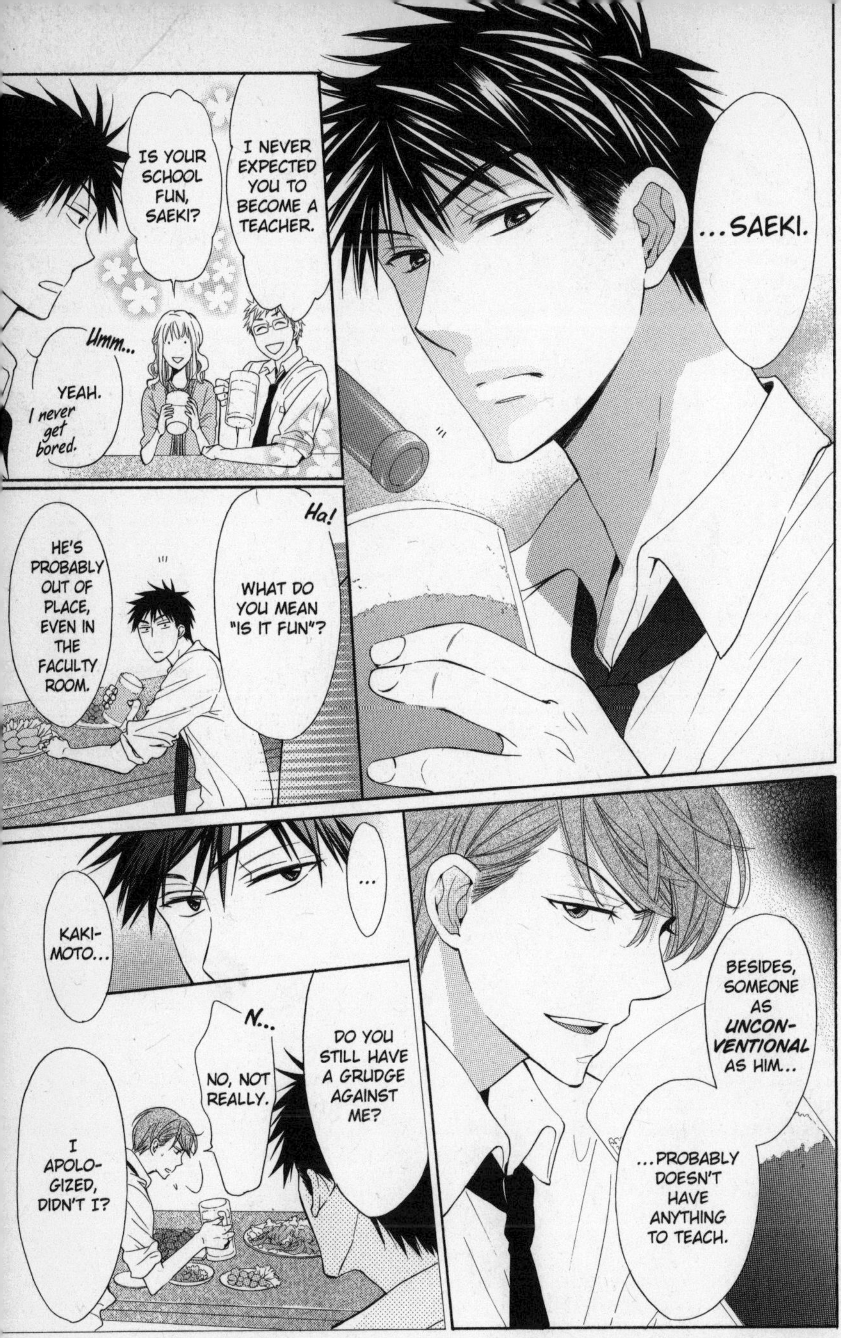
...SAEKI.
I NEVER EXPECTED YOU TO BECOME A TEACHER.
IS YOUR SCHOOL FUN, SAEKI?
Umm...
YEAH. I never get bored.
Ha!
WHAT DO YOU MEAN "IS IT FUN"?
HE'S PROBABLY OUT OF PLACE, EVEN IN THE FACULTY ROOM.
BESIDES, SOMEONE AS *UNCONVENTIONAL* AS HIM...
...PROBABLY DOESN'T HAVE ANYTHING TO TEACH.
...
KAKI-MOTO...
DO YOU STILL HAVE A GRUDGE AGAINST ME?
N...
NO, NOT REALLY.
I APOLOGIZED, DIDN'T I?

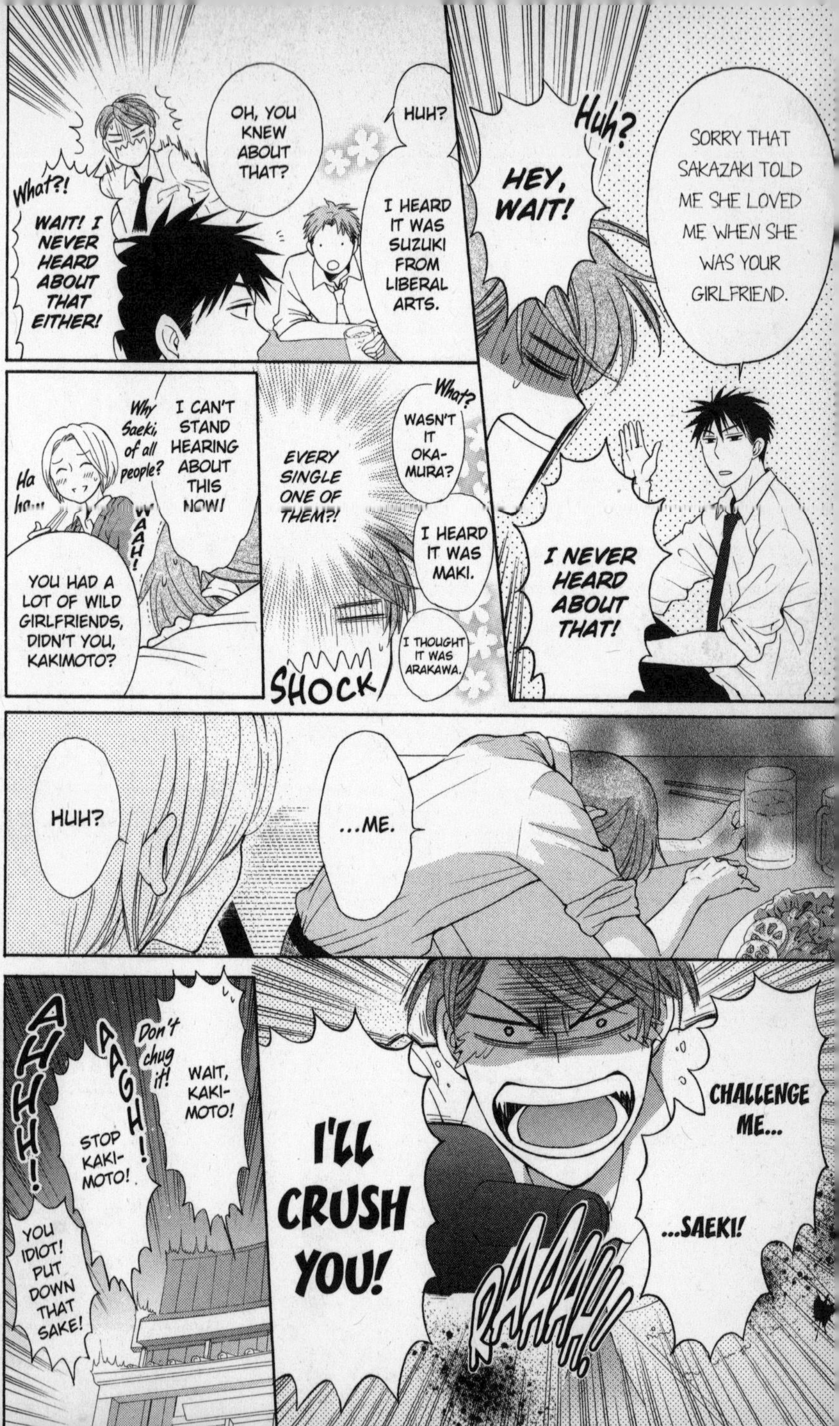
SORRY THAT SAKAZAKI TOLD ME SHE LOVED ME WHEN SHE WAS YOUR GIRLFRIEND.
Huh?
HEY, WAIT!
I NEVER HEARD ABOUT THAT!
HUH?
I HEARD IT WAS SUZUKI FROM LIBERAL ARTS.
OH, YOU KNEW ABOUT THAT?
What?!
WAIT! I NEVER HEARD ABOUT THAT EITHER!
What?
WASN'T IT OKAMURA?
I HEARD IT WAS MAKI.
I THOUGHT IT WAS ARAKAWA.
EVERY SINGLE ONE OF THEM?!
SHOCK
I CAN'T STAND HEARING ABOUT THIS NOW!
Why Saeki, of all people?
WAAH!
Ha ha...
YOU HAD A LOT OF WILD GIRLFRIENDS, DIDN'T YOU, KAKIMOTO?
...ME.
HUH?
CHALLENGE ME...
...SAEKI!
I'LL CRUSH YOU!
WAIT, KAKIMOTO!
Don't chug it!
AAGH!
AHHHH!
STOP KAKIMOTO!
YOU IDIOT! PUT DOWN THAT SAKE!

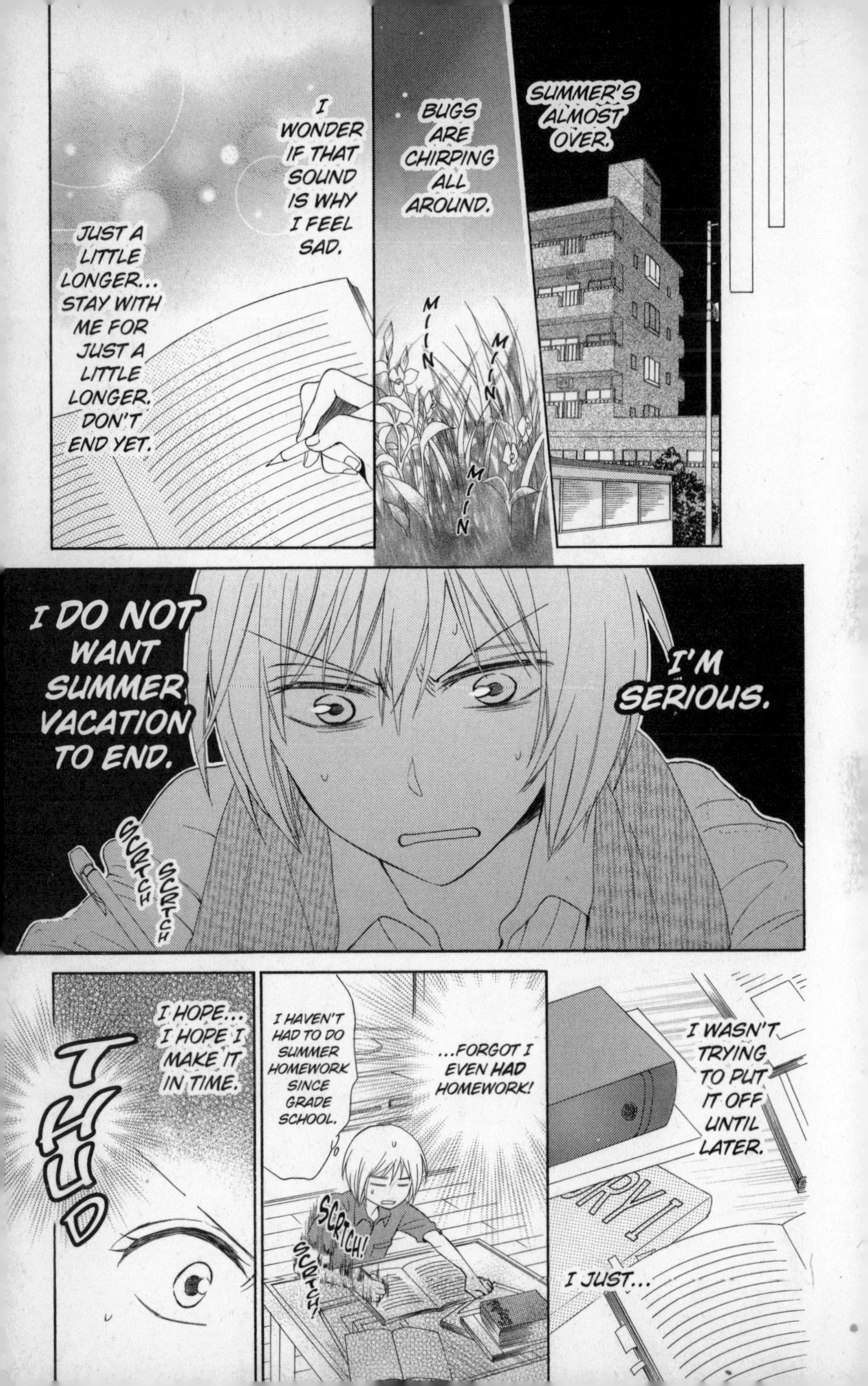

SUMMER'S ALMOST OVER.
BUGS ARE CHIRPING ALL AROUND.
MIIN
MIIN
MIIN
I WONDER IF THAT SOUND IS WHY I FEEL SAD.
JUST A LITTLE LONGER... STAY WITH ME FOR JUST A LITTLE LONGER. DON'T END YET.
I DO NOT WANT SUMMER VACATION TO END.
I'M SERIOUS.
SCRATCH
SCRATCH
I WASN'T TRYING TO PUT IT OFF UNTIL LATER.
I JUST...
...FORGOT I EVEN HAD HOMEWORK!
I HAVEN'T HAD TO DO SUMMER HOMEWORK SINCE GRADE SCHOOL.
SCRITCH!
SCRITCH!
I HOPE... I HOPE I MAKE IT IN TIME.
THUD

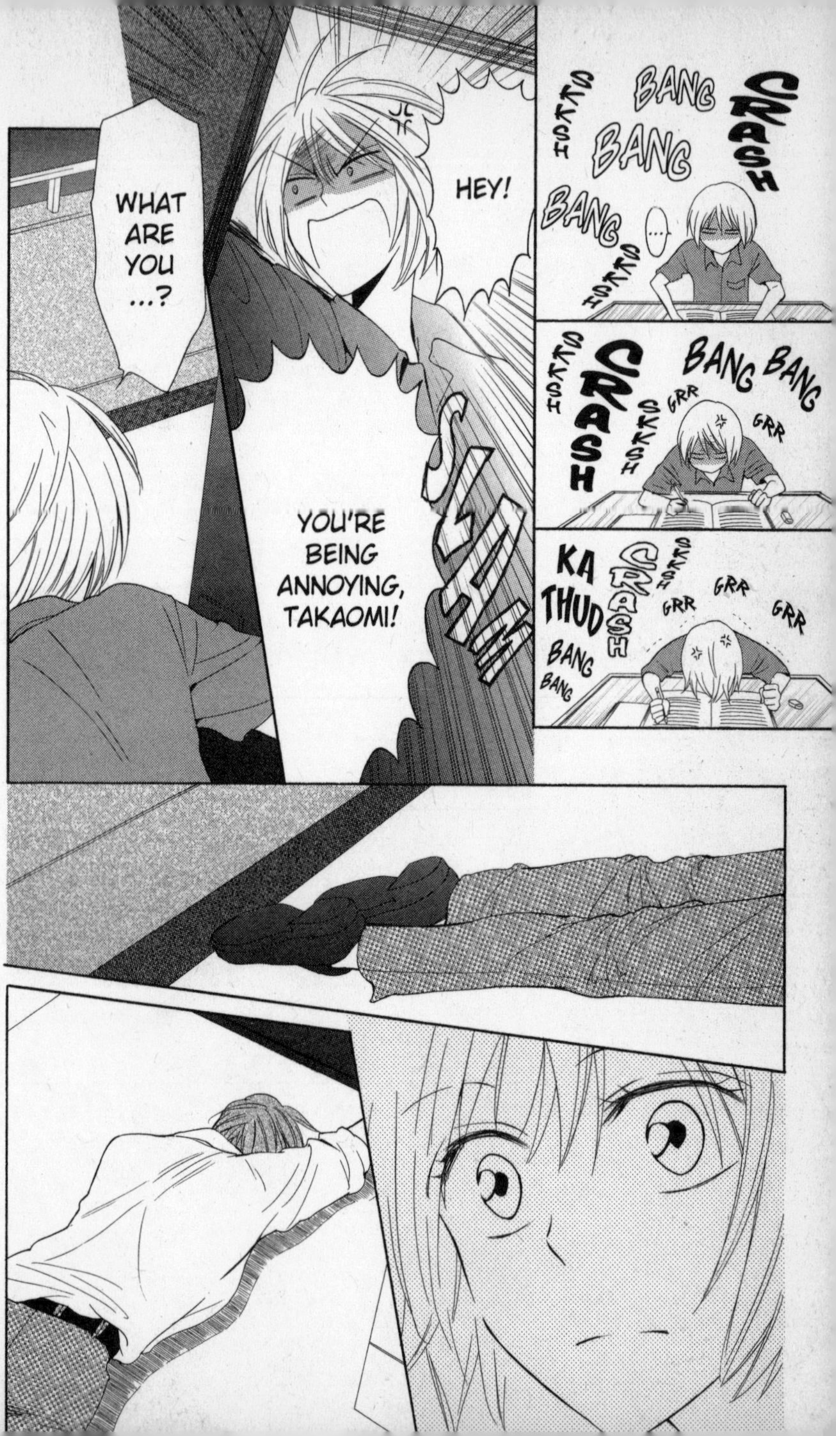
CRASH
BANG
SKKSH
BANG
BANG
...
SKKSH
SKKSH
BANG
BANG
BANG
CRASH
SKKSH
GRR
GRR
SKKSH
SKKSH
CRASH
GRR
GRR
GRR
KA THUD
BANG
BANG
HEY!
YOU'RE BEING ANNOYING, TAKAOMI!
SLAM
WHAT ARE YOU ...?

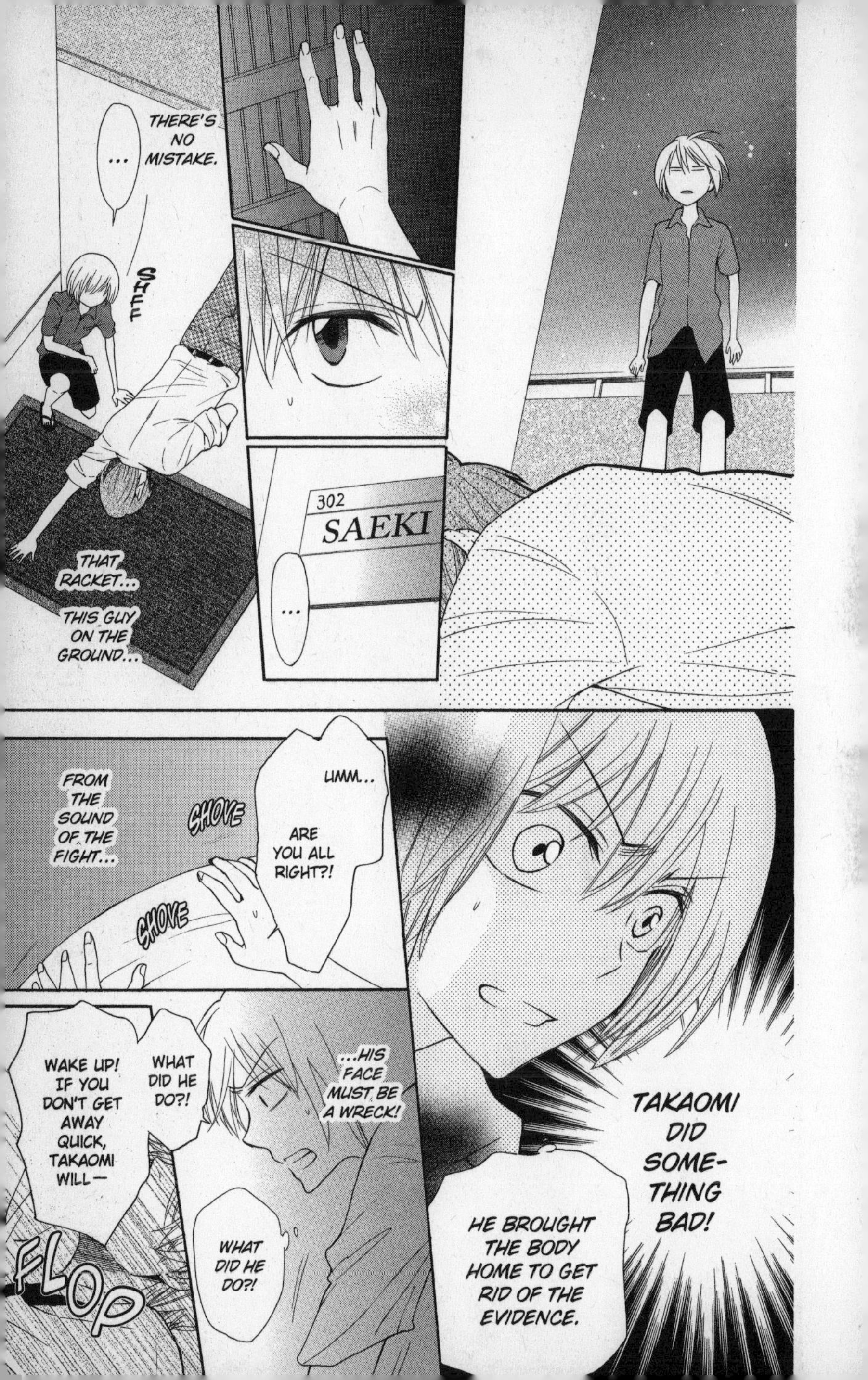

...
THERE'S NO MISTAKE.
SHFF
SAEKI
302
...
THAT RACKET...
THIS GUY ON THE GROUND...
UMM...
ARE YOU ALL RIGHT?!
SHOVE
SHOVE
FROM THE SOUND OF THE FIGHT...
TAKAOMI DID SOME-THING BAD!
HE BROUGHT THE BODY HOME TO GET RID OF THE EVIDENCE.
...HIS FACE MUST BE A WRECK!
WHAT DID HE DO?!
WAKE UP! IF YOU DON'T GET AWAY QUICK, TAKAOMI WILL—
WHAT DID HE DO?!
FLOP

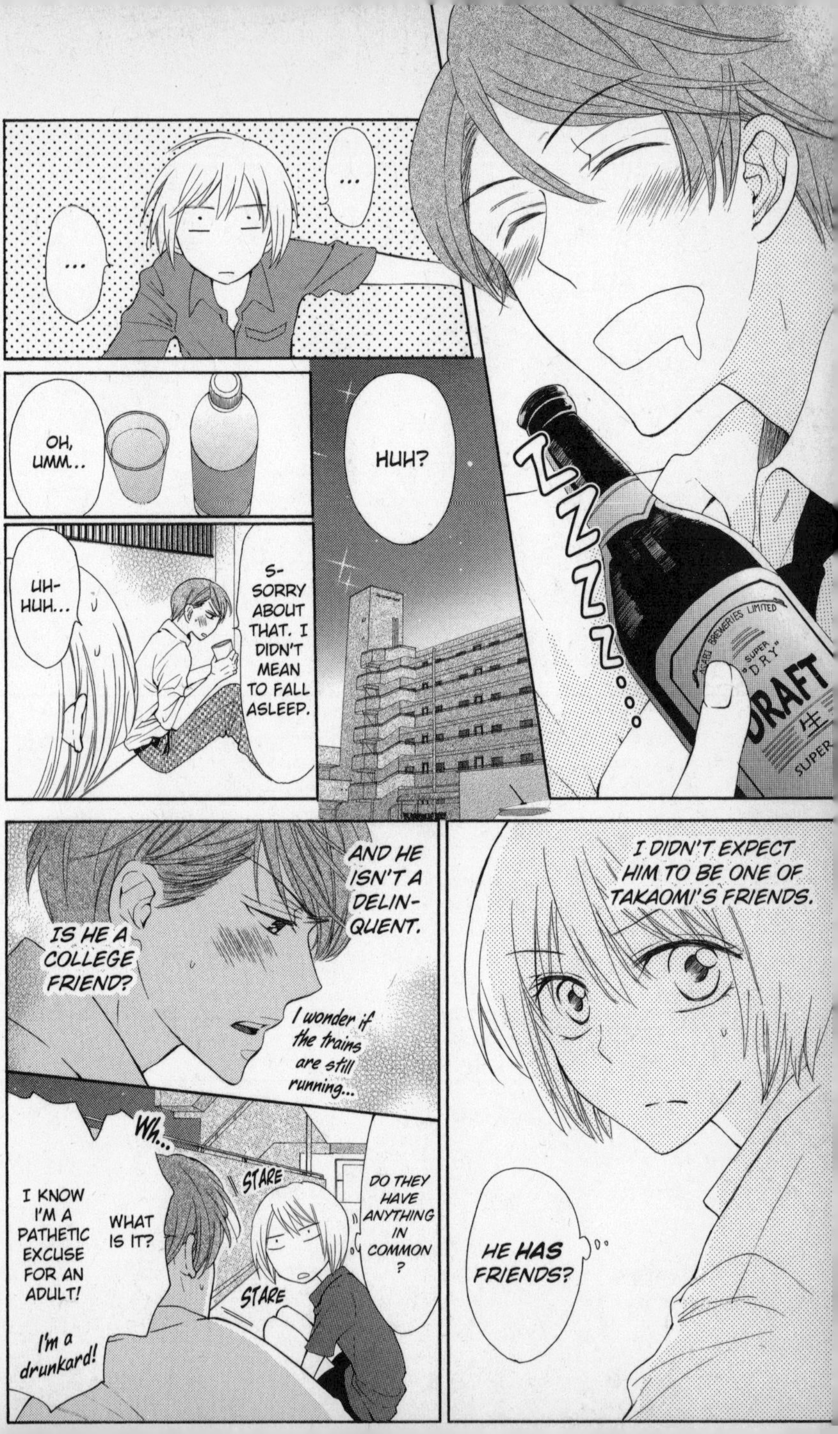
ZZZZ...
...
...
HUH?
OH, UMM...
S-SORRY ABOUT THAT. I DIDN'T MEAN TO FALL ASLEEP.
UH-HUH...
I DIDN'T EXPECT HIM TO BE ONE OF TAKAOMI'S FRIENDS.
HE HAS FRIENDS?
AND HE ISN'T A DELINQUENT.
IS HE A COLLEGE FRIEND?
I wonder if the trains are still running...
DO THEY HAVE ANYTHING IN COMMON?
STARE
STARE
Wh...
WHAT IS IT?
I KNOW I'M A PATHETIC EXCUSE FOR AN ADULT!
I'm a drunkard!

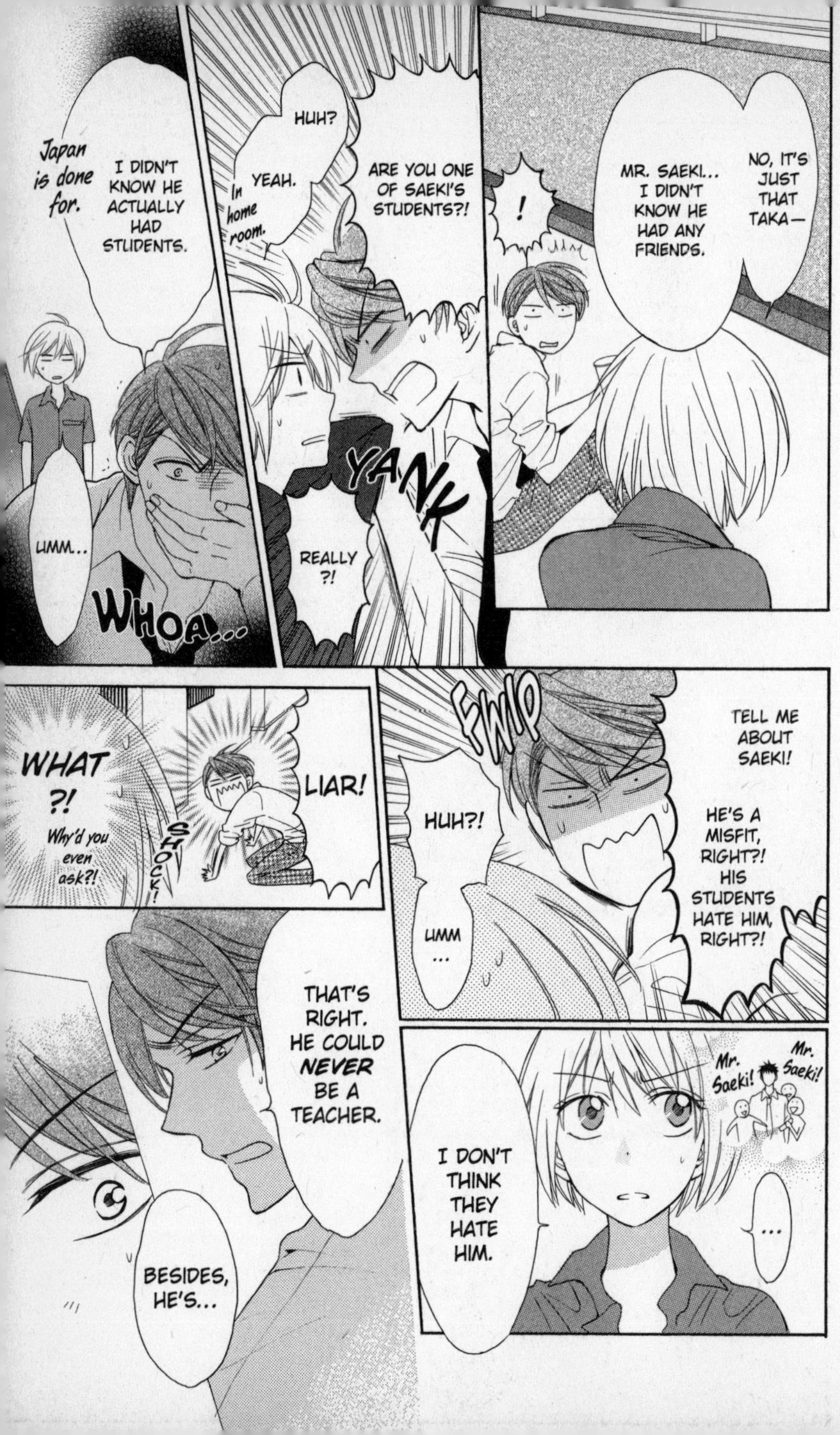
NO, IT'S JUST THAT TAKA—
MR. SAEKI... I DIDN'T KNOW HE HAD ANY FRIENDS.
!
HUH?
ARE YOU ONE OF SAEKI'S STUDENTS?!
YEAH.
In home room.
YANK
REALLY ?!
I DIDN'T KNOW HE ACTUALLY HAD STUDENTS.
Japan is done for.
UMM...
WHOA...
TELL ME ABOUT SAEKI!
HE'S A MISFIT, RIGHT?! HIS STUDENTS HATE HIM, RIGHT?!
FWIP
HUH?!
UMM ...
LIAR!
WHAT ?!
Why'd you even ask?!
SHOCK!
Mr. Saeki!
Mr. Saeki!
...
I DON'T THINK THEY HATE HIM.
THAT'S RIGHT. HE COULD NEVER BE A TEACHER.
BESIDES, HE'S...

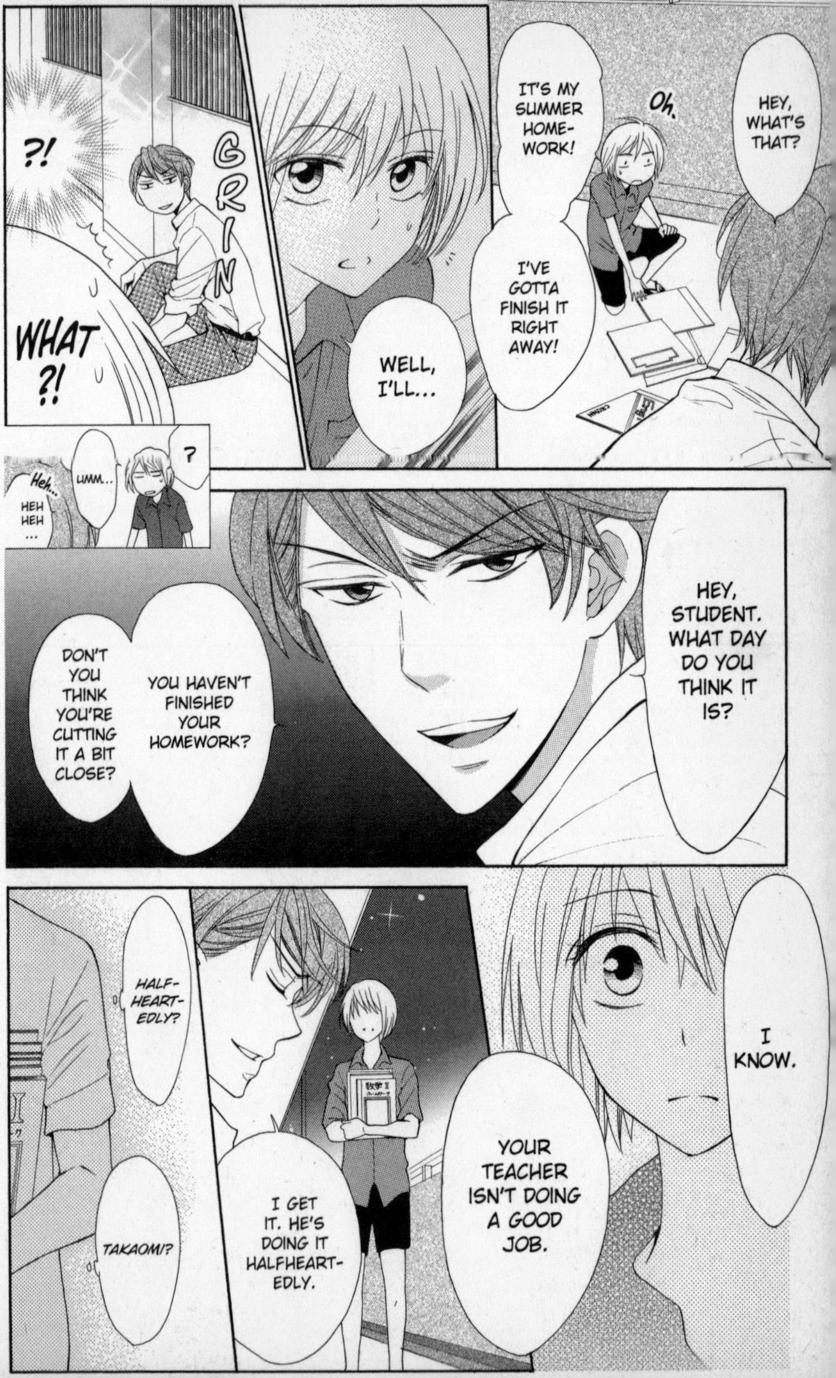
HEY, WHAT'S THAT?
Oh.
IT'S MY SUMMER HOME-WORK!
I'VE GOTTA FINISH IT RIGHT AWAY!
WELL, I'LL...
GRIN
?!
WHAT ?!
?
UMM...
Heh... HEH HEH...
HEY, STUDENT. WHAT DAY DO YOU THINK IT IS?
YOU HAVEN'T FINISHED YOUR HOMEWORK?
DON'T YOU THINK YOU'RE CUTTING IT A BIT CLOSE?
I KNOW.
YOUR TEACHER ISN'T DOING A GOOD JOB.
I GET IT. HE'S DOING IT HALFHEART-EDLY.
HALF-HEART-EDLY?
TAKAOMI?

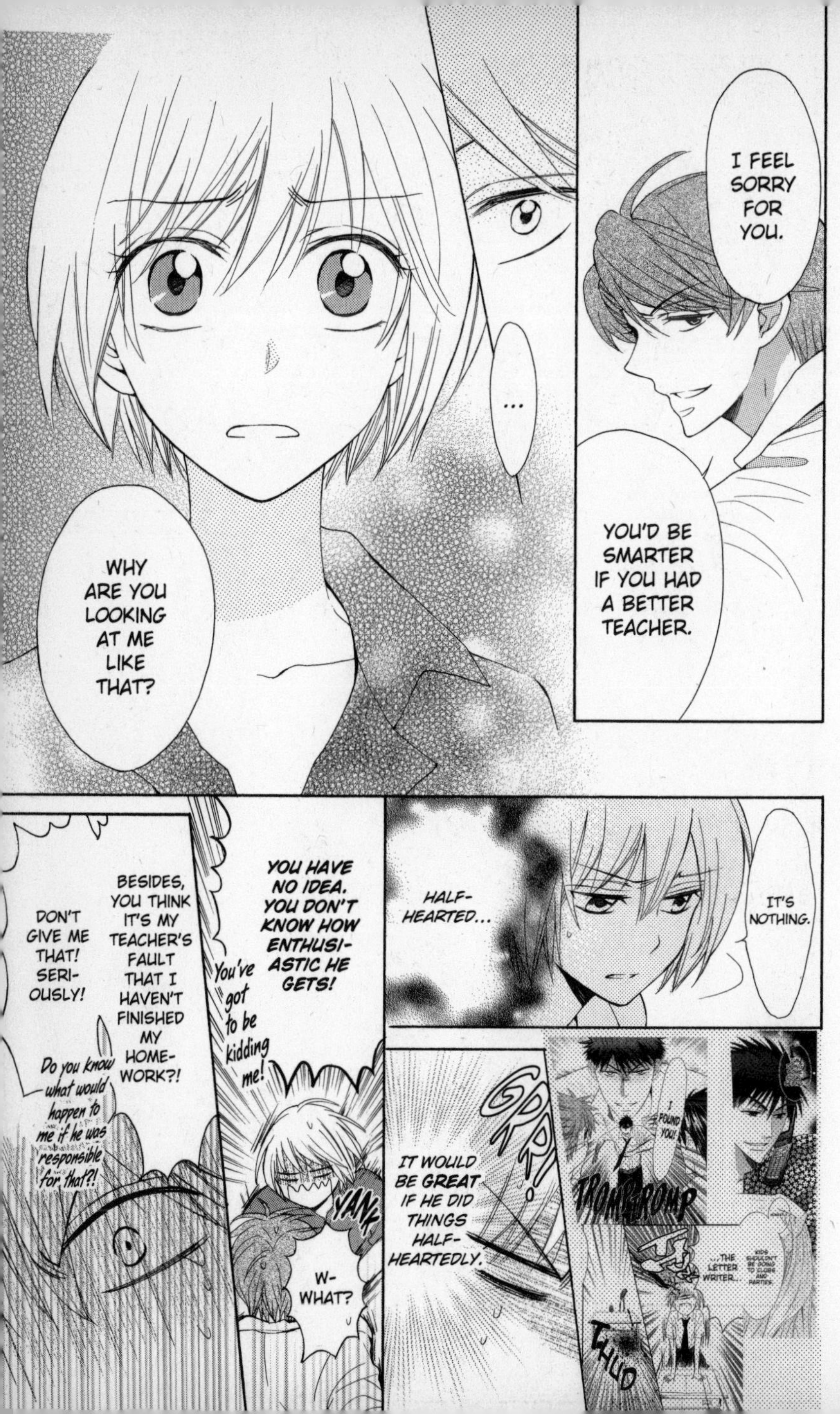
I FEEL SORRY FOR YOU.
YOU'D BE SMARTER IF YOU HAD A BETTER TEACHER.
...
WHY ARE YOU LOOKING AT ME LIKE THAT?
IT'S NOTHING.
HALF-HEARTED...
I FOUND YOU!
TROMP TROMP
KIDS SHOULDN'T BE GOING TO CLUBS AND PARTIES.
...THE LETTER WRITER...
THUD
GRR!
IT WOULD BE GREAT IF HE DID THINGS HALF-HEARTEDLY.
YOU HAVE NO IDEA. YOU DON'T KNOW HOW ENTHUSI-ASTIC HE GETS!
You've got to be kidding me!
YANK
W-WHAT?
BESIDES, YOU THINK IT'S MY TEACHER'S FAULT THAT I HAVEN'T FINISHED MY HOME-WORK?!
DON'T GIVE ME THAT! SERI-OUSLY!
Do you know what would happen to me if he was responsible for that?!

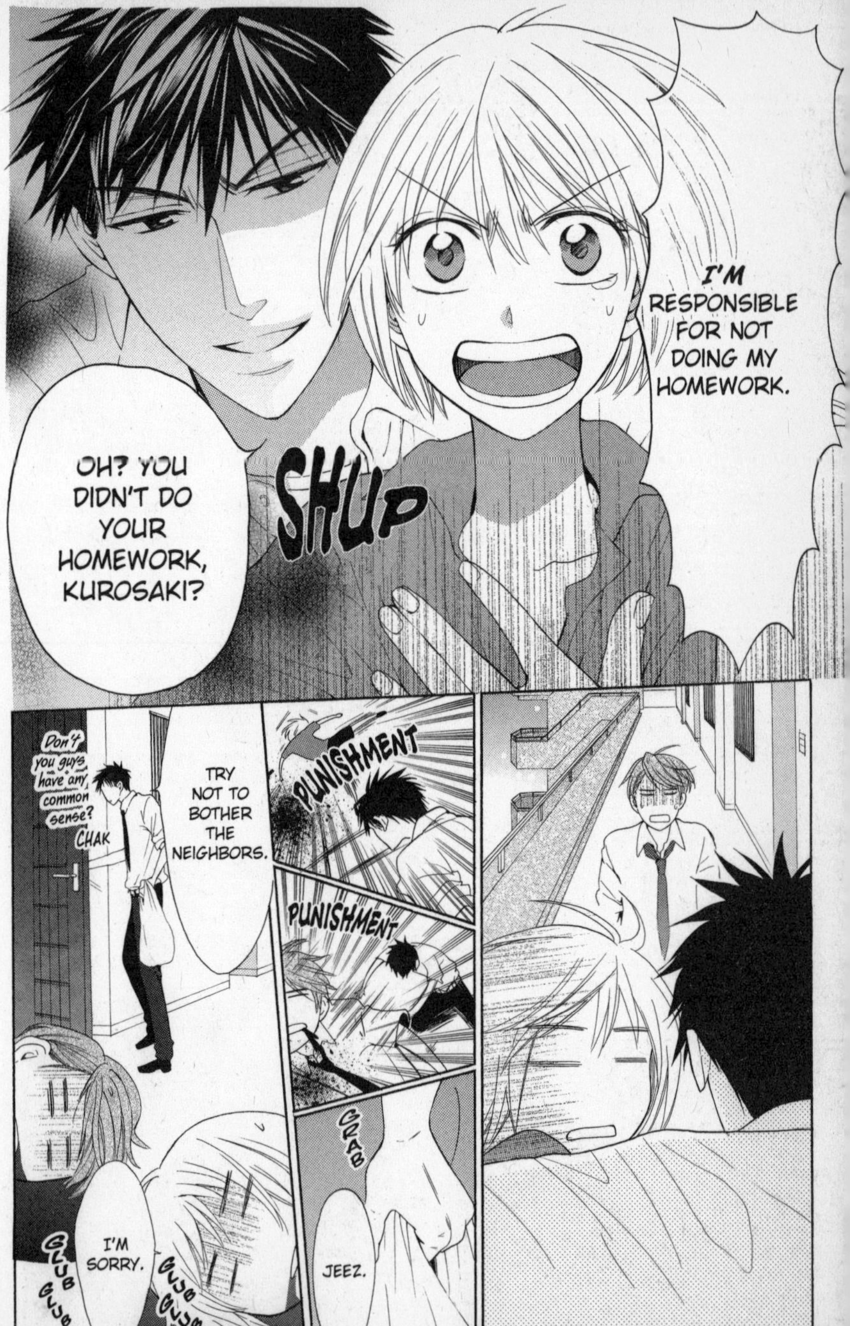
I'M RESPONSIBLE FOR NOT DOING MY HOMEWORK.
SHUP
OH? YOU DIDN'T DO YOUR HOMEWORK, KUROSAKI?
PUNISHMENT
PUNISHMENT
GRAB
JEEZ.
TRY NOT TO BOTHER THE NEIGHBORS.
Don't you guys have any common sense?
CHAK
GLUB GLUB
I'M SORRY.
GLUB GLUB

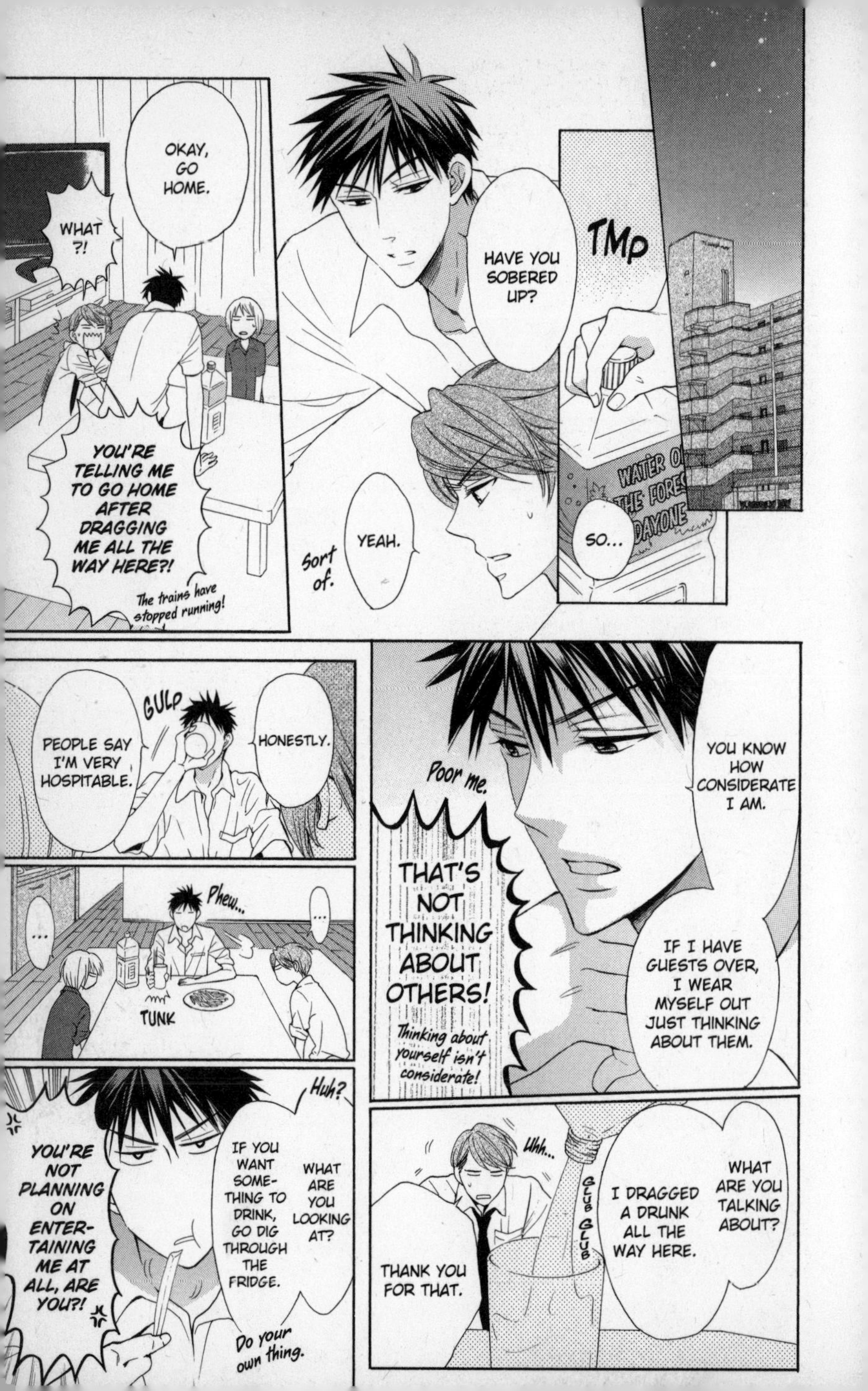

TMp
SO...
WATER OF THE FORES DAYONE
HAVE YOU SOBERED UP?
YEAH.
Sort of.
OKAY, GO HOME.
WHAT ?!
YOU'RE TELLING ME TO GO HOME AFTER DRAGGING ME ALL THE WAY HERE?!
The trains have stopped running!
YOU KNOW HOW CONSIDERATE I AM.
IF I HAVE GUESTS OVER, I WEAR MYSELF OUT JUST THINKING ABOUT THEM.
Poor me.
THAT'S NOT THINKING ABOUT OTHERS!
Thinking about yourself isn't considerate!
HONESTLY.
GULP
PEOPLE SAY I'M VERY HOSPITABLE.
...
Phew...
...
TUNK
WHAT ARE YOU TALKING ABOUT?
I DRAGGED A DRUNK ALL THE WAY HERE.
Uhh...
GLUB GLUB
THANK YOU FOR THAT.
Huh?
WHAT ARE YOU LOOKING AT?
IF YOU WANT SOME-THING TO DRINK, GO DIG THROUGH THE FRIDGE.
Do your own thing.
YOU'RE NOT PLANNING ON ENTER-TAINING ME AT ALL, ARE YOU?!

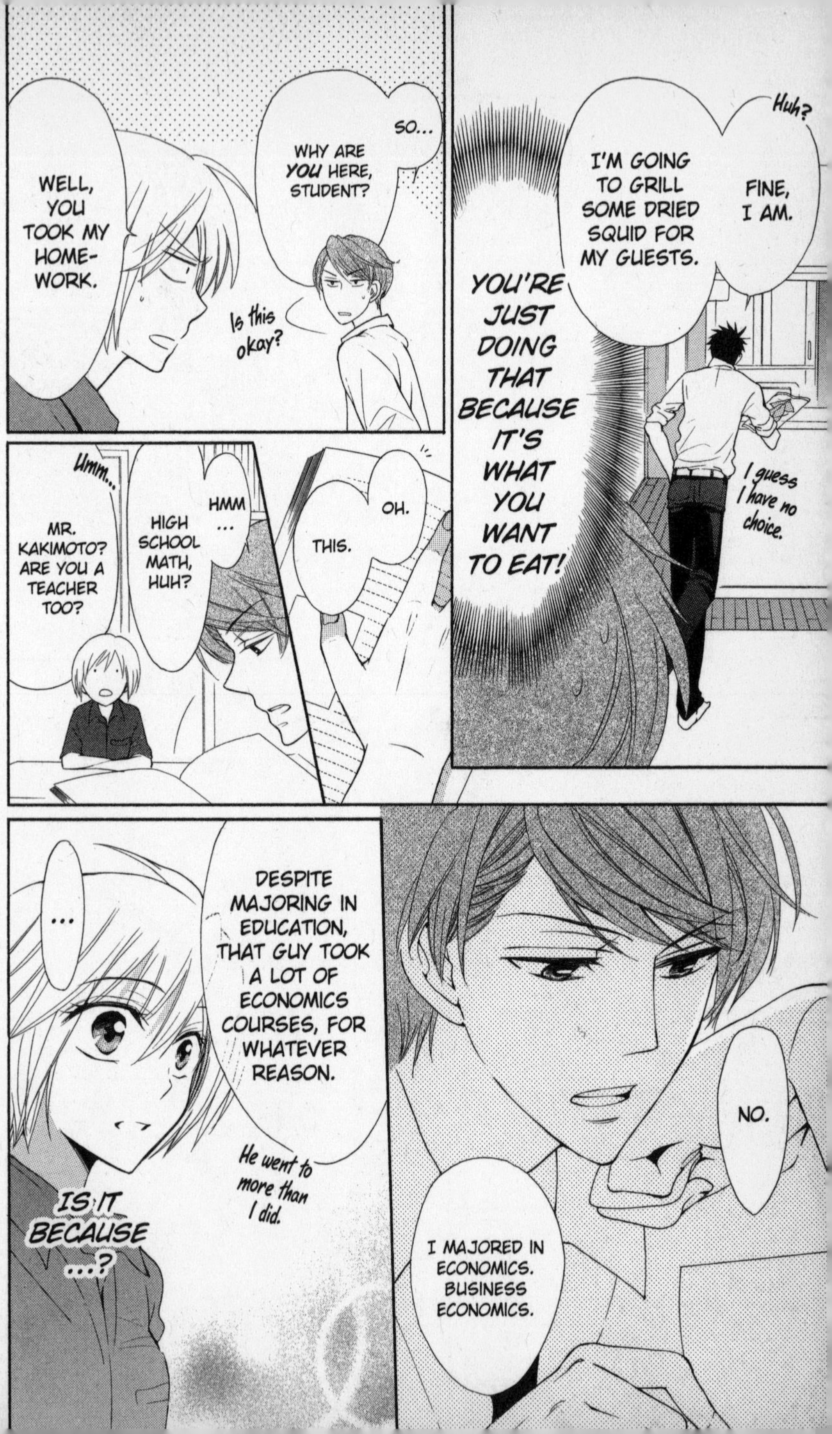
I'M GOING TO GRILL SOME DRIED SQUID FOR MY GUESTS.
Huh?
FINE, I AM.
YOU'RE JUST DOING THAT BECAUSE IT'S WHAT YOU WANT TO EAT!
I guess I have no choice.
SO...
WHY ARE *YOU* HERE, STUDENT?
Is this okay?
WELL, YOU TOOK MY HOMEWORK.
OH.
THIS.
HMM...
HIGH SCHOOL MATH, HUH?
Umm...
MR. KAKIMOTO? ARE YOU A TEACHER TOO?
NO.
I MAJORED IN ECONOMICS. BUSINESS ECONOMICS.
DESPITE MAJORING IN EDUCATION, THAT GUY TOOK A LOT OF ECONOMICS COURSES, FOR WHATEVER REASON.
He went to more than I did.
...
IS IT BECAUSE ...?

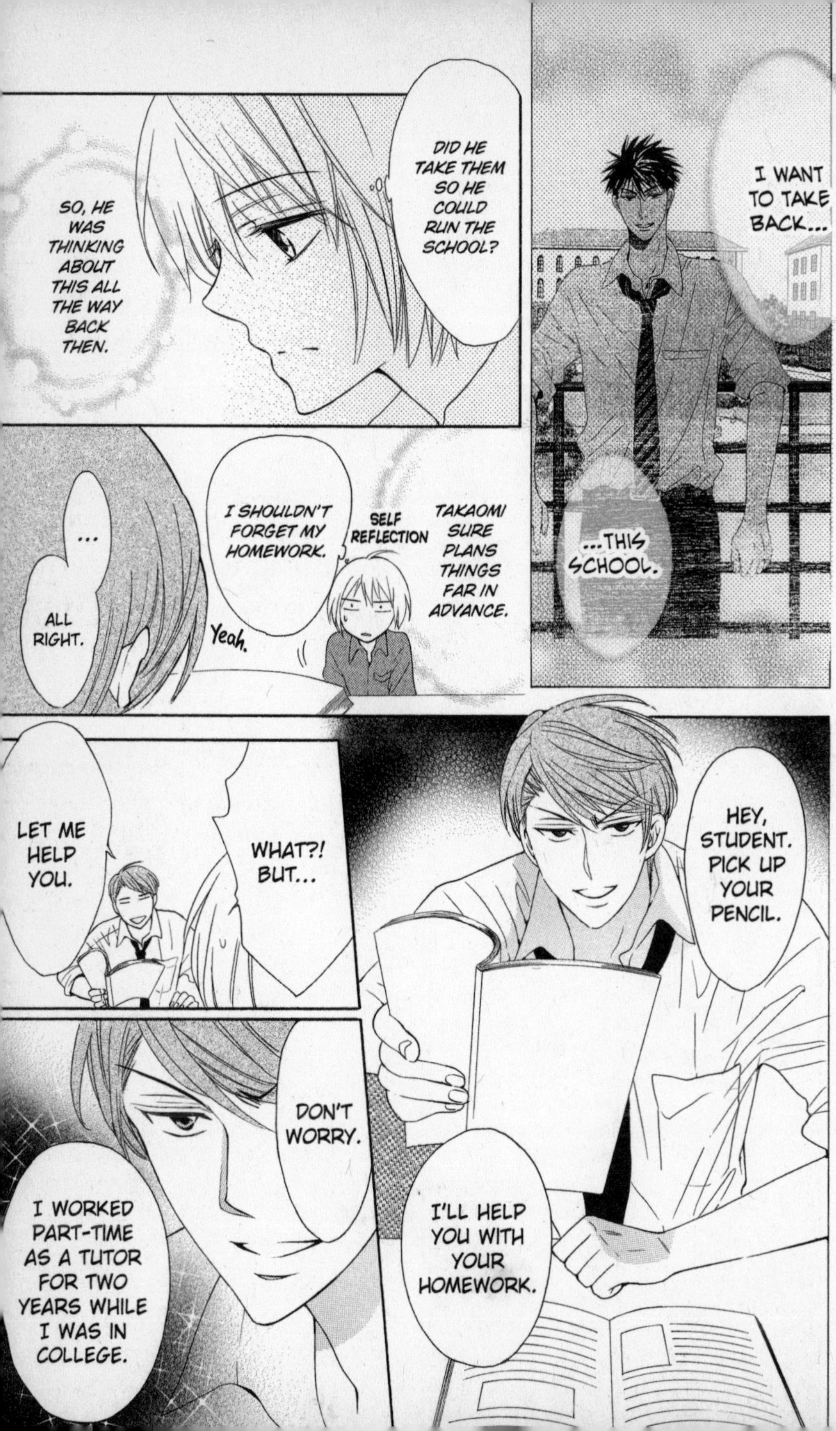
I WANT TO TAKE BACK...
...THIS SCHOOL.
DID HE TAKE THEM SO HE COULD RUN THE SCHOOL?
SO, HE WAS THINKING ABOUT THIS ALL THE WAY BACK THEN.
TAKAOMI SURE PLANS THINGS FAR IN ADVANCE.
SELF REFLECTION
I SHOULDN'T FORGET MY HOMEWORK.
Yeah.
...
ALL RIGHT.
HEY, STUDENT. PICK UP YOUR PENCIL.
I'LL HELP YOU WITH YOUR HOMEWORK.
WHAT?! BUT...
LET ME HELP YOU.
DON'T WORRY.
I WORKED PART-TIME AS A TUTOR FOR TWO YEARS WHILE I WAS IN COLLEGE.

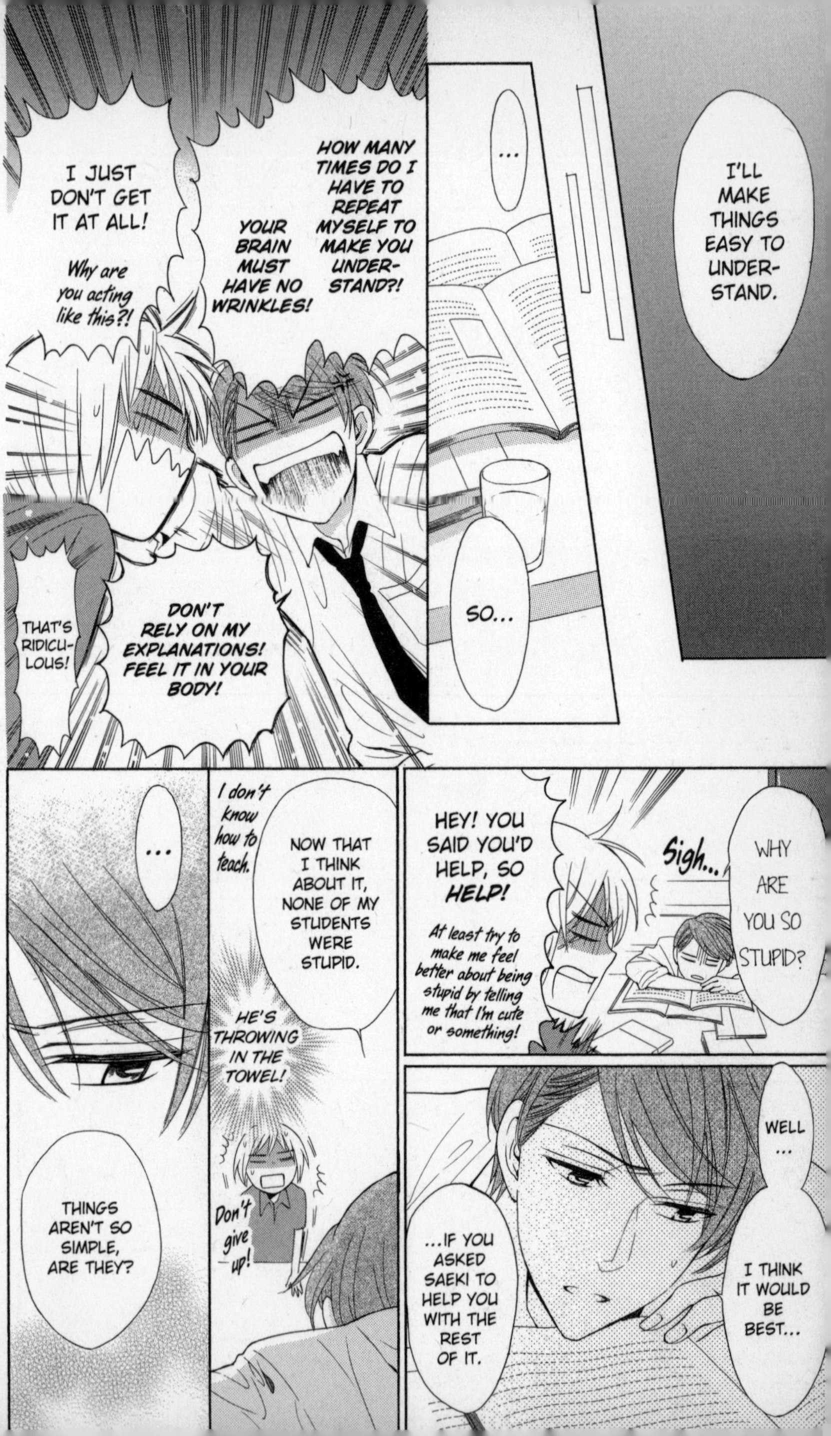
I'LL MAKE THINGS EASY TO UNDERSTAND.
...
SO...
HOW MANY TIMES DO I HAVE TO REPEAT MYSELF TO MAKE YOU UNDERSTAND?!
YOUR BRAIN MUST HAVE NO WRINKLES!
I JUST DON'T GET IT AT ALL!
Why are you acting like this?!
DON'T RELY ON MY EXPLANATIONS! FEEL IT IN YOUR BODY!
THAT'S RIDICULOUS!
WHY ARE YOU SO STUPID?
Sigh...
HEY! YOU SAID YOU'D HELP, SO HELP!
At least try to make me feel better about being stupid by telling me that I'm cute or something!
WELL...
I THINK IT WOULD BE BEST...
...IF YOU ASKED SAEKI TO HELP YOU WITH THE REST OF IT.
NOW THAT I THINK ABOUT IT, NONE OF MY STUDENTS WERE STUPID.
I don't know how to teach.
HE'S THROWING IN THE TOWEL!
Don't give up!
...
THINGS AREN'T SO SIMPLE, ARE THEY?

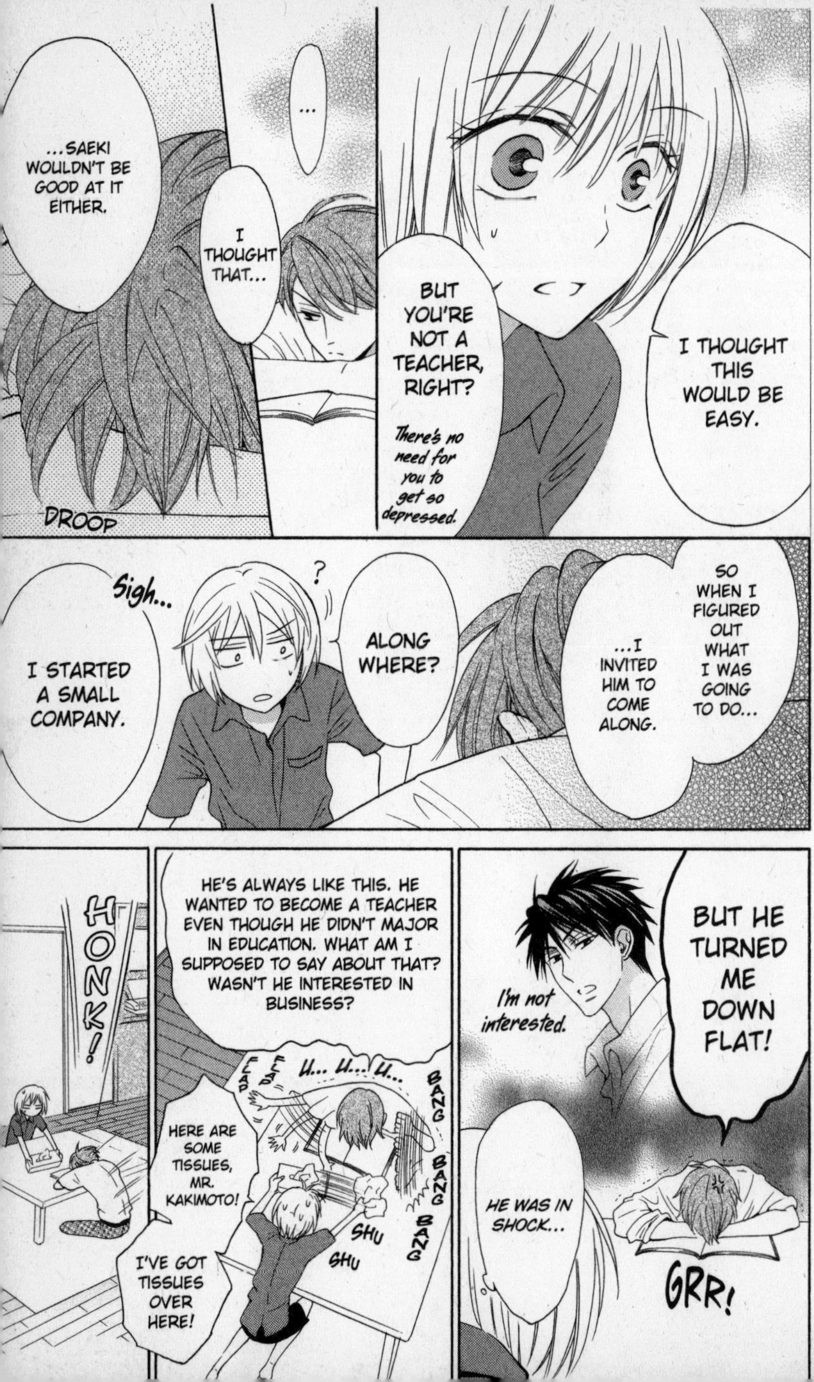
I THOUGHT THIS WOULD BE EASY.
BUT YOU'RE NOT A TEACHER, RIGHT?
There's no need for you to get so depressed.
...
I THOUGHT THAT...
...SAEKI WOULDN'T BE GOOD AT IT EITHER.
DROOP
SO WHEN I FIGURED OUT WHAT I WAS GOING TO DO...
...I INVITED HIM TO COME ALONG.
?
ALONG WHERE?
Sigh...
I STARTED A SMALL COMPANY.
BUT HE TURNED ME DOWN FLAT!
I'm not interested.
HE WAS IN SHOCK...
GRR!
HE'S ALWAYS LIKE THIS. HE WANTED TO BECOME A TEACHER EVEN THOUGH HE DIDN'T MAJOR IN EDUCATION. WHAT AM I SUPPOSED TO SAY ABOUT THAT? WASN'T HE INTERESTED IN BUSINESS?
U... U... U...
BANG
BANG
BANG
FLAP FLAP
HERE ARE SOME TISSUES, MR. KAKIMOTO!
SHU
SHU
I'VE GOT TISSUES OVER HERE!
HONK!

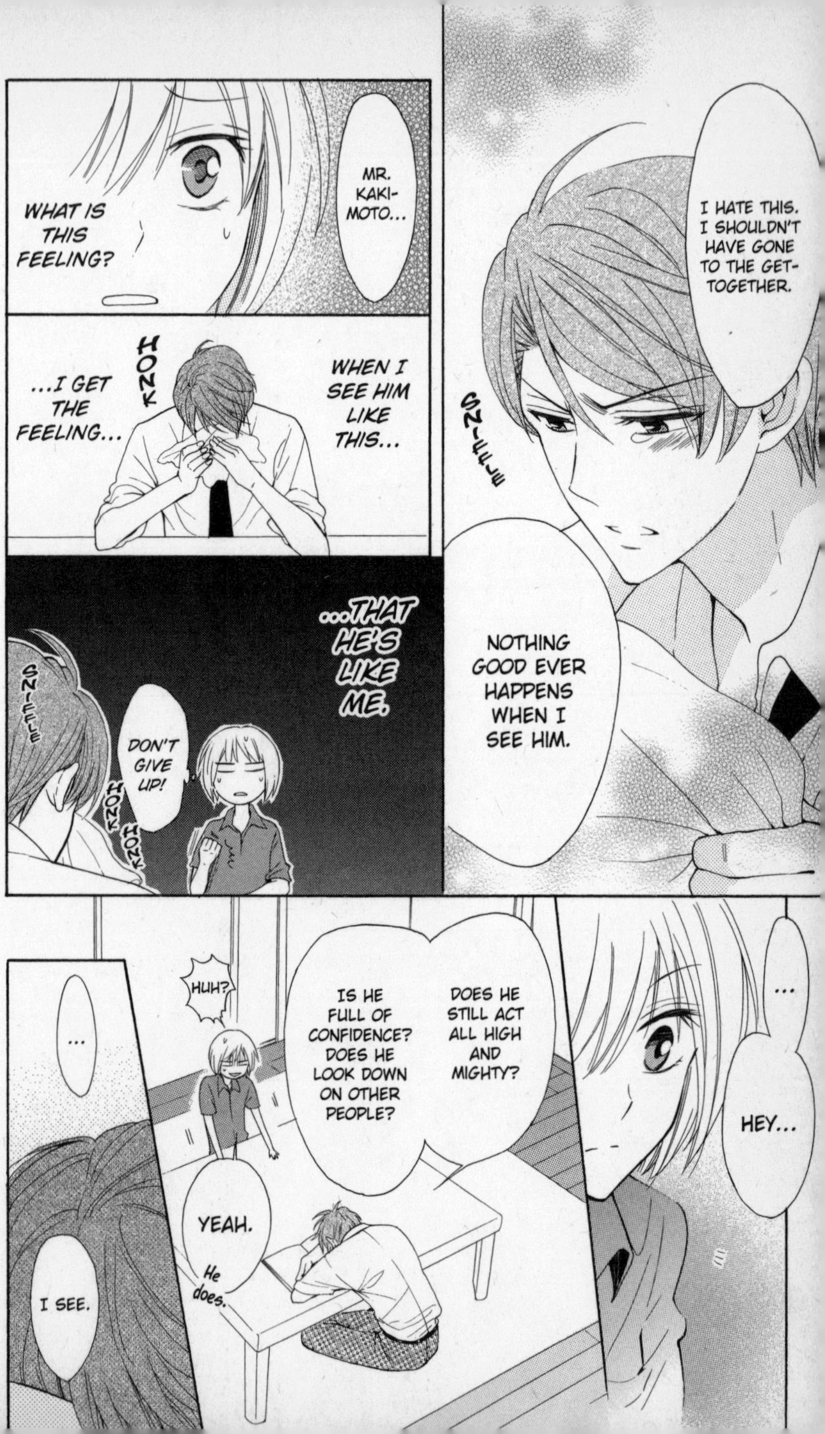
I HATE THIS. I SHOULDN'T HAVE GONE TO THE GET-TOGETHER.
SNIFFLE
NOTHING GOOD EVER HAPPENS WHEN I SEE HIM.
MR. KAKI-MOTO...
WHAT IS THIS FEELING?
WHEN I SEE HIM LIKE THIS...
HONK
...I GET THE FEELING...
...THAT HE'S LIKE ME.
DON'T GIVE UP!
SNIFFLE
HONK HONK
...
HEY...
DOES HE STILL ACT ALL HIGH AND MIGHTY?
IS HE FULL OF CONFIDENCE? DOES HE LOOK DOWN ON OTHER PEOPLE?
HUH?
YEAH.
He does.
...
I SEE.

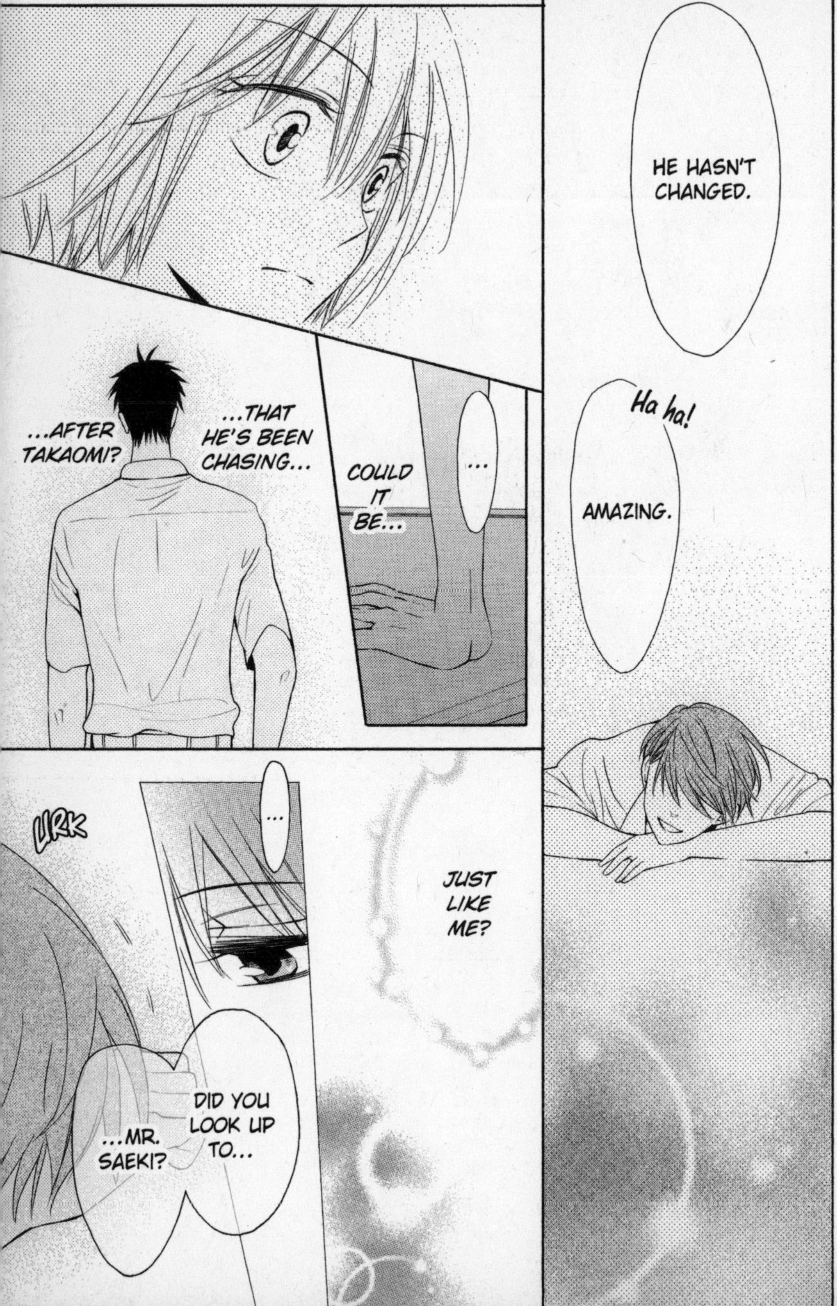
HE HASN'T CHANGED.
Ha ha!
AMAZING.
...
COULD IT BE...
...THAT HE'S BEEN CHASING...
...AFTER TAKAOMI?
JUST LIKE ME?
...
URK
DID YOU LOOK UP TO...
...MR. SAEKI?

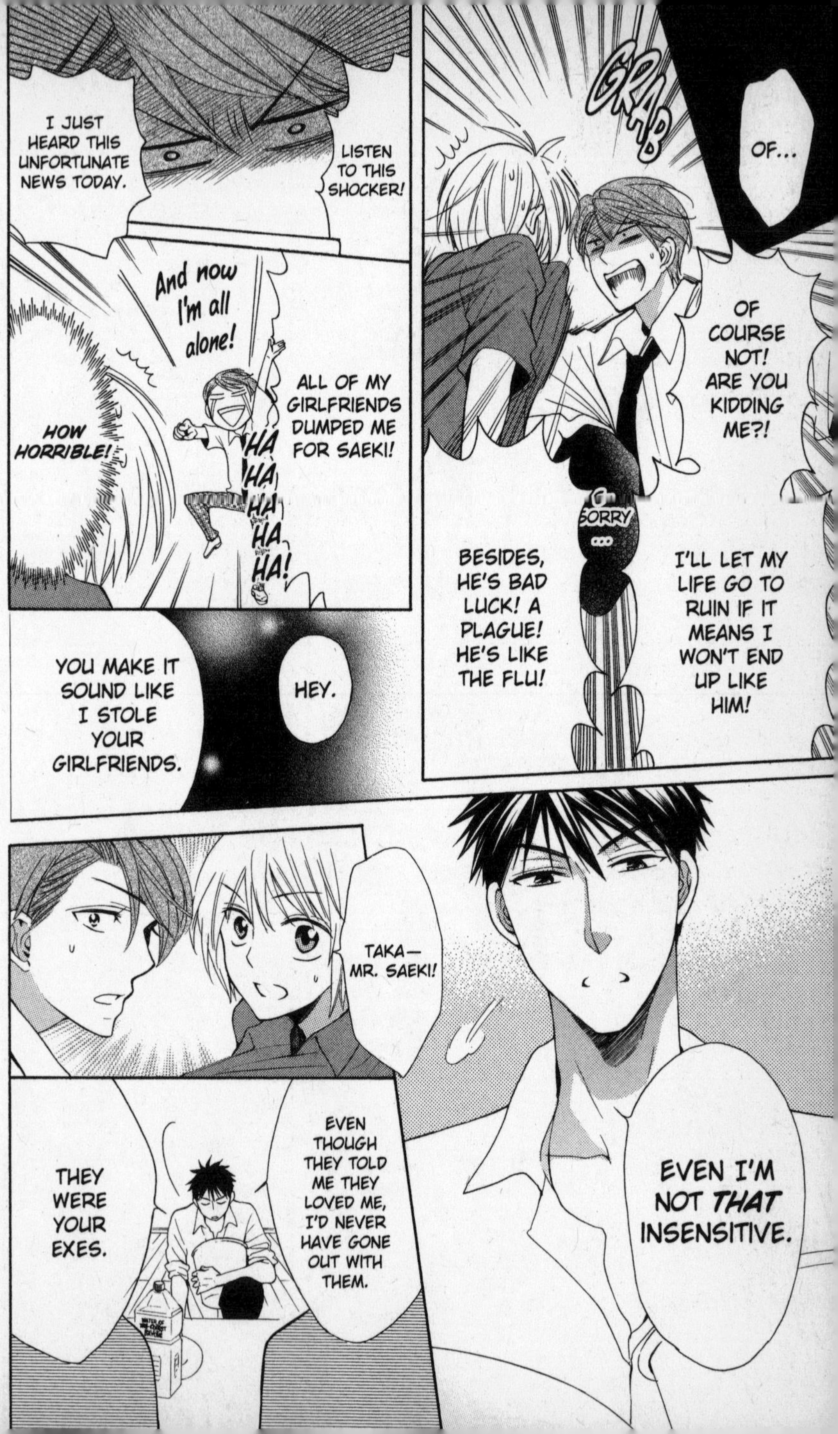
LISTEN TO THIS SHOCKER!
I JUST HEARD THIS UNFORTUNATE NEWS TODAY.
ALL OF MY GIRLFRIENDS DUMPED ME FOR SAEKI!
And now I'm all alone!
HA HA HA HA HA!
HOW HORRIBLE!
HEY.
YOU MAKE IT SOUND LIKE I STOLE YOUR GIRLFRIENDS.
GRAB
OF...
OF COURSE NOT! ARE YOU KIDDING ME?!
SORRY...
I'LL LET MY LIFE GO TO RUIN IF IT MEANS I WON'T END UP LIKE HIM!
BESIDES, HE'S BAD LUCK! A PLAGUE! HE'S LIKE THE FLU!
EVEN I'M NOT *THAT* INSENSITIVE.
TAKA— MR. SAEKI!
EVEN THOUGH THEY TOLD ME THEY LOVED ME, I'D NEVER HAVE GONE OUT WITH THEM.
THEY WERE YOUR EXES.

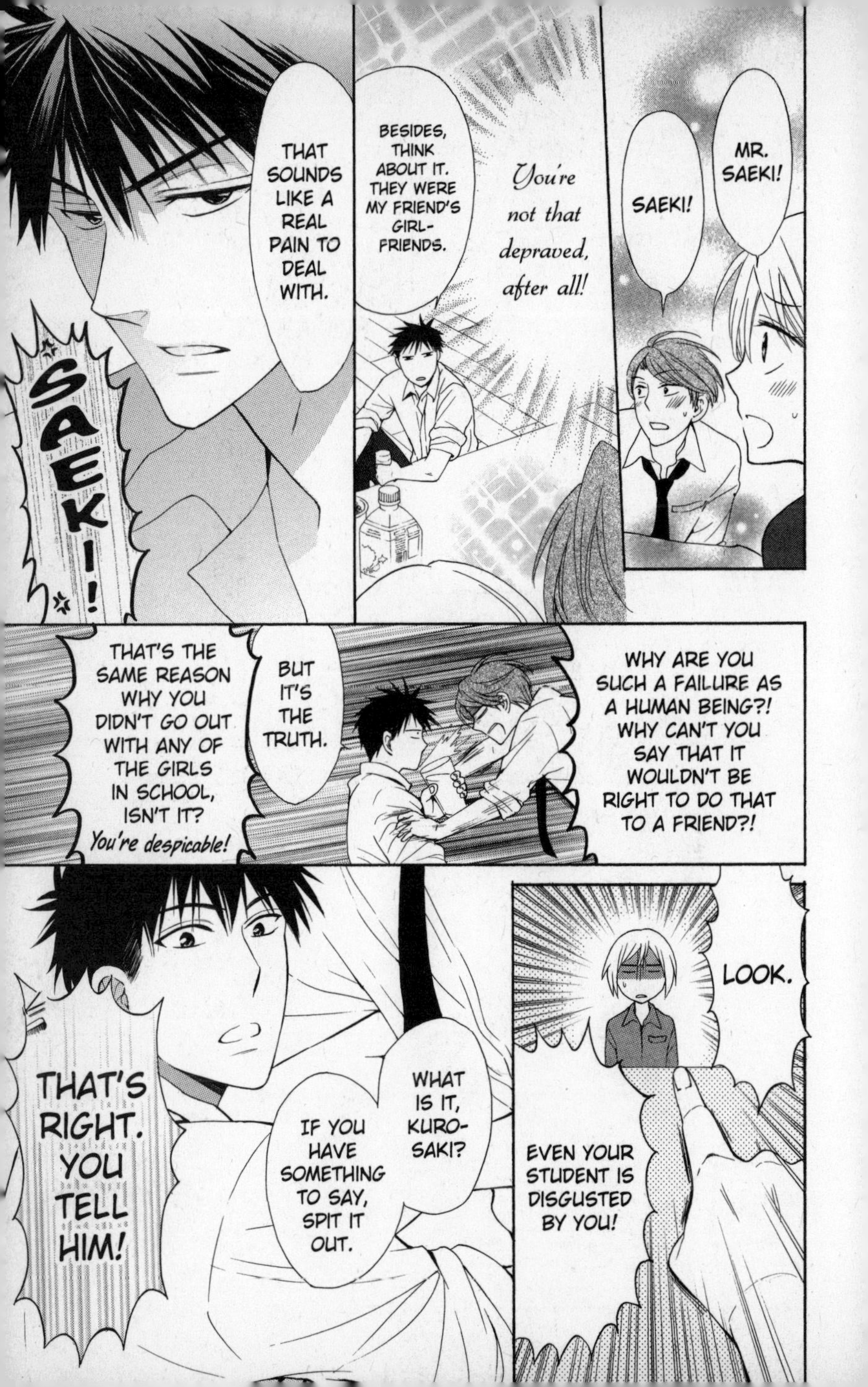
MR. SAEKI!
SAEKI!
You're not that depraved, after all!
BESIDES, THINK ABOUT IT. THEY WERE MY FRIEND'S GIRL-FRIENDS.
THAT SOUNDS LIKE A REAL PAIN TO DEAL WITH.
SAEKI!
WHY ARE YOU SUCH A FAILURE AS A HUMAN BEING?! WHY CAN'T YOU SAY THAT IT WOULDN'T BE RIGHT TO DO THAT TO A FRIEND?!
BUT IT'S THE TRUTH.
THAT'S THE SAME REASON WHY YOU DIDN'T GO OUT WITH ANY OF THE GIRLS IN SCHOOL, ISN'T IT? You're despicable!
LOOK.
EVEN YOUR STUDENT IS DISGUSTED BY YOU!
WHAT IS IT, KURO-SAKI?
IF YOU HAVE SOMETHING TO SAY, SPIT IT OUT.
THAT'S RIGHT. YOU TELL HIM!

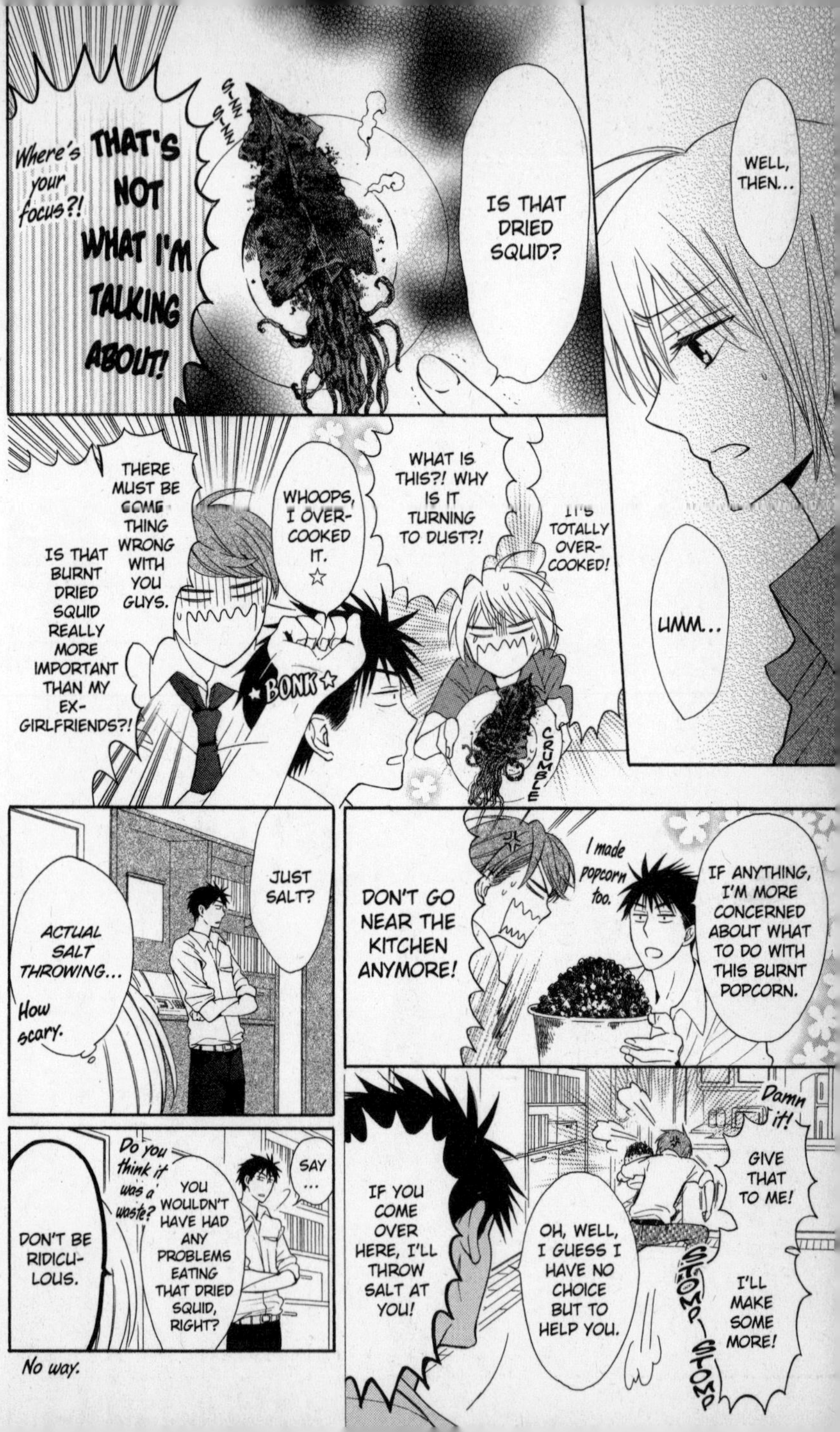
WELL, THEN...
UMM...
IS THAT DRIED SQUID?
SIZZ SIZZ
THAT'S NOT WHAT I'M TALKING ABOUT!
Where's your focus?!
IT'S TOTALLY OVER-COOKED!
WHAT IS THIS?! WHY IS IT TURNING TO DUST?!
CRUMBLE
WHOOPS, I OVER-COOKED IT. ☆
BONK☆
THERE MUST BE SOME-THING WRONG WITH YOU GUYS.
IS THAT BURNT DRIED SQUID REALLY MORE IMPORTANT THAN MY EX-GIRLFRIENDS?!
IF ANYTHING, I'M MORE CONCERNED ABOUT WHAT TO DO WITH THIS BURNT POPCORN.
I made popcorn too.
DON'T GO NEAR THE KITCHEN ANYMORE!
JUST SALT?
ACTUAL SALT THROWING...
How scary.
Damn it!
GIVE THAT TO ME!
I'LL MAKE SOME MORE!
STOMP STOMP
OH, WELL, I GUESS I HAVE NO CHOICE BUT TO HELP YOU.
IF YOU COME OVER HERE, I'LL THROW SALT AT YOU!
SAY...
YOU WOULDN'T HAVE HAD ANY PROBLEMS EATING THAT DRIED SQUID, RIGHT?
Do you think it was a waste?
DON'T BE RIDICU-LOUS.
No way.

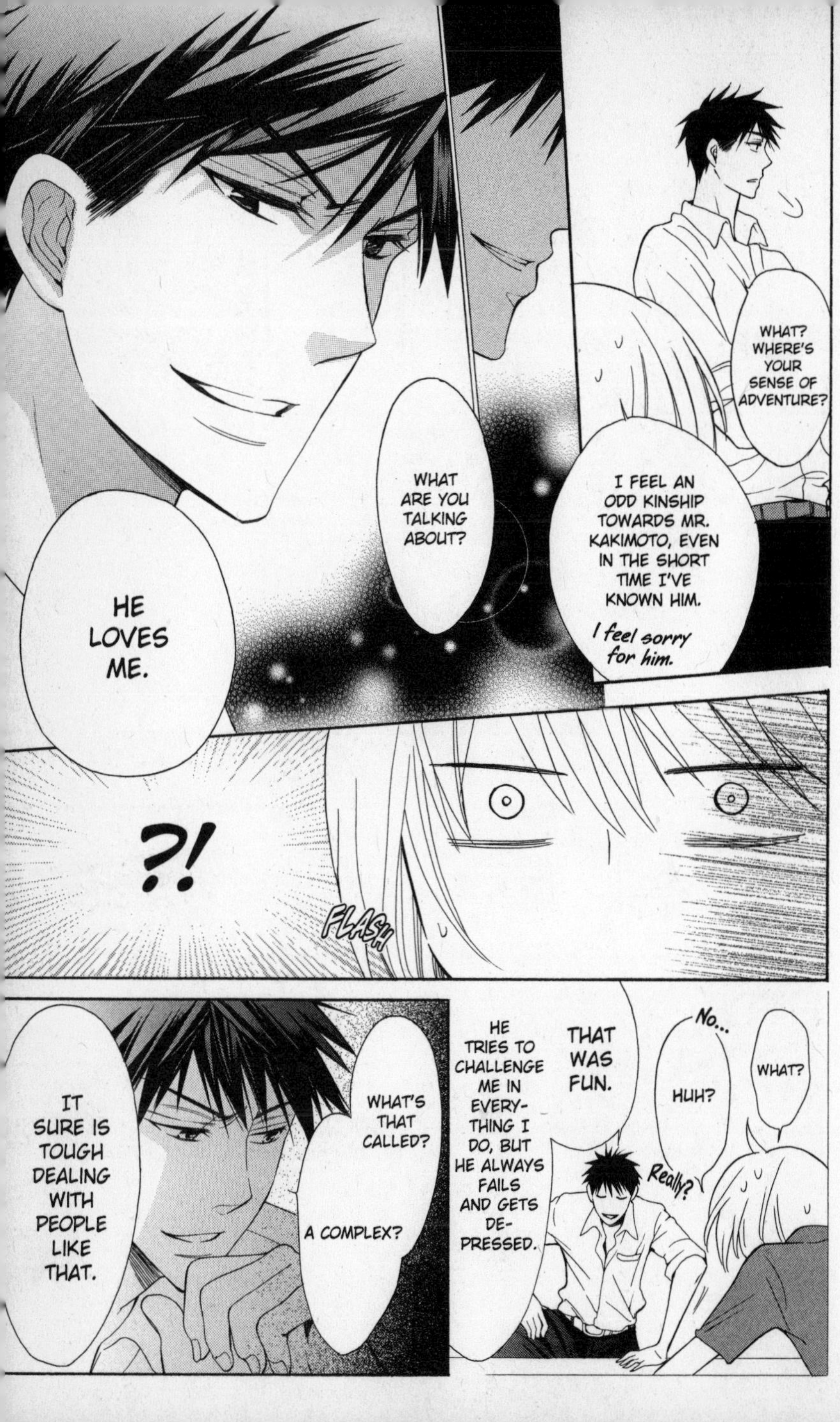
WHAT? WHERE'S YOUR SENSE OF ADVENTURE?
I FEEL AN ODD KINSHIP TOWARDS MR. KAKIMOTO, EVEN IN THE SHORT TIME I'VE KNOWN HIM.
I feel sorry for him.
WHAT ARE YOU TALKING ABOUT?
HE LOVES ME.
?!
FLASH
WHAT?
No...
HUH?
Really?
THAT WAS FUN.
HE TRIES TO CHALLENGE ME IN EVERY-THING I DO, BUT HE ALWAYS FAILS AND GETS DE-PRESSED.
WHAT'S THAT CALLED?
A COMPLEX?
IT SURE IS TOUGH DEALING WITH PEOPLE LIKE THAT.

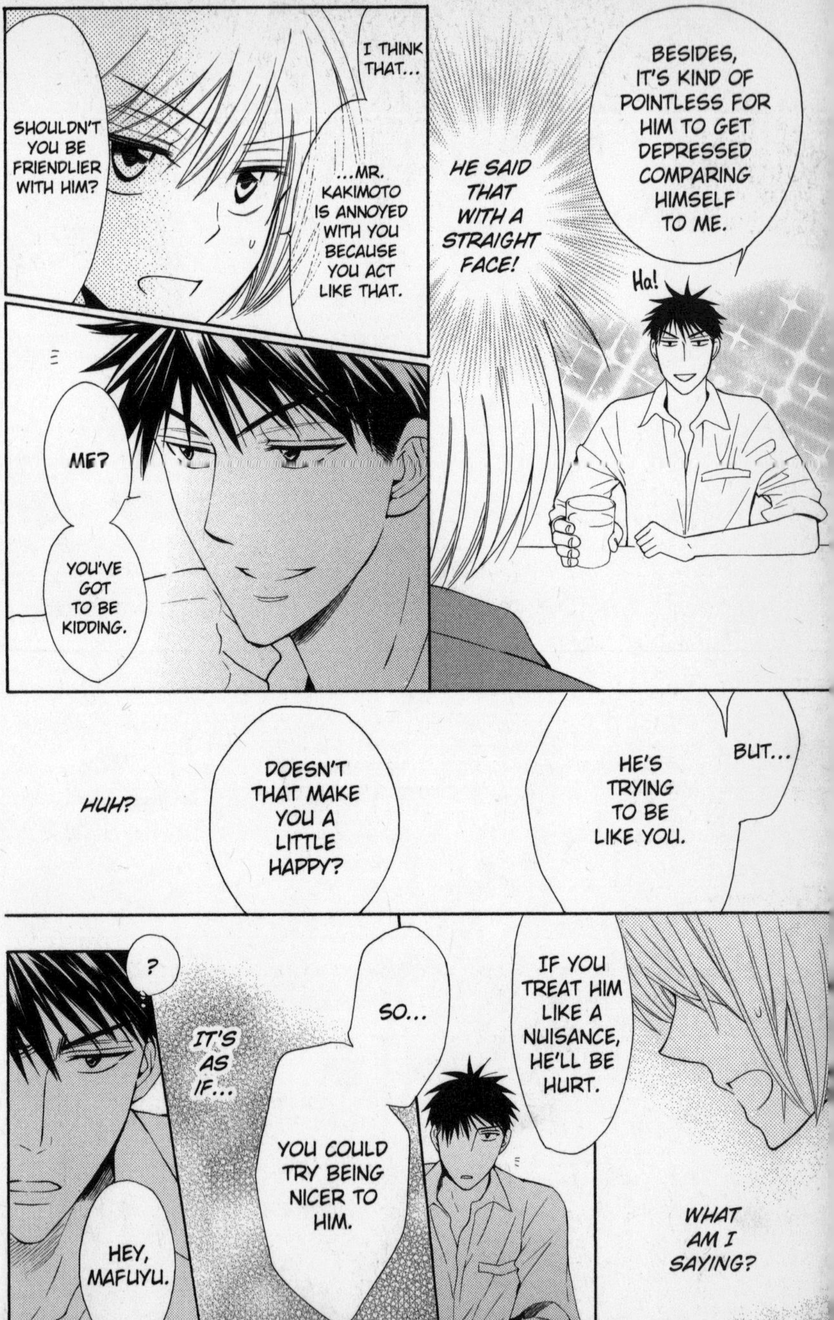
BESIDES, IT'S KIND OF POINTLESS FOR HIM TO GET DEPRESSED COMPARING HIMSELF TO ME.
Ha!
HE SAID THAT WITH A STRAIGHT FACE!
I THINK THAT...
...MR. KAKIMOTO IS ANNOYED WITH YOU BECAUSE YOU ACT LIKE THAT.
SHOULDN'T YOU BE FRIENDLIER WITH HIM?
ME?
YOU'VE GOT TO BE KIDDING.
BUT...
HE'S TRYING TO BE LIKE YOU.
DOESN'T THAT MAKE YOU A LITTLE HAPPY?
HUH?
IF YOU TREAT HIM LIKE A NUISANCE, HE'LL BE HURT.
WHAT AM I SAYING?
SO...
YOU COULD TRY BEING NICER TO HIM.
?
IT'S AS IF...
HEY, MAFUYU.

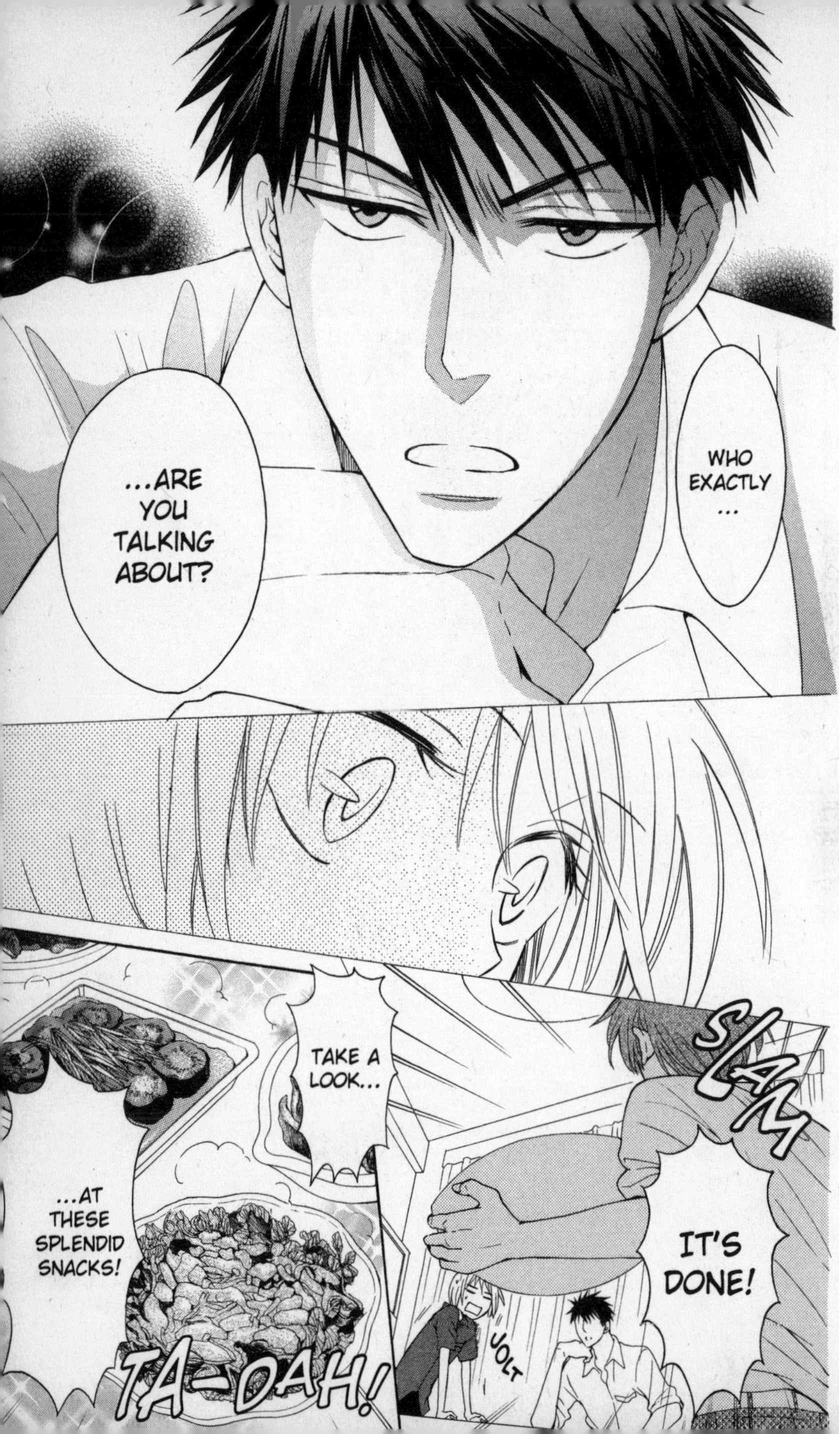
WHO EXACTLY ...
...ARE YOU TALKING ABOUT?
SLAM
IT'S DONE!
JOLT
TAKE A LOOK...
...AT THESE SPLENDID SNACKS!
TA-DAH!

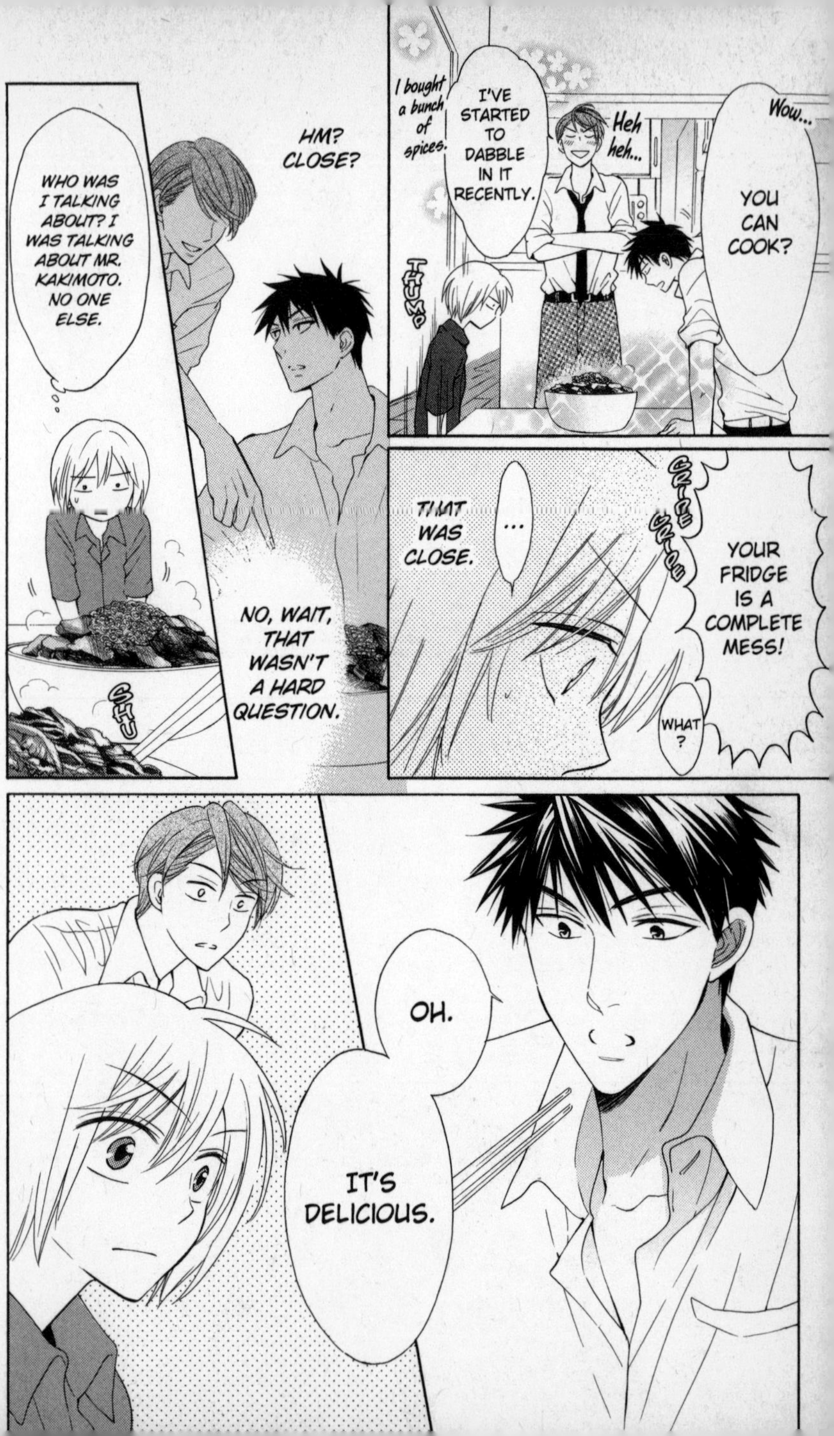
Wow...
YOU CAN COOK?
Heh heh...
I'VE STARTED TO DABBLE IN IT RECENTLY.
I bought a bunch of spices.
THUMP
YOUR FRIDGE IS A COMPLETE MESS!
WHAT?
...
THAT WAS CLOSE.
HM? CLOSE?
WHO WAS I TALKING ABOUT? I WAS TALKING ABOUT MR. KAKIMOTO. NO ONE ELSE.
NO, WAIT, THAT WASN'T A HARD QUESTION.
SHU
OH.
IT'S DELICIOUS.

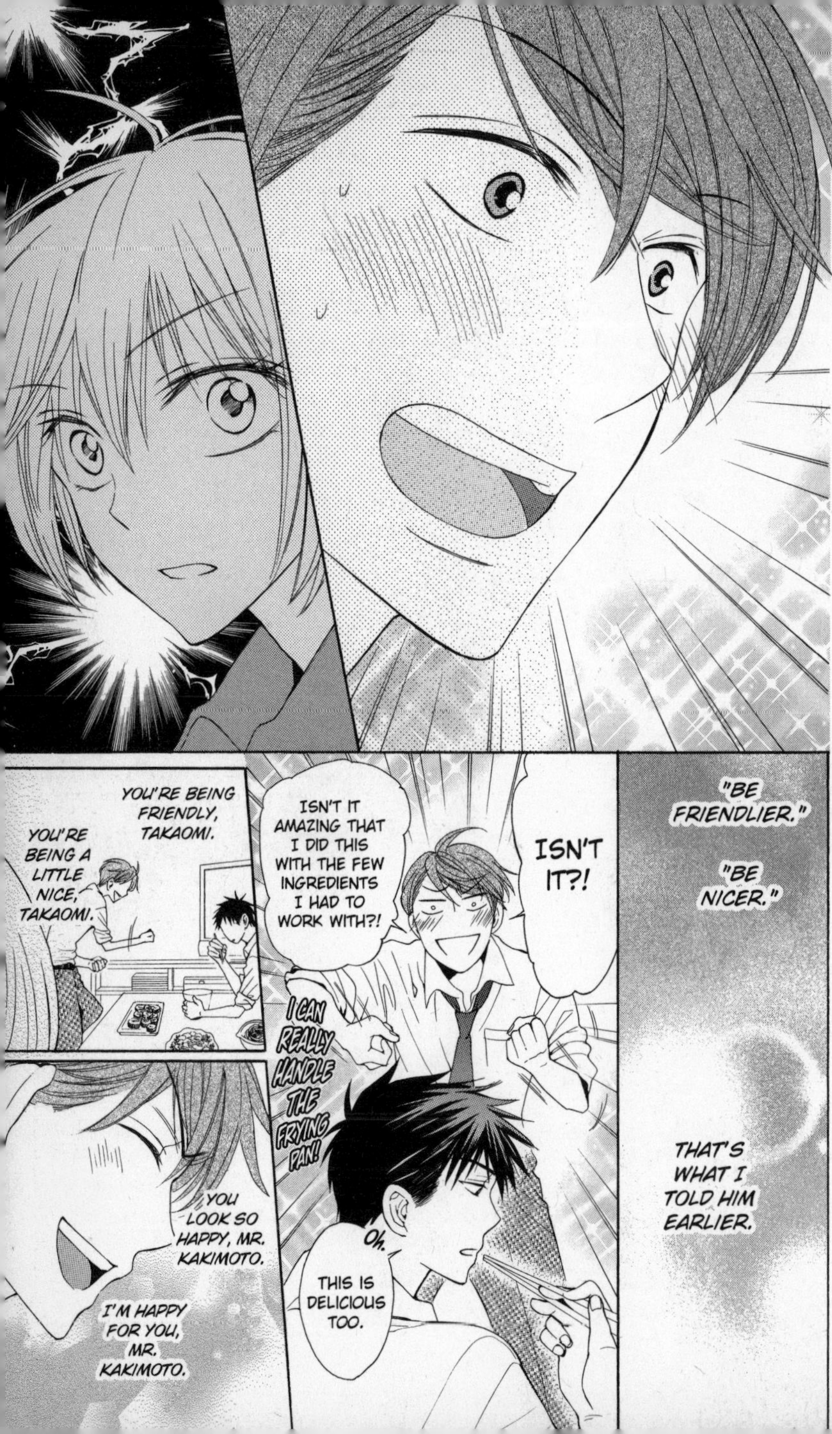
"BE FRIENDLIER."
"BE NICER."
THAT'S WHAT I TOLD HIM EARLIER.
ISN'T IT?!
ISN'T IT AMAZING THAT I DID THIS WITH THE FEW INGREDIENTS I HAD TO WORK WITH?!
I CAN REALLY HANDLE THE FRYING PAN!
Oh.
THIS IS DELICIOUS TOO.
YOU'RE BEING FRIENDLY, TAKAOMI.
YOU'RE BEING A LITTLE NICE, TAKAOMI.
YOU LOOK SO HAPPY, MR. KAKIMOTO.
I'M HAPPY FOR YOU, MR. KAKIMOTO.

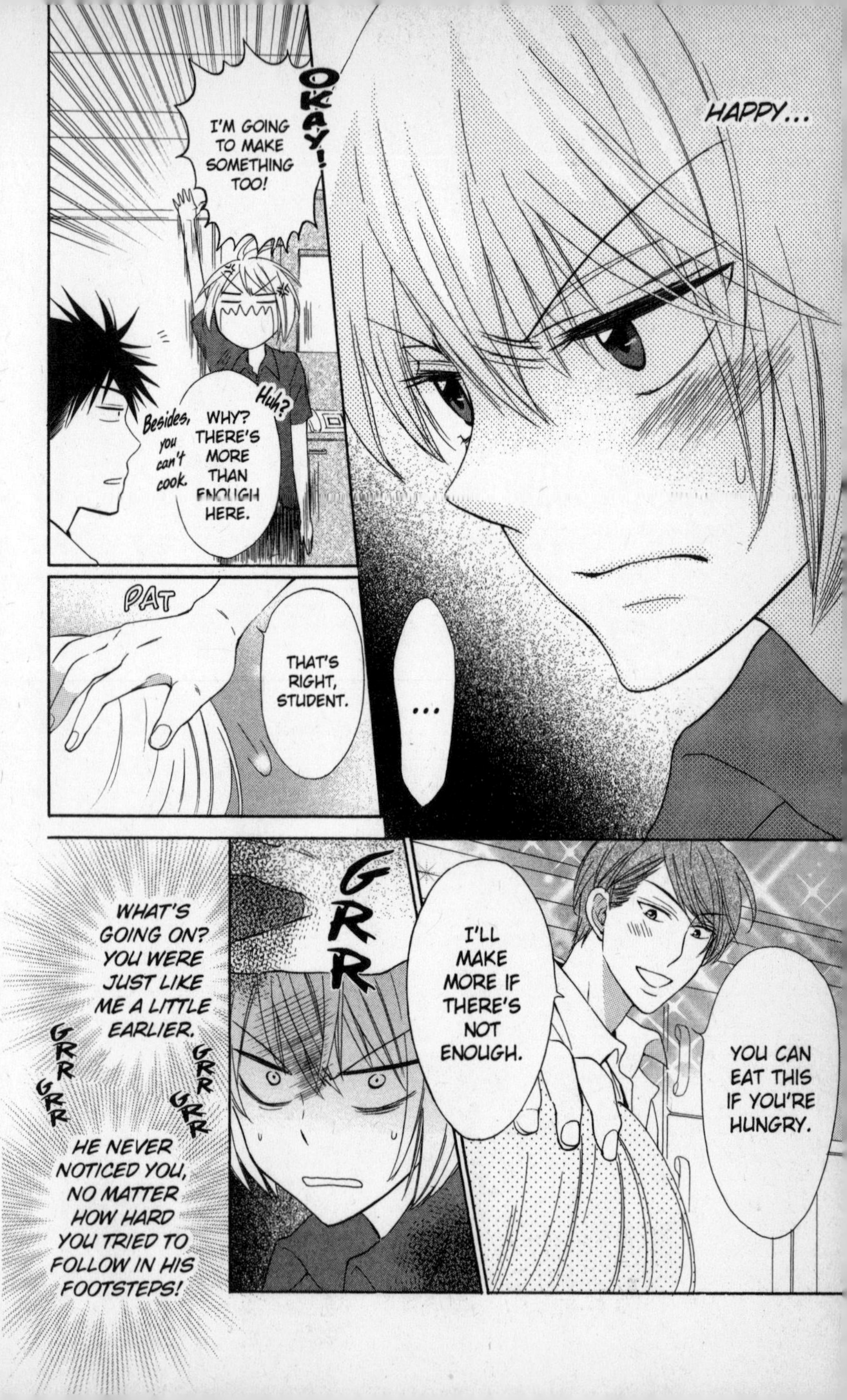
HAPPY...
...
OKAY!
I'M GOING TO MAKE SOMETHING TOO!
Huh?
WHY? THERE'S MORE THAN ENOUGH HERE.
Besides, you can't cook.
PAT
THAT'S RIGHT, STUDENT.
YOU CAN EAT THIS IF YOU'RE HUNGRY.
I'LL MAKE MORE IF THERE'S NOT ENOUGH.
GRR
WHAT'S GOING ON? YOU WERE JUST LIKE ME A LITTLE EARLIER.
GRR GRR
GRR GRR
HE NEVER NOTICED YOU, NO MATTER HOW HARD YOU TRIED TO FOLLOW IN HIS FOOTSTEPS!

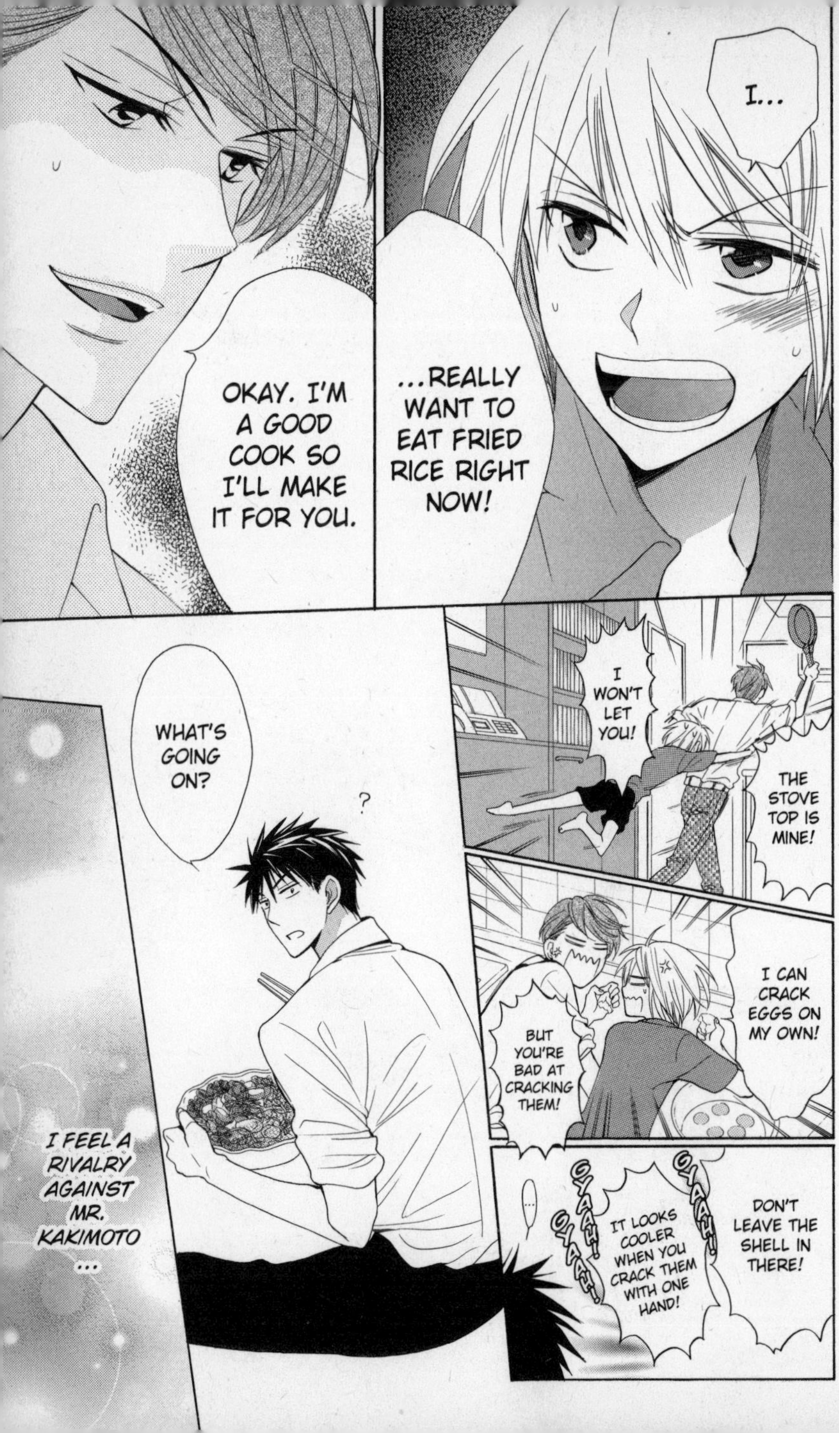
I...
...REALLY WANT TO EAT FRIED RICE RIGHT NOW!
OKAY. I'M A GOOD COOK SO I'LL MAKE IT FOR YOU.
I WON'T LET YOU!
THE STOVE TOP IS MINE!
I CAN CRACK EGGS ON MY OWN!
BUT YOU'RE BAD AT CRACKING THEM!
DON'T LEAVE THE SHELL IN THERE!
GYAAH!
IT LOOKS COOLER WHEN YOU CRACK THEM WITH ONE HAND!
GYAAH! GYAAH!
...
WHAT'S GOING ON?
?
I FEEL A RIVALRY AGAINST MR. KAKIMOTO ...

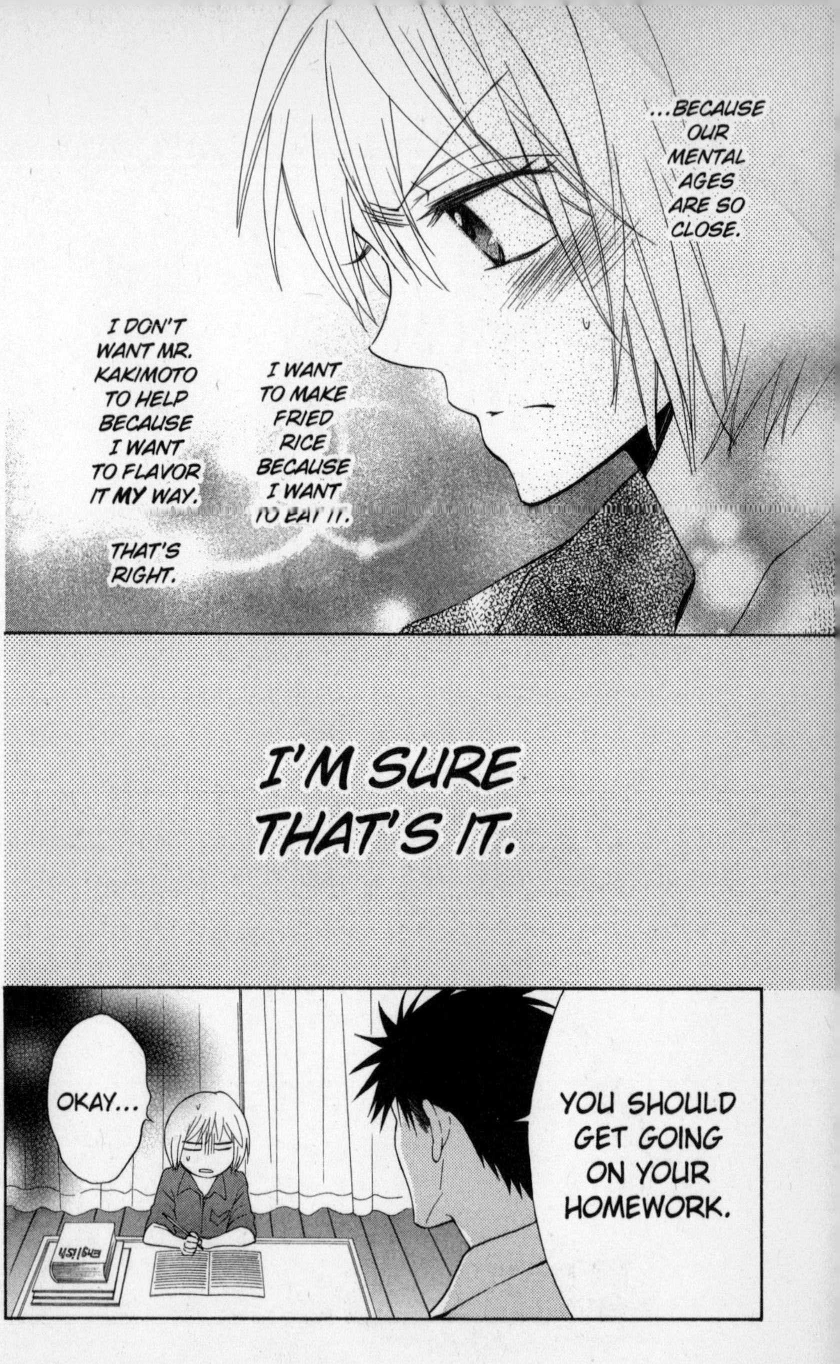
...BECAUSE OUR MENTAL AGES ARE SO CLOSE.
I WANT TO MAKE FRIED RICE BECAUSE I WANT TO EAT IT.
I DON'T WANT MR. KAKIMOTO TO HELP BECAUSE I WANT TO FLAVOR IT MY WAY.
THAT'S RIGHT.
I'M SURE THAT'S IT.
YOU SHOULD GET GOING ON YOUR HOMEWORK.
OKAY...
English

Chapter 42

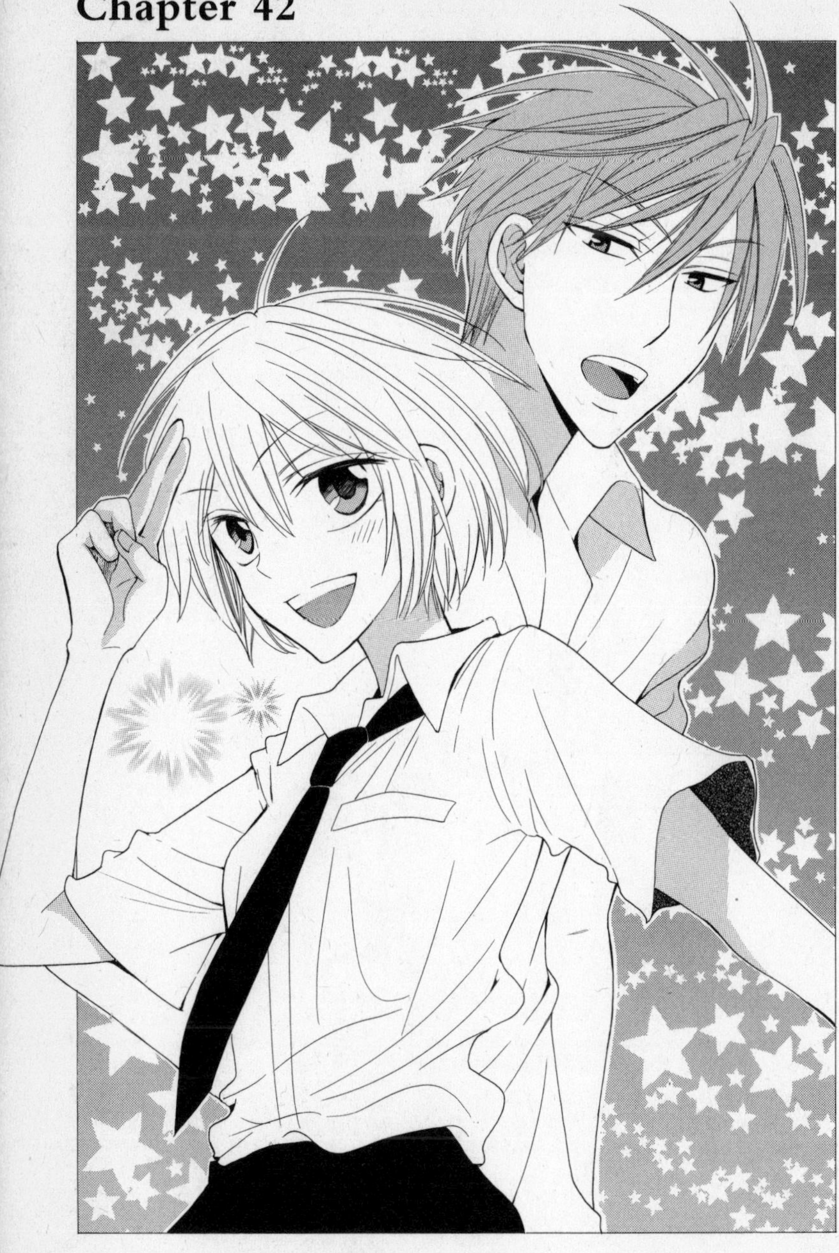

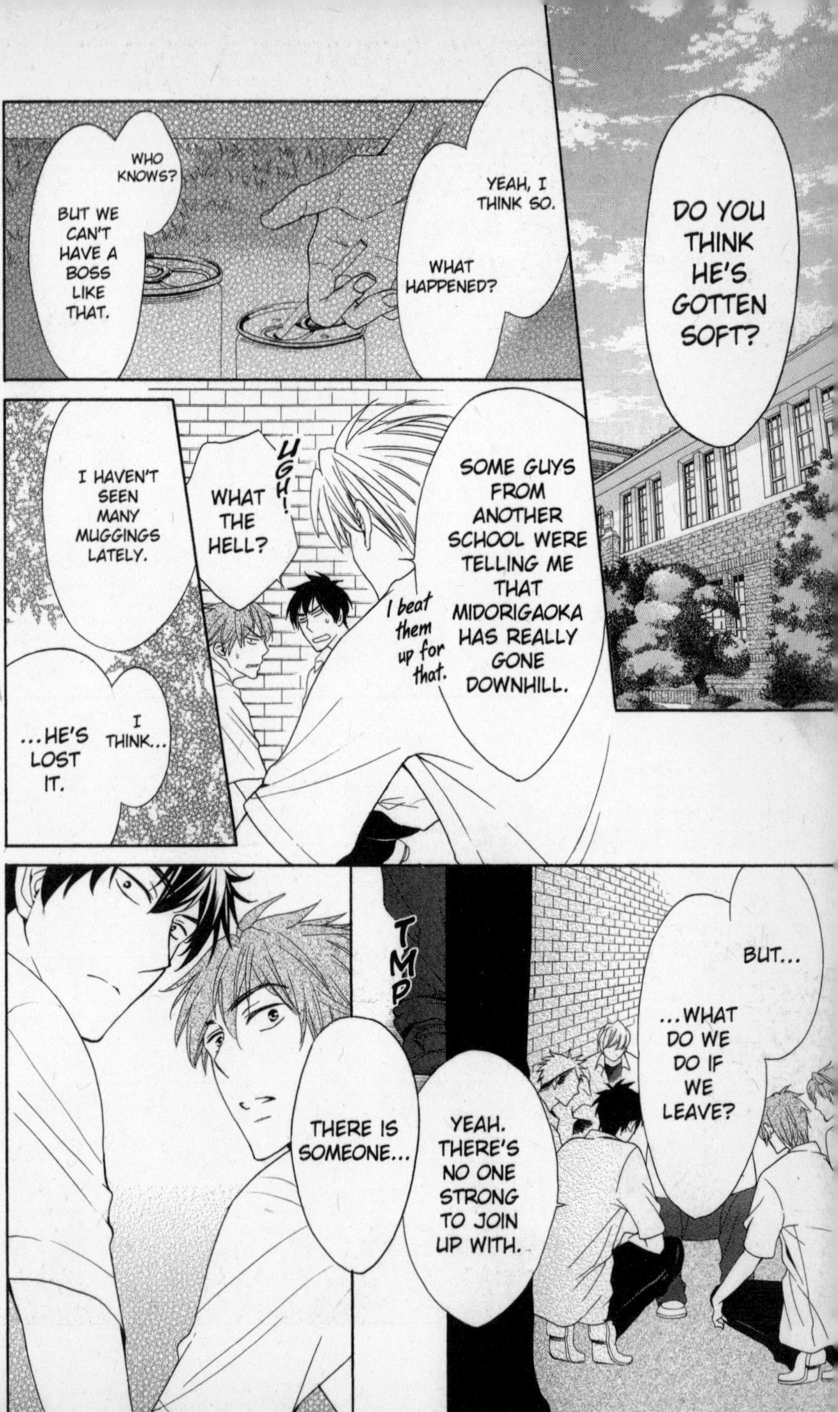
DO YOU THINK HE'S GOTTEN SOFT?
YEAH, I THINK SO.
WHAT HAPPENED?
WHO KNOWS?
BUT WE CAN'T HAVE A BOSS LIKE THAT.
SOME GUYS FROM ANOTHER SCHOOL WERE TELLING ME THAT MIDORIGAOKA HAS REALLY GONE DOWNHILL.
I beat them up for that.
UGH!
WHAT THE HELL?
I HAVEN'T SEEN MANY MUGGINGS LATELY.
I THINK...
...HE'S LOST IT.
BUT...
...WHAT DO WE DO IF WE LEAVE?
YEAH. THERE'S NO ONE STRONG TO JOIN UP WITH.
TMP
THERE IS SOMEONE...

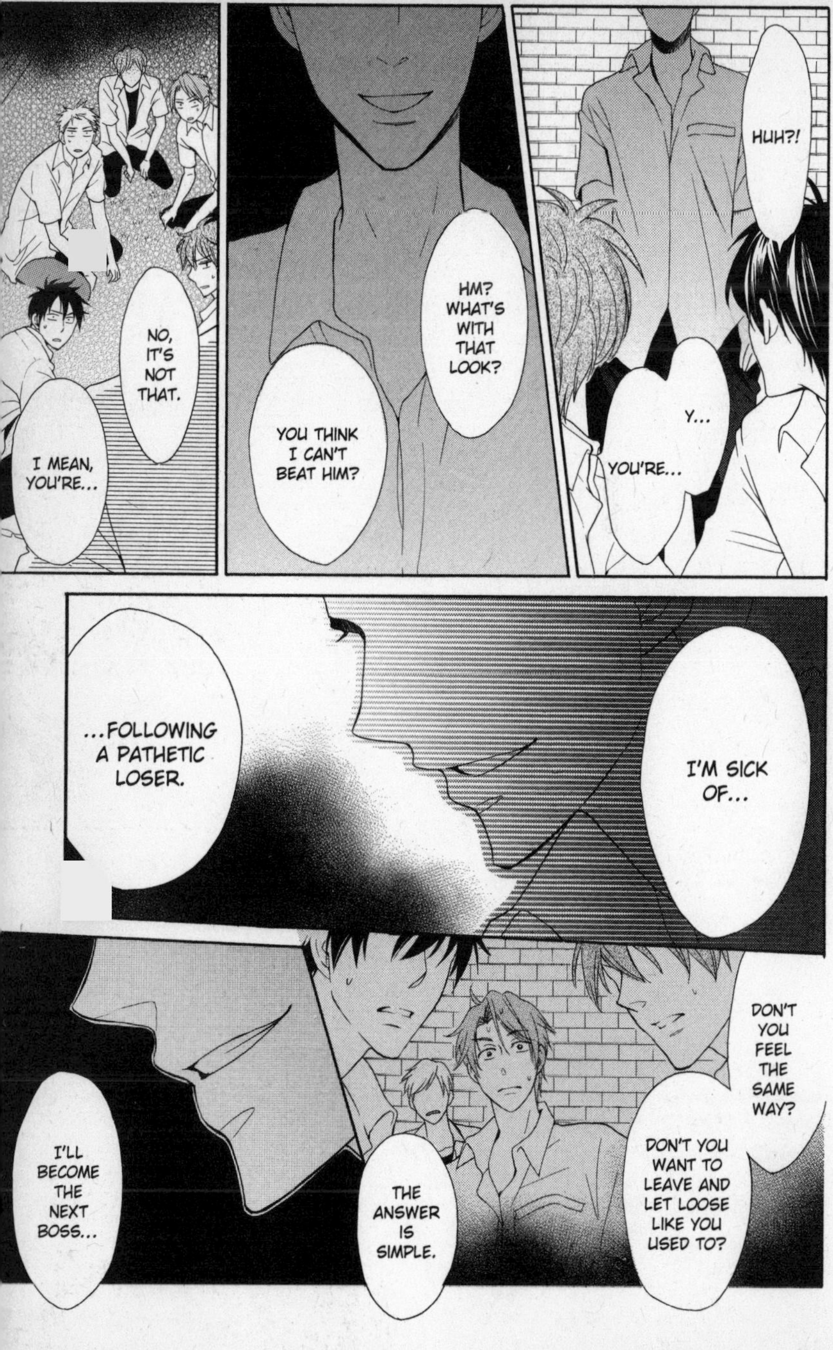
HUH?!
Y... YOU'RE...
HM? WHAT'S WITH THAT LOOK?
YOU THINK I CAN'T BEAT HIM?
NO, IT'S NOT THAT.
I MEAN, YOU'RE...
I'M SICK OF...
...FOLLOWING A PATHETIC LOSER.
DON'T YOU FEEL THE SAME WAY?
DON'T YOU WANT TO LEAVE AND LET LOOSE LIKE YOU USED TO?
THE ANSWER IS SIMPLE.
I'LL BECOME THE NEXT BOSS...

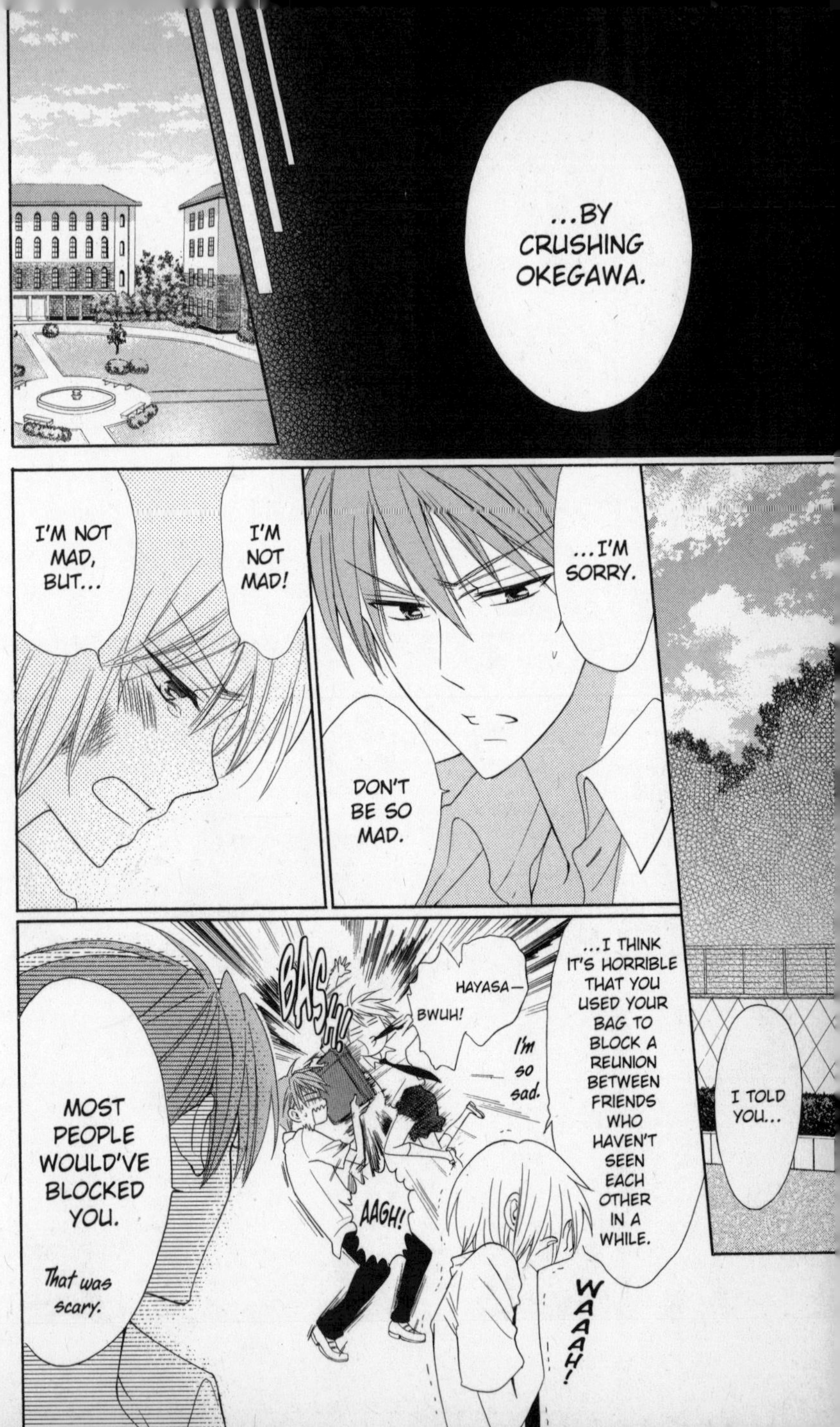
...BY CRUSHING OKEGAWA.
...I'M SORRY.
DON'T BE SO MAD.
I'M NOT MAD!
I'M NOT MAD, BUT...
I TOLD YOU...
...I THINK IT'S HORRIBLE THAT YOU USED YOUR BAG TO BLOCK A REUNION BETWEEN FRIENDS WHO HAVEN'T SEEN EACH OTHER IN A WHILE.
HAYASA—
BWUH!
BASH!
I'm so sad.
WAAAAH!
AAGH!
MOST PEOPLE WOULD'VE BLOCKED YOU.
That was scary.

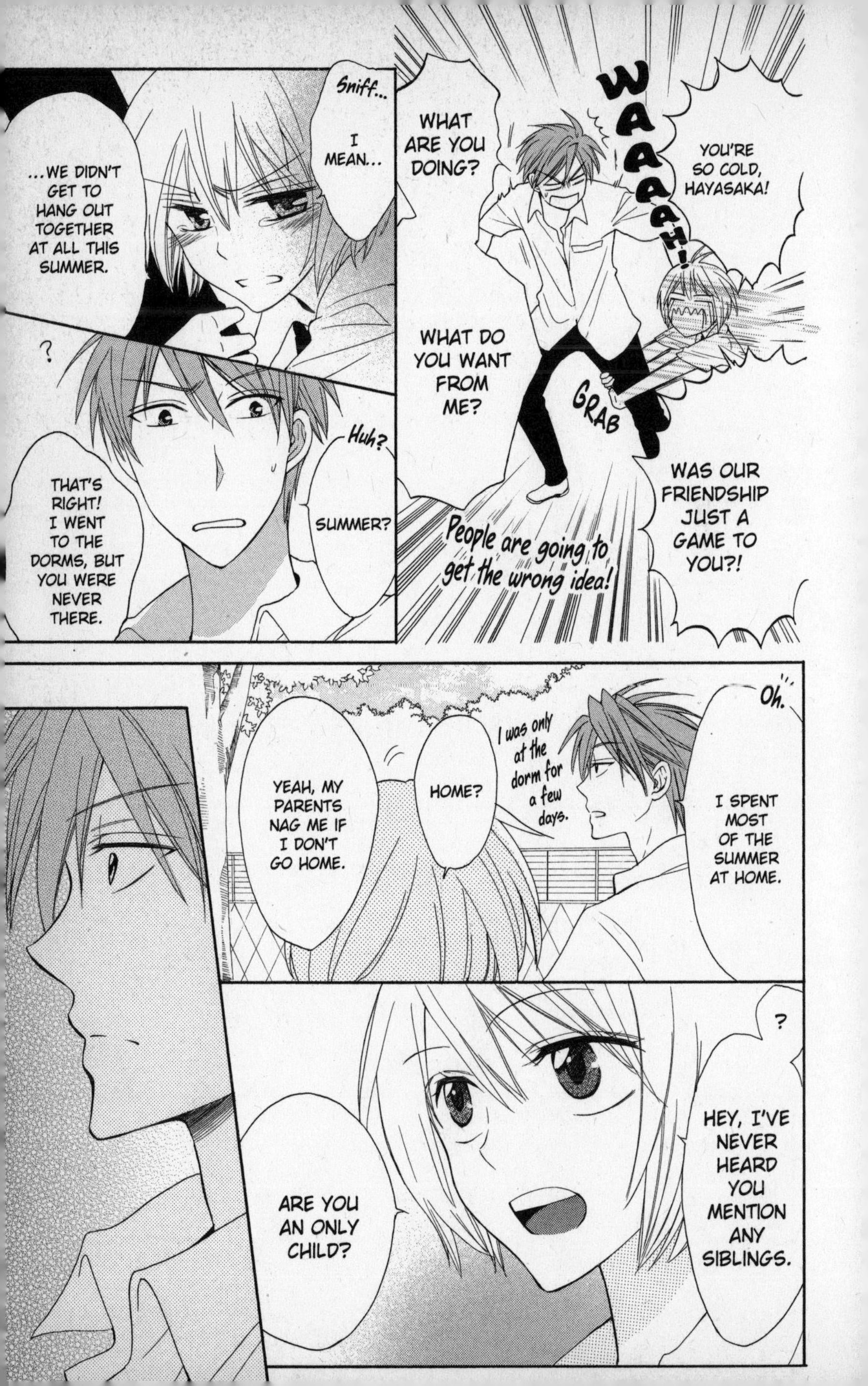
YOU'RE SO COLD, HAYASAKA!
WAAAAH!
WHAT ARE YOU DOING?
WHAT DO YOU WANT FROM ME?
GRAB
WAS OUR FRIENDSHIP JUST A GAME TO YOU?!
People are going to get the wrong idea!
Sniff...
I MEAN...
...WE DIDN'T GET TO HANG OUT TOGETHER AT ALL THIS SUMMER.
Huh?
SUMMER?
?
THAT'S RIGHT! I WENT TO THE DORMS, BUT YOU WERE NEVER THERE.
Oh.
I SPENT MOST OF THE SUMMER AT HOME.
I was only at the dorm for a few days.
HOME?
YEAH, MY PARENTS NAG ME IF I DON'T GO HOME.
?
HEY, I'VE NEVER HEARD YOU MENTION ANY SIBLINGS.
ARE YOU AN ONLY CHILD?

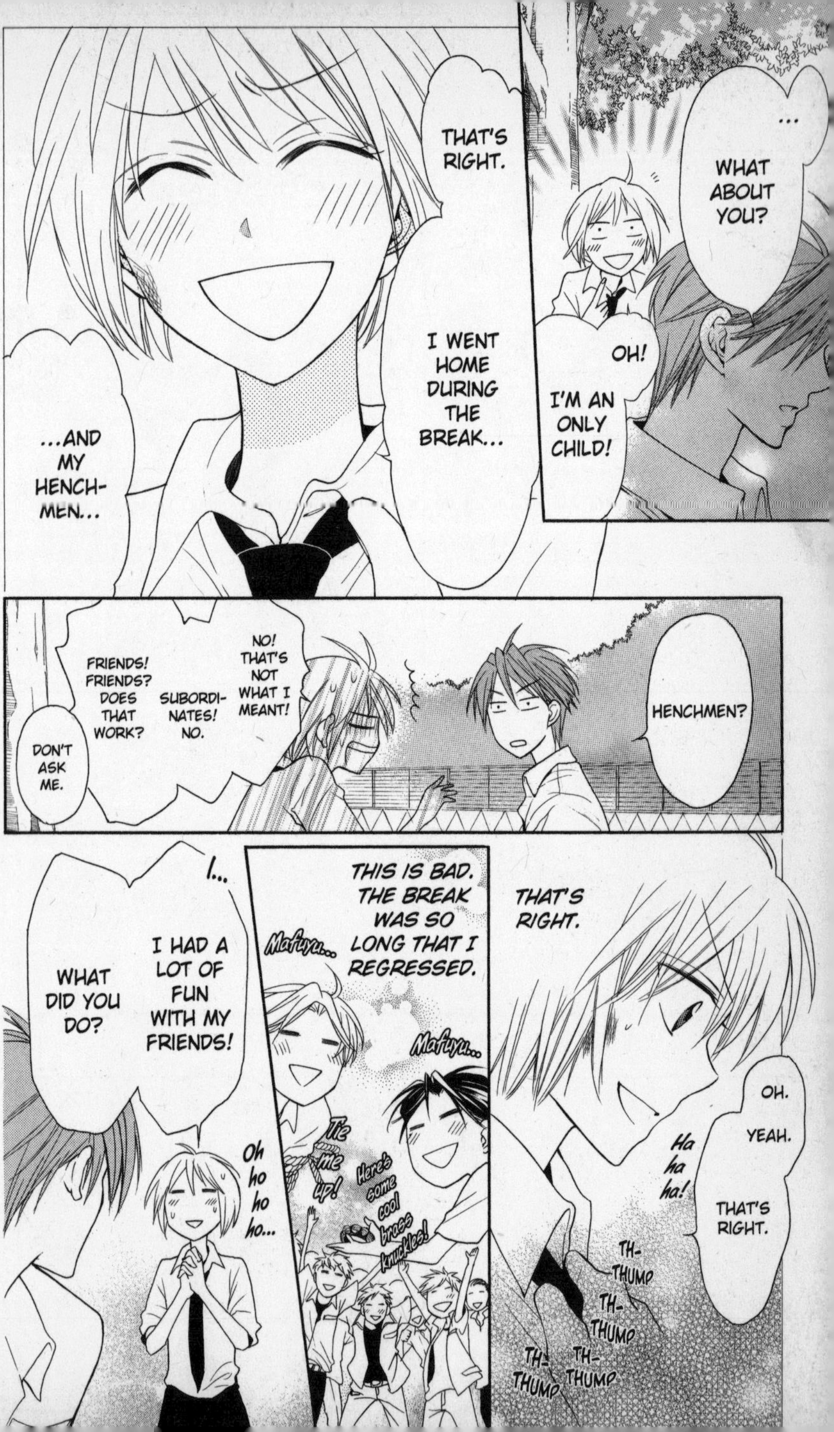
...
WHAT ABOUT YOU?
OH!
I'M AN ONLY CHILD!
THAT'S RIGHT.
I WENT HOME DURING THE BREAK...
...AND MY HENCH-MEN...
HENCHMEN?
NO! THAT'S NOT WHAT I MEANT!
SUBORDI-NATES! NO.
FRIENDS! FRIENDS? DOES THAT WORK?
DON'T ASK ME.
THAT'S RIGHT.
OH.
YEAH.
THAT'S RIGHT.
Ha ha ha!
TH-THUMP
TH-THUMP
TH-THUMP
TH-THUMP
THIS IS BAD. THE BREAK WAS SO LONG THAT I REGRESSED.
Mafuyu...
Mafuyu...
Tie me up!
Here's some cool brass knuckles!
I...
I HAD A LOT OF FUN WITH MY FRIENDS!
WHAT DID YOU DO?
Oh ho ho ho...

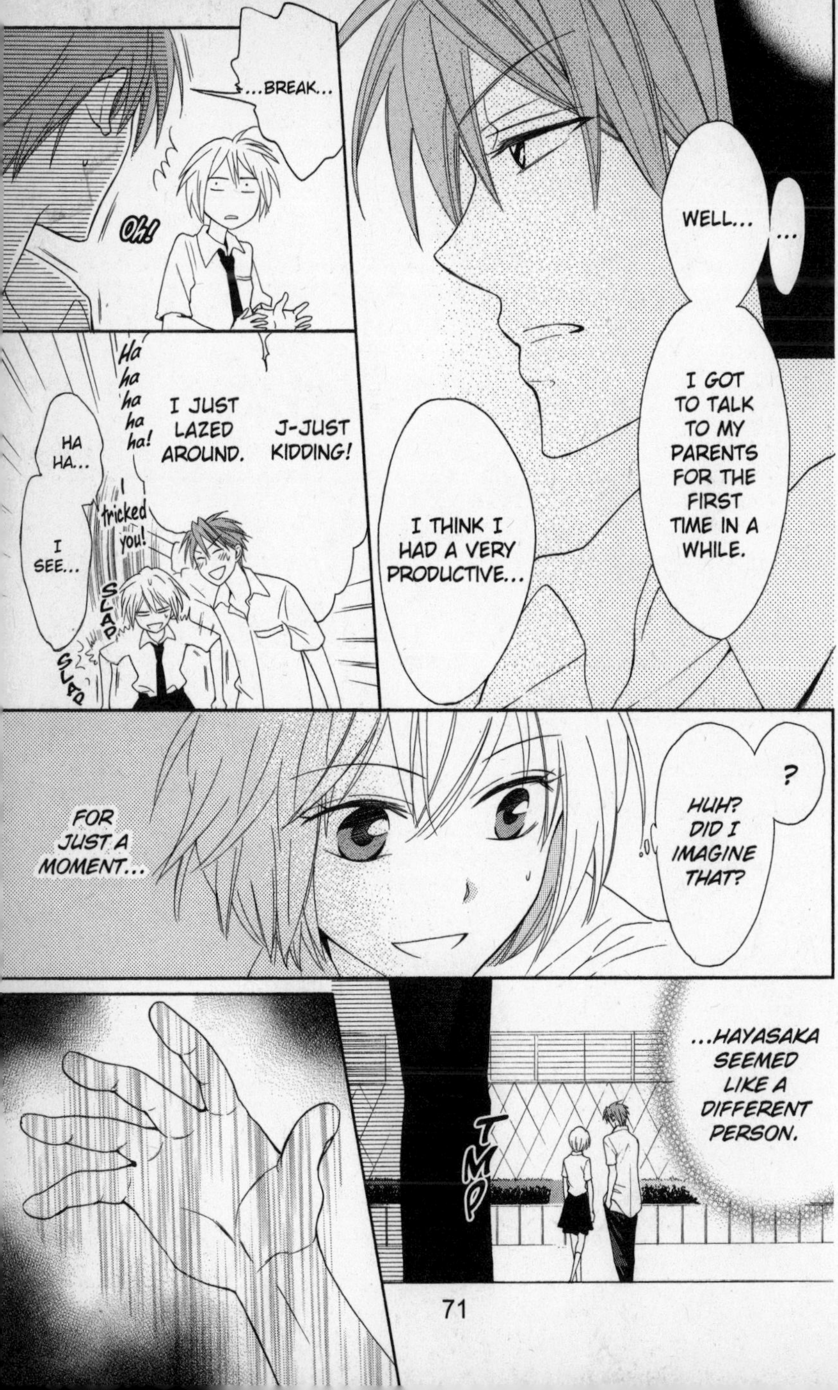
WELL...
...
I GOT TO TALK TO MY PARENTS FOR THE FIRST TIME IN A WHILE.
I THINK I HAD A VERY PRODUCTIVE...
...BREAK...
Oh!
J-JUST KIDDING!
I JUST LAZED AROUND.
Ha ha ha ha ha!
HA HA... I SEE...
I tricked you!
SLAP
SLAP
?
HUH? DID I IMAGINE THAT?
FOR JUST A MOMENT...
...HAYASAKA SEEMED LIKE A DIFFERENT PERSON.
TMP

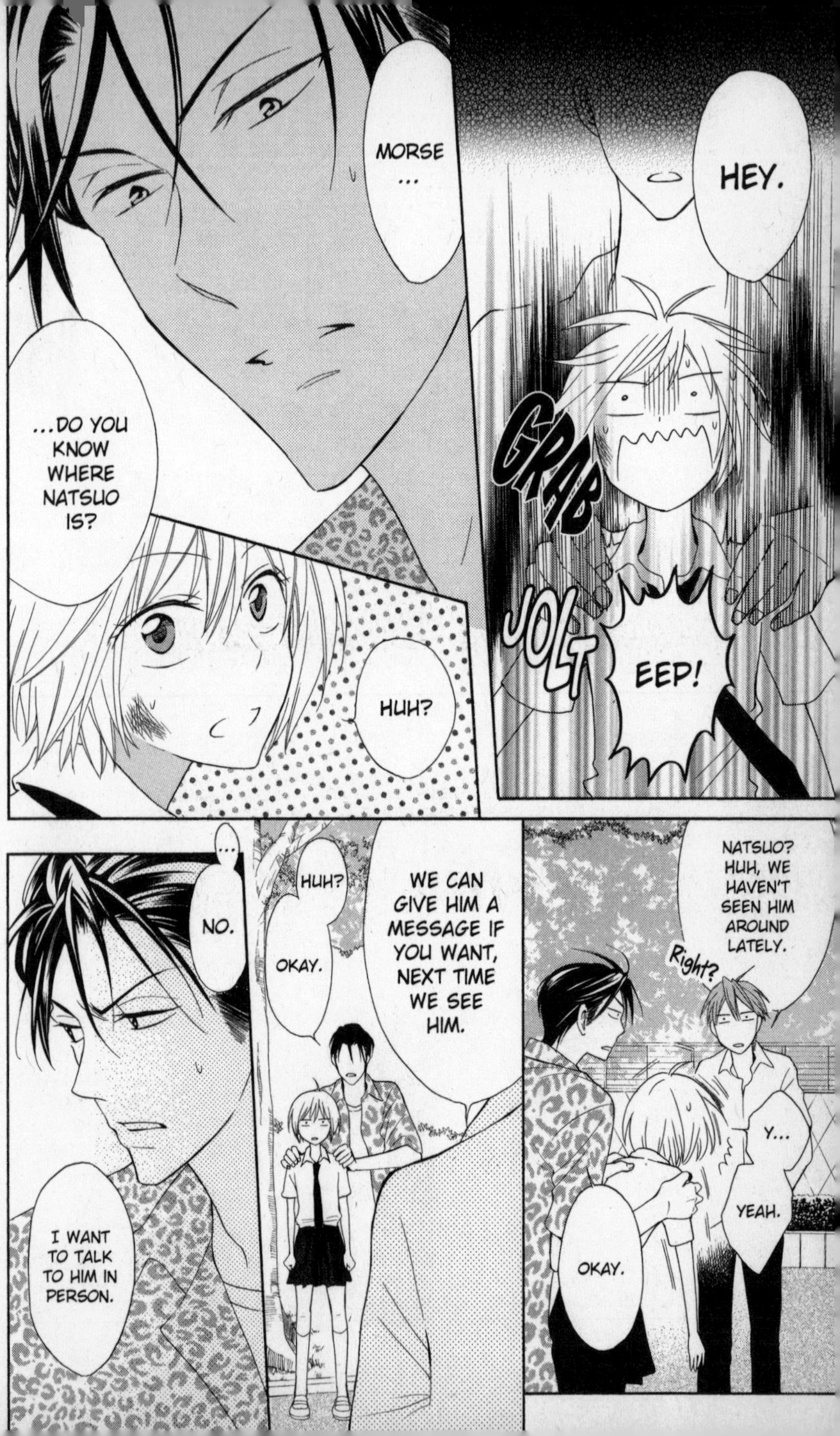
HEY.
GRAB
JOLT
EEP!
MORSE ...
...DO YOU KNOW WHERE NATSUO IS?
HUH?
NATSUO? HUH, WE HAVEN'T SEEN HIM AROUND LATELY.
Right?
Y...
YEAH.
OKAY.
WE CAN GIVE HIM A MESSAGE IF YOU WANT, NEXT TIME WE SEE HIM.
HUH?
OKAY.
...
NO.
I WANT TO TALK TO HIM IN PERSON.

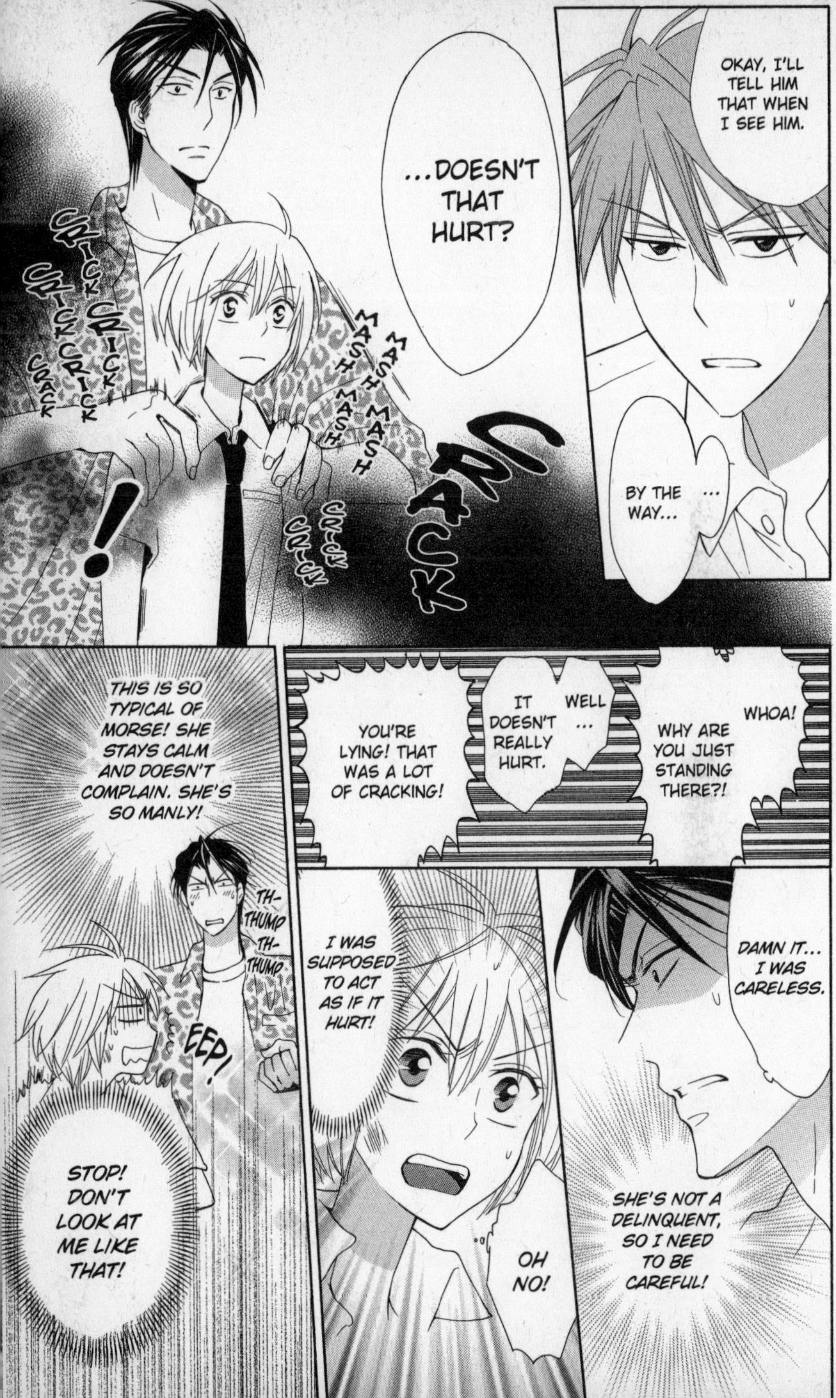

OKAY, I'LL TELL HIM THAT WHEN I SEE HIM.
BY THE WAY... ...
...DOESN'T THAT HURT?
CRICK CRICK
CRICK CRICK CRACK
MASH MASH MASH MASH
CRACK
!
WHOA!
WHY ARE YOU JUST STANDING THERE?!
WELL ...
IT DOESN'T REALLY HURT.
YOU'RE LYING! THAT WAS A LOT OF CRACKING!
DAMN IT... I WAS CARELESS.
SHE'S NOT A DELINQUENT, SO I NEED TO BE CAREFUL!
I WAS SUPPOSED TO ACT AS IF IT HURT!
OH NO!
THIS IS SO TYPICAL OF MORSE! SHE STAYS CALM AND DOESN'T COMPLAIN. SHE'S SO MANLY!
TH-THUMP TH-THUMP
EEP!
STOP! DON'T LOOK AT ME LIKE THAT!

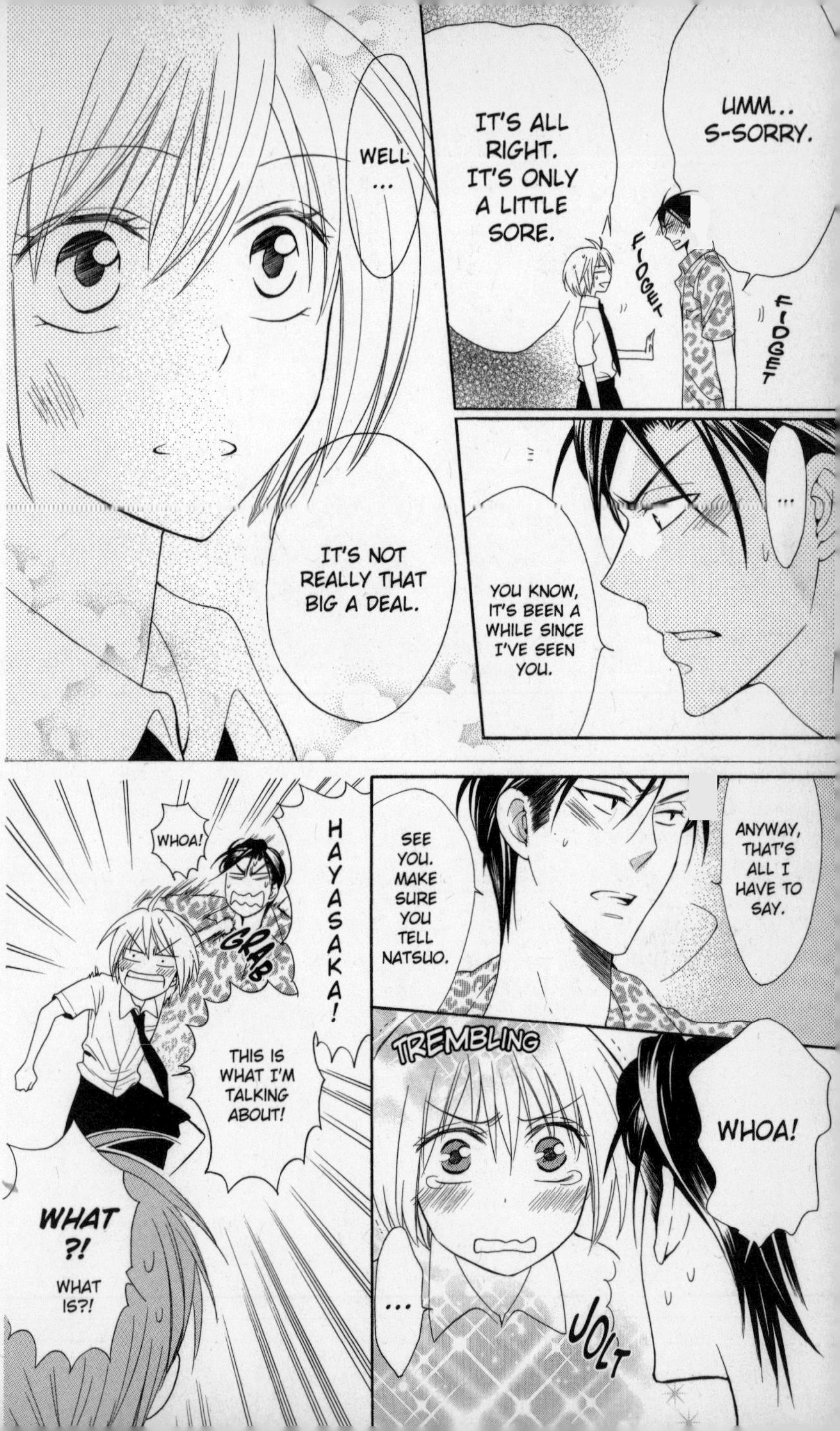
UMM... S-SORRY.
IT'S ALL RIGHT. IT'S ONLY A LITTLE SORE.
FIDGET
FIDGET
...
YOU KNOW, IT'S BEEN A WHILE SINCE I'VE SEEN YOU.
WELL ...
IT'S NOT REALLY THAT BIG A DEAL.
ANYWAY, THAT'S ALL I HAVE TO SAY.
SEE YOU. MAKE SURE YOU TELL NATSUO.
TREMBLING
WHOA!
...
JOLT
HAYASAKA!
WHOA!
GRAB
THIS IS WHAT I'M TALKING ABOUT!
WHAT ?!
WHAT IS?!

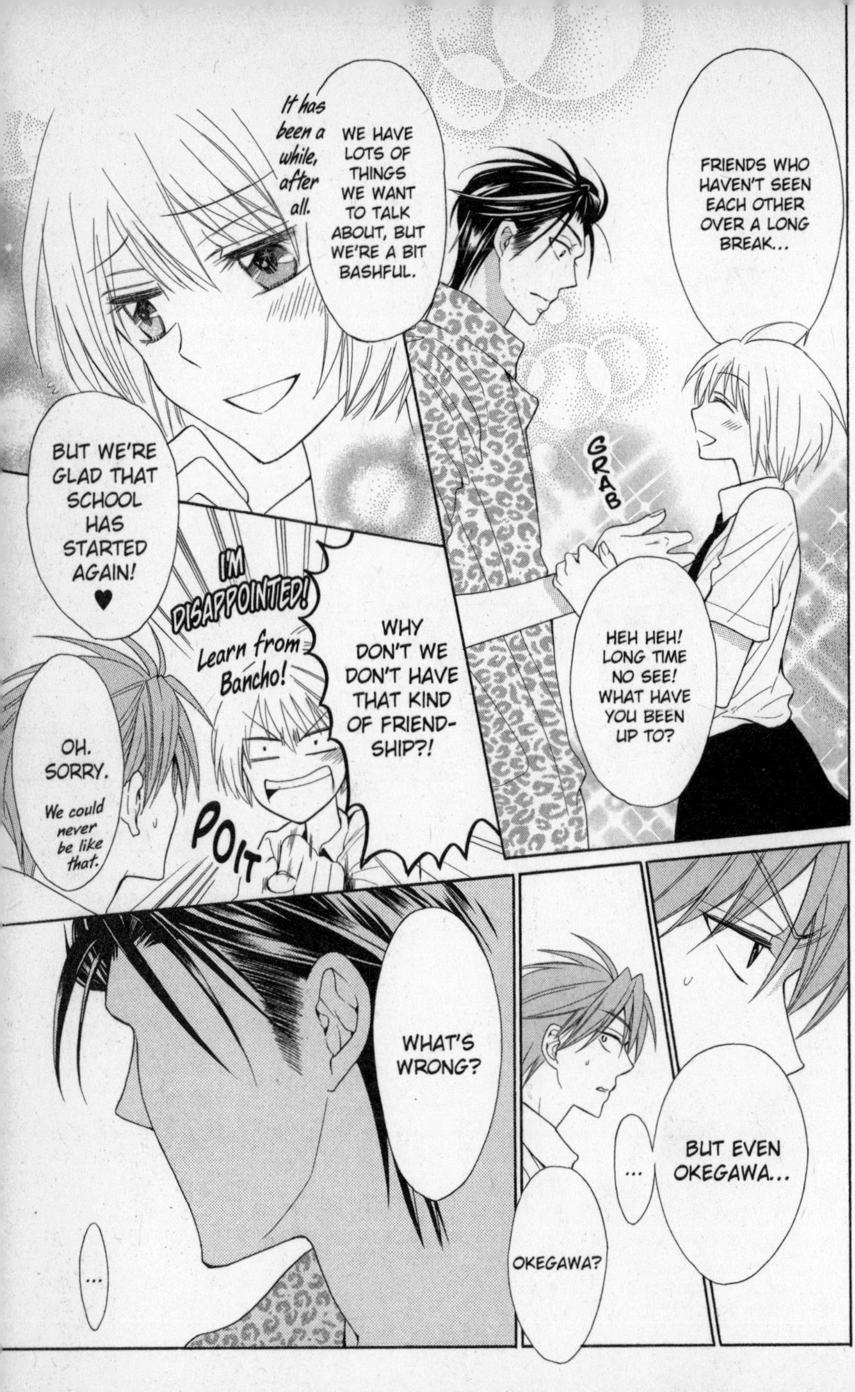

FRIENDS WHO HAVEN'T SEEN EACH OTHER OVER A LONG BREAK...
GRAB
HEH HEH! LONG TIME NO SEE! WHAT HAVE YOU BEEN UP TO?
WE HAVE LOTS OF THINGS WE WANT TO TALK ABOUT, BUT WE'RE A BIT BASHFUL.
It has been a while, after all.
BUT WE'RE GLAD THAT SCHOOL HAS STARTED AGAIN! ♥
WHY DON'T WE DON'T HAVE THAT KIND OF FRIEND-SHIP?!
I'M DISAPPOINTED!
Learn from Bancho!
OH. SORRY.
We could never be like that.
POIT
BUT EVEN OKEGAWA...
...
OKEGAWA?
WHAT'S WRONG?
...

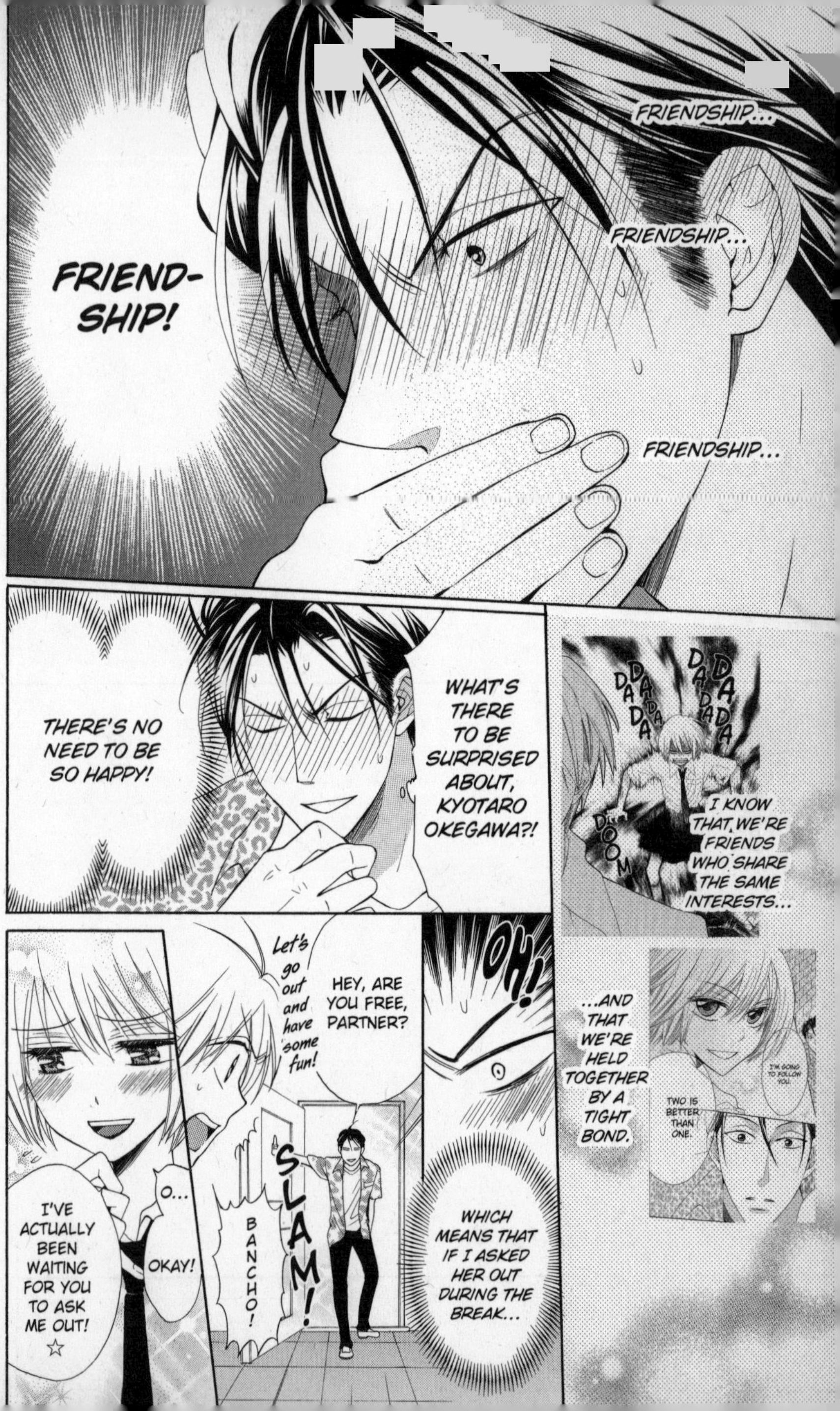
FRIENDSHIP...
FRIENDSHIP...
FRIENDSHIP...
FRIEND-SHIP!
DADADA DADADA DADADA
DOOM
I KNOW THAT WE'RE FRIENDS WHO SHARE THE SAME INTERESTS...
WHAT'S THERE TO BE SURPRISED ABOUT, KYOTARO OKEGAWA?!
THERE'S NO NEED TO BE SO HAPPY!
...AND THAT WE'RE HELD TOGETHER BY A TIGHT BOND.
I'M GOING TO FOLLOW YOU.
TWO IS BETTER THAN ONE.
OH!
WHICH MEANS THAT IF I ASKED HER OUT DURING THE BREAK...
HEY, ARE YOU FREE, PARTNER?
Let's go out and have some fun!
SLAM!
BANCHO!
O... OKAY!
I'VE ACTUALLY BEEN WAITING FOR YOU TO ASK ME OUT! ☆

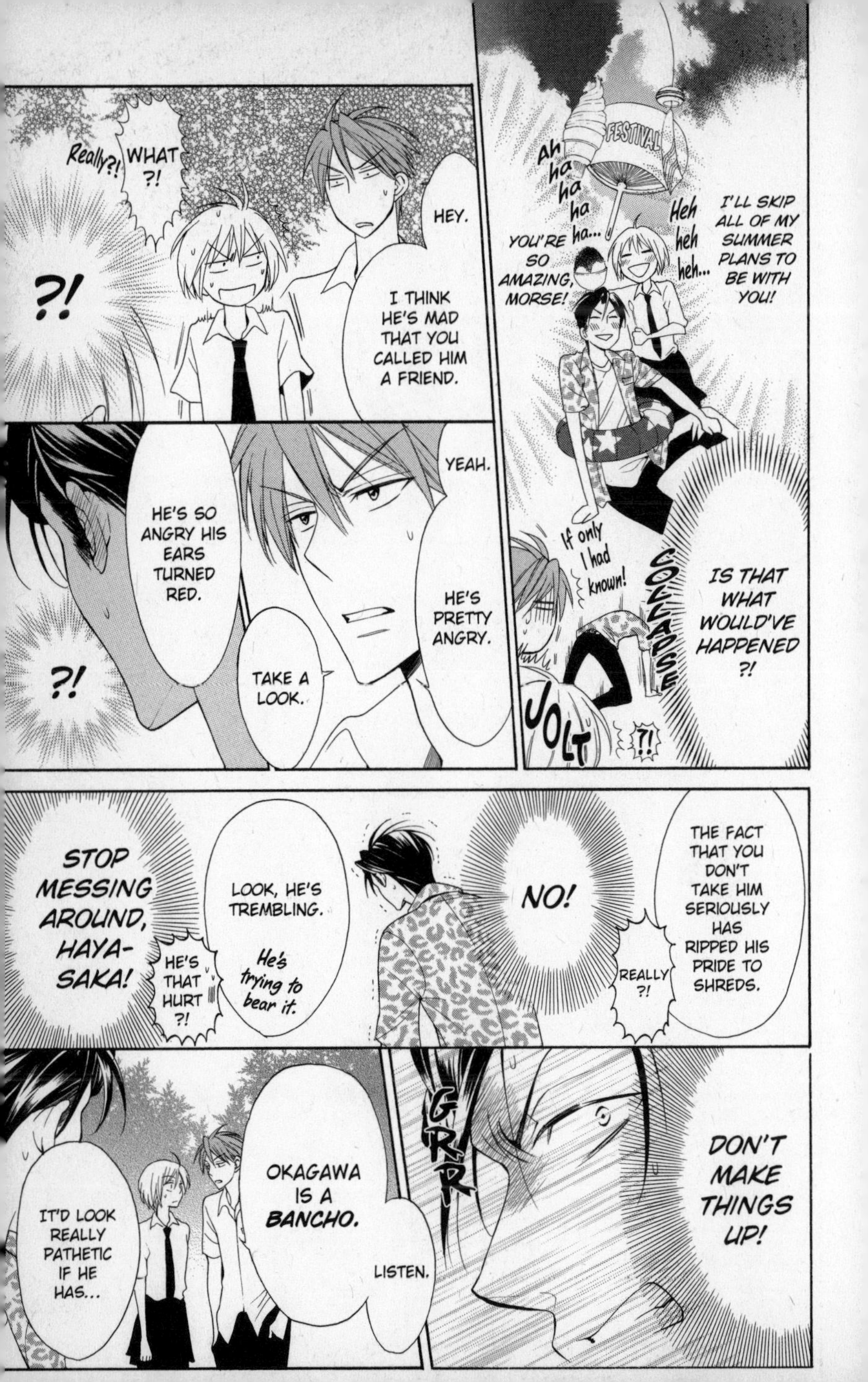
I'LL SKIP ALL OF MY SUMMER PLANS TO BE WITH YOU!
Heh heh heh...
Ah ha ha ha ha...
YOU'RE SO AMAZING, MORSE!
IS THAT WHAT WOULD'VE HAPPENED?!
COLLAPSE
If only I had known!
?!
JOLT
HEY.
I THINK HE'S MAD THAT YOU CALLED HIM A FRIEND.
WHAT?!
Really?!
?!
YEAH.
HE'S PRETTY ANGRY.
TAKE A LOOK.
HE'S SO ANGRY HIS EARS TURNED RED.
?!
THE FACT THAT YOU DON'T TAKE HIM SERIOUSLY HAS RIPPED HIS PRIDE TO SHREDS.
REALLY?!
NO!
LOOK, HE'S TREMBLING.
He's trying to bear it.
HE'S THAT HURT?!
STOP MESSING AROUND, HAYA-SAKA!
DON'T MAKE THINGS UP!
GRR
LISTEN.
OKAGAWA IS A BANCHO.
IT'D LOOK REALLY PATHETIC IF HE HAS...

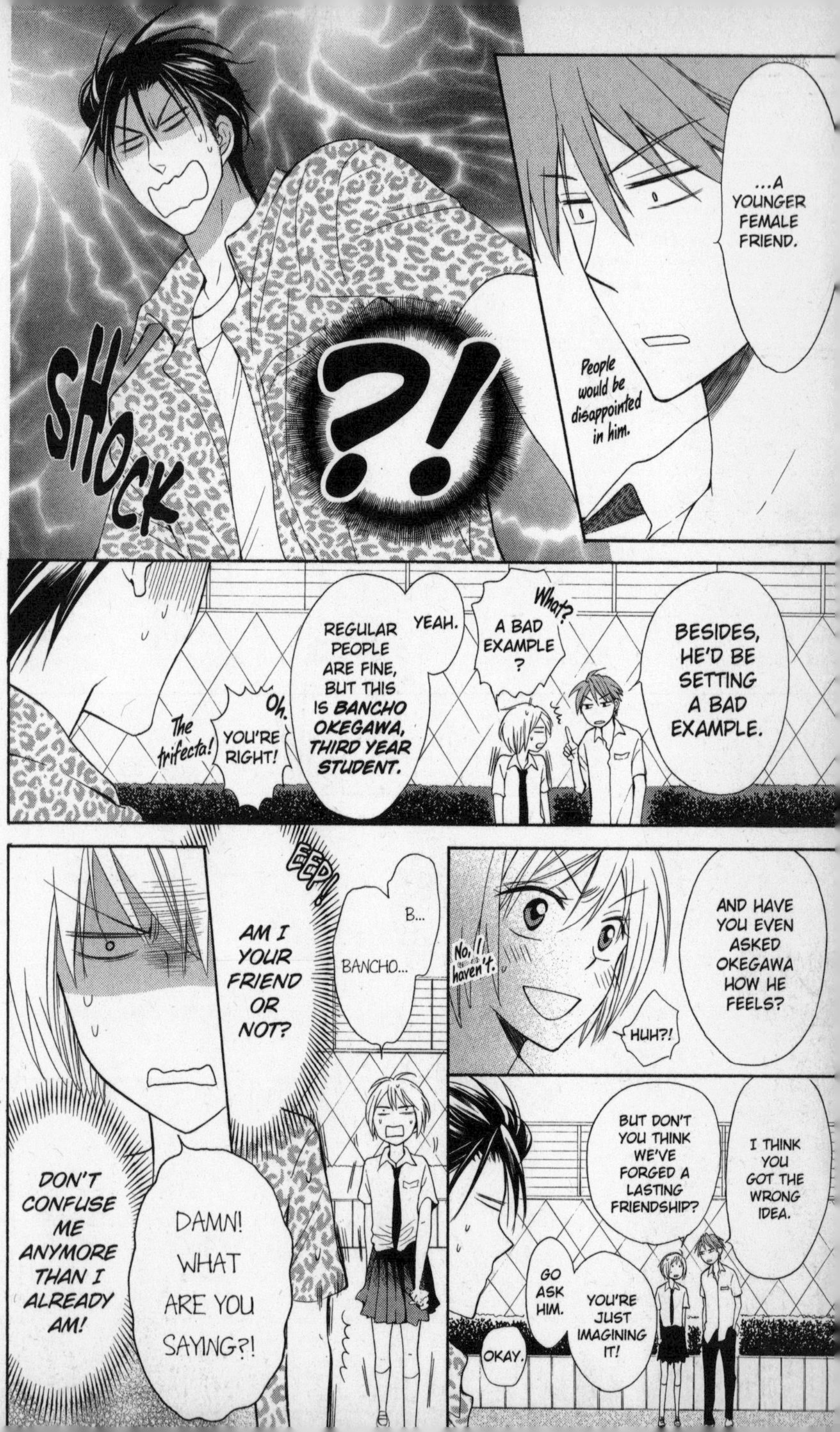
...A YOUNGER FEMALE FRIEND.
People would be disappointed in him.
SHOCK
?!
BESIDES, HE'D BE SETTING A BAD EXAMPLE.
What?
A BAD EXAMPLE?
YEAH.
REGULAR PEOPLE ARE FINE, BUT THIS IS BANCHO OKEGAWA, THIRD YEAR STUDENT.
Oh. YOU'RE RIGHT!
The trifecta!
AND HAVE YOU EVEN ASKED OKEGAWA HOW HE FEELS?
HUH?!
No, I haven't.
I THINK YOU GOT THE WRONG IDEA.
BUT DON'T YOU THINK WE'VE FORGED A LASTING FRIENDSHIP?
YOU'RE JUST IMAGINING IT!
GO ASK HIM.
OKAY.
EEP!
B... BANCHO...
AM I YOUR FRIEND OR NOT?
DAMN! WHAT ARE YOU SAYING?!
DON'T CONFUSE ME ANYMORE THAN I ALREADY AM!

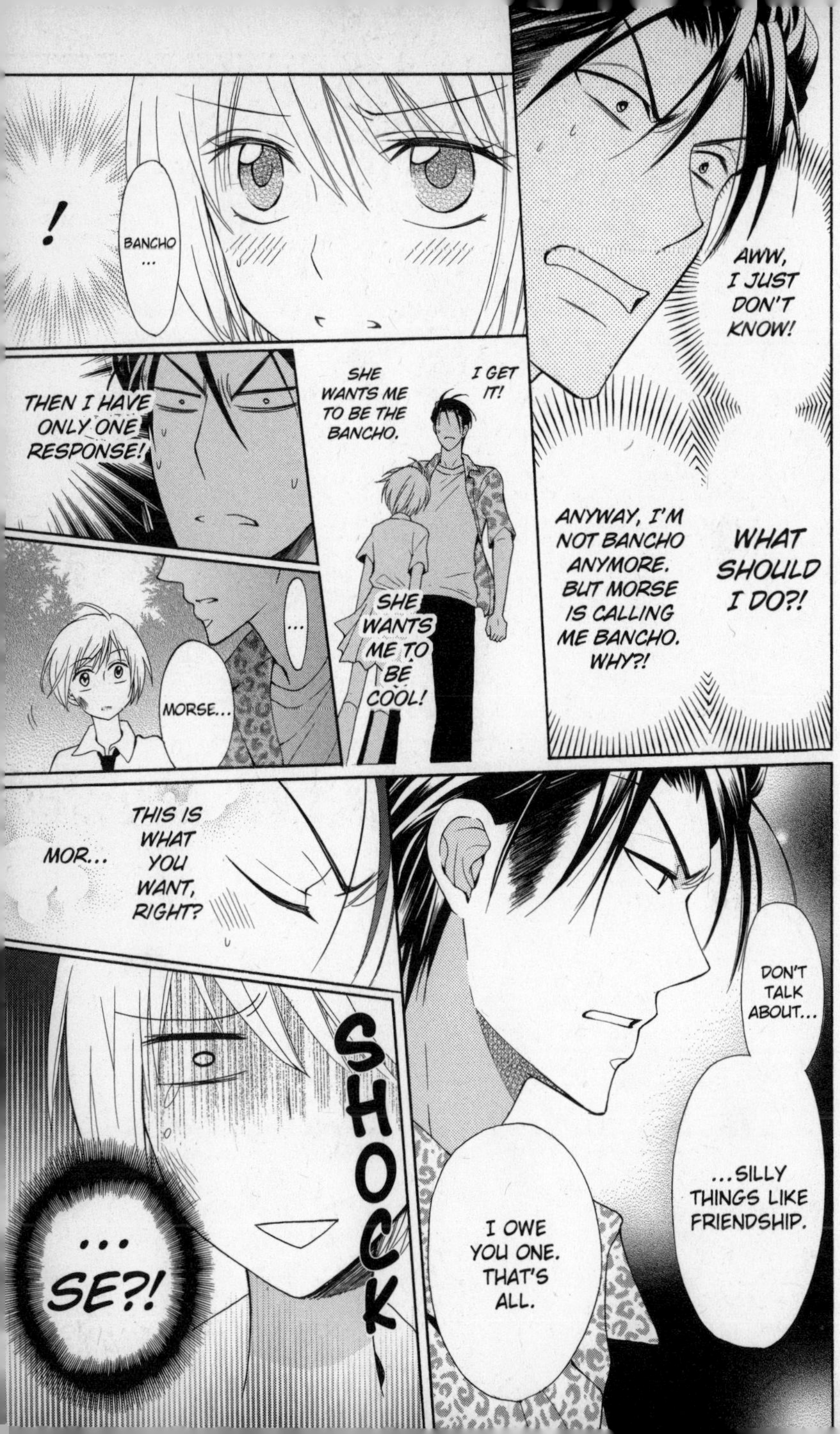
AWW, I JUST DON'T KNOW!
WHAT SHOULD I DO?!
ANYWAY, I'M NOT BANCHO ANYMORE. BUT MORSE IS CALLING ME BANCHO. WHY?!
BANCHO ...
!
I GET IT!
SHE WANTS ME TO BE THE BANCHO.
SHE WANTS ME TO BE COOL!
THEN I HAVE ONLY ONE RESPONSE!
...
MORSE...
DON'T TALK ABOUT...
...SILLY THINGS LIKE FRIENDSHIP.
I OWE YOU ONE. THAT'S ALL.
THIS IS WHAT YOU WANT, RIGHT?
MOR...
SHOCK
... SE?!

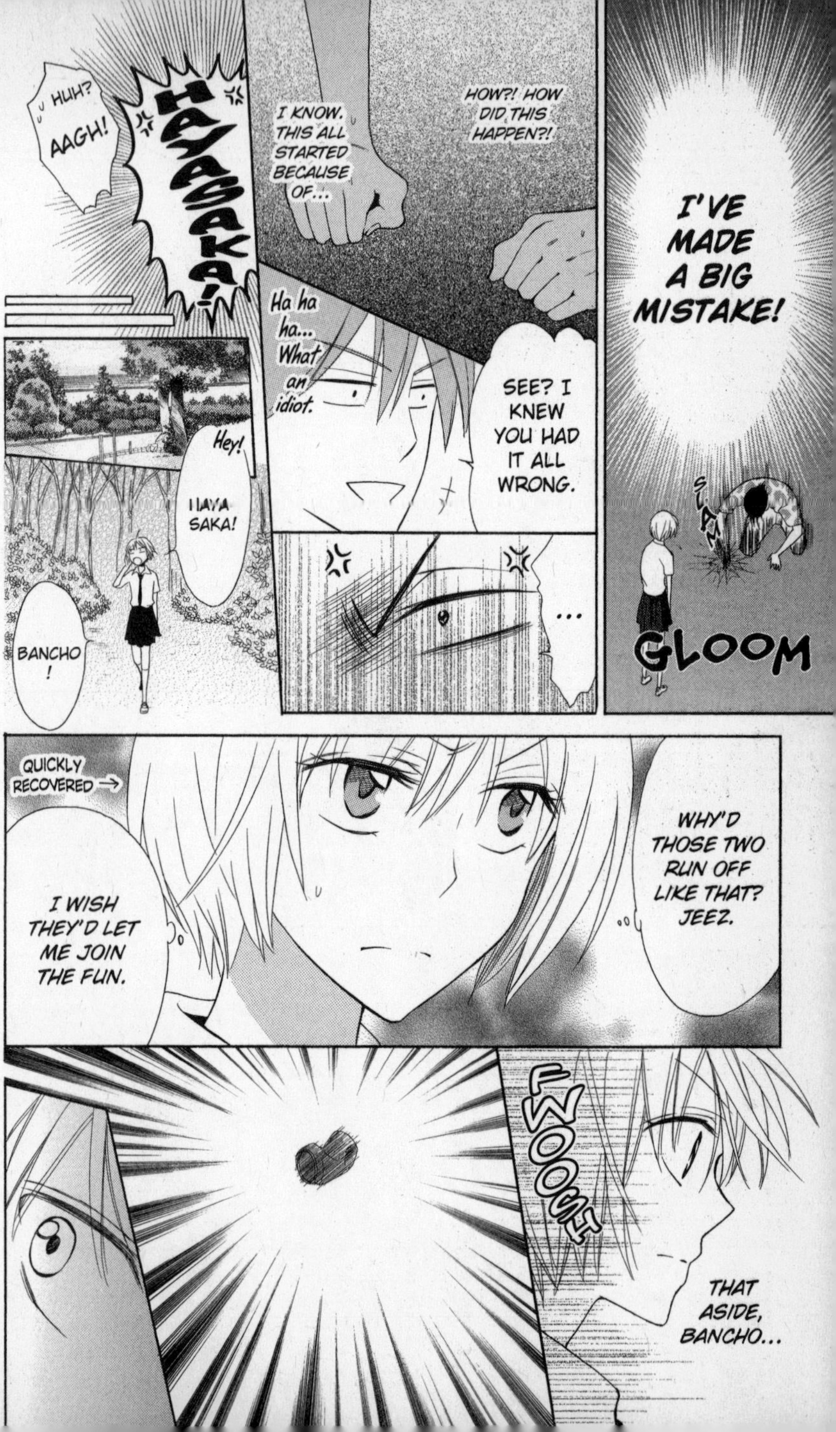
I'VE MADE A BIG MISTAKE!
SLAM
GLOOM
HOW?! HOW DID THIS HAPPEN?!
I KNOW. THIS ALL STARTED BECAUSE OF...
SEE? I KNEW YOU HAD IT ALL WRONG.
Ha ha ha... What an idiot.
...
HAYASAKA!
HUH? AAGH!
Hey!
HAYA SAKA!
BANCHO!
WHY'D THOSE TWO RUN OFF LIKE THAT? JEEZ.
I WISH THEY'D LET ME JOIN THE FUN.
QUICKLY RECOVERED →
THAT ASIDE, BANCHO...
FWOOSH

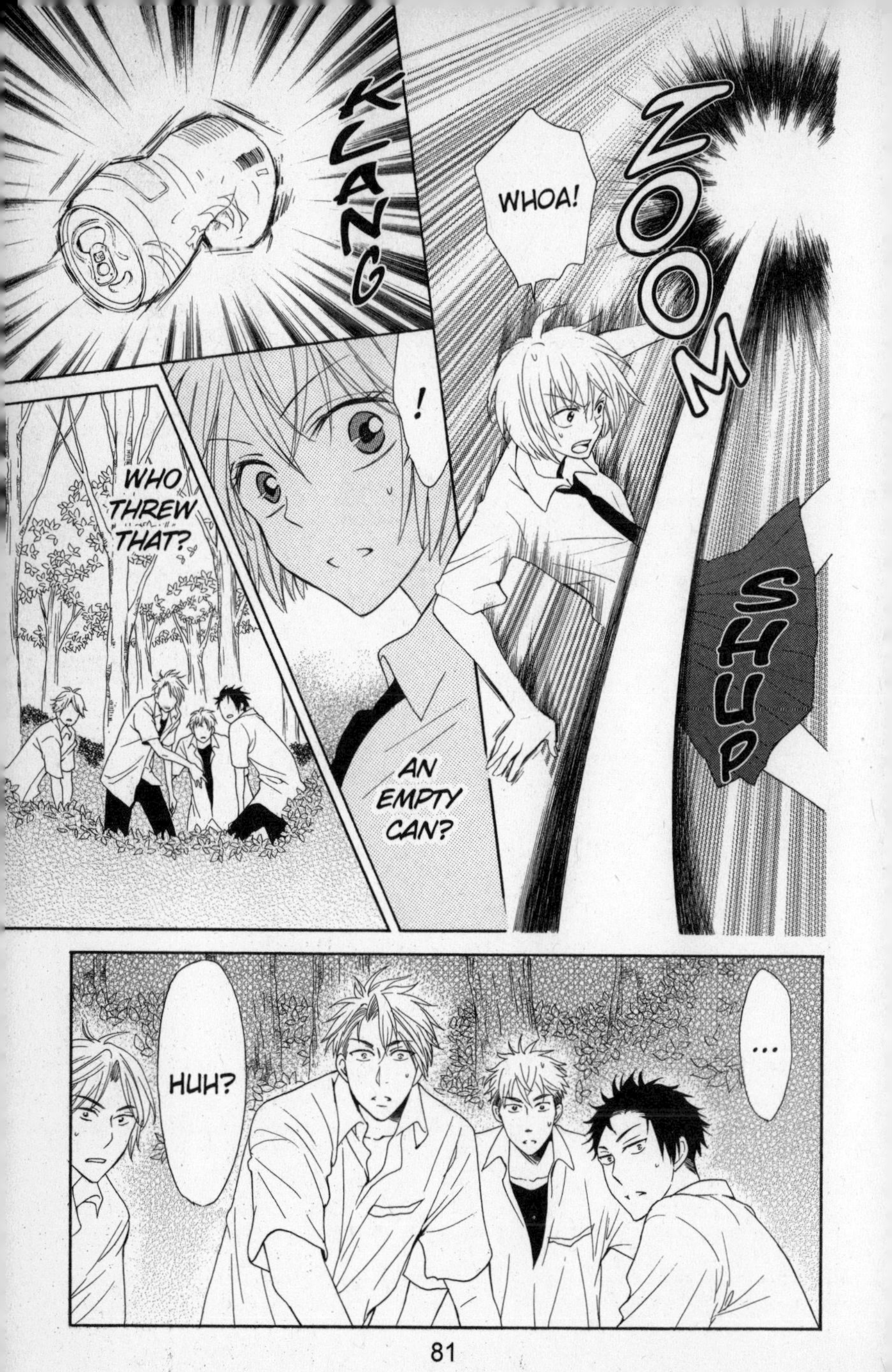
ZOOM
WHOA!
SHUP
KLANG
!
AN EMPTY CAN?
WHO THREW THAT?
...
HUH?

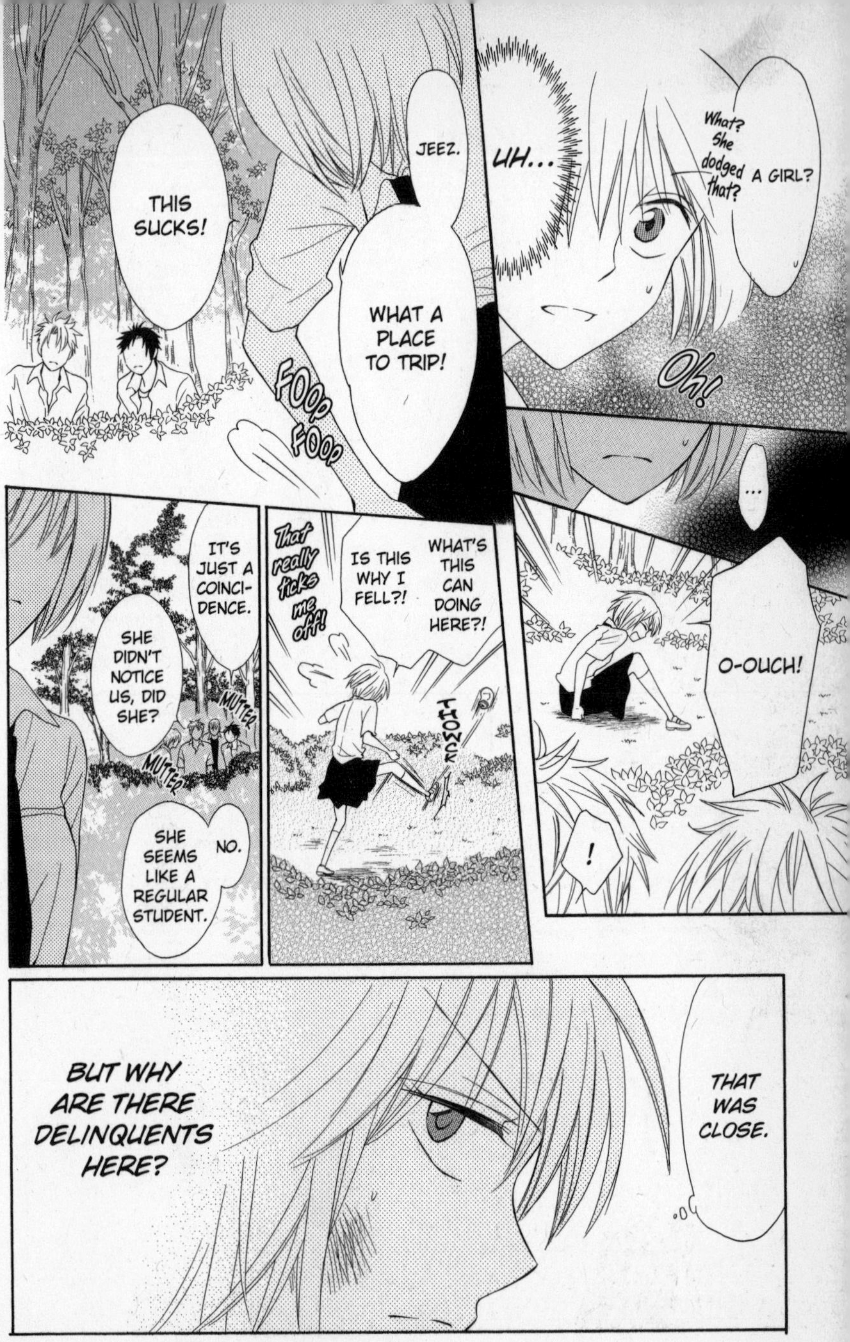

UH...
What? She dodged that?
A GIRL?
Oh!
JEEZ.
WHAT A PLACE TO TRIP!
FOOp FOOp
THIS SUCKS!
...
O-OUCH!
!
WHAT'S THIS CAN DOING HERE?!
IS THIS WHY I FELL?!
That really ticks me off!
THOWCK
IT'S JUST A COINCIDENCE.
SHE DIDN'T NOTICE US, DID SHE?
MUTTER
MUTTER
NO.
SHE SEEMS LIKE A REGULAR STUDENT.
THAT WAS CLOSE.
BUT WHY ARE THERE DELINQUENTS HERE?

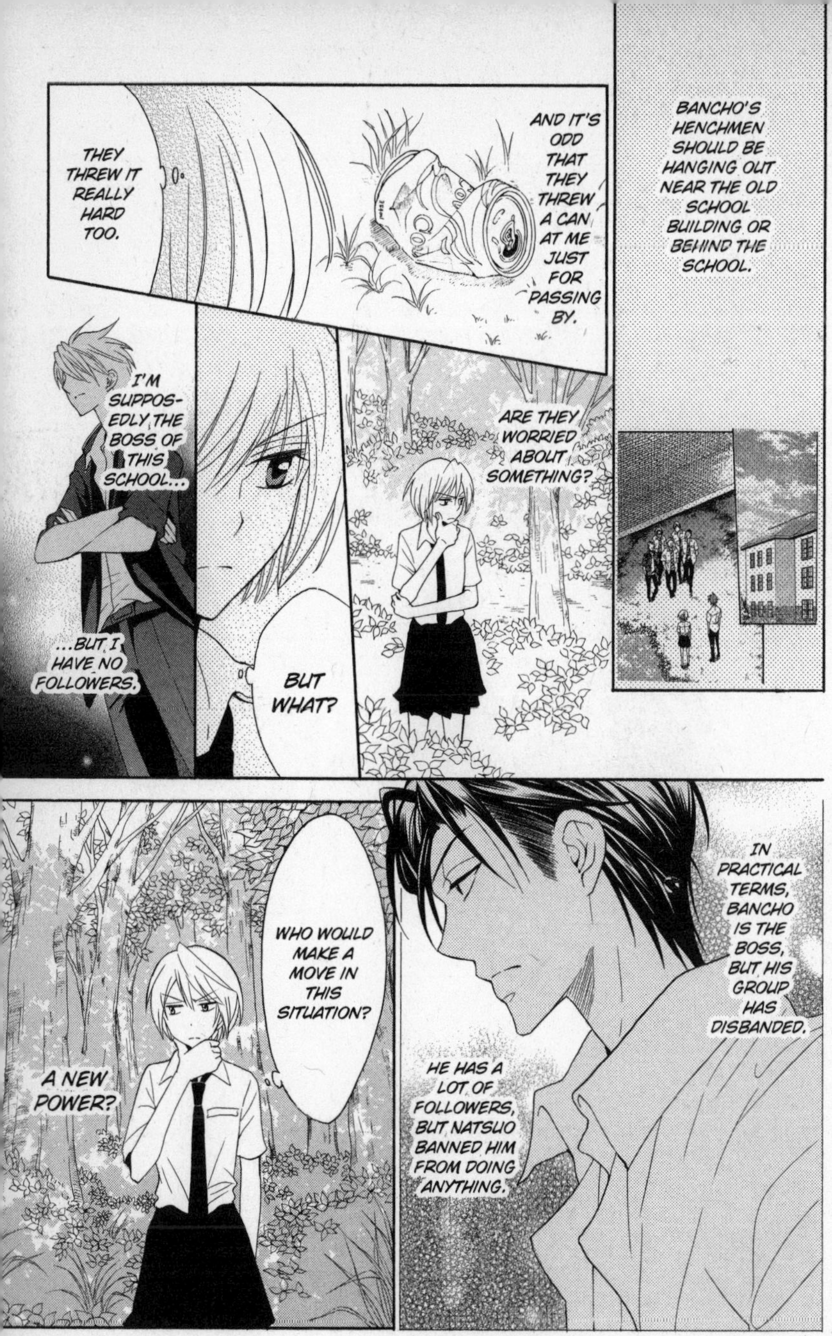
BANCHO'S HENCHMEN SHOULD BE HANGING OUT NEAR THE OLD SCHOOL BUILDING OR BEHIND THE SCHOOL.
AND IT'S ODD THAT THEY THREW A CAN AT ME JUST FOR PASSING BY.
THEY THREW IT REALLY HARD TOO.
ARE THEY WORRIED ABOUT SOMETHING?
BUT WHAT?
I'M SUPPOSEDLY THE BOSS OF THIS SCHOOL...
...BUT I HAVE NO FOLLOWERS.
IN PRACTICAL TERMS, BANCHO IS THE BOSS, BUT HIS GROUP HAS DISBANDED.
HE HAS A LOT OF FOLLOWERS, BUT NATSUO BANNED HIM FROM DOING ANYTHING.
WHO WOULD MAKE A MOVE IN THIS SITUATION?
A NEW POWER?

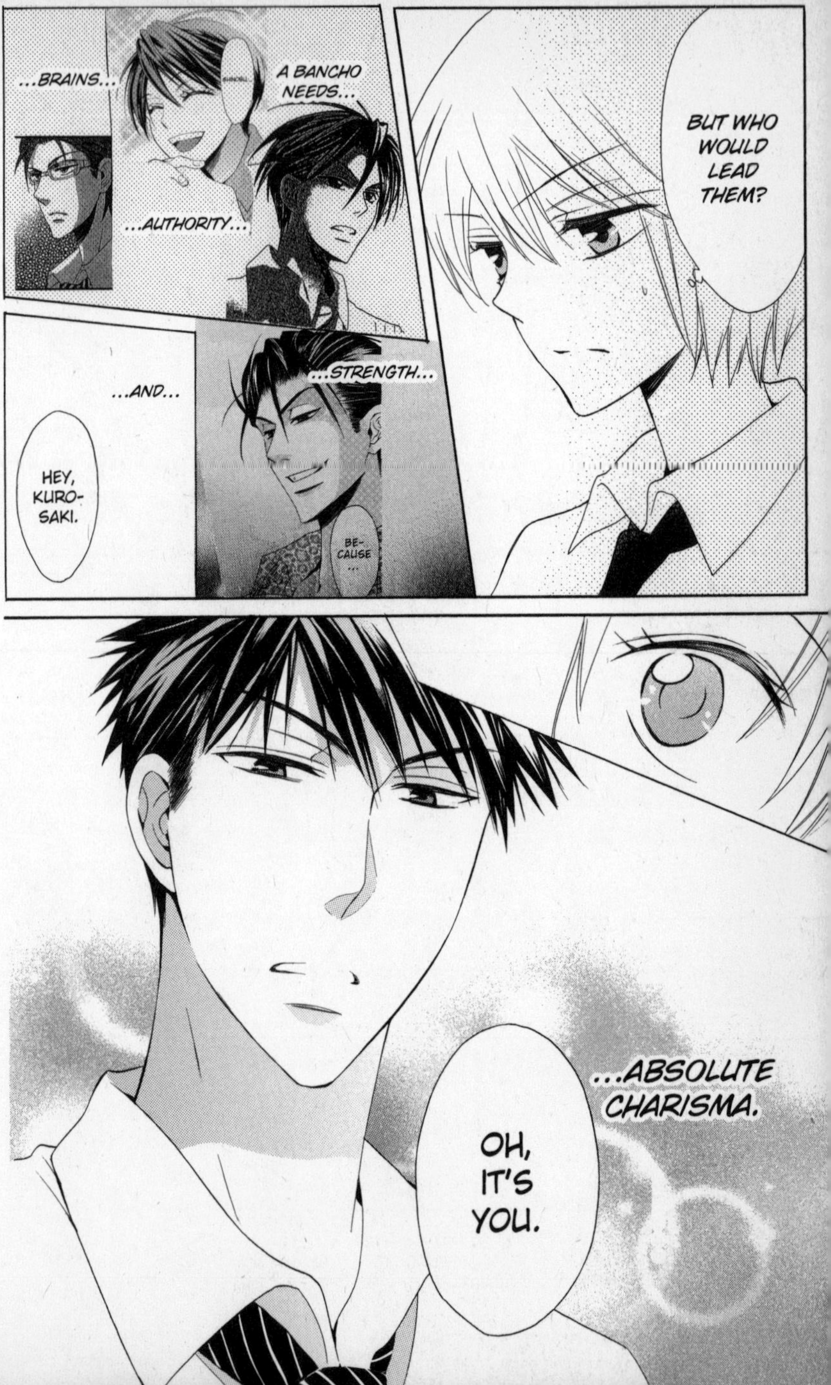
BUT WHO WOULD LEAD THEM?
A BANCHO NEEDS...
...BRAINS...
...AUTHORITY...
...STRENGTH...
BE-CAUSE...
...AND...
HEY, KURO-SAKI.
...ABSOLUTE CHARISMA.
OH, IT'S YOU.

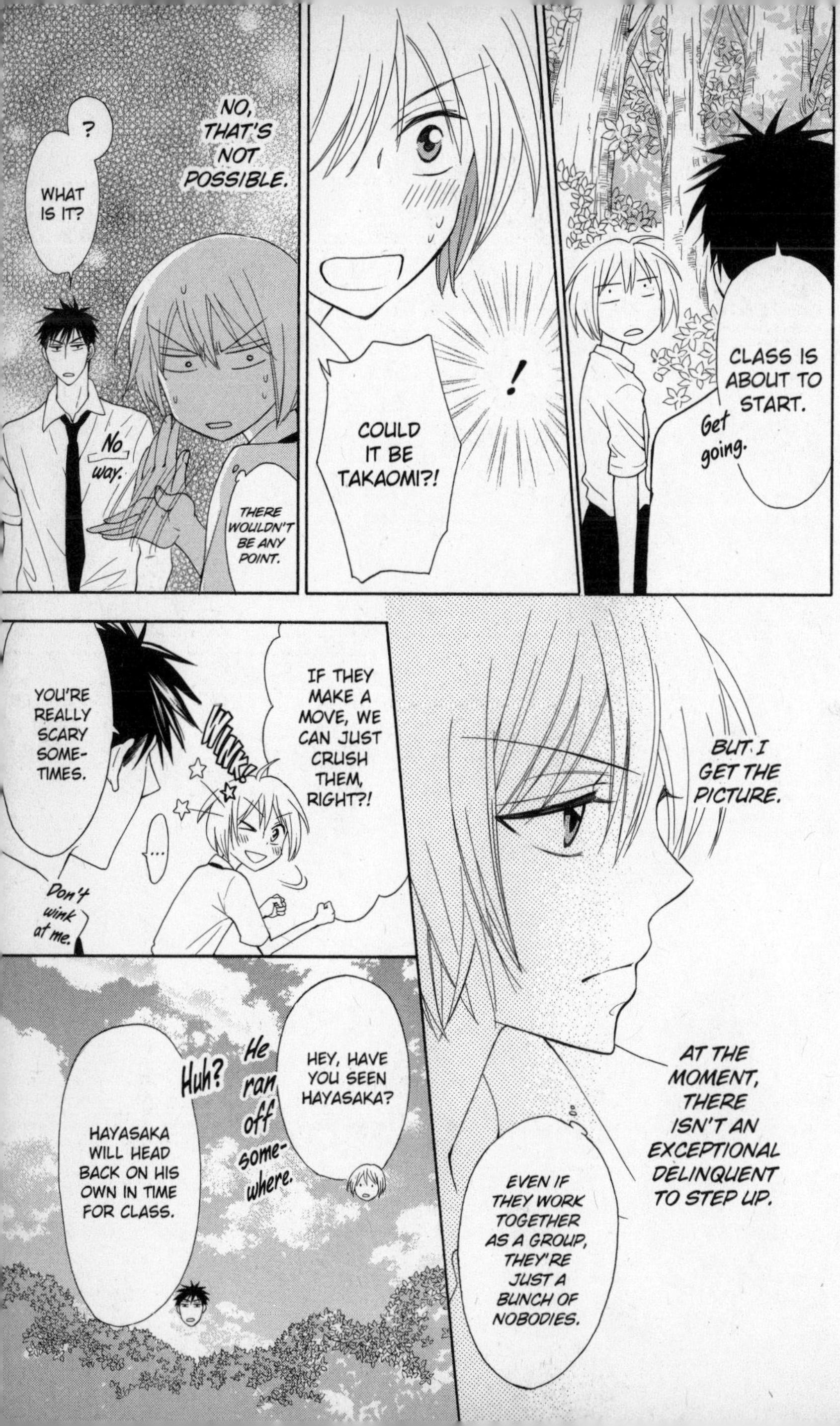

CLASS IS ABOUT TO START.
Get going.
!
COULD IT BE TAKAOMI?!
NO, THAT'S NOT POSSIBLE.
?
WHAT IS IT?
No way.
THERE WOULDN'T BE ANY POINT.
BUT I GET THE PICTURE.
AT THE MOMENT, THERE ISN'T AN EXCEPTIONAL DELINQUENT TO STEP UP.
EVEN IF THEY WORK TOGETHER AS A GROUP, THEY'RE JUST A BUNCH OF NOBODIES.
IF THEY MAKE A MOVE, WE CAN JUST CRUSH THEM, RIGHT?!
WINK
...
YOU'RE REALLY SCARY SOMETIMES.
Don't wink at me.
HEY, HAVE YOU SEEN HAYASAKA?
He ran off somewhere.
Huh?
HAYASAKA WILL HEAD BACK ON HIS OWN IN TIME FOR CLASS.

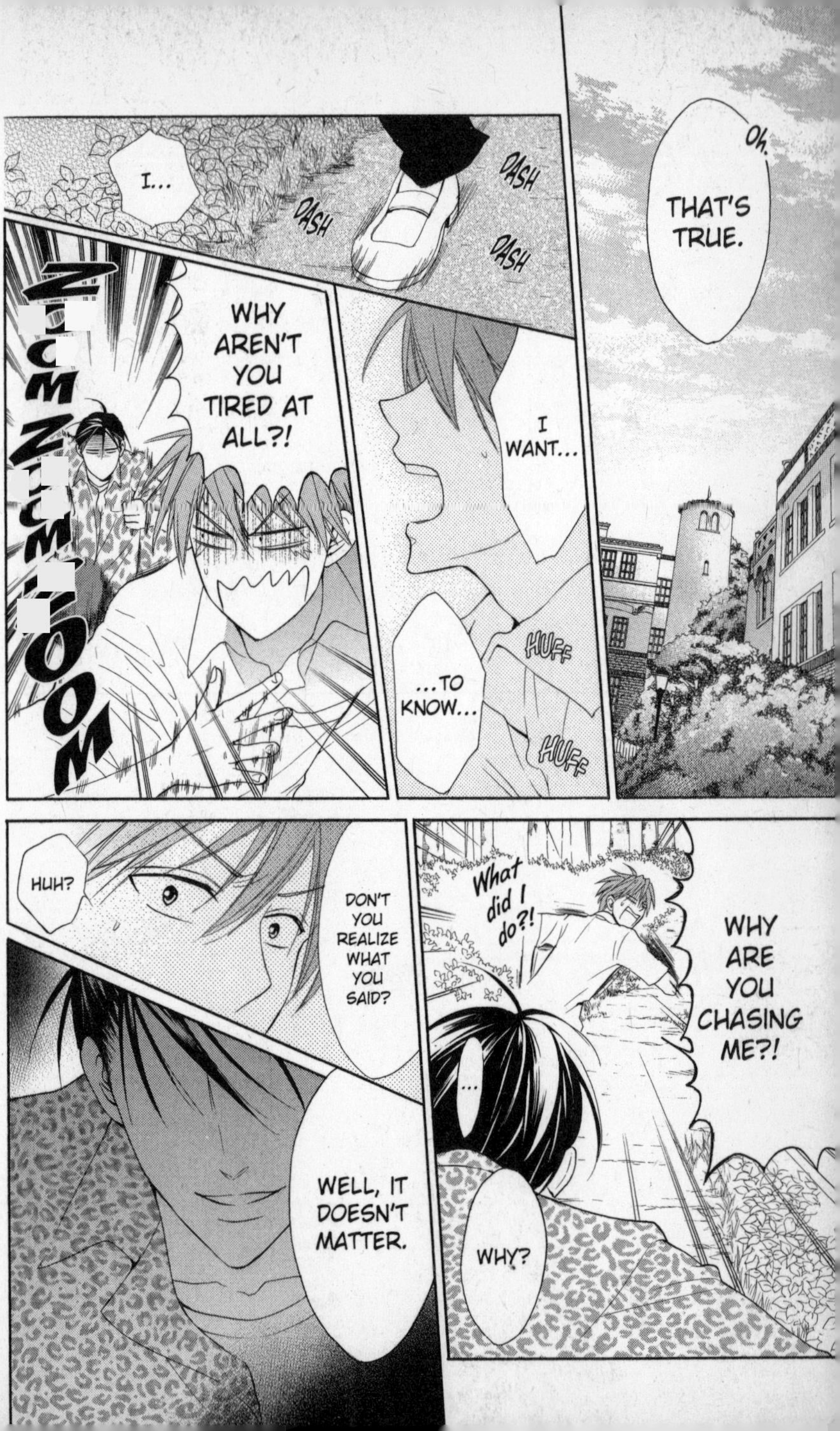

Oh.
THAT'S TRUE.
I...
DASH
DASH
DASH
I WANT...
...TO KNOW...
HUFF
HUFF
WHY AREN'T YOU TIRED AT ALL?!
WHY ARE YOU CHASING ME?!
What did I do?!
...
WHY?
HUH?
DON'T YOU REALIZE WHAT YOU SAID?
WELL, IT DOESN'T MATTER.

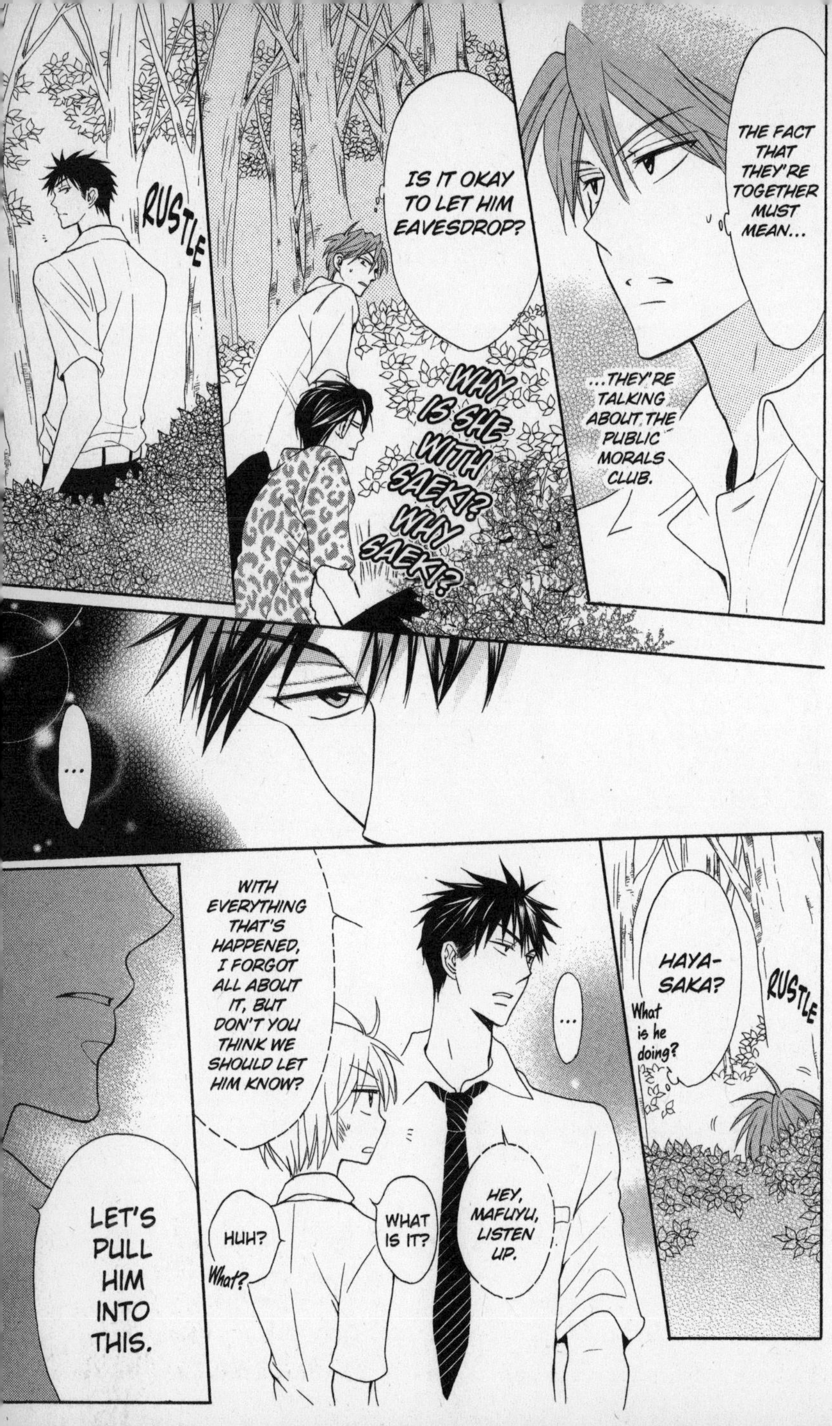
THE FACT THAT THEY'RE TOGETHER MUST MEAN...
...THEY'RE TALKING ABOUT THE PUBLIC MORALS CLUB.
IS IT OKAY TO LET HIM EAVESDROP?
WHY IS SHE WITH SAEKI? WHY SAEKI!?
RUSTLE
...
HAYA-SAKA?
What is he doing?
RUSTLE
...
WITH EVERYTHING THAT'S HAPPENED, I FORGOT ALL ABOUT IT, BUT DON'T YOU THINK WE SHOULD LET HIM KNOW?
HEY, MAFUYU, LISTEN UP.
WHAT IS IT?
HUH?
What?
LET'S PULL HIM INTO THIS.

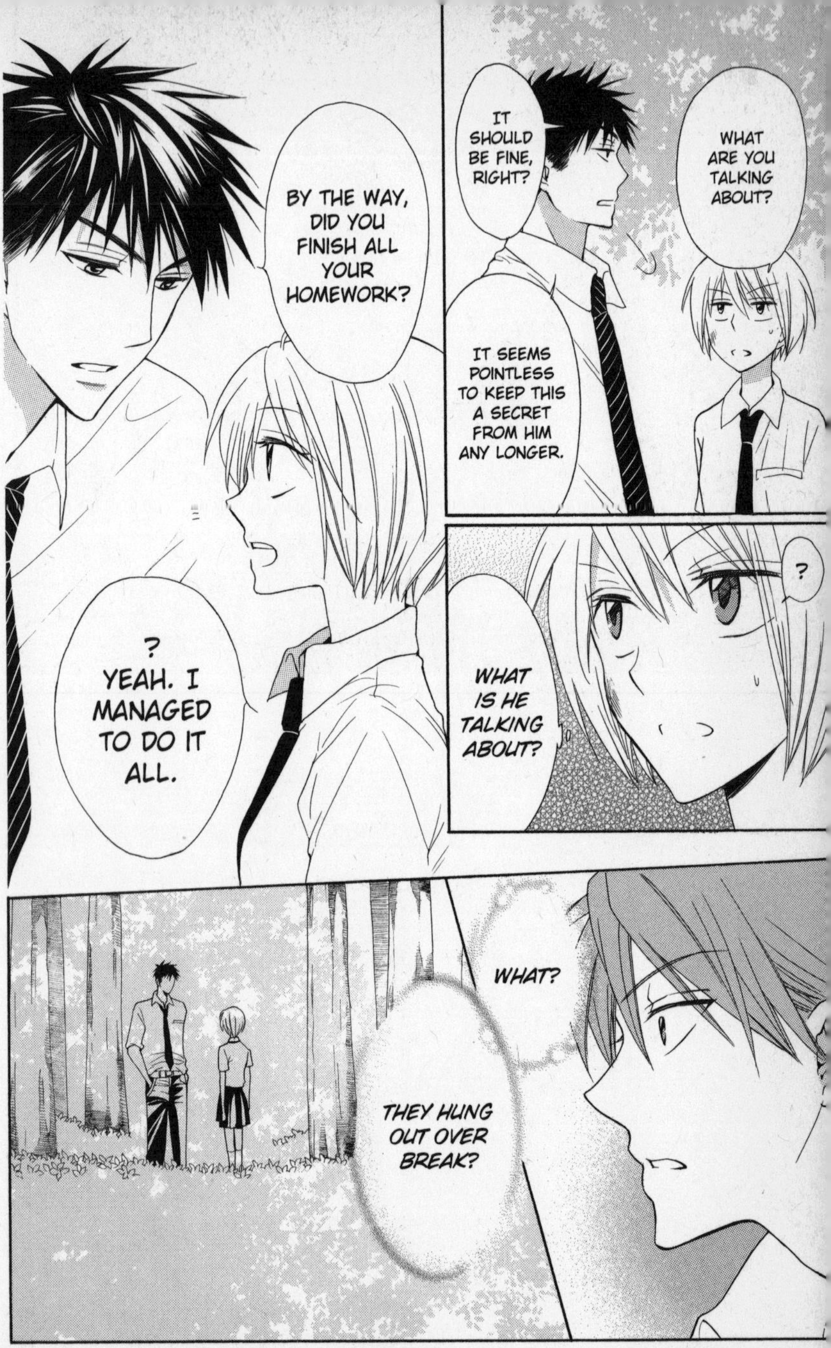
WHAT ARE YOU TALKING ABOUT?
IT SHOULD BE FINE, RIGHT?
IT SEEMS POINTLESS TO KEEP THIS A SECRET FROM HIM ANY LONGER.
?
WHAT IS HE TALKING ABOUT?
BY THE WAY, DID YOU FINISH ALL YOUR HOMEWORK?
? YEAH. I MANAGED TO DO IT ALL.
WHAT?
THEY HUNG OUT OVER BREAK?

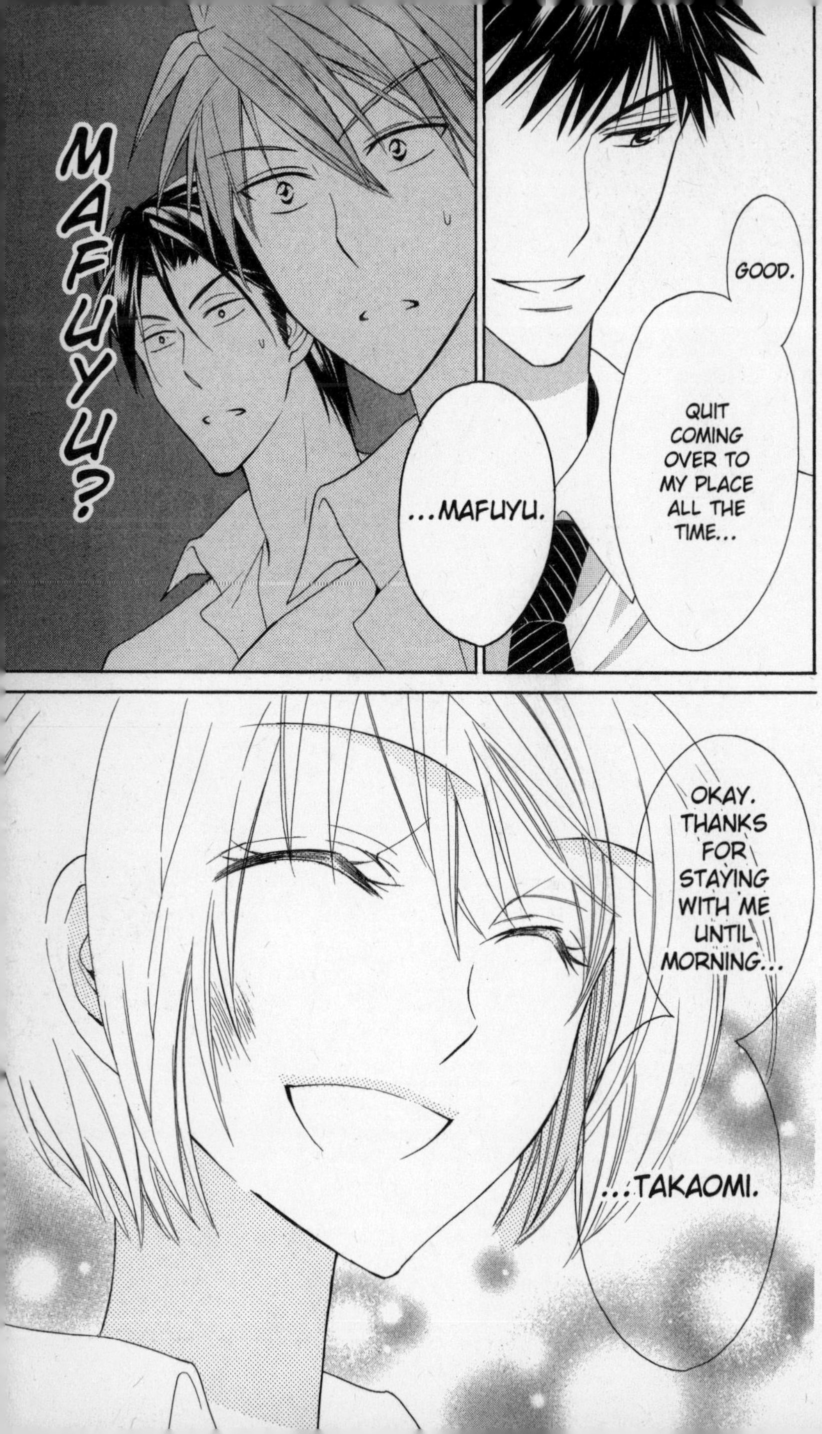
GOOD.
QUIT COMING OVER TO MY PLACE ALL THE TIME...
...MAFUYU.
MAFUYU?
OKAY. THANKS FOR STAYING WITH ME UNTIL MORNING...
...TAKAOMI.

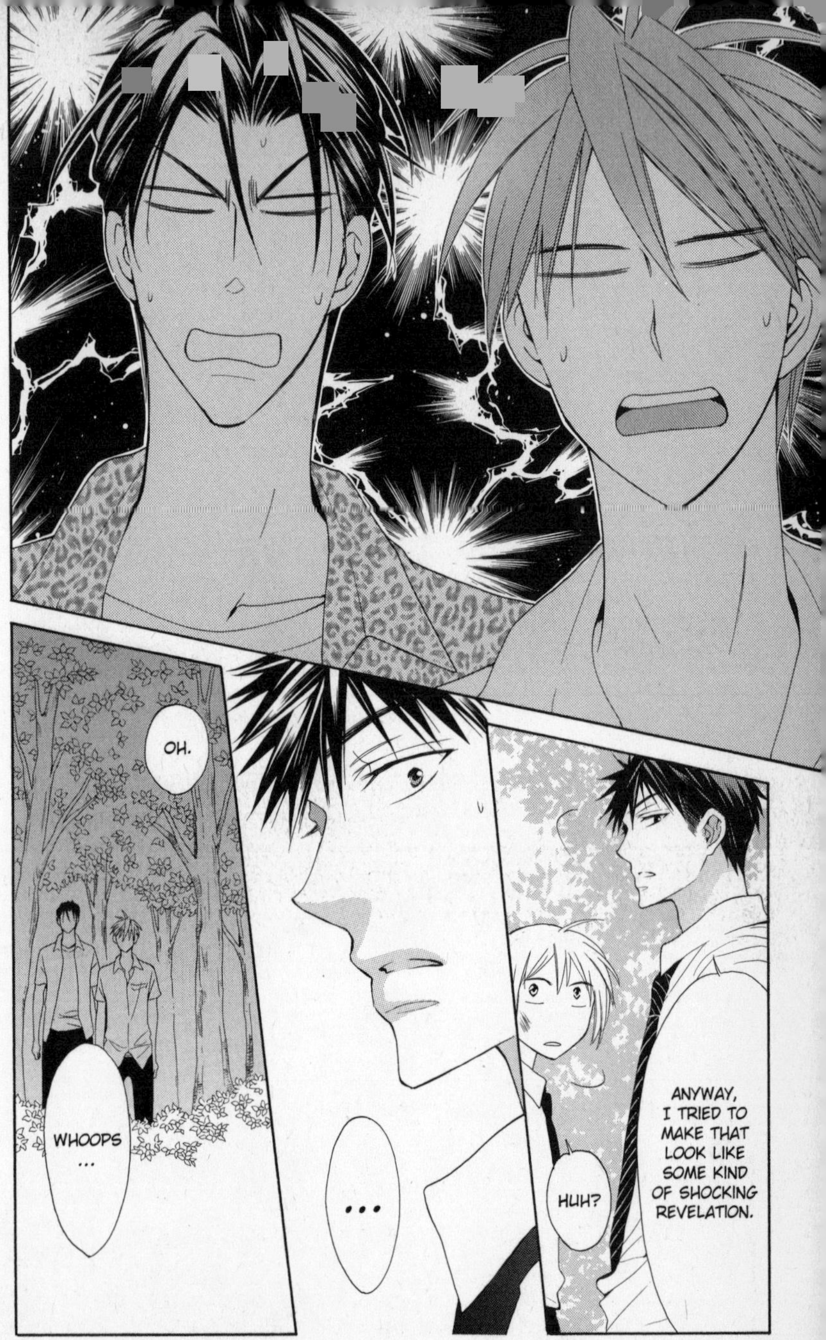
ANYWAY, I TRIED TO MAKE THAT LOOK LIKE SOME KIND OF SHOCKING REVELATION.
HUH?
...
OH.
WHOOPS ...

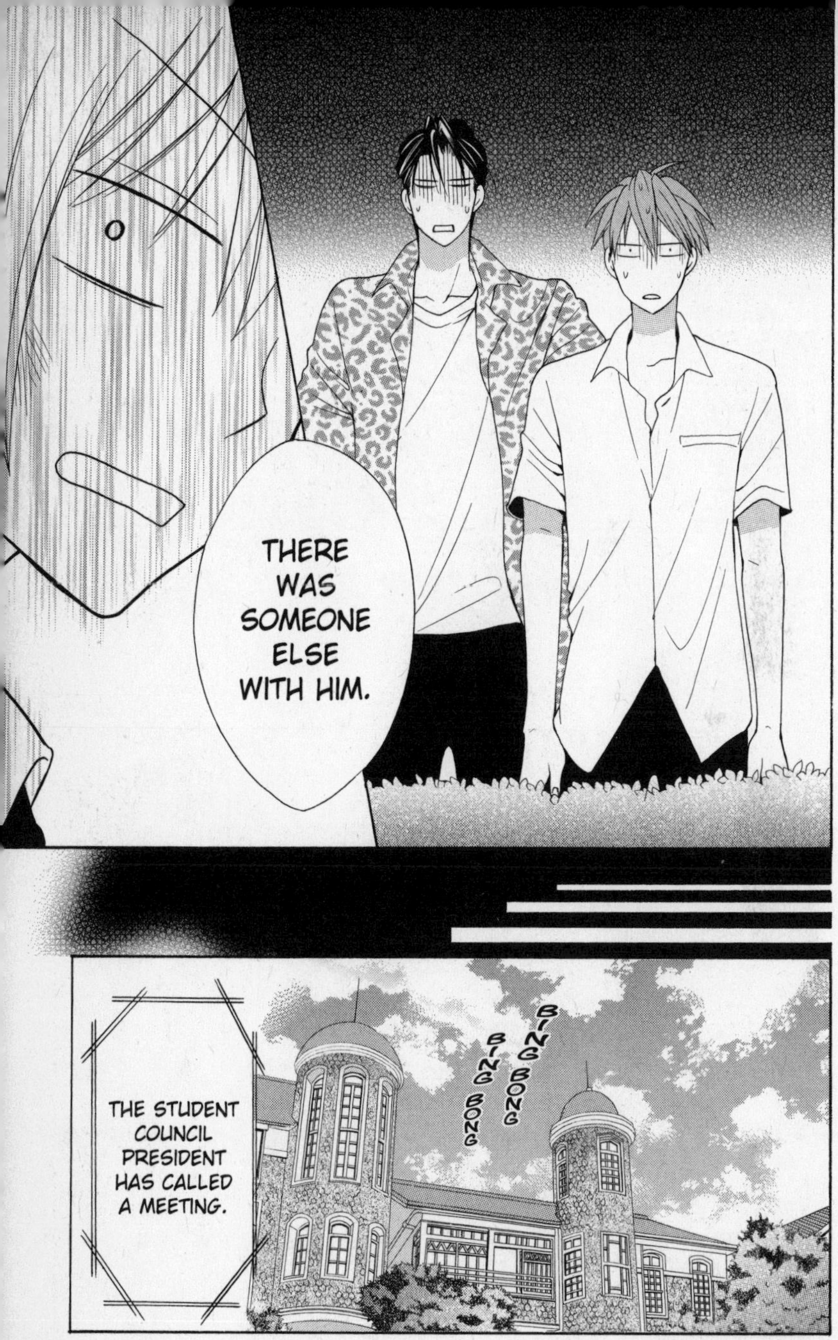
THERE WAS SOMEONE ELSE WITH HIM.
BING BONG
BING BONG
THE STUDENT COUNCIL PRESIDENT HAS CALLED A MEETING.

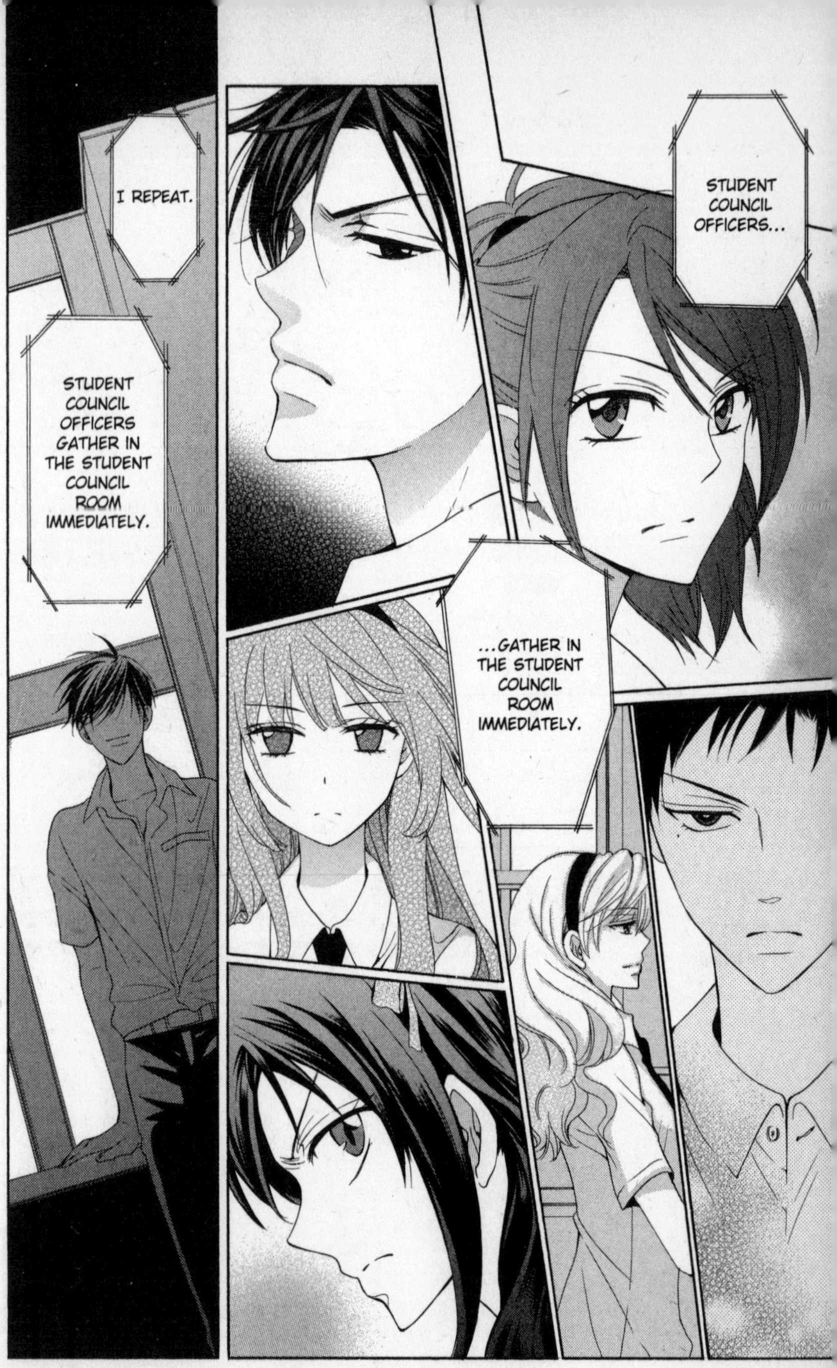
STUDENT COUNCIL OFFICERS...
...GATHER IN THE STUDENT COUNCIL ROOM IMMEDIATELY.
I REPEAT.
STUDENT COUNCIL OFFICERS GATHER IN THE STUDENT COUNCIL ROOM IMMEDIATELY.

A POPULAR MAN

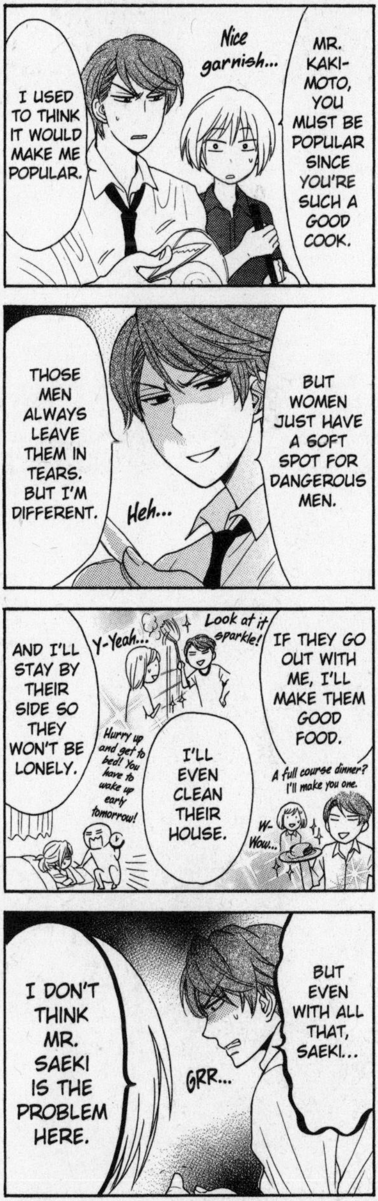
MR. KAKIMOTO, YOU MUST BE POPULAR SINCE YOU'RE SUCH A GOOD COOK.
Nice garnish...
I USED TO THINK IT WOULD MAKE ME POPULAR.
BUT WOMEN JUST HAVE A SOFT SPOT FOR DANGEROUS MEN.
THOSE MEN ALWAYS LEAVE THEM IN TEARS. BUT I'M DIFFERENT.
Heh...
IF THEY GO OUT WITH ME, I'LL MAKE THEM GOOD FOOD.
Look at it sparkle!
Y-Yeah...
A full course dinner? I'll make you one.
W-Wow...
I'LL EVEN CLEAN THEIR HOUSE.
AND I'LL STAY BY THEIR SIDE SO THEY WON'T BE LONELY.
Hurry up and get to bed! You have to wake up early tomorrow!
BUT EVEN WITH ALL THAT, SAEKI...
GRR...
I DON'T THINK MR. SAEKI IS THE PROBLEM HERE.

A LOVED MAN

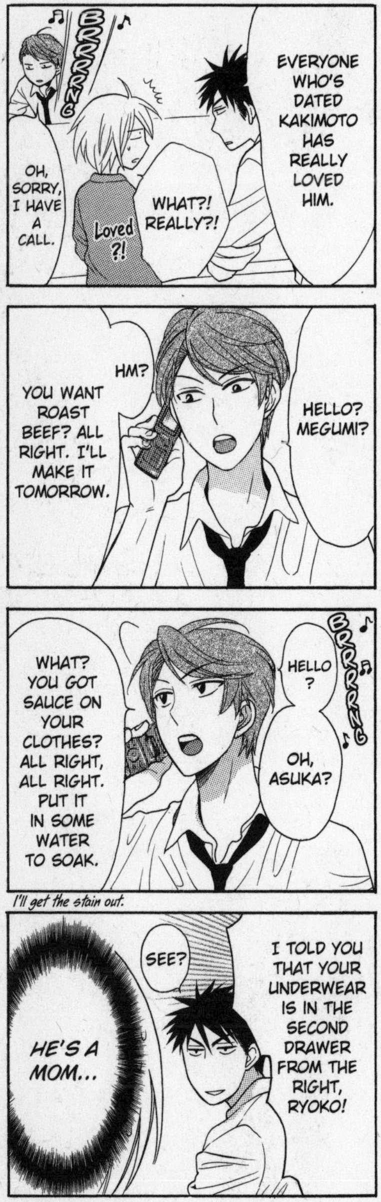
EVERYONE WHO'S DATED KAKIMOTO HAS REALLY LOVED HIM.
BRRRRNG
WHAT?! REALLY?!
Loved?!
OH, SORRY, I HAVE A CALL.
HELLO? MEGUMI?
HM?
YOU WANT ROAST BEEF? ALL RIGHT. I'LL MAKE IT TOMORROW.
BRRRRNG
OH, ASUKA?
HELLO?
WHAT? YOU GOT SAUCE ON YOUR CLOTHES? ALL RIGHT, ALL RIGHT. PUT IT IN SOME WATER TO SOAK.
I'll get the stain out.
I TOLD YOU THAT YOUR UNDERWEAR IS IN THE SECOND DRAWER FROM THE RIGHT, RYOKO!
SEE?
HE'S A MOM...

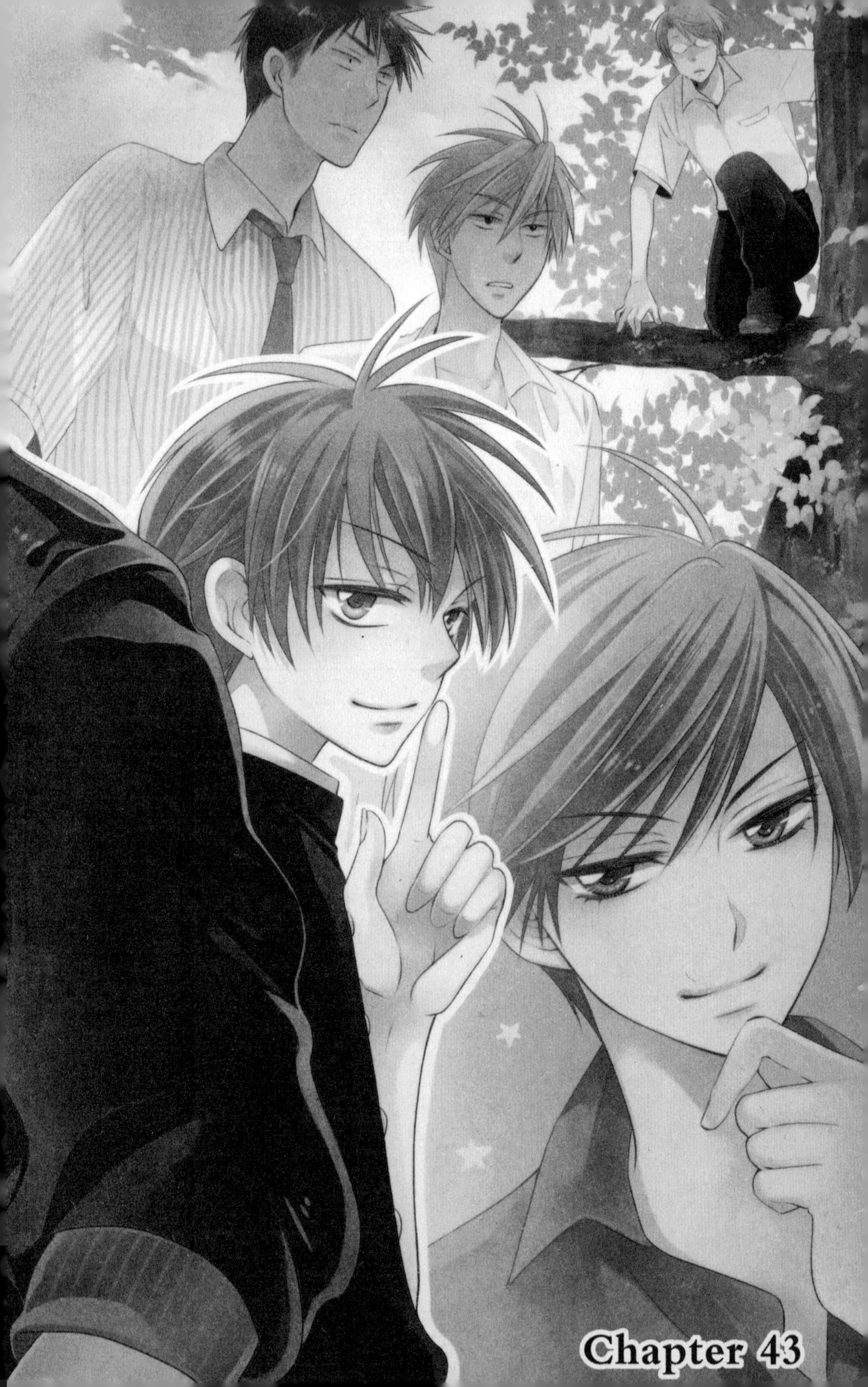

Chapter 43

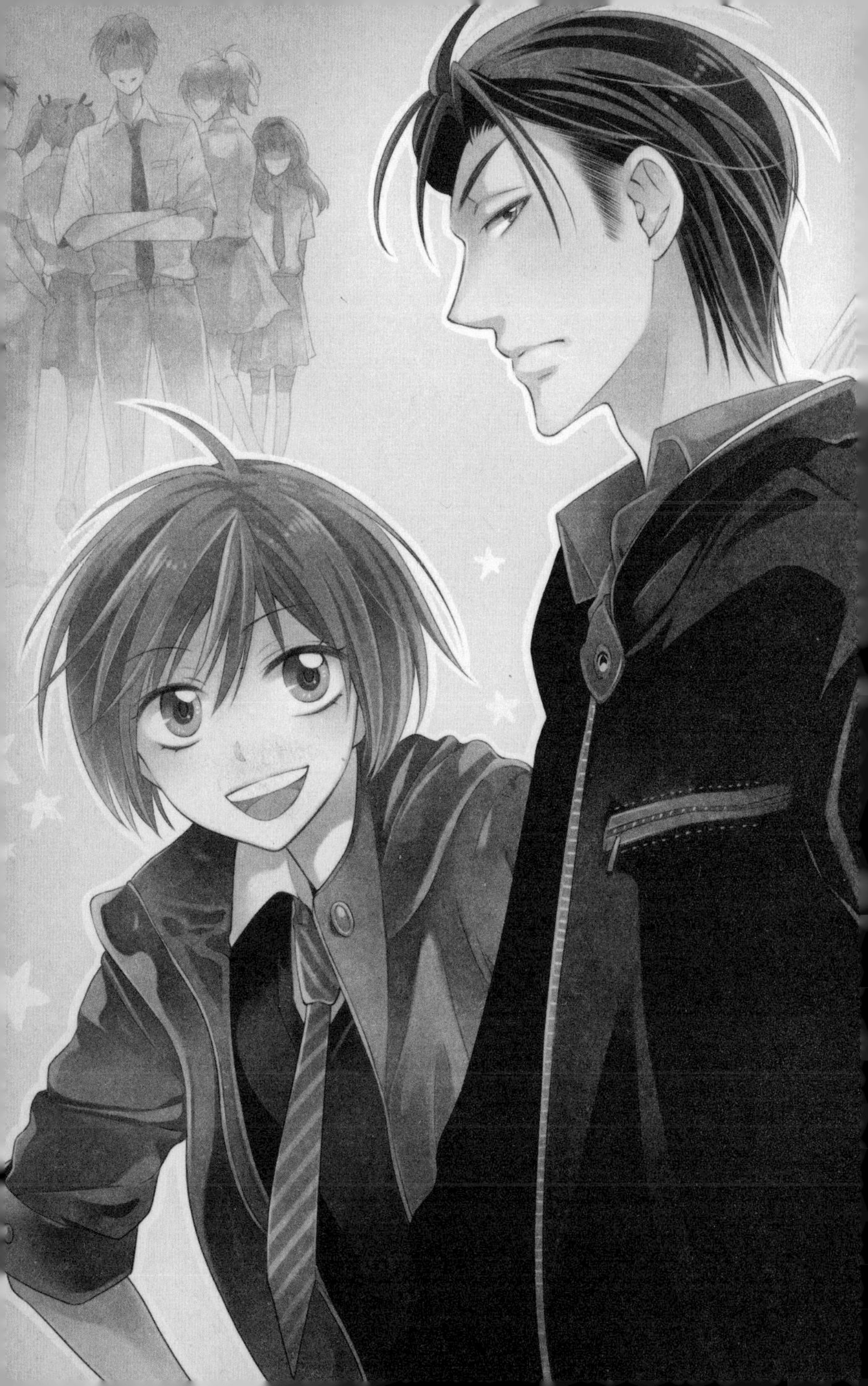

THEY REALLY EXIST!

SIDE CHARACTER INTRODUCTION Part 2

WE'RE TAKING A LOOK AT CHARACTERS THAT DIDN'T HAVE NAMES WHEN THEY FIRST APPEARED.

Part 1 is on page 4.

Volume 1 page 15

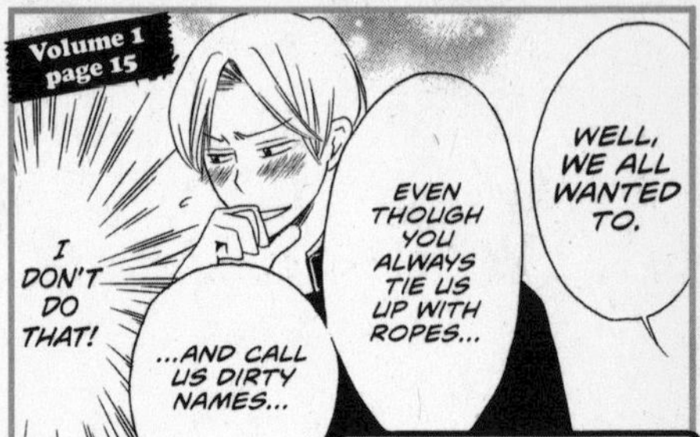
WELL, WE ALL WANTED TO.
EVEN THOUGH YOU ALWAYS TIE US UP WITH ROPES...
...AND CALL US DIRTY NAMES...
I DON'T DO THAT!

Yuto Maizono

HE WAS AN UNEXPECTEDLY SUCCESSFUL CHARACTER. I NEVER THOUGHT I WOULD WRITE AN EXTRA CHAPTER STARRING HIM. ON A SIDE NOTE, MAIZONO NEVER GOES ALL OUT IN A FIGHT FOR CERTAIN REASONS.

Volume 3 page 113

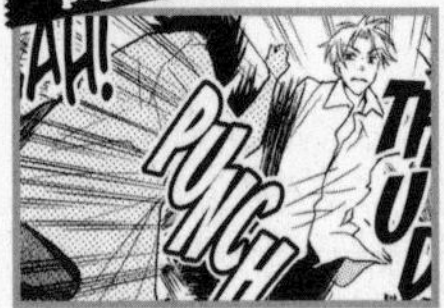
AH!
PUNCH

HE ONLY FIGHTS WHEN HE'S IN A GROUP AND DOESN'T STAND OUT.

Volume 3 page 75

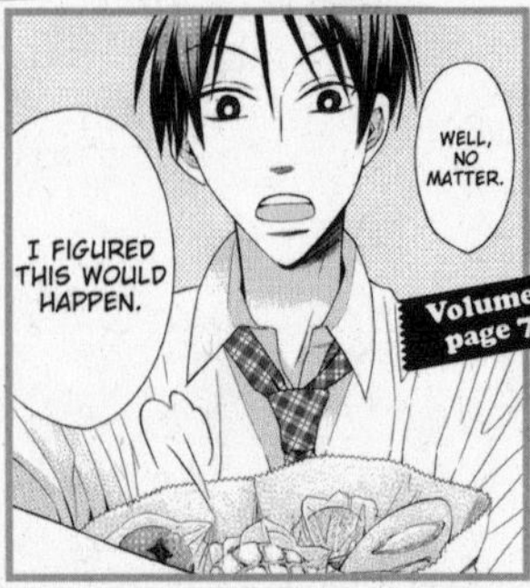
WELL, NO MATTER.
I FIGURED THIS WOULD HAPPEN.

Masayoshi Omiya

HIS JOB WAS TO BUY BREAD WHEN HE FIRST APPEARED. LATER ON HE SHOWS UP IN A FEW FOUR-PANEL STRIPS. HE'S VERY CALM AND CALCULATING. HE'S A SURVIVOR OF WEST HIGH.

Volume 5 page 98

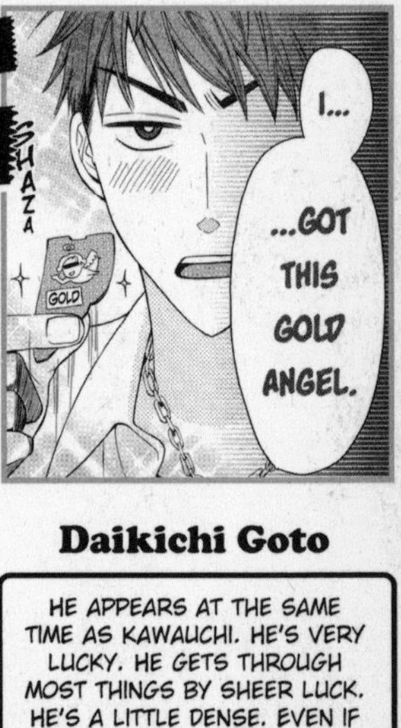
I...
...GOT THIS GOLD ANGEL.
SHAZA
GOLD

Daikichi Goto

HE APPEARS AT THE SAME TIME AS KAWAUCHI. HE'S VERY LUCKY. HE GETS THROUGH MOST THINGS BY SHEER LUCK. HE'S A LITTLE DENSE. EVEN IF HE GETS INTO A FIGHT, HE'LL END UP WITH FEWER INJURIES THAN MOST PEOPLE BECAUSE HE'S SO LUCKY.

Bancho's Two Henchmen

Volume 5 page 111

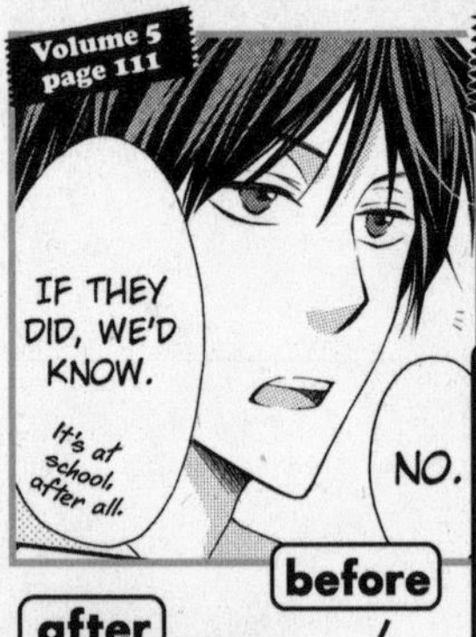
NO.
IF THEY DID, WE'D KNOW.
It's at school, after all.

before

after

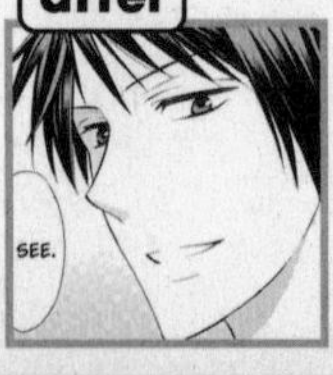
SEE.

Tomohiro Kawauchi

HE APPEARED IN VOLUME 5 CHAPTER 27 AND VOLUME 7 CHAPTER 38. HE CUT HIS BANGS BEFORE SUMMER VACATION. IT LOOKS NICE! HE'S THE NUMBER TWO GUY AT MIDORIGAOKA. HE'S QUITE WELL INFORMED.

ON A SIDE NOTE, THE BANCHO ARC (CHAPTER 42~) STARTED BEHIND THE SCENES IN CHAPTER 27.

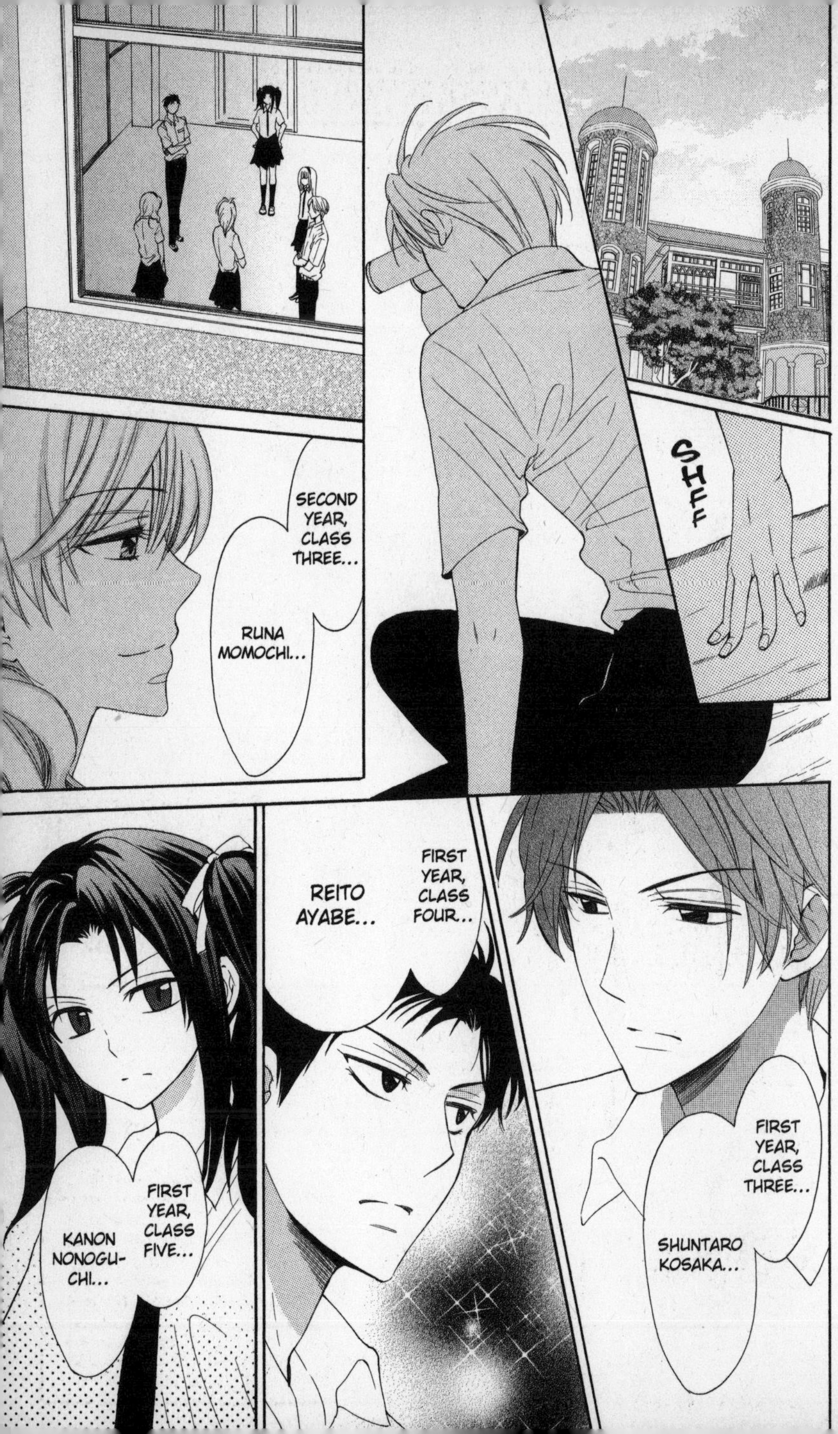
SHFF
SECOND YEAR, CLASS THREE...
RUNA MOMOCHI...
FIRST YEAR, CLASS THREE...
SHUNTARO KOSAKA...
FIRST YEAR, CLASS FOUR...
REITO AYABE...
FIRST YEAR, CLASS FIVE...
KANON NONOGU-CHI...

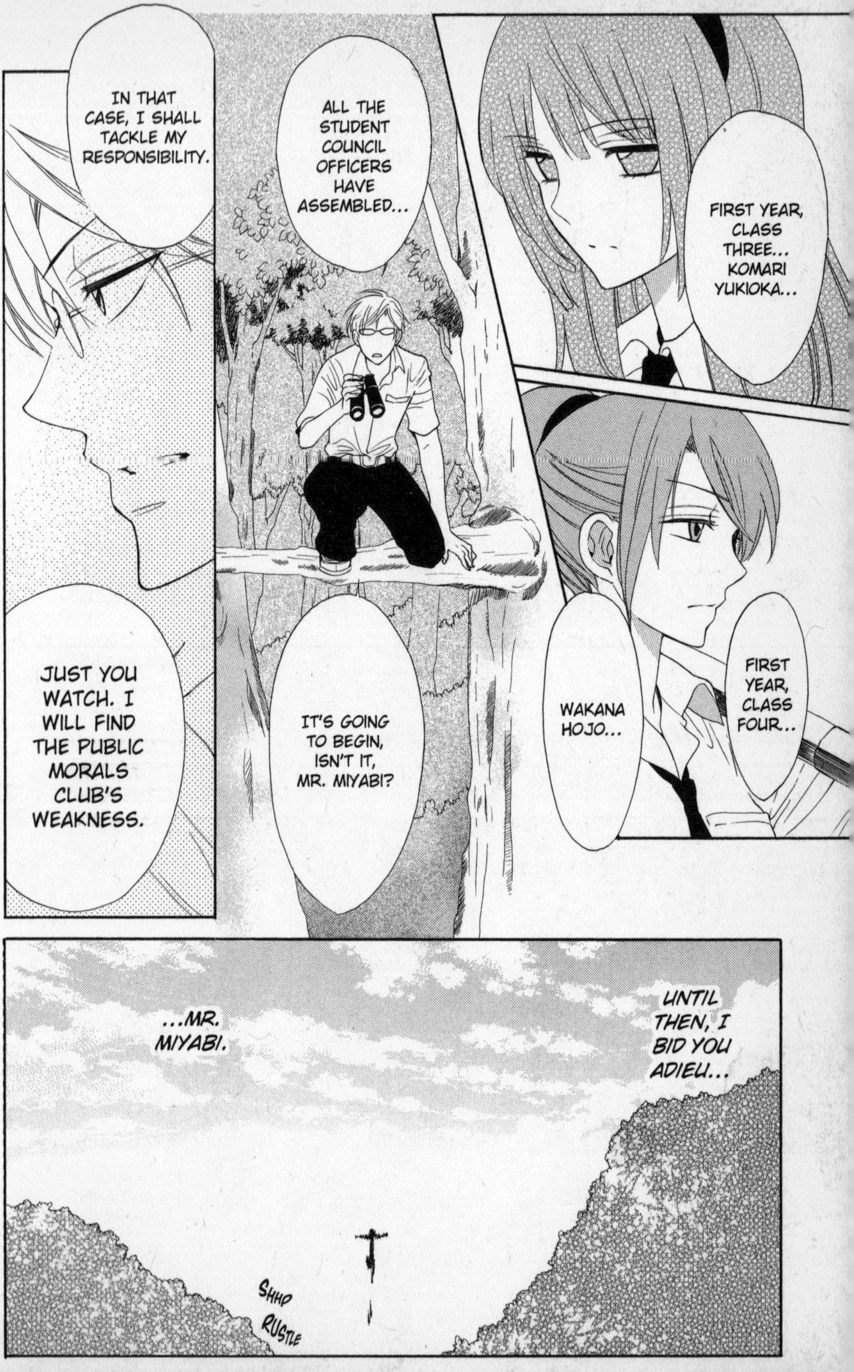
FIRST YEAR, CLASS THREE... KOMARI YUKIOKA...
FIRST YEAR, CLASS FOUR...
WAKANA HOJO...
ALL THE STUDENT COUNCIL OFFICERS HAVE ASSEMBLED...
IT'S GOING TO BEGIN, ISN'T IT, MR. MIYABI?
IN THAT CASE, I SHALL TACKLE MY RESPONSIBILITY.
JUST YOU WATCH. I WILL FIND THE PUBLIC MORALS CLUB'S WEAKNESS.
UNTIL THEN, I BID YOU ADIEU...
...MR. MIYABI.
SHHP
RUSTLE

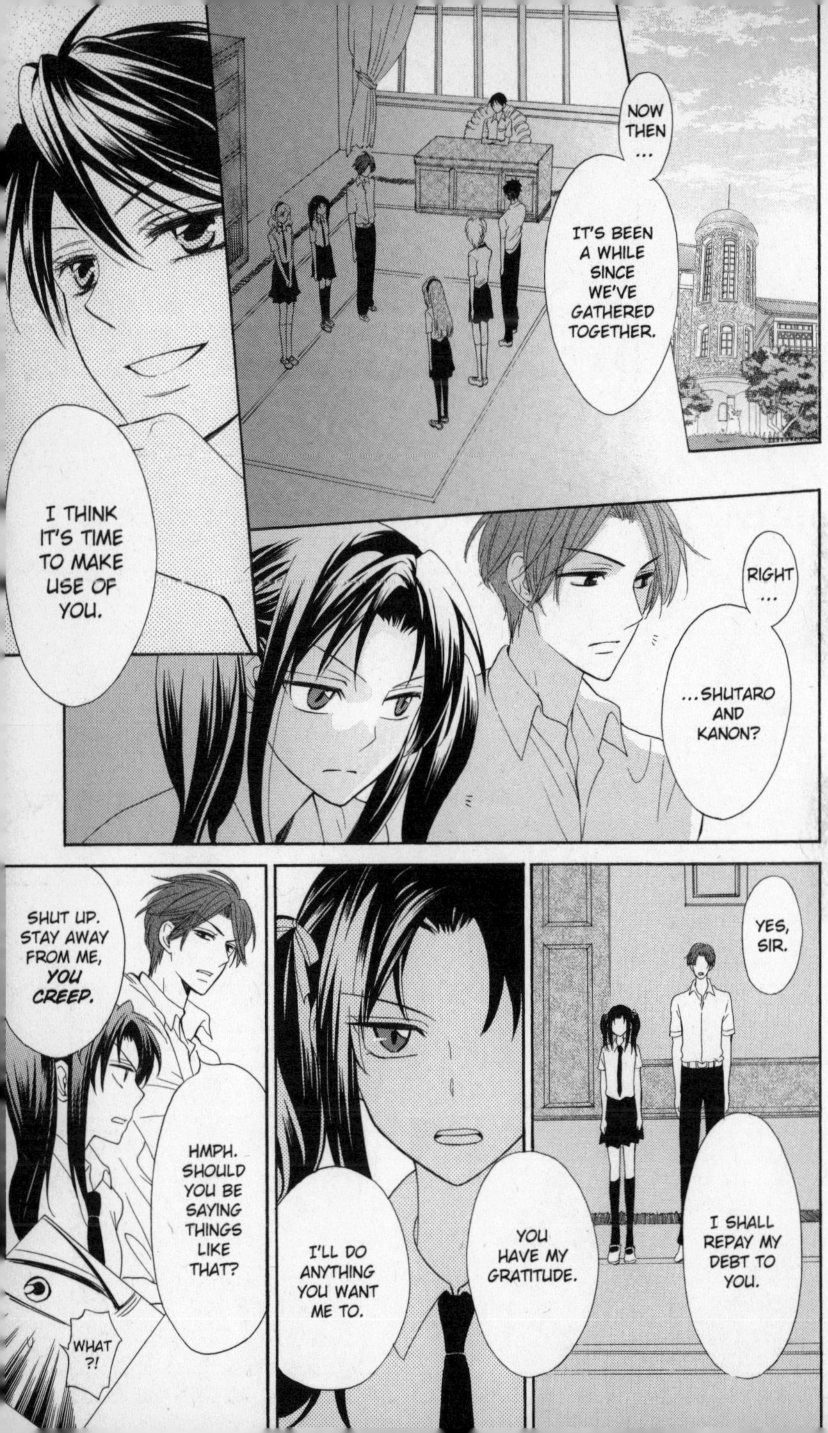
NOW THEN...
IT'S BEEN A WHILE SINCE WE'VE GATHERED TOGETHER.
I THINK IT'S TIME TO MAKE USE OF YOU.
RIGHT...
...SHUTARO AND KANON?
YES, SIR.
I SHALL REPAY MY DEBT TO YOU.
YOU HAVE MY GRATITUDE.
I'LL DO ANYTHING YOU WANT ME TO.
SHUT UP. STAY AWAY FROM ME, YOU CREEP.
HMPH. SHOULD YOU BE SAYING THINGS LIKE THAT?
WHAT?!

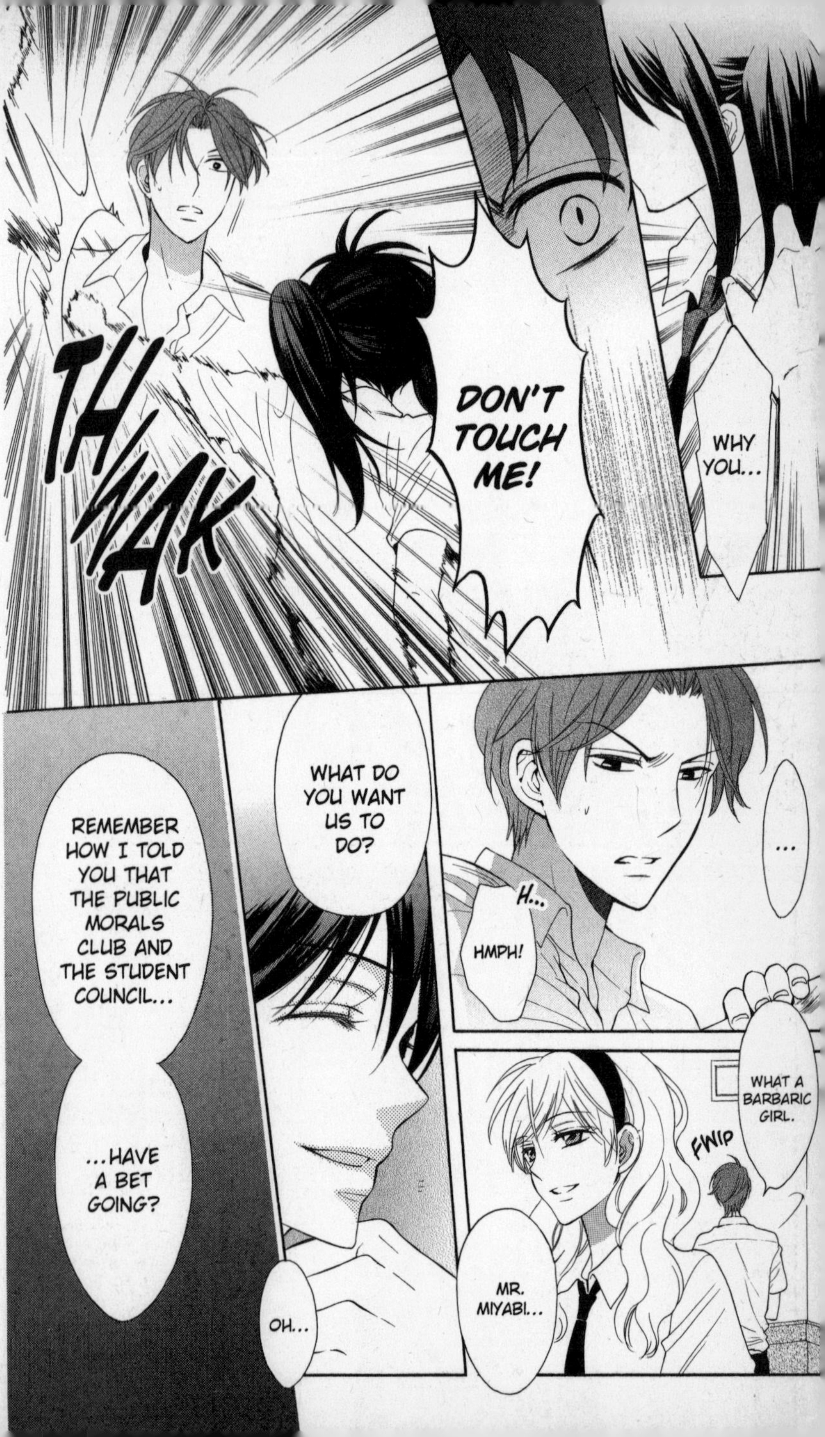
WHY YOU...
DON'T TOUCH ME!
THWAK
...
H...
HMPH!
WHAT A BARBARIC GIRL.
FWIP
MR. MIYABI...
WHAT DO YOU WANT US TO DO?
OH...
REMEMBER HOW I TOLD YOU THAT THE PUBLIC MORALS CLUB AND THE STUDENT COUNCIL...
...HAVE A BET GOING?

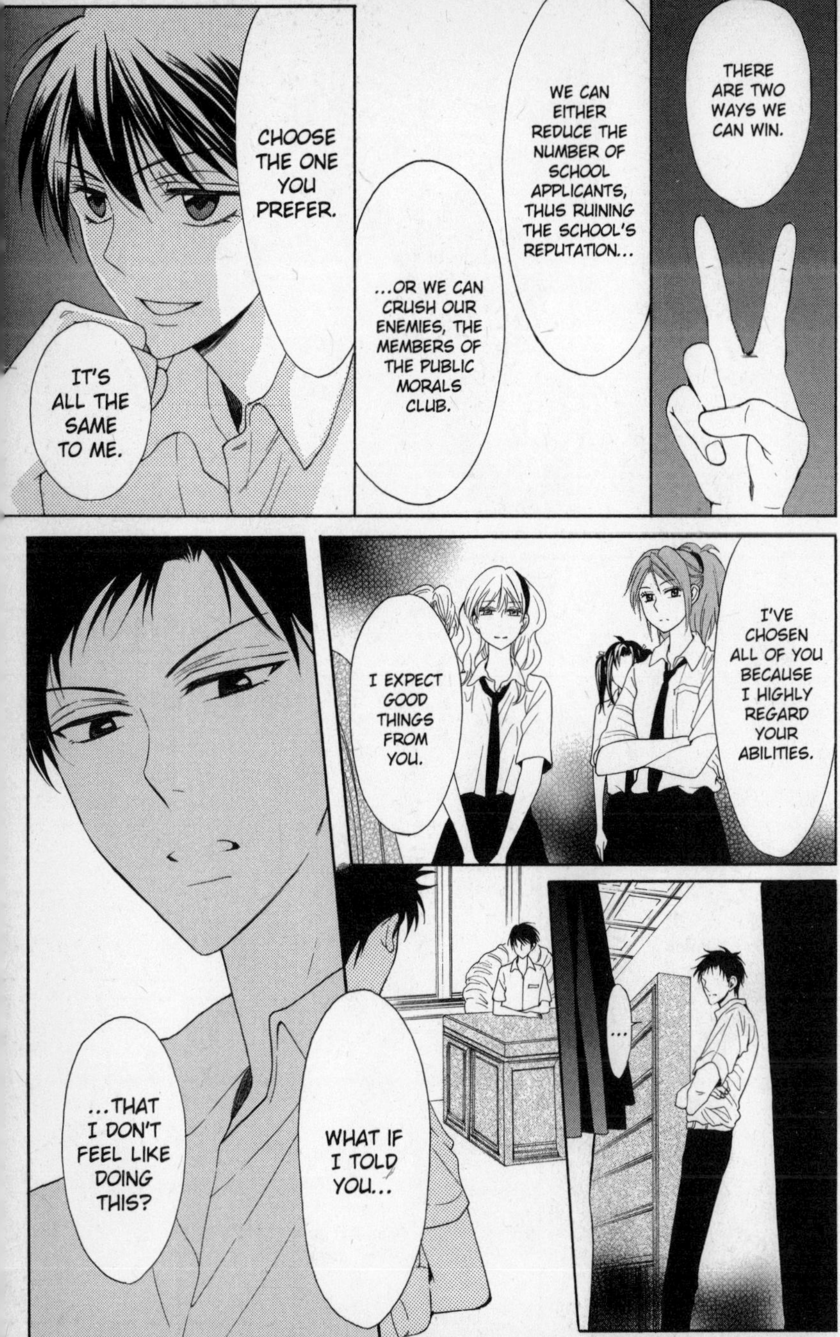
THERE ARE TWO WAYS WE CAN WIN.
WE CAN EITHER REDUCE THE NUMBER OF SCHOOL APPLICANTS, THUS RUINING THE SCHOOL'S REPUTATION...
...OR WE CAN CRUSH OUR ENEMIES, THE MEMBERS OF THE PUBLIC MORALS CLUB.
CHOOSE THE ONE YOU PREFER.
IT'S ALL THE SAME TO ME.
I'VE CHOSEN ALL OF YOU BECAUSE I HIGHLY REGARD YOUR ABILITIES.
I EXPECT GOOD THINGS FROM YOU.
...
WHAT IF I TOLD YOU...
...THAT I DON'T FEEL LIKE DOING THIS?

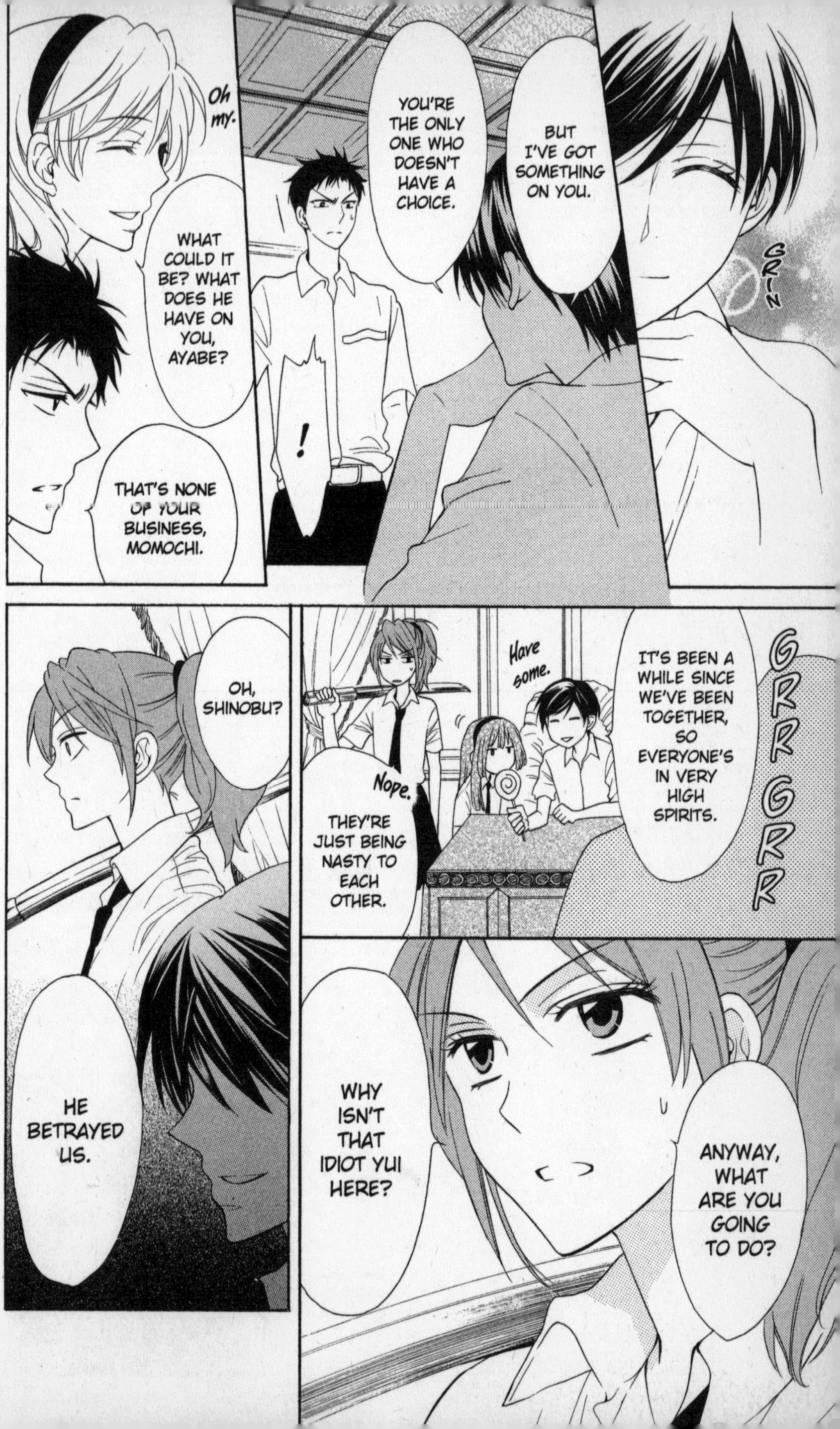
BUT I'VE GOT SOMETHING ON YOU.
GRIN
YOU'RE THE ONLY ONE WHO DOESN'T HAVE A CHOICE.
!
Oh my.
WHAT COULD IT BE? WHAT DOES HE HAVE ON YOU, AYABE?
THAT'S NONE OF YOUR BUSINESS, MOMOCHI.
GRR GRR GRR
IT'S BEEN A WHILE SINCE WE'VE BEEN TOGETHER, SO EVERYONE'S IN VERY HIGH SPIRITS.
Have some.
Nope.
THEY'RE JUST BEING NASTY TO EACH OTHER.
ANYWAY, WHAT ARE YOU GOING TO DO?
WHY ISN'T THAT IDIOT YUI HERE?
OH, SHINOBU?
HE BETRAYED US.

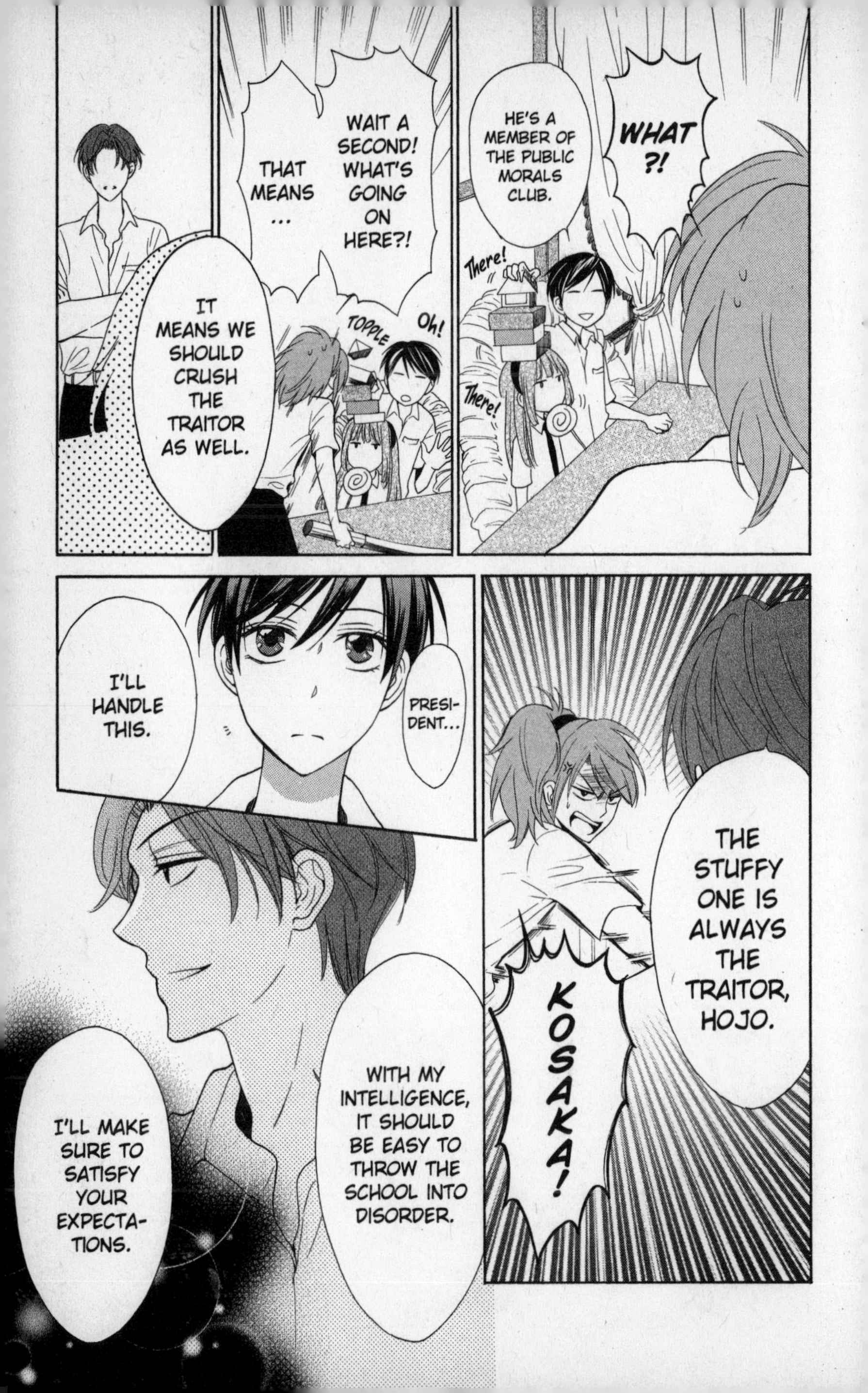
WHAT ?!
HE'S A MEMBER OF THE PUBLIC MORALS CLUB.
There!
There!
WAIT A SECOND! WHAT'S GOING ON HERE?!
THAT MEANS ...
TOPPLE
Oh!
IT MEANS WE SHOULD CRUSH THE TRAITOR AS WELL.
THE STUFFY ONE IS ALWAYS THE TRAITOR, HOJO.
KOSAKA!
PRESI-DENT...
I'LL HANDLE THIS.
WITH MY INTELLIGENCE, IT SHOULD BE EASY TO THROW THE SCHOOL INTO DISORDER.
I'LL MAKE SURE TO SATISFY YOUR EXPECTA-TIONS.

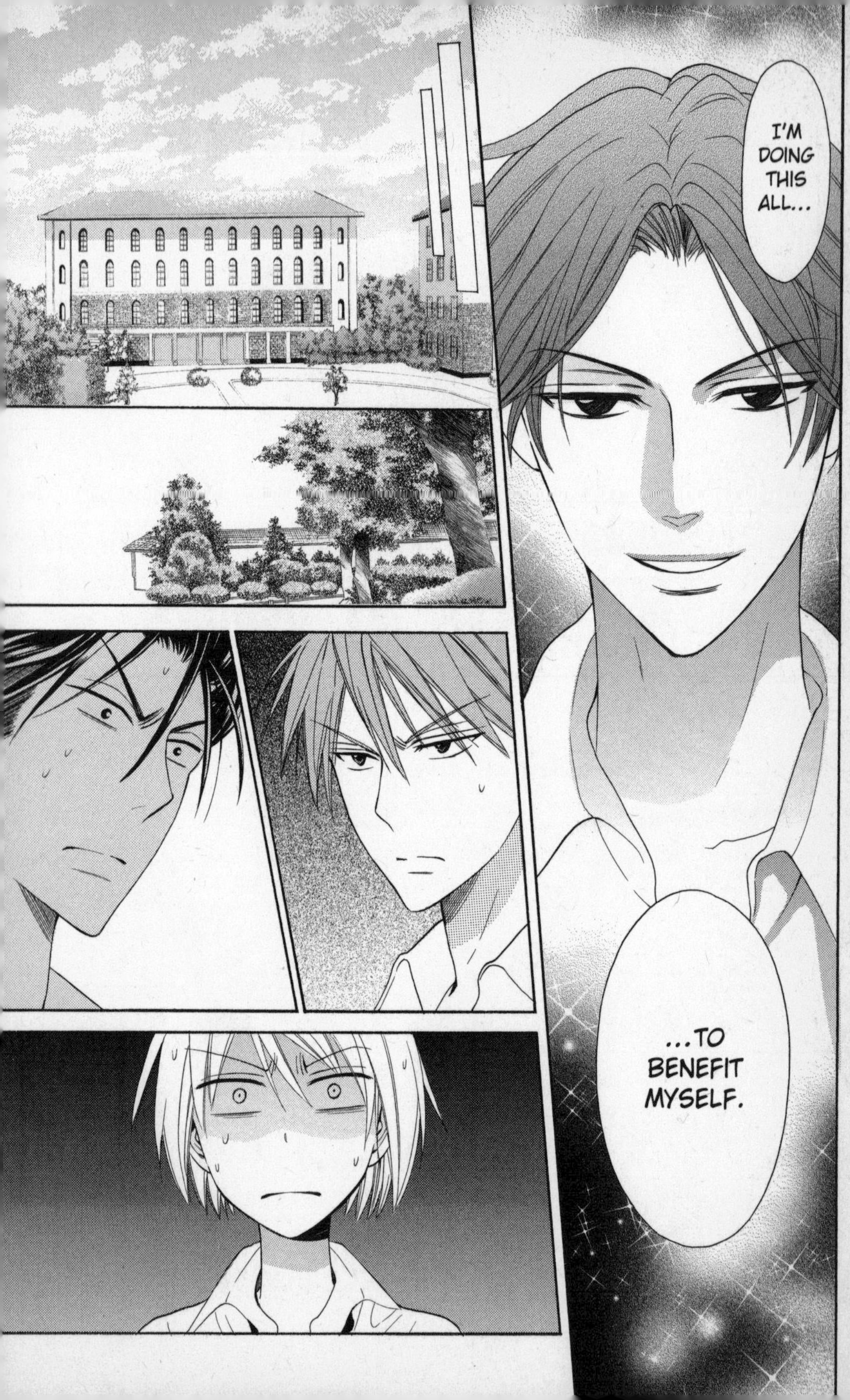
I'M DOING THIS ALL...
...TO BENEFIT MYSELF.

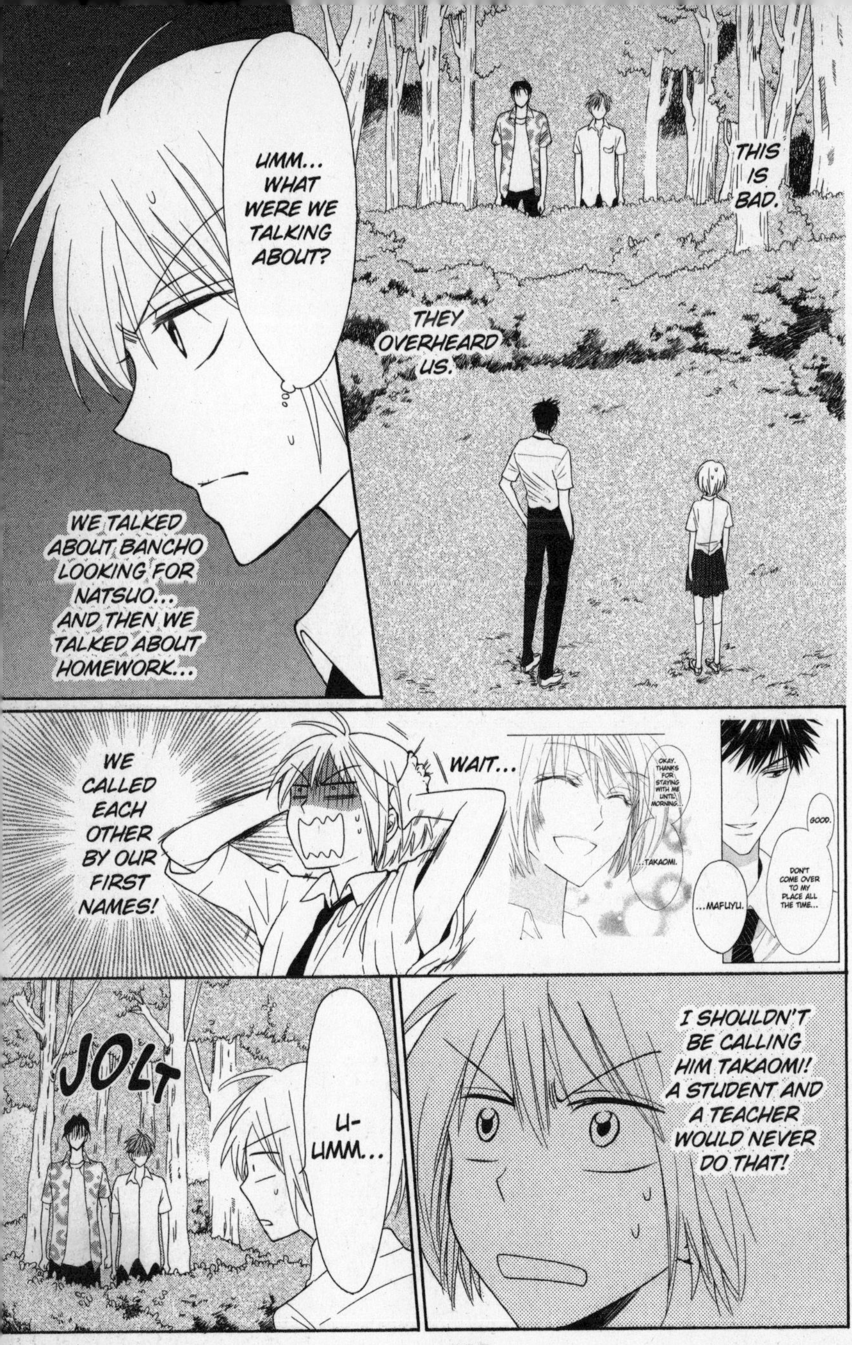
THIS IS BAD.
THEY OVERHEARD US.
UMM... WHAT WERE WE TALKING ABOUT?
WE TALKED ABOUT BANCHO LOOKING FOR NATSUO... AND THEN WE TALKED ABOUT HOMEWORK...
GOOD.
DON'T COME OVER TO MY PLACE ALL THE TIME...
...MAFUYU.
OKAY. THANKS FOR STAYING WITH ME UNTIL MORNING...
...TAKAOMI.
WAIT...
WE CALLED EACH OTHER BY OUR FIRST NAMES!
I SHOULDN'T BE CALLING HIM TAKAOMI! A STUDENT AND A TEACHER WOULD NEVER DO THAT!
U-UMM...
JOLT

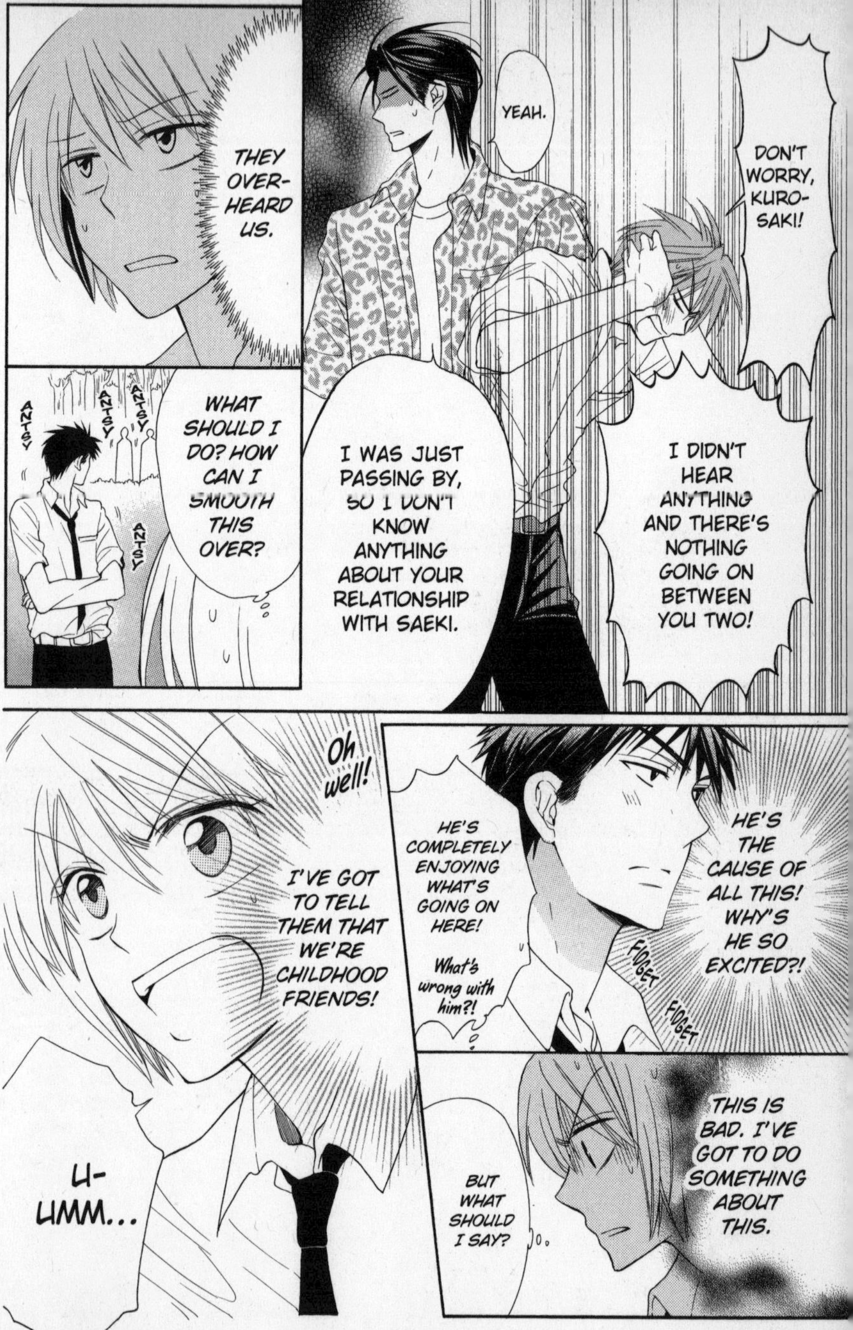
DON'T WORRY, KURO-SAKI!
YEAH.
I DIDN'T HEAR ANYTHING AND THERE'S NOTHING GOING ON BETWEEN YOU TWO!
I WAS JUST PASSING BY, SO I DON'T KNOW ANYTHING ABOUT YOUR RELATIONSHIP WITH SAEKI.
THEY OVER-HEARD US.
WHAT SHOULD I DO? HOW CAN I SMOOTH THIS OVER?
ANTSY
ANTSY
ANTSY
ANTSY
HE'S THE CAUSE OF ALL THIS! WHY'S HE SO EXCITED?!
FIDGET
FIDGET
HE'S COMPLETELY ENJOYING WHAT'S GOING ON HERE!
What's wrong with him?!
THIS IS BAD. I'VE GOT TO DO SOMETHING ABOUT THIS.
BUT WHAT SHOULD I SAY?
Oh well!
I'VE GOT TO TELL THEM THAT WE'RE CHILDHOOD FRIENDS!
U-UMM...

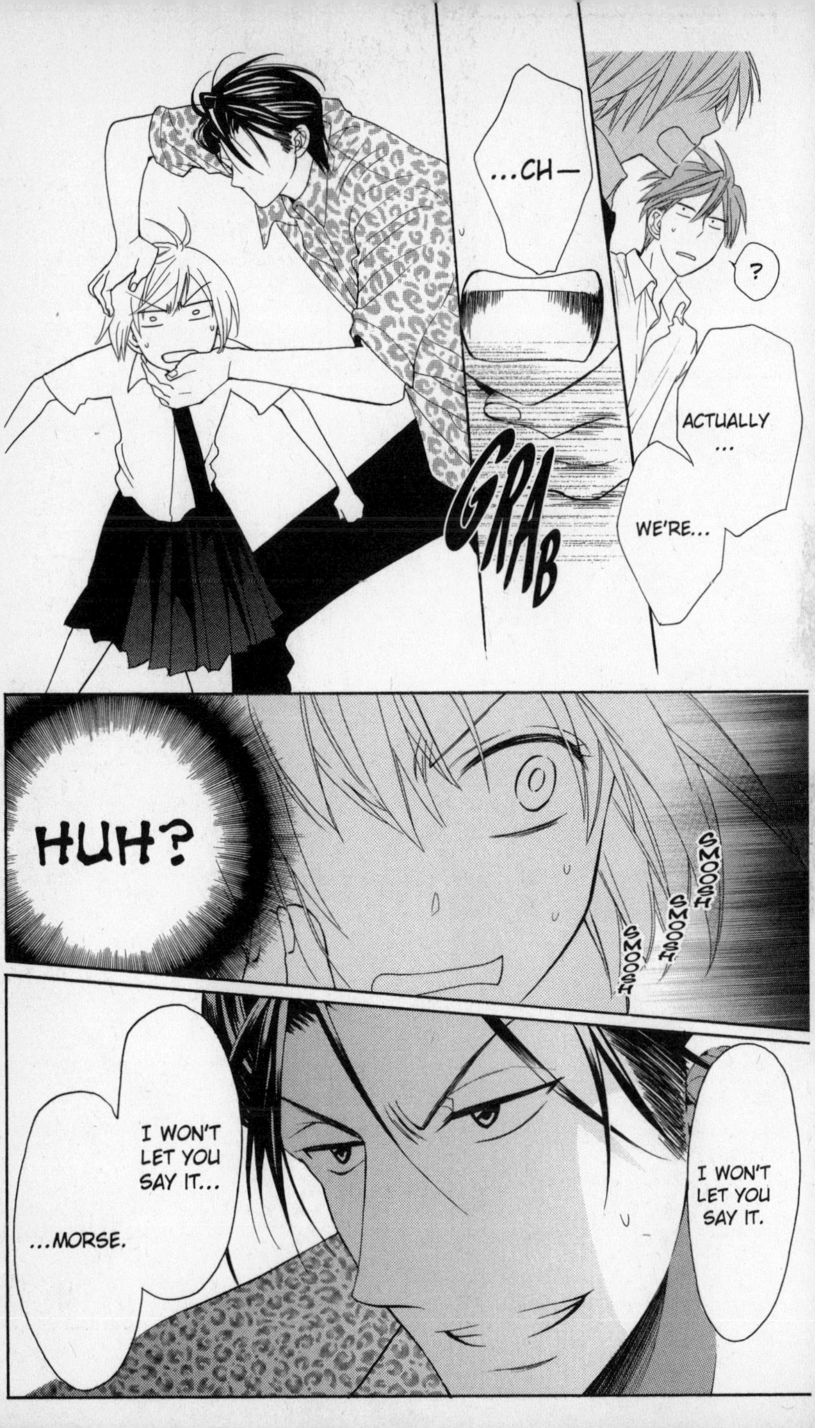
?
ACTUALLY... WE'RE...
...CH—
GRAB
HUH?
SMOOSH SMOOSH SMOOSH
I WON'T LET YOU SAY IT.
I WON'T LET YOU SAY IT...
...MORSE.

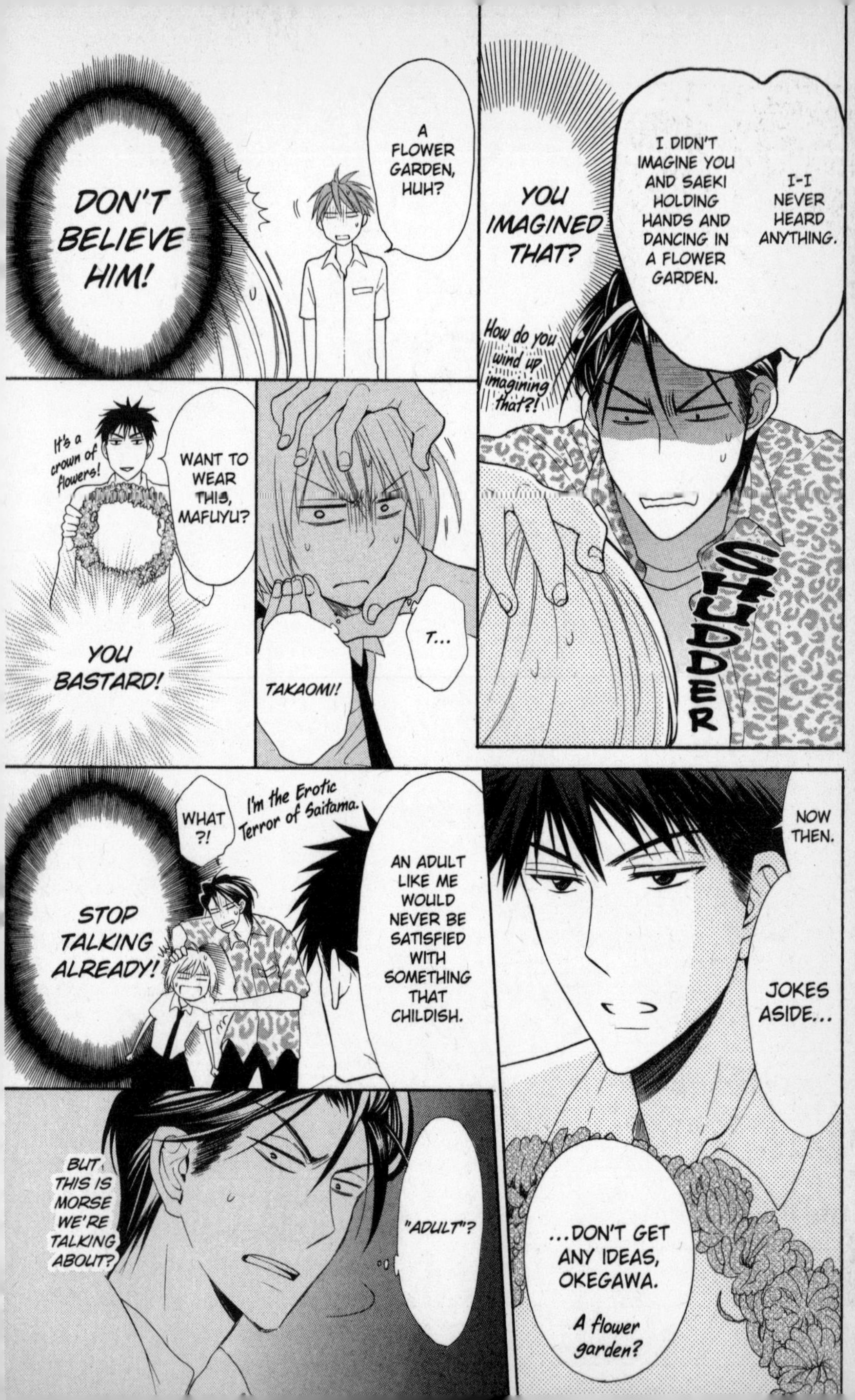
I-I NEVER HEARD ANYTHING.
I DIDN'T IMAGINE YOU AND SAEKI HOLDING HANDS AND DANCING IN A FLOWER GARDEN.
YOU IMAGINED THAT?
How do you wind up imagining that?!
SHUDDER
A FLOWER GARDEN, HUH?
DON'T BELIEVE HIM!
T...
TAKAOMI!
WANT TO WEAR THIS, MAFUYU?
It's a crown of flowers!
YOU BASTARD!
NOW THEN.
JOKES ASIDE...
...DON'T GET ANY IDEAS, OKEGAWA.
A flower garden?
AN ADULT LIKE ME WOULD NEVER BE SATISFIED WITH SOMETHING THAT CHILDISH.
I'm the Erotic Terror of Saitama.
WHAT ?!
STOP TALKING ALREADY!
"ADULT"?
BUT THIS IS MORSE WE'RE TALKING ABOUT?

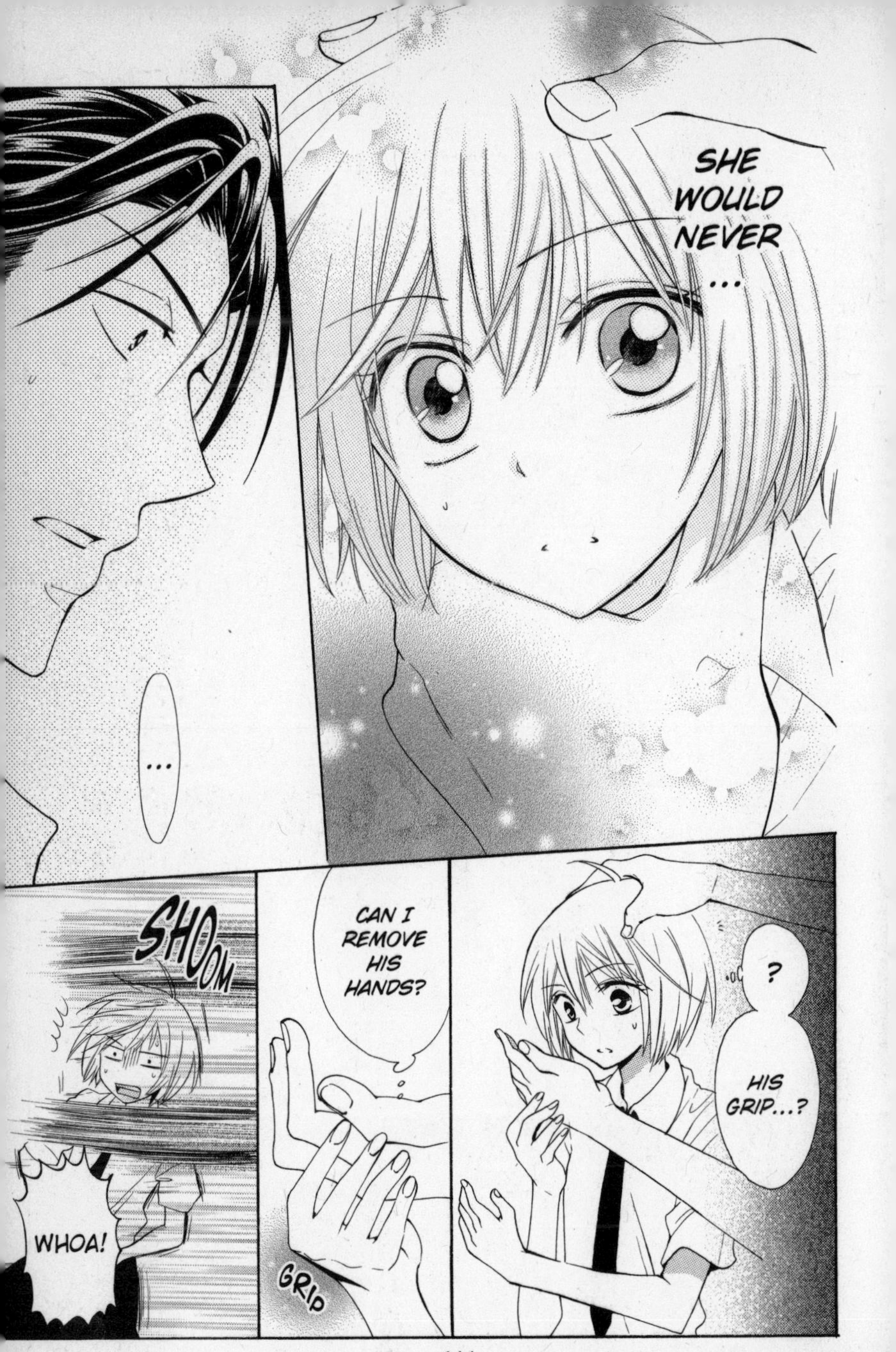
SHE WOULD NEVER ...
...
?
HIS GRIP...?
CAN I REMOVE HIS HANDS?
GRIP
SHOOM
WHOA!

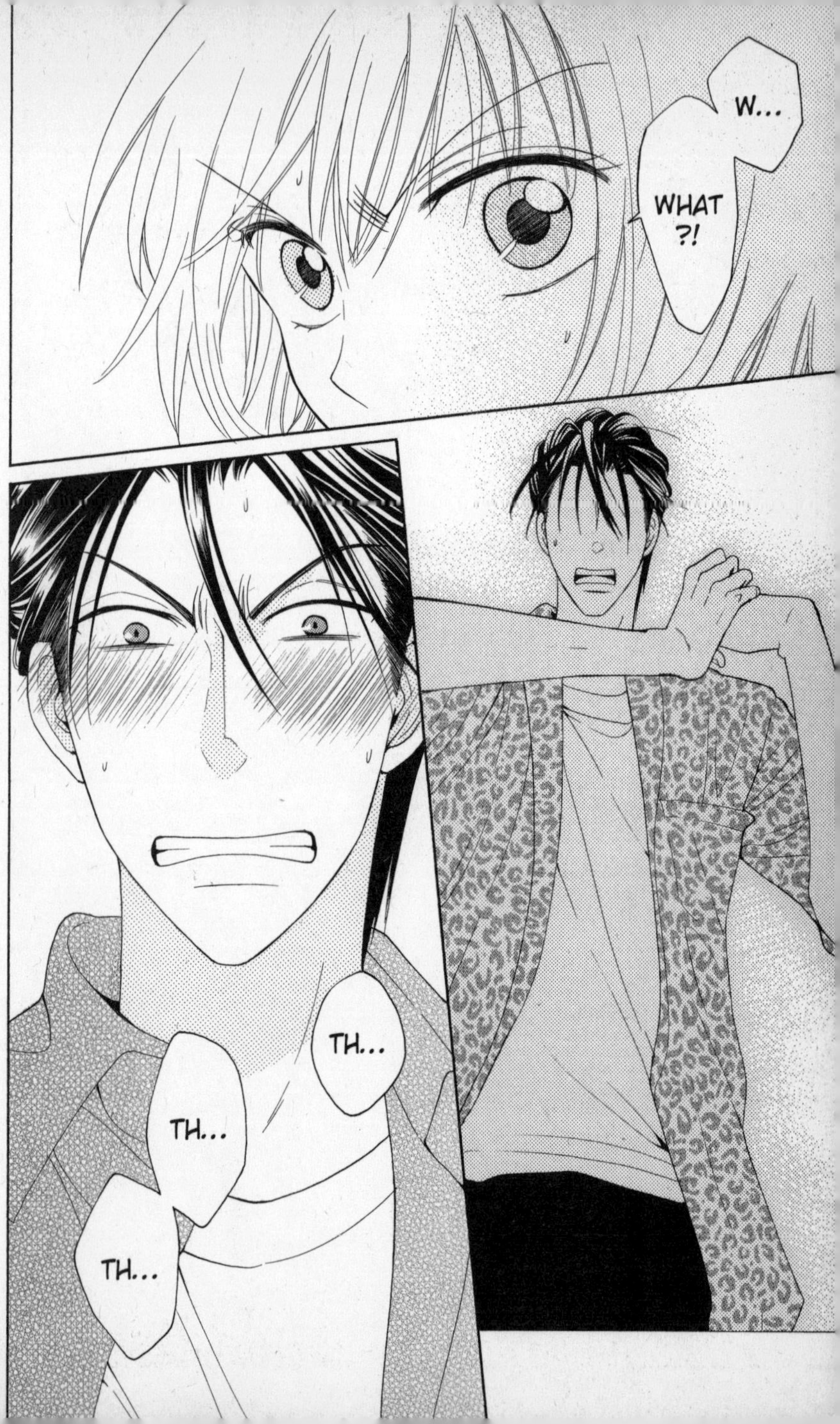
W...
WHAT ?!
TH...
TH...
TH...

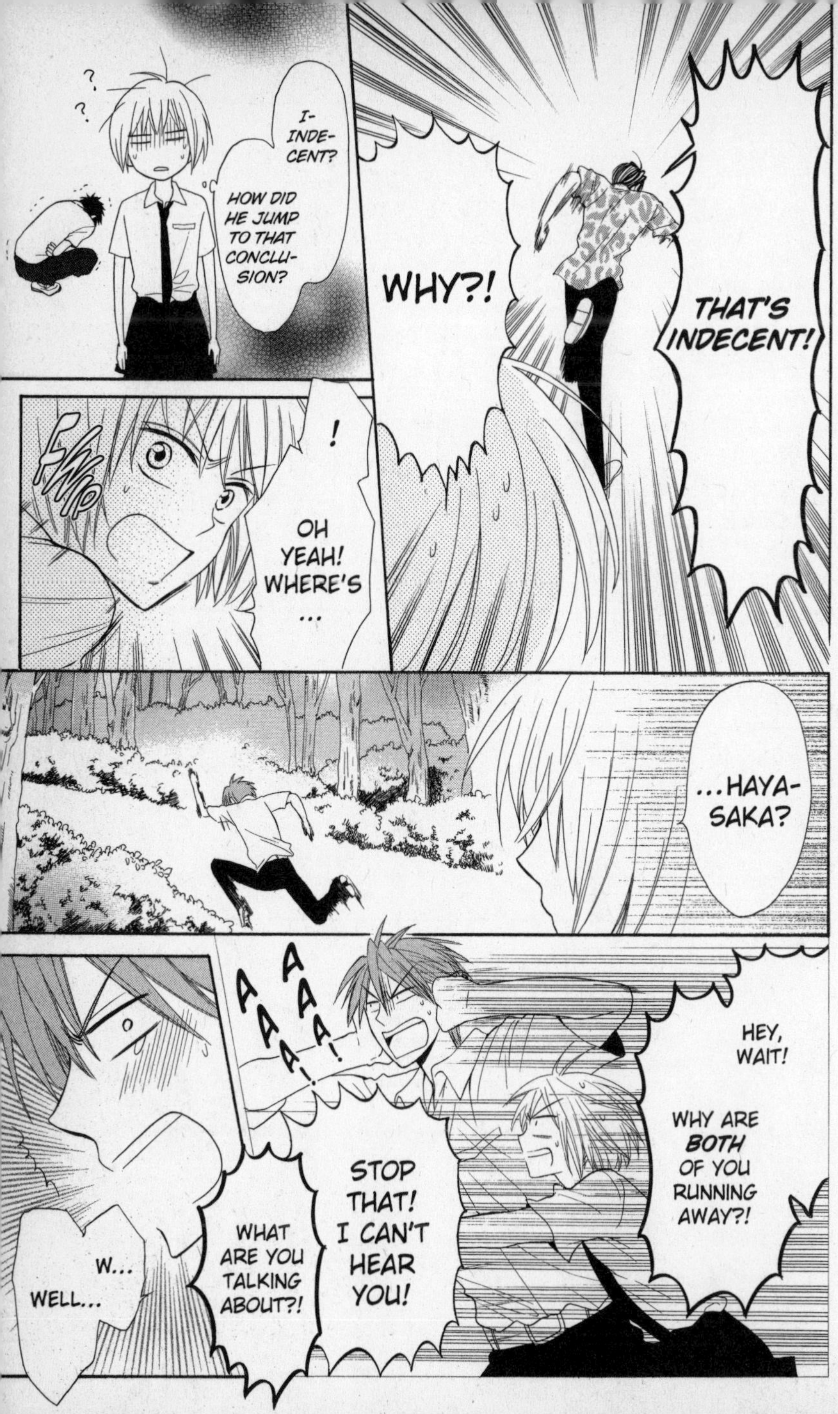
THAT'S INDECENT!
WHY?!
I- INDE- CENT?
HOW DID HE JUMP TO THAT CONCLU- SION?
!
OH YEAH! WHERE'S ...
FWIP
...HAYA- SAKA?
HEY, WAIT!
WHY ARE *BOTH* OF YOU RUNNING AWAY?!
AAAAAA!
STOP THAT! I CAN'T HEAR YOU!
WHAT ARE YOU TALKING ABOUT?!
W... WELL...

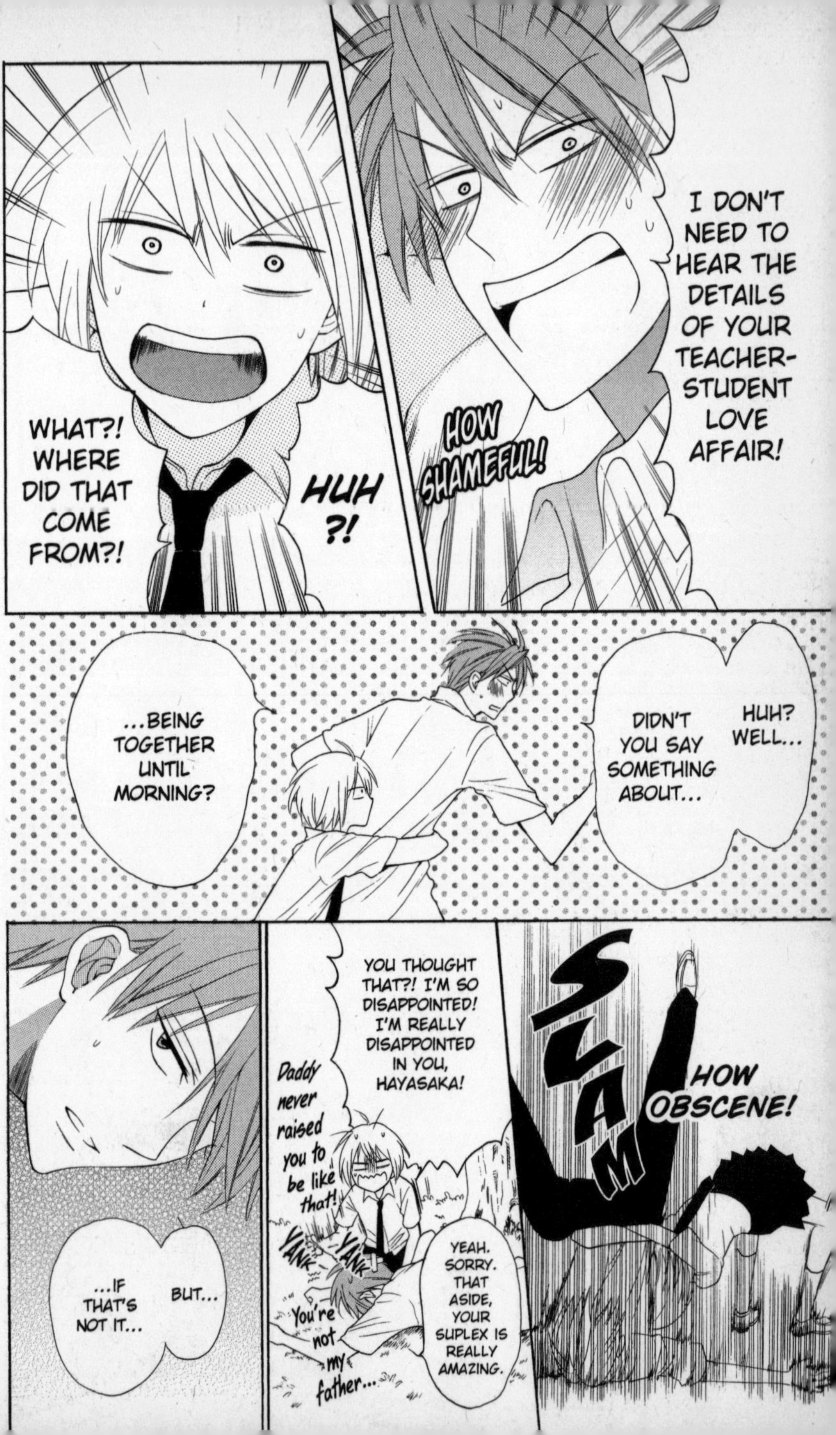
I DON'T NEED TO HEAR THE DETAILS OF YOUR TEACHER-STUDENT LOVE AFFAIR!
HOW SHAMEFUL!
HUH ?!
WHAT?! WHERE DID THAT COME FROM?!
HUH? WELL...
DIDN'T YOU SAY SOMETHING ABOUT...
...BEING TOGETHER UNTIL MORNING?
SLAM
HOW OBSCENE!
YOU THOUGHT THAT?! I'M SO DISAPPOINTED! I'M REALLY DISAPPOINTED IN YOU, HAYASAKA!
Daddy never raised you to be like that!
YANK
YANK
YEAH. SORRY. THAT ASIDE, YOUR SUPLEX IS REALLY AMAZING.
You're not my father...
BUT...
...IF THAT'S NOT IT...

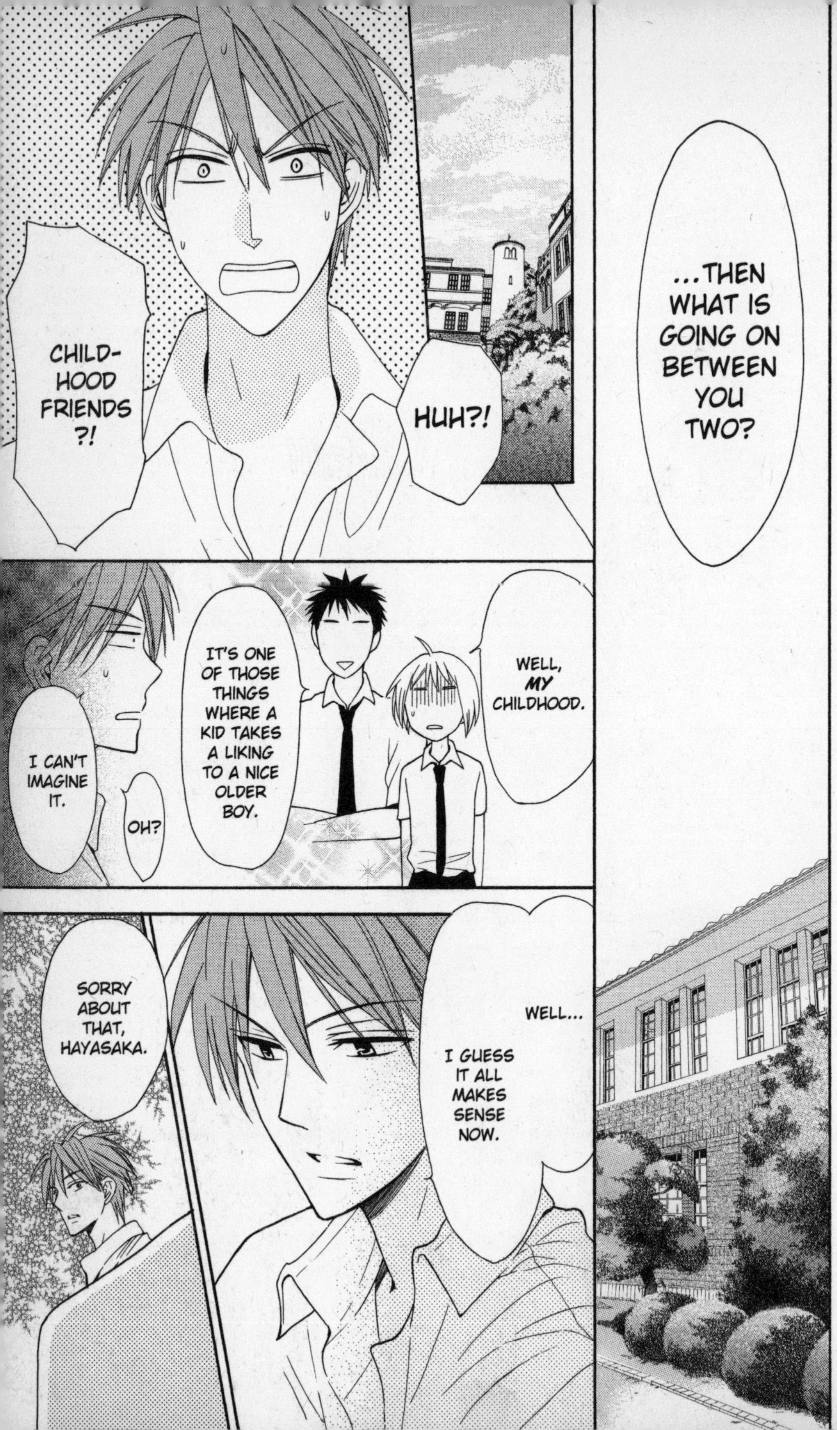
...THEN WHAT IS GOING ON BETWEEN YOU TWO?
HUH?!
CHILD-HOOD FRIENDS?!
WELL, MY CHILDHOOD.
IT'S ONE OF THOSE THINGS WHERE A KID TAKES A LIKING TO A NICE OLDER BOY.
OH?
I CAN'T IMAGINE IT.
WELL...
I GUESS IT ALL MAKES SENSE NOW.
SORRY ABOUT THAT, HAYASAKA.

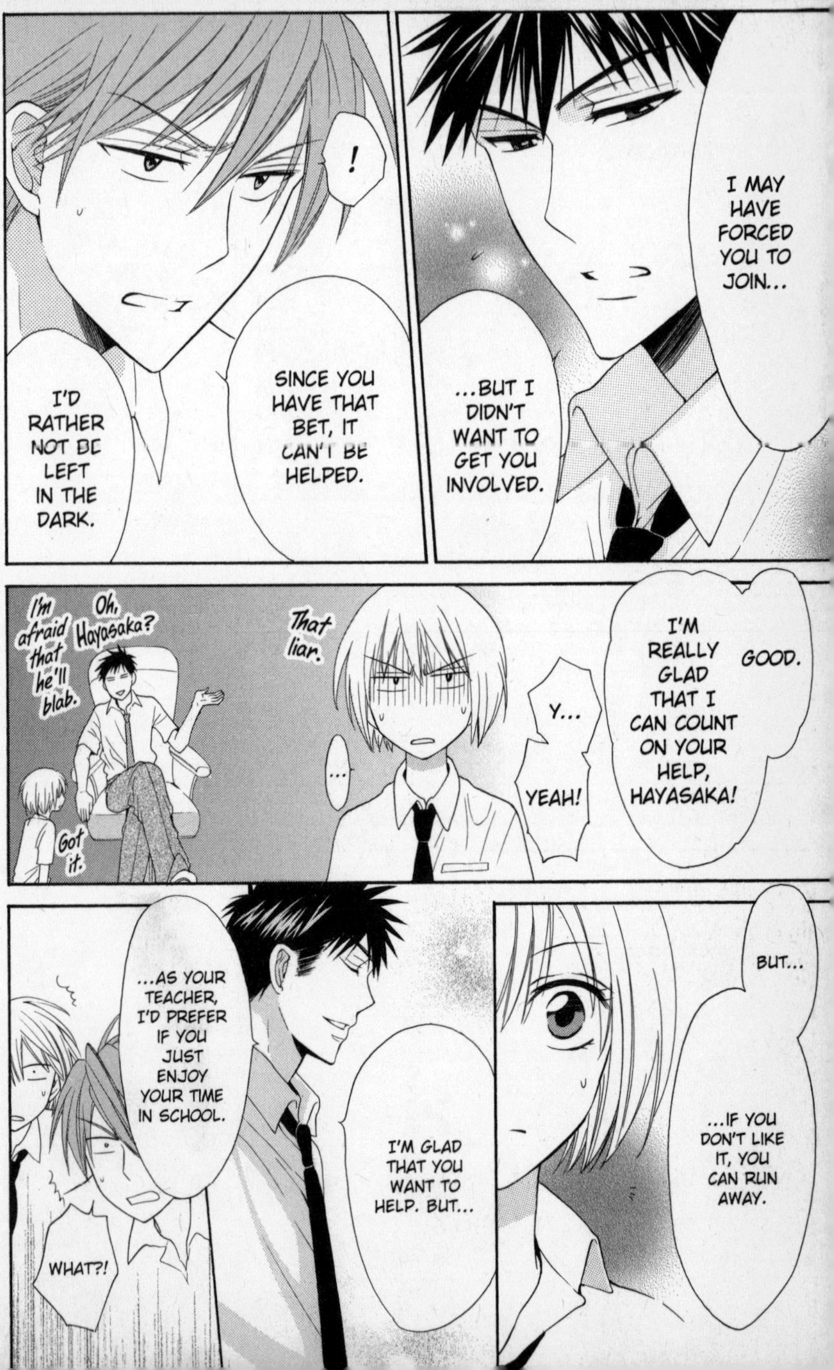
I MAY HAVE FORCED YOU TO JOIN...
...BUT I DIDN'T WANT TO GET YOU INVOLVED.
!
SINCE YOU HAVE THAT BET, IT CAN'T BE HELPED.
I'D RATHER NOT BE LEFT IN THE DARK.
GOOD.
I'M REALLY GLAD THAT I CAN COUNT ON YOUR HELP, HAYASAKA!
Y... YEAH!
...
That liar.
Oh, Hayasaka?
I'm afraid that he'll blab.
Got it.
BUT...
...IF YOU DON'T LIKE IT, YOU CAN RUN AWAY.
I'M GLAD THAT YOU WANT TO HELP. BUT...
...AS YOUR TEACHER, I'D PREFER IF YOU JUST ENJOY YOUR TIME IN SCHOOL.
WHAT?!

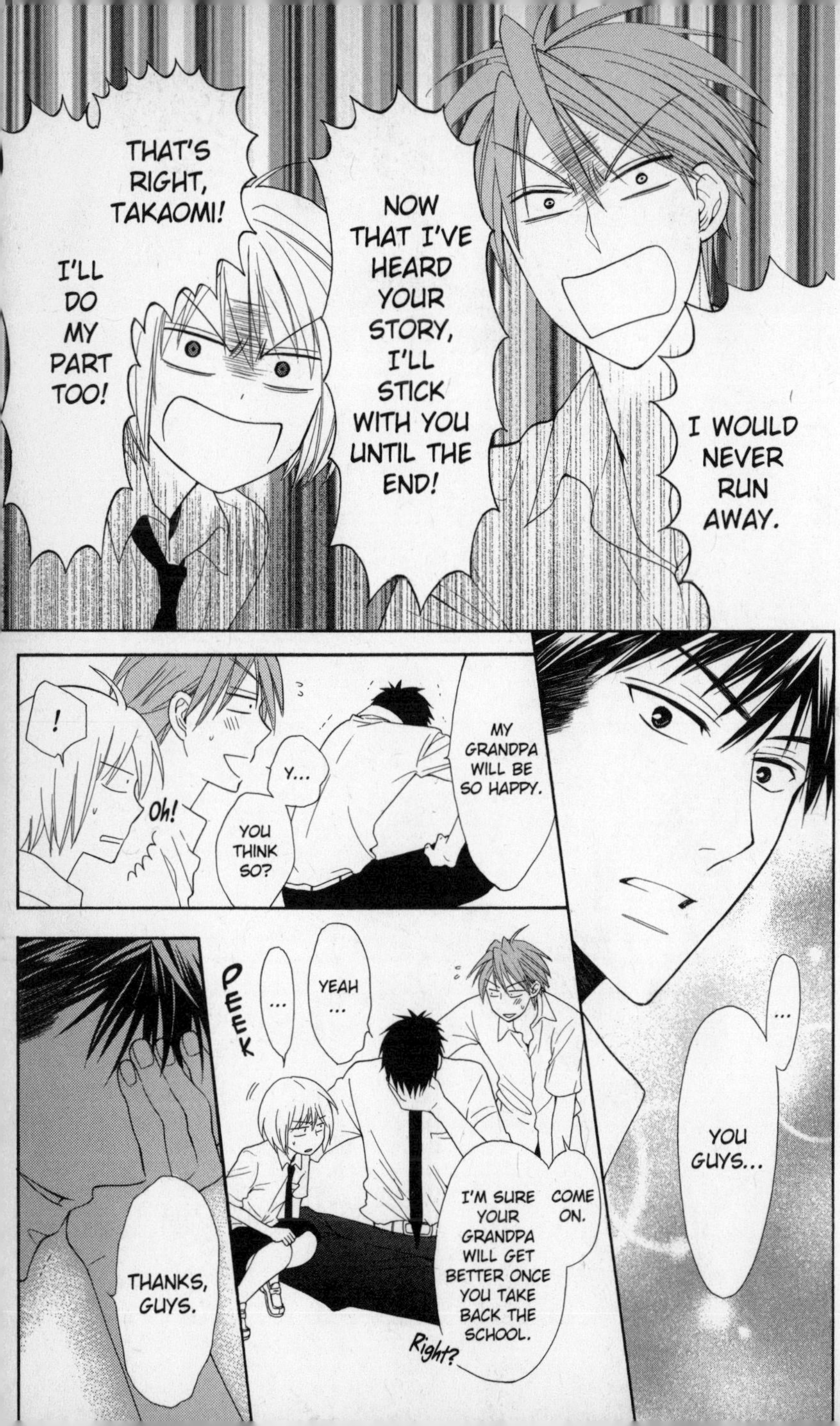
I WOULD NEVER RUN AWAY.
NOW THAT I'VE HEARD YOUR STORY, I'LL STICK WITH YOU UNTIL THE END!
THAT'S RIGHT, TAKAOMI!
I'LL DO MY PART TOO!
...
YOU GUYS...
MY GRANDPA WILL BE SO HAPPY.
Y...
YOU THINK SO?
!
Oh!
COME ON.
I'M SURE YOUR GRANDPA WILL GET BETTER ONCE YOU TAKE BACK THE SCHOOL.
Right?
YEAH...
...
PEEK
THANKS, GUYS.

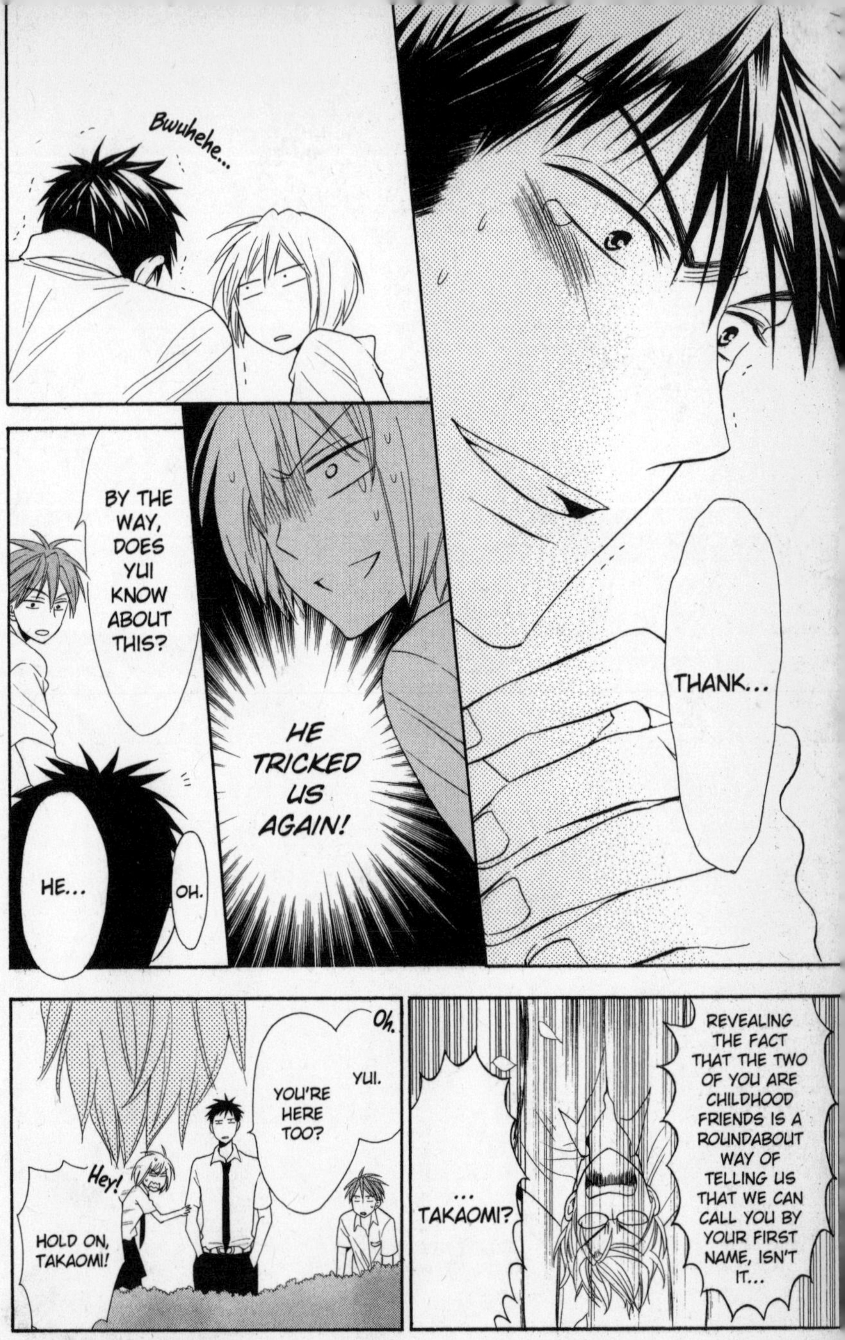
THANK...
Bwuhehe...
HE TRICKED US AGAIN!
BY THE WAY, DOES YUI KNOW ABOUT THIS?
OH.
HE...
REVEALING THE FACT THAT THE TWO OF YOU ARE CHILDHOOD FRIENDS IS A ROUNDABOUT WAY OF TELLING US THAT WE CAN CALL YOU BY YOUR FIRST NAME, ISN'T IT...
... TAKAOMI?
Oh.
YUI.
YOU'RE HERE TOO?
Hey!
HOLD ON, TAKAOMI!

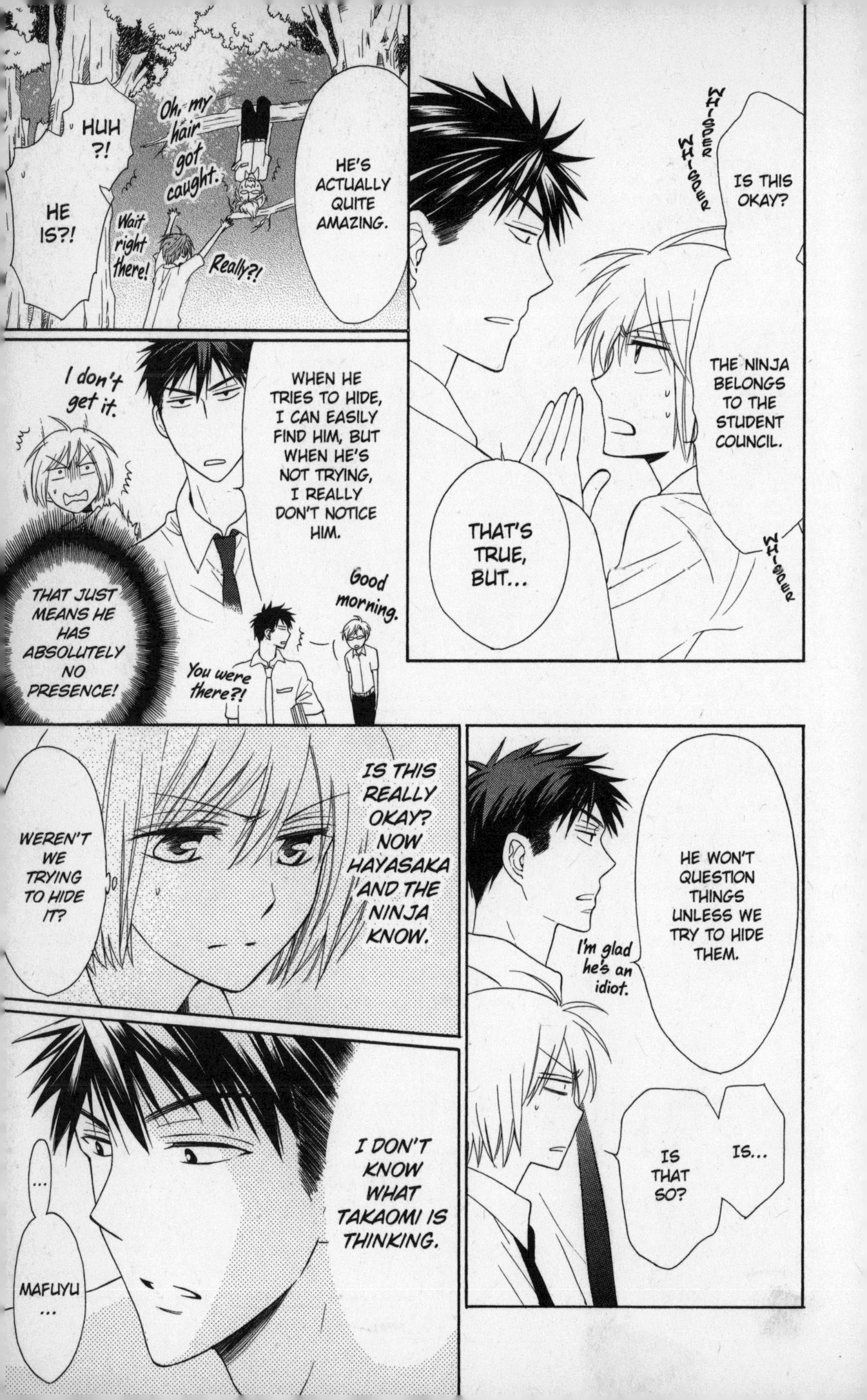
WHISPER WHISPER
IS THIS OKAY?
THE NINJA BELONGS TO THE STUDENT COUNCIL.
THAT'S TRUE, BUT...
WHISPER
HE'S ACTUALLY QUITE AMAZING.
Oh, my hair got caught.
HUH?!
HE IS?!
Really?!
Wait right there!
WHEN HE TRIES TO HIDE, I CAN EASILY FIND HIM, BUT WHEN HE'S NOT TRYING, I REALLY DON'T NOTICE HIM.
I don't get it.
Good morning.
You were there?!
THAT JUST MEANS HE HAS ABSOLUTELY NO PRESENCE!
HE WON'T QUESTION THINGS UNLESS WE TRY TO HIDE THEM.
I'm glad he's an idiot.
IS...
IS THAT SO?
IS THIS REALLY OKAY? NOW HAYASAKA AND THE NINJA KNOW.
WEREN'T WE TRYING TO HIDE IT?
I DON'T KNOW WHAT TAKAOMI IS THINKING.
... MAFUYU...

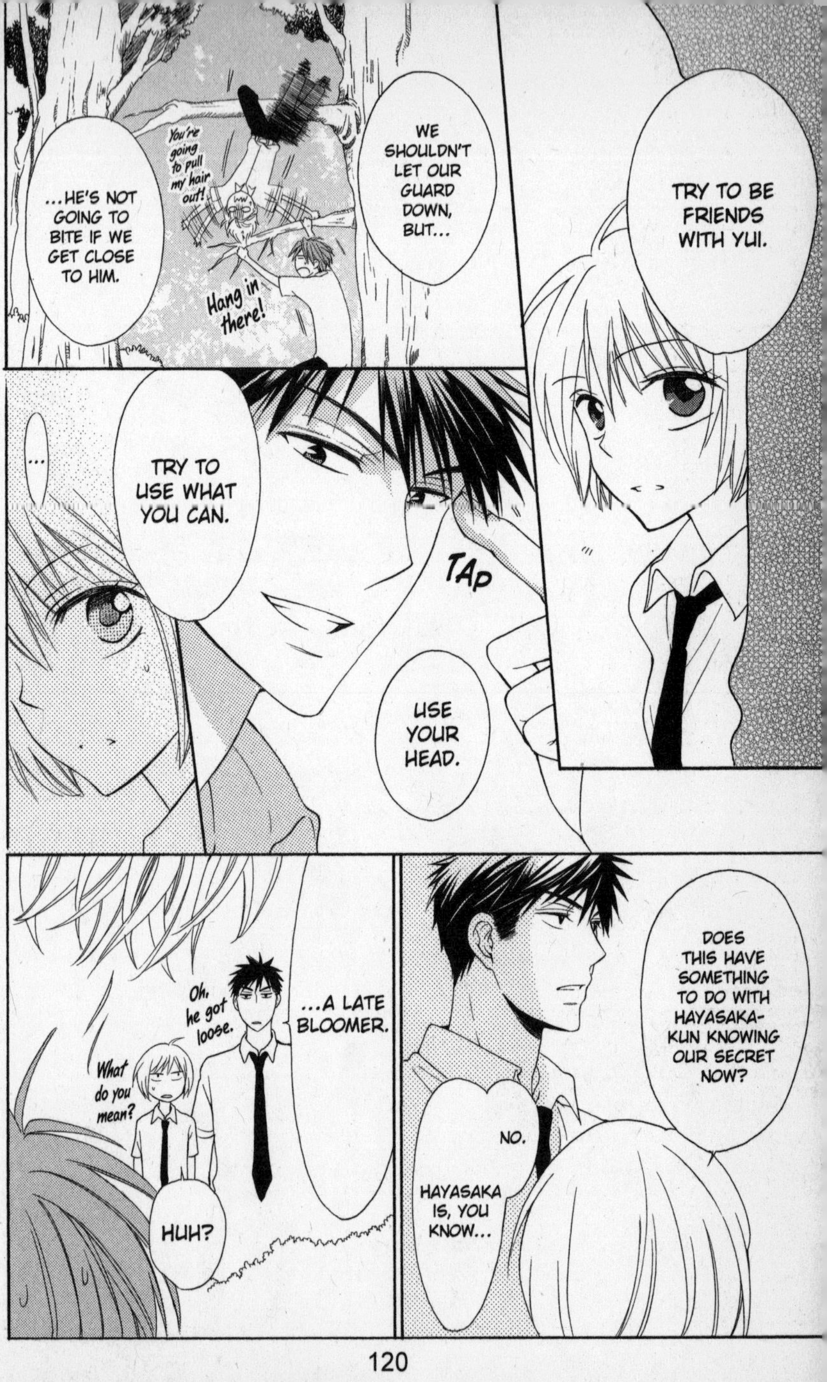
TRY TO BE FRIENDS WITH YUI.
WE SHOULDN'T LET OUR GUARD DOWN, BUT...
You're going to pull my hair out!
Hang in there!
...HE'S NOT GOING TO BITE IF WE GET CLOSE TO HIM.
TRY TO USE WHAT YOU CAN.
TAP
USE YOUR HEAD.
...
DOES THIS HAVE SOMETHING TO DO WITH HAYASAKA-KUN KNOWING OUR SECRET NOW?
NO.
HAYASAKA IS, YOU KNOW...
...A LATE BLOOMER.
Oh, he got loose.
What do you mean?
HUH?

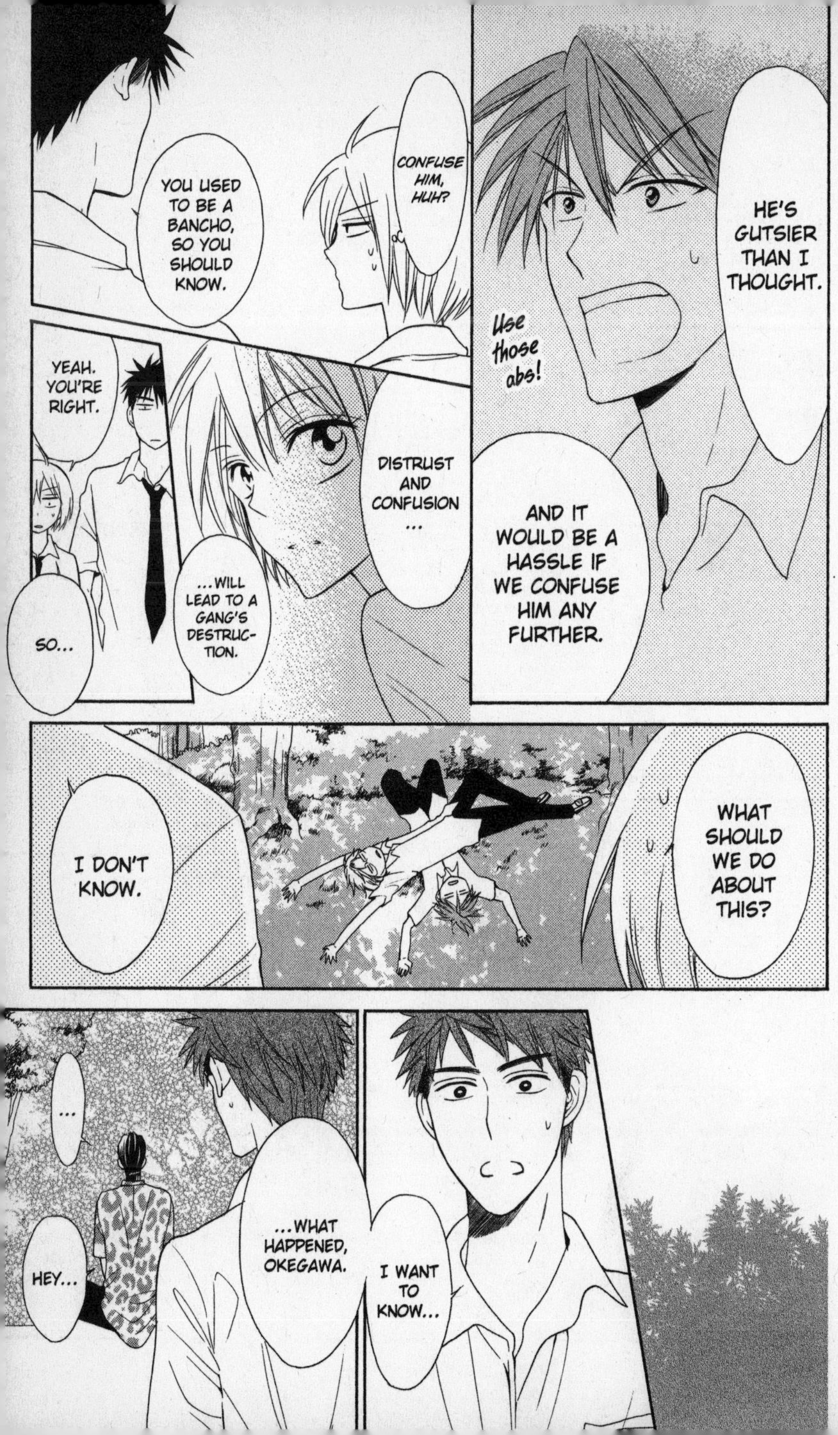
HE'S GUTSIER THAN I THOUGHT.
Use those abs!
AND IT WOULD BE A HASSLE IF WE CONFUSE HIM ANY FURTHER.
CONFUSE HIM, HUH?
YOU USED TO BE A BANCHO, SO YOU SHOULD KNOW.
DISTRUST AND CONFUSION ...
...WILL LEAD TO A GANG'S DESTRUCTION.
YEAH. YOU'RE RIGHT.
SO...
WHAT SHOULD WE DO ABOUT THIS?
I DON'T KNOW.
I WANT TO KNOW...
...WHAT HAPPENED, OKEGAWA.
...
HEY...

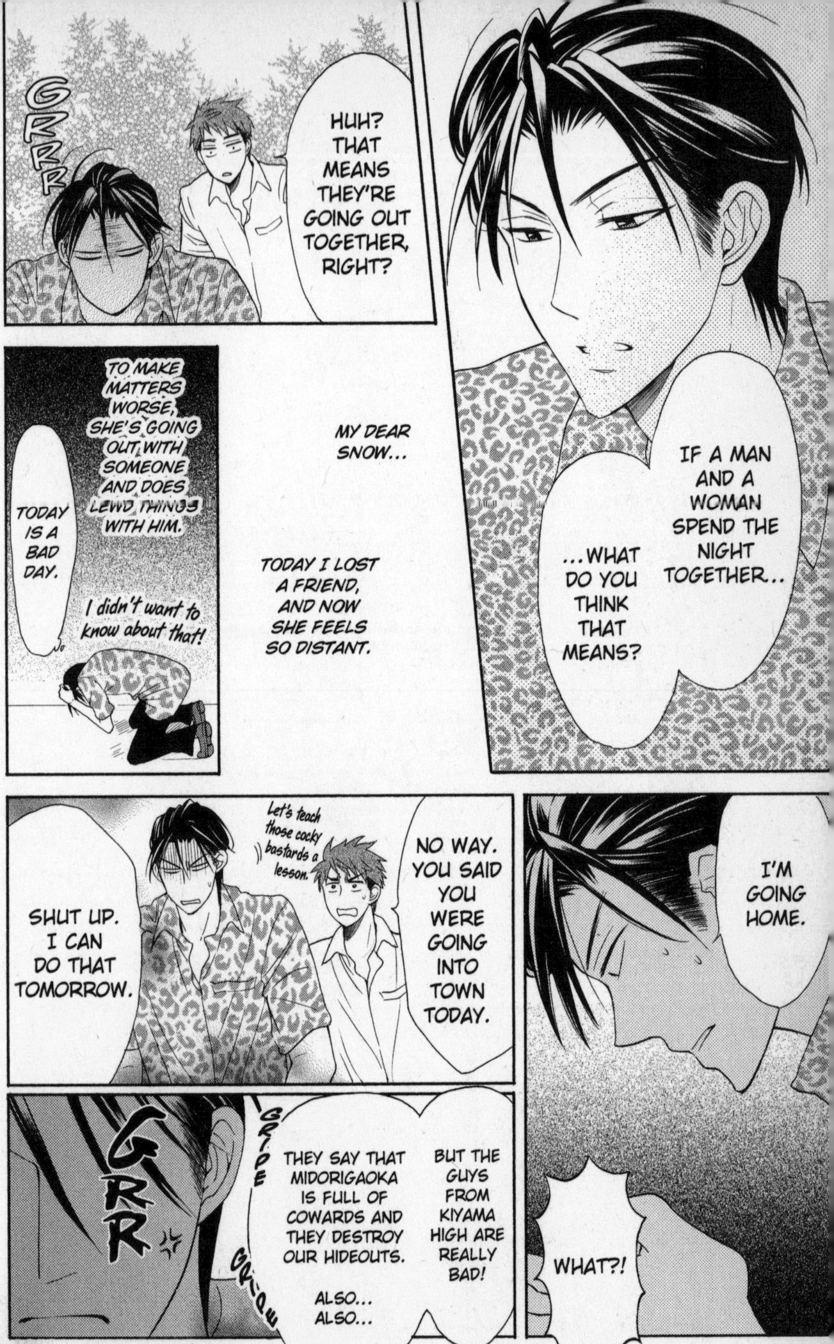
IF A MAN AND A WOMAN SPEND THE NIGHT TOGETHER...
...WHAT DO YOU THINK THAT MEANS?
HUH? THAT MEANS THEY'RE GOING OUT TOGETHER, RIGHT?
GRRR
MY DEAR SNOW...
TODAY I LOST A FRIEND, AND NOW SHE FEELS SO DISTANT.
TO MAKE MATTERS WORSE, SHE'S GOING OUT WITH SOMEONE AND DOES LEWD THINGS WITH HIM.
TODAY IS A BAD DAY.
I didn't want to know about that!
I'M GOING HOME.
WHAT?!
NO WAY. YOU SAID YOU WERE GOING INTO TOWN TODAY.
Let's teach those cocky bastards a lesson.
SHUT UP. I CAN DO THAT TOMORROW.
BUT THE GUYS FROM KIYAMA HIGH ARE REALLY BAD!
THEY SAY THAT MIDORIGAOKA IS FULL OF COWARDS AND THEY DESTROY OUR HIDEOUTS.
ALSO... ALSO...
GRIDE
GRR

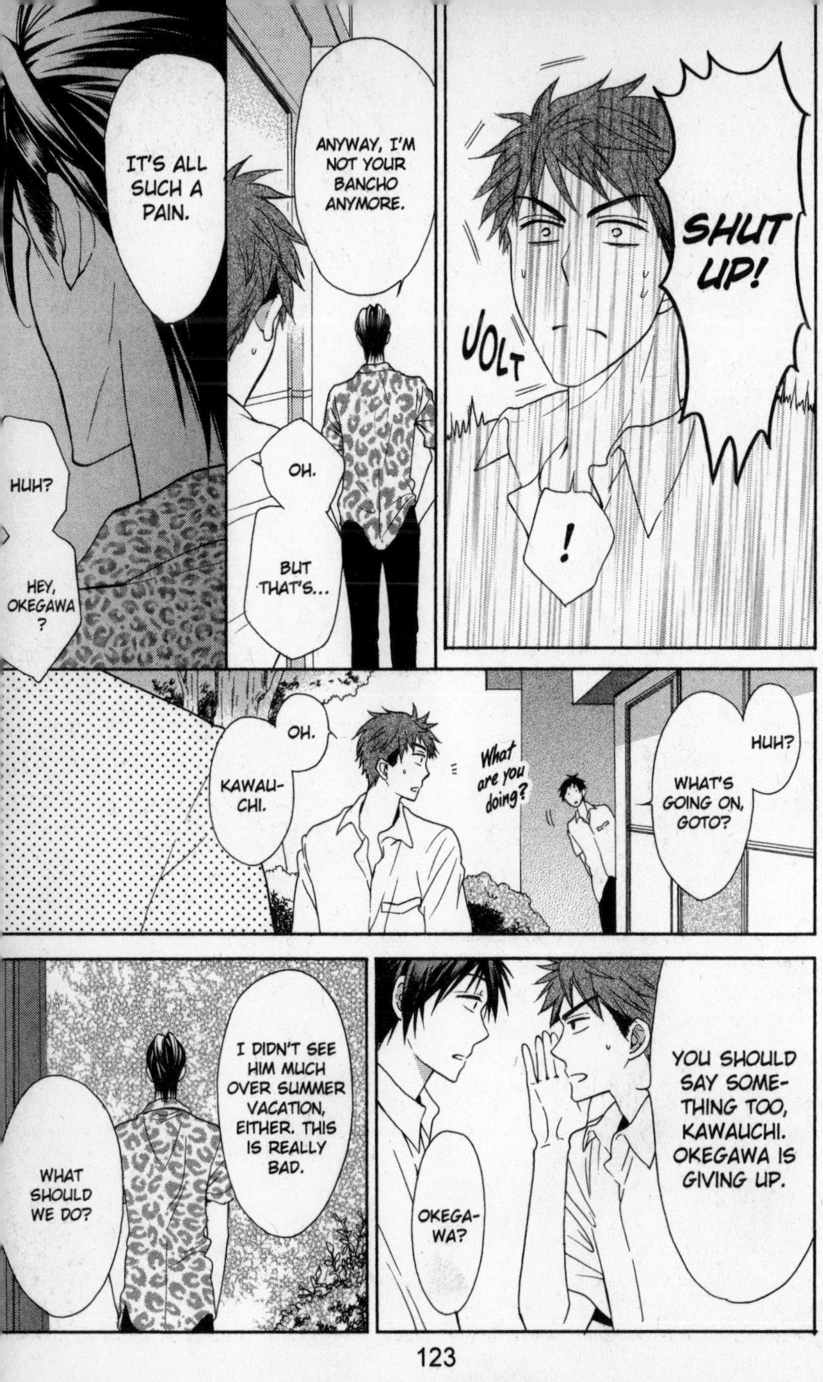
SHUT UP!
JOLT
!
ANYWAY, I'M NOT YOUR BANCHO ANYMORE.
OH.
BUT THAT'S...
IT'S ALL SUCH A PAIN.
HUH?
HEY, OKEGAWA?
HUH?
WHAT'S GOING ON, GOTO?
What are you doing?
OH.
KAWAUCHI.
YOU SHOULD SAY SOMETHING TOO, KAWAUCHI. OKEGAWA IS GIVING UP.
OKEGAWA?
I DIDN'T SEE HIM MUCH OVER SUMMER VACATION, EITHER. THIS IS REALLY BAD.
WHAT SHOULD WE DO?

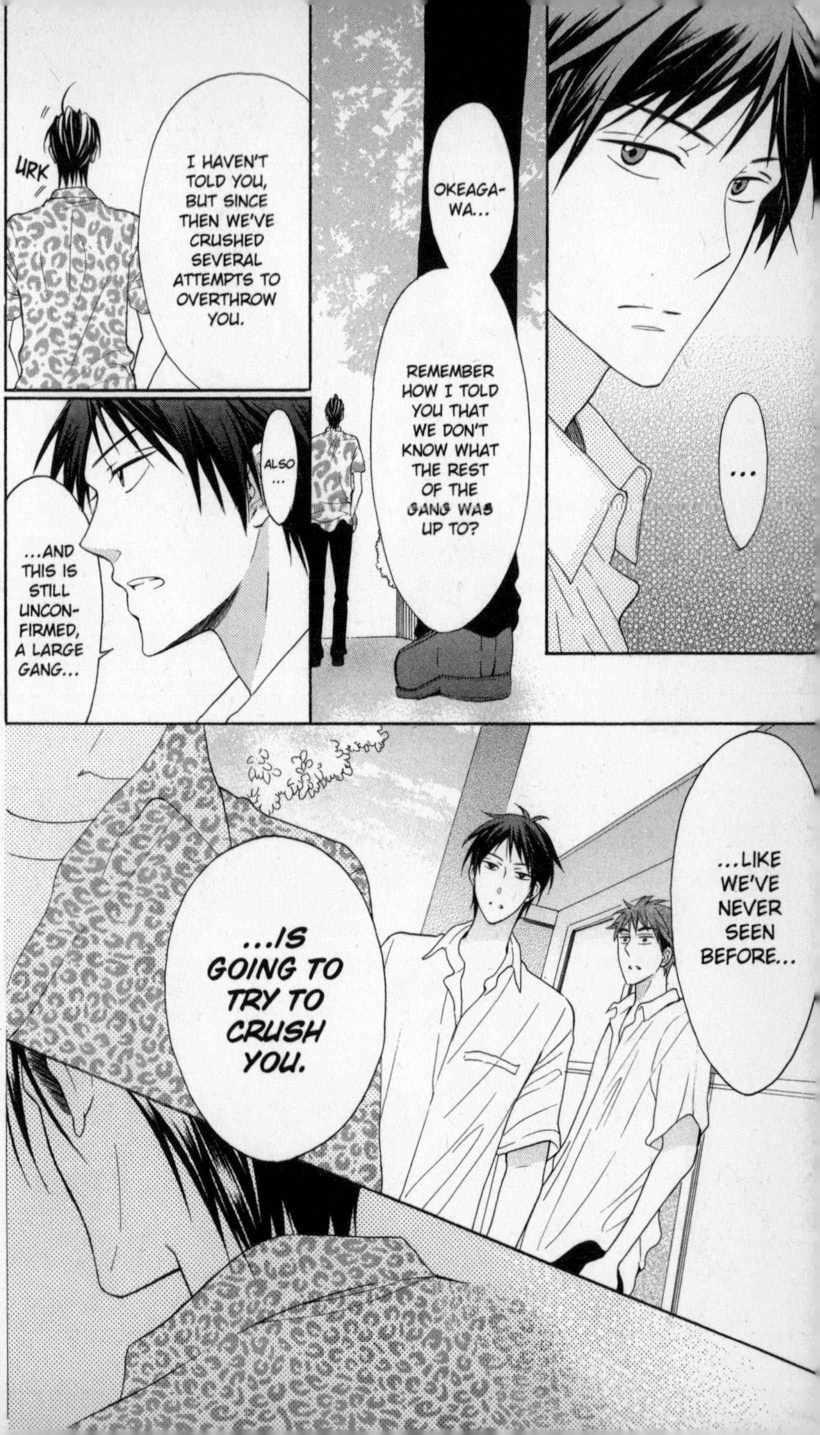

...
OKEAGAWA...
REMEMBER HOW I TOLD YOU THAT WE DON'T KNOW WHAT THE REST OF THE GANG WAS UP TO?
URK
I HAVEN'T TOLD YOU, BUT SINCE THEN WE'VE CRUSHED SEVERAL ATTEMPTS TO OVERTHROW YOU.
ALSO...
...AND THIS IS STILL UNCONFIRMED, A LARGE GANG...
...LIKE WE'VE NEVER SEEN BEFORE...
...IS GOING TO TRY TO CRUSH YOU.

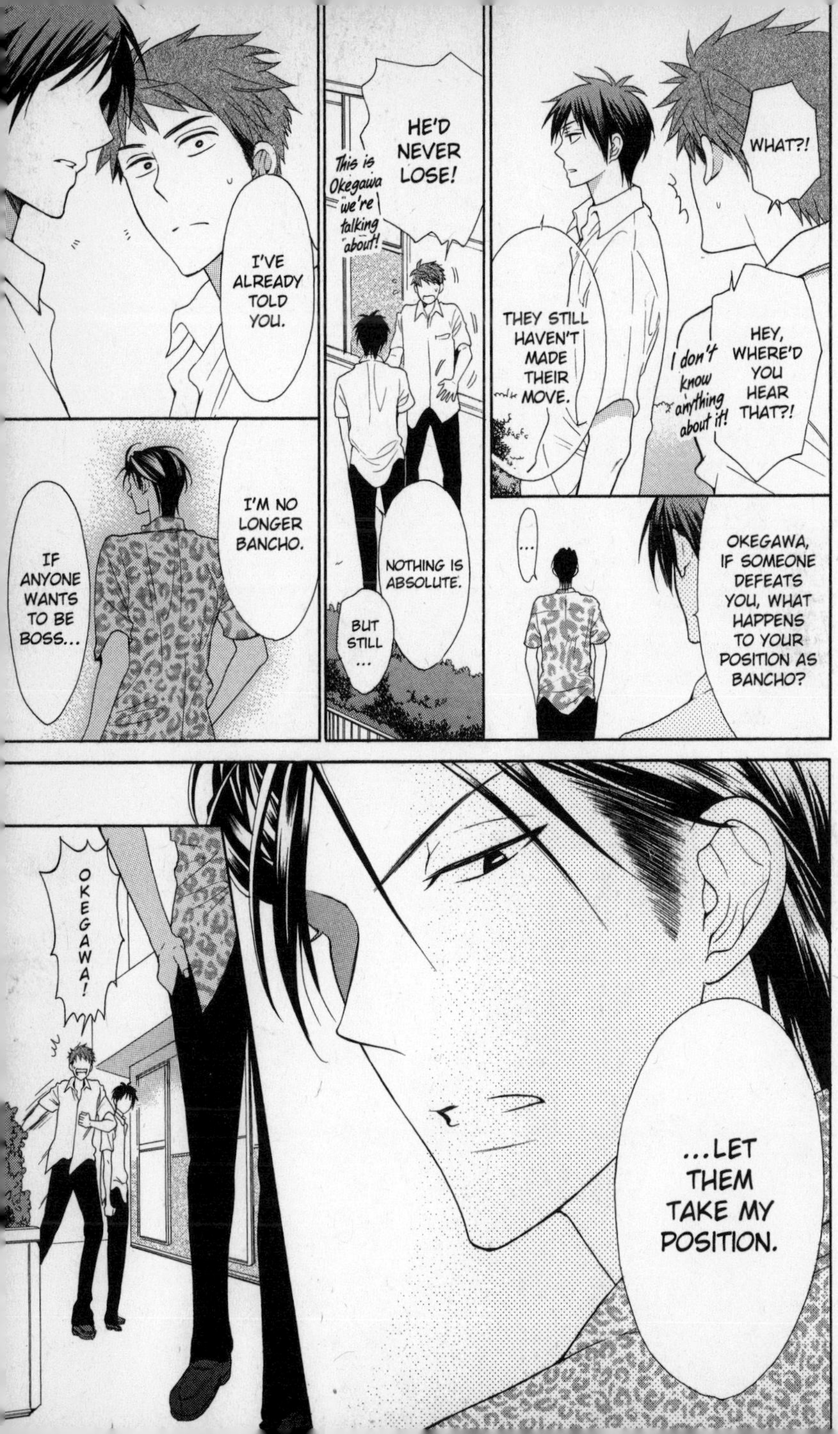
WHAT?!
HEY, WHERE'D YOU HEAR THAT?!
I don't know anything about it!
THEY STILL HAVEN'T MADE THEIR MOVE.
OKEGAWA, IF SOMEONE DEFEATS YOU, WHAT HAPPENS TO YOUR POSITION AS BANCHO?
...
HE'D NEVER LOSE!
This is Okegawa we're talking about!
NOTHING IS ABSOLUTE.
BUT STILL...
I'VE ALREADY TOLD YOU.
I'M NO LONGER BANCHO.
IF ANYONE WANTS TO BE BOSS...
...LET THEM TAKE MY POSITION.
OKEGAWA!

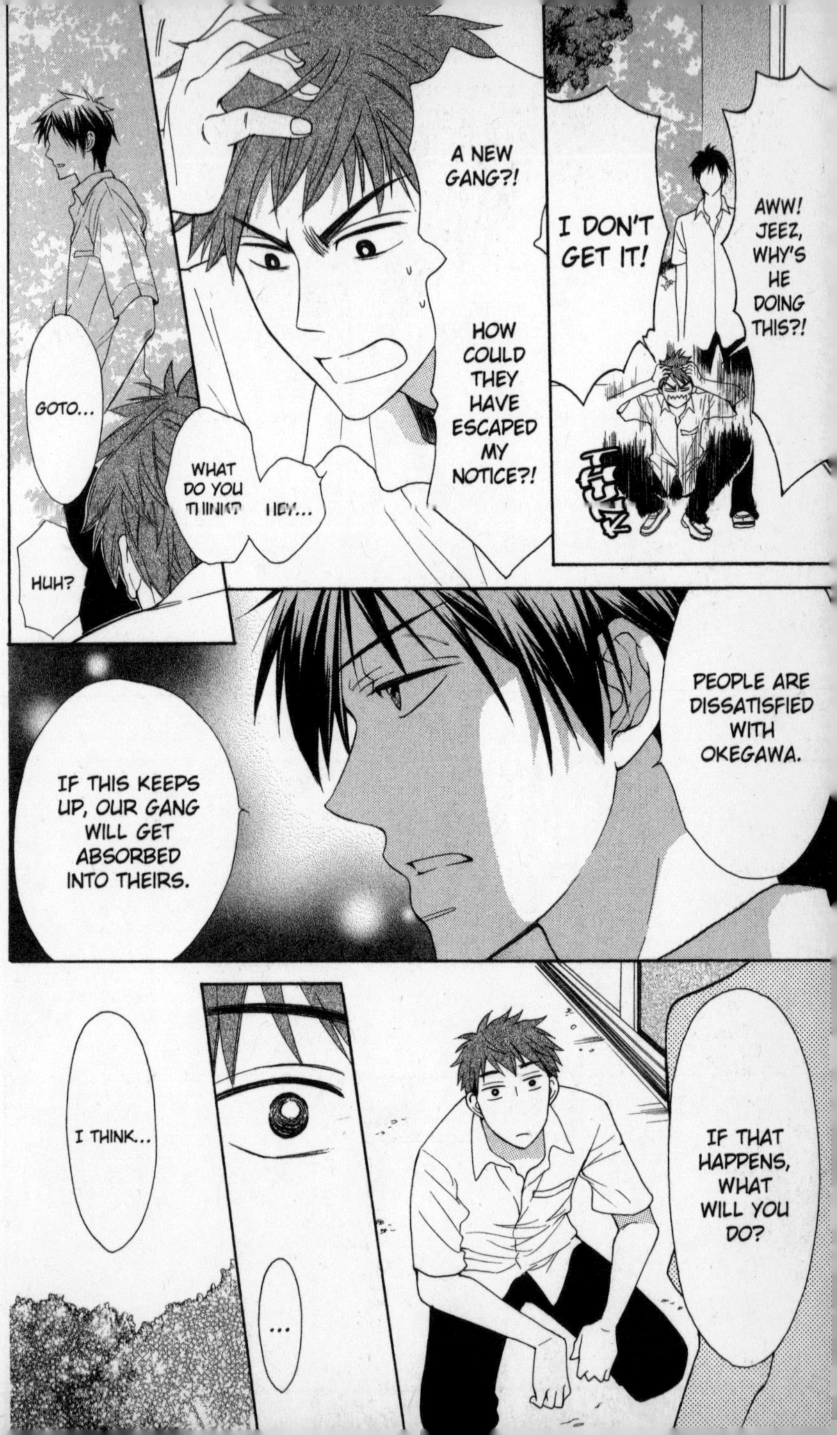
AWW! JEEZ, WHY'S HE DOING THIS?!
I DON'T GET IT!
A NEW GANG?!
HOW COULD THEY HAVE ESCAPED MY NOTICE?!
HEY...
WHAT DO YOU THINK?
GOTO...
HUH?
PEOPLE ARE DISSATISFIED WITH OKEGAWA.
IF THIS KEEPS UP, OUR GANG WILL GET ABSORBED INTO THEIRS.
IF THAT HAPPENS, WHAT WILL YOU DO?
I THINK...
...

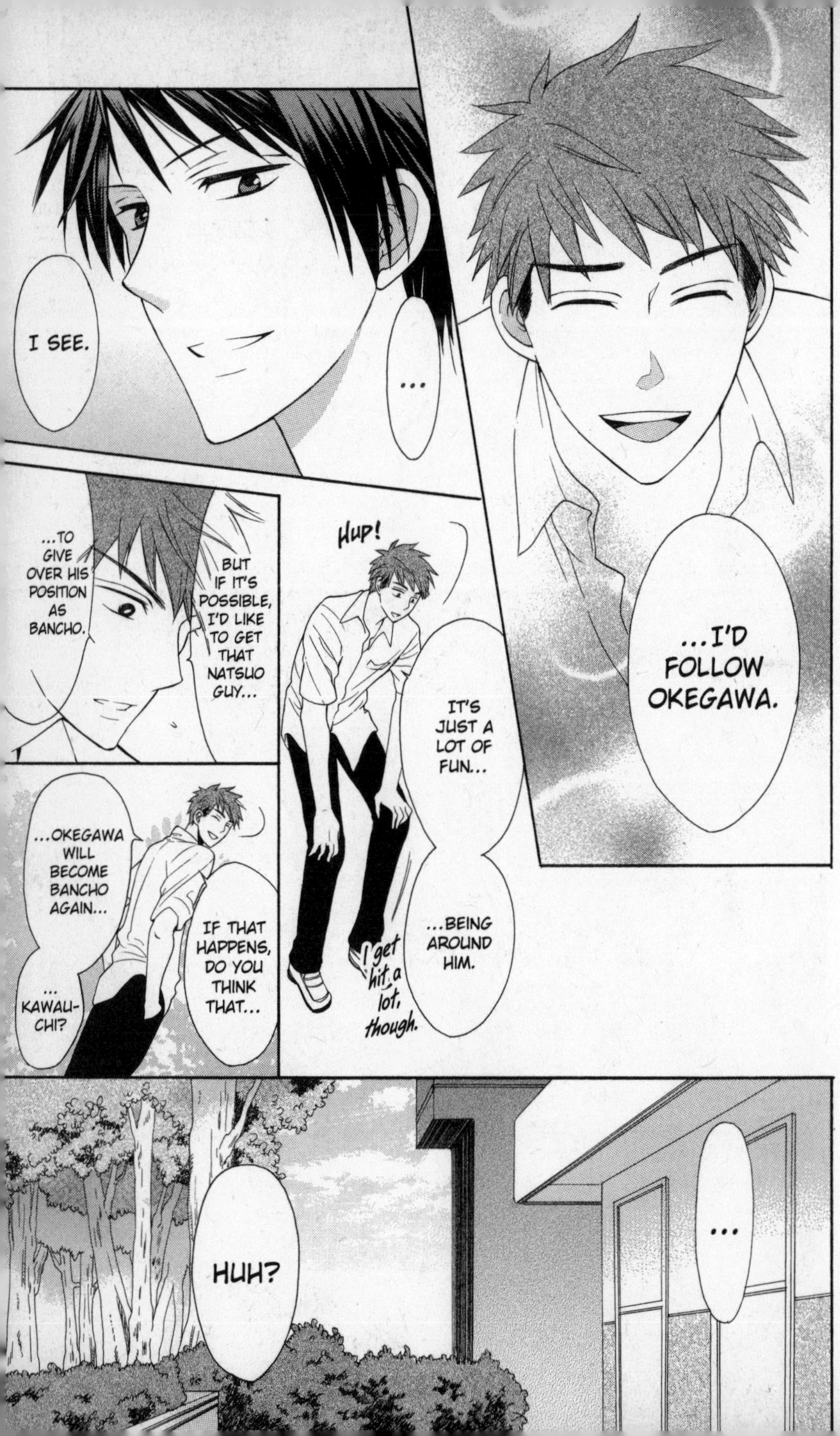
...I'D FOLLOW OKEGAWA.
...
I SEE.
Hup!
IT'S JUST A LOT OF FUN...
...BEING AROUND HIM.
I get hit a lot, though.
BUT IF IT'S POSSIBLE, I'D LIKE TO GET THAT NATSUO GUY...
...TO GIVE OVER HIS POSITION AS BANCHO.
IF THAT HAPPENS, DO YOU THINK THAT...
...OKEGAWA WILL BECOME BANCHO AGAIN...
...KAWAUCHI?
...
HUH?

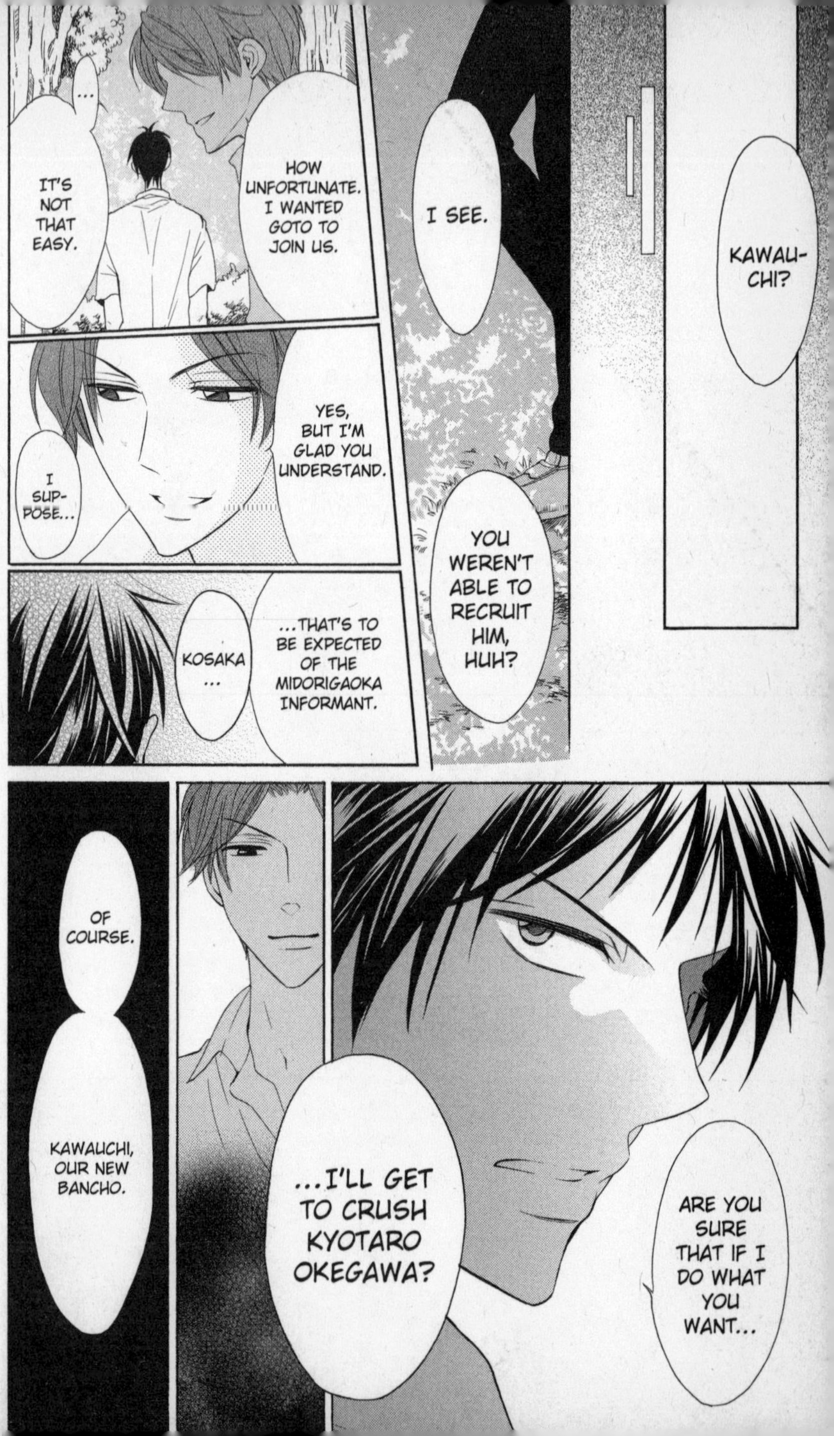
KAWAUCHI?
I SEE.
YOU WEREN'T ABLE TO RECRUIT HIM, HUH?
HOW UNFORTUNATE. I WANTED GOTO TO JOIN US.
...
IT'S NOT THAT EASY.
YES, BUT I'M GLAD YOU UNDERSTAND.
I SUPPOSE...
...THAT'S TO BE EXPECTED OF THE MIDORIGAOKA INFORMANT.
KOSAKA...
ARE YOU SURE THAT IF I DO WHAT YOU WANT...
...I'LL GET TO CRUSH KYOTARO OKEGAWA?
OF COURSE.
KAWAUCHI, OUR NEW BANCHO.

Chapter 44

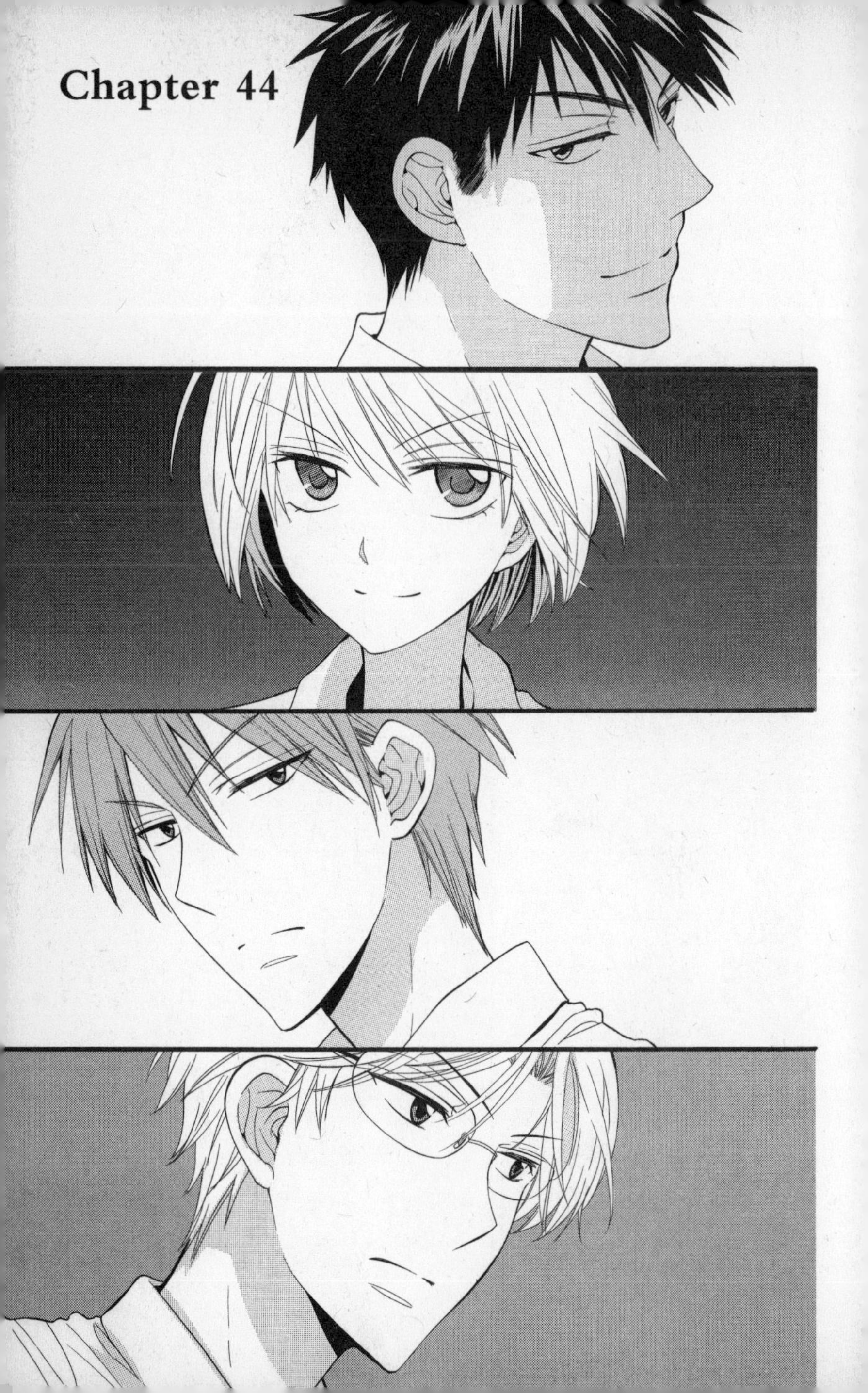

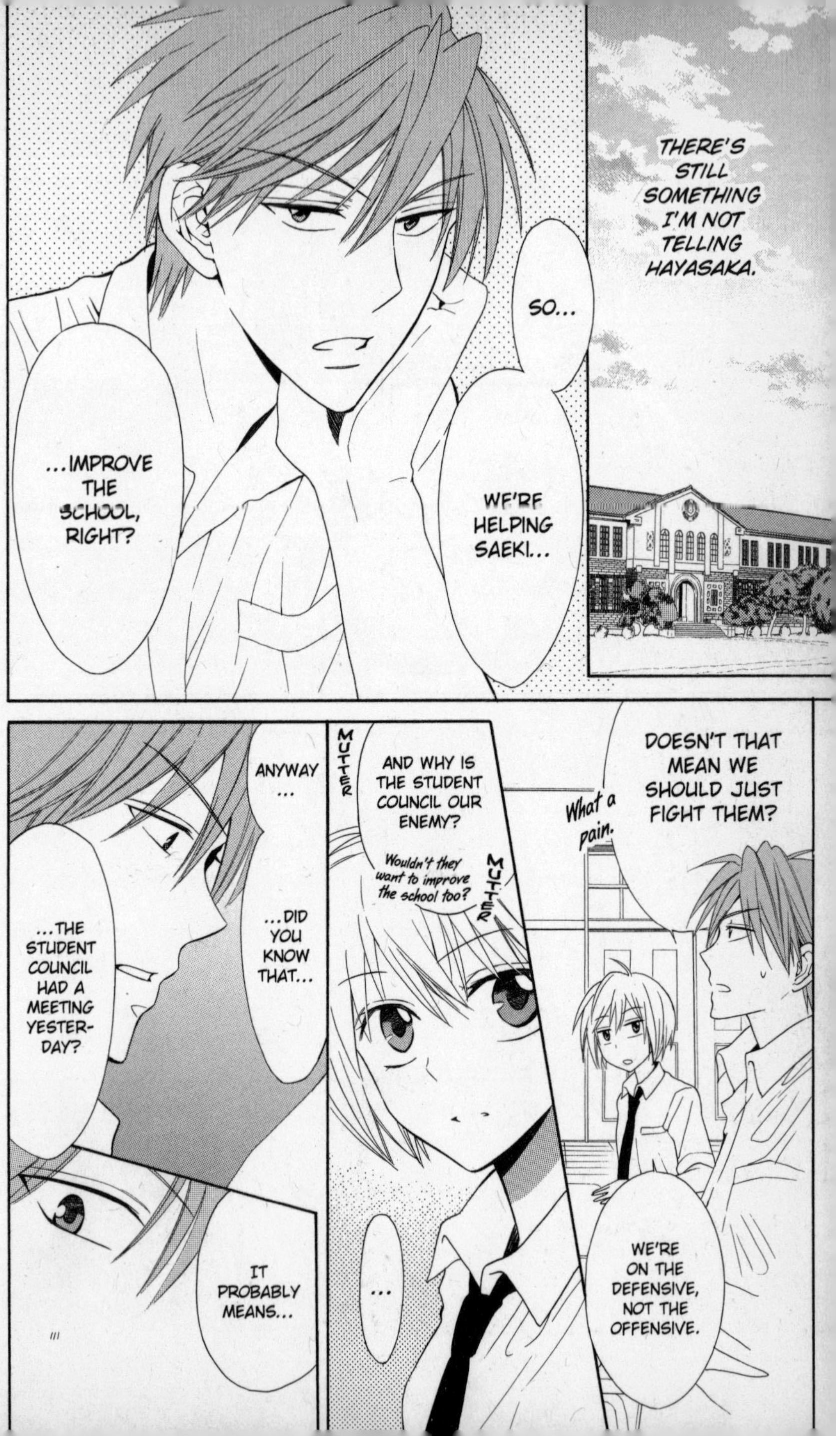
THERE'S STILL SOMETHING I'M NOT TELLING HAYASAKA.
SO...
WE'RE HELPING SAEKI...
...IMPROVE THE SCHOOL, RIGHT?
DOESN'T THAT MEAN WE SHOULD JUST FIGHT THEM?
What a pain.
WE'RE ON THE DEFENSIVE, NOT THE OFFENSIVE.
MUTTER
AND WHY IS THE STUDENT COUNCIL OUR ENEMY?
Wouldn't they want to improve the school too?
MUTTER
...
ANYWAY ...
...DID YOU KNOW THAT...
...THE STUDENT COUNCIL HAD A MEETING YESTER-DAY?
IT PROBABLY MEANS...

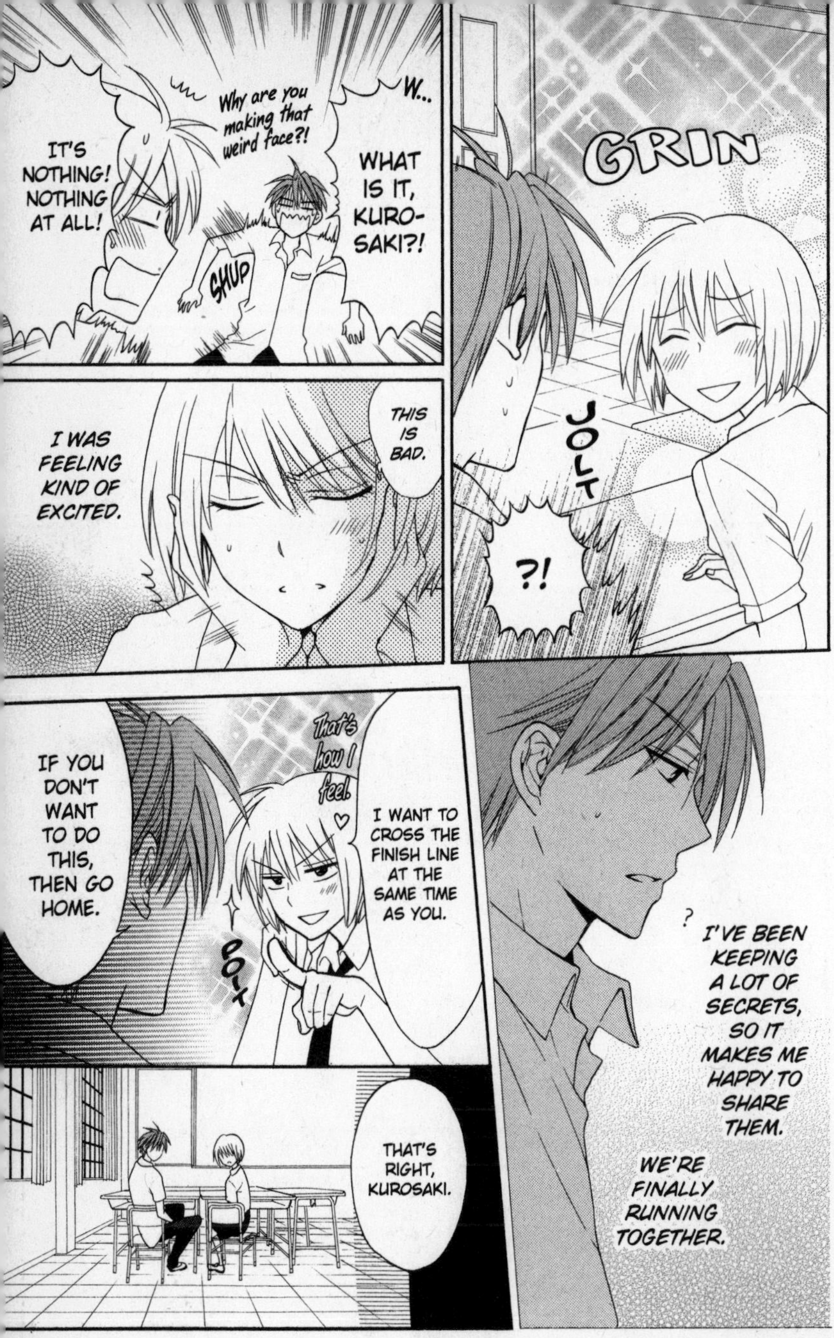
GRIN
JOLT
?!
W...
WHAT IS IT, KURO-SAKI?!
Why are you making that weird face?!
IT'S NOTHING! NOTHING AT ALL!
SHUP
THIS IS BAD.
I WAS FEELING KIND OF EXCITED.
?
I'VE BEEN KEEPING A LOT OF SECRETS, SO IT MAKES ME HAPPY TO SHARE THEM.
WE'RE FINALLY RUNNING TOGETHER.
That's how I feel. ♡
I WANT TO CROSS THE FINISH LINE AT THE SAME TIME AS YOU.
POIT
IF YOU DON'T WANT TO DO THIS, THEN GO HOME.
THAT'S RIGHT, KUROSAKI.

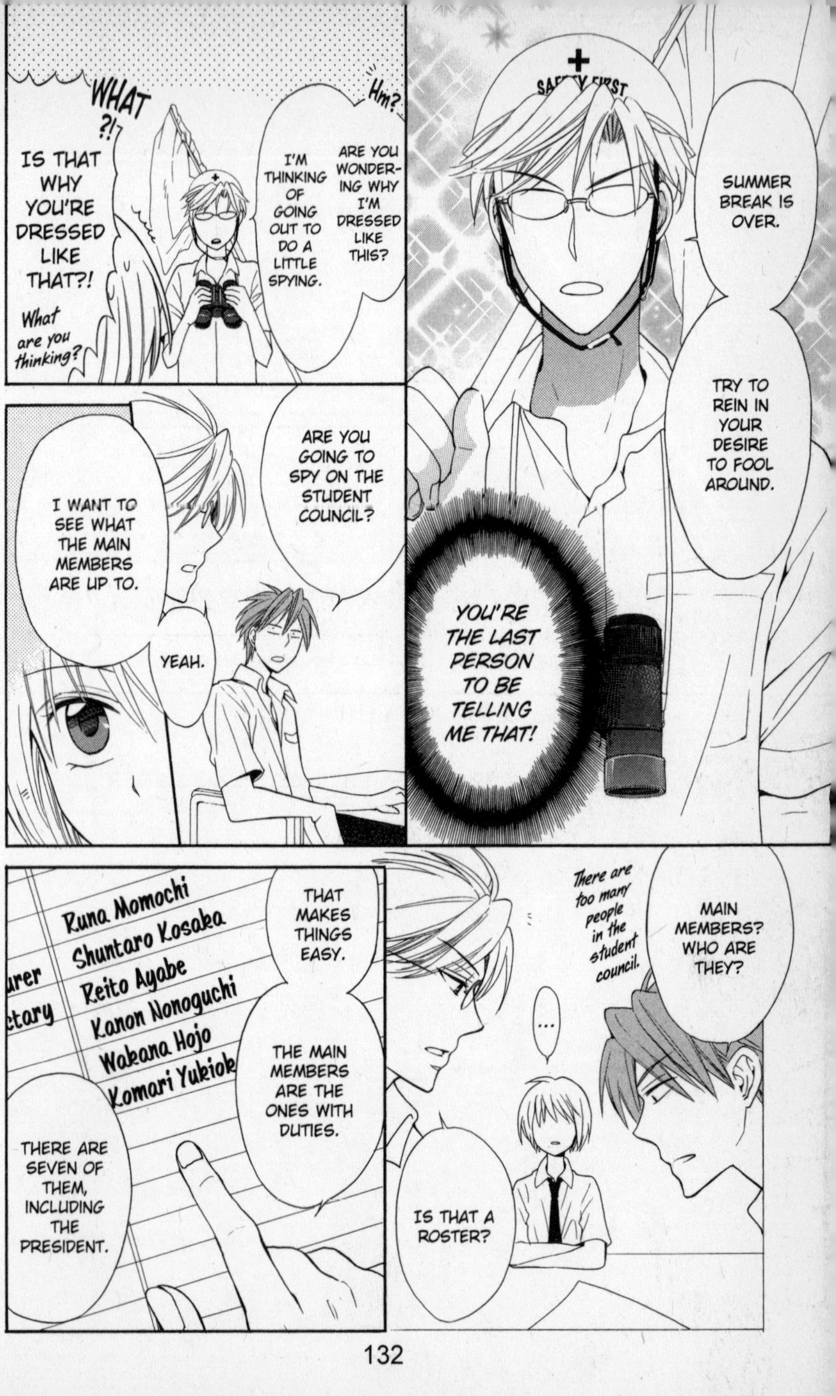
SUMMER BREAK IS OVER.
TRY TO REIN IN YOUR DESIRE TO FOOL AROUND.
YOU'RE THE LAST PERSON TO BE TELLING ME THAT!
Hm?
ARE YOU WONDERING WHY I'M DRESSED LIKE THIS?
I'M THINKING OF GOING OUT TO DO A LITTLE SPYING.
WHAT ?!
IS THAT WHY YOU'RE DRESSED LIKE THAT?!
What are you thinking?
ARE YOU GOING TO SPY ON THE STUDENT COUNCIL?
I WANT TO SEE WHAT THE MAIN MEMBERS ARE UP TO.
YEAH.
MAIN MEMBERS? WHO ARE THEY?
There are too many people in the student council.
...
IS THAT A ROSTER?
THAT MAKES THINGS EASY.
THE MAIN MEMBERS ARE THE ONES WITH DUTIES.
THERE ARE SEVEN OF THEM, INCLUDING THE PRESIDENT.
Runa Momochi
Shuntaro Kosaka
Reito Ayabe
Kanon Nonoguchi
Wakana Hojo
Komari Yukiok

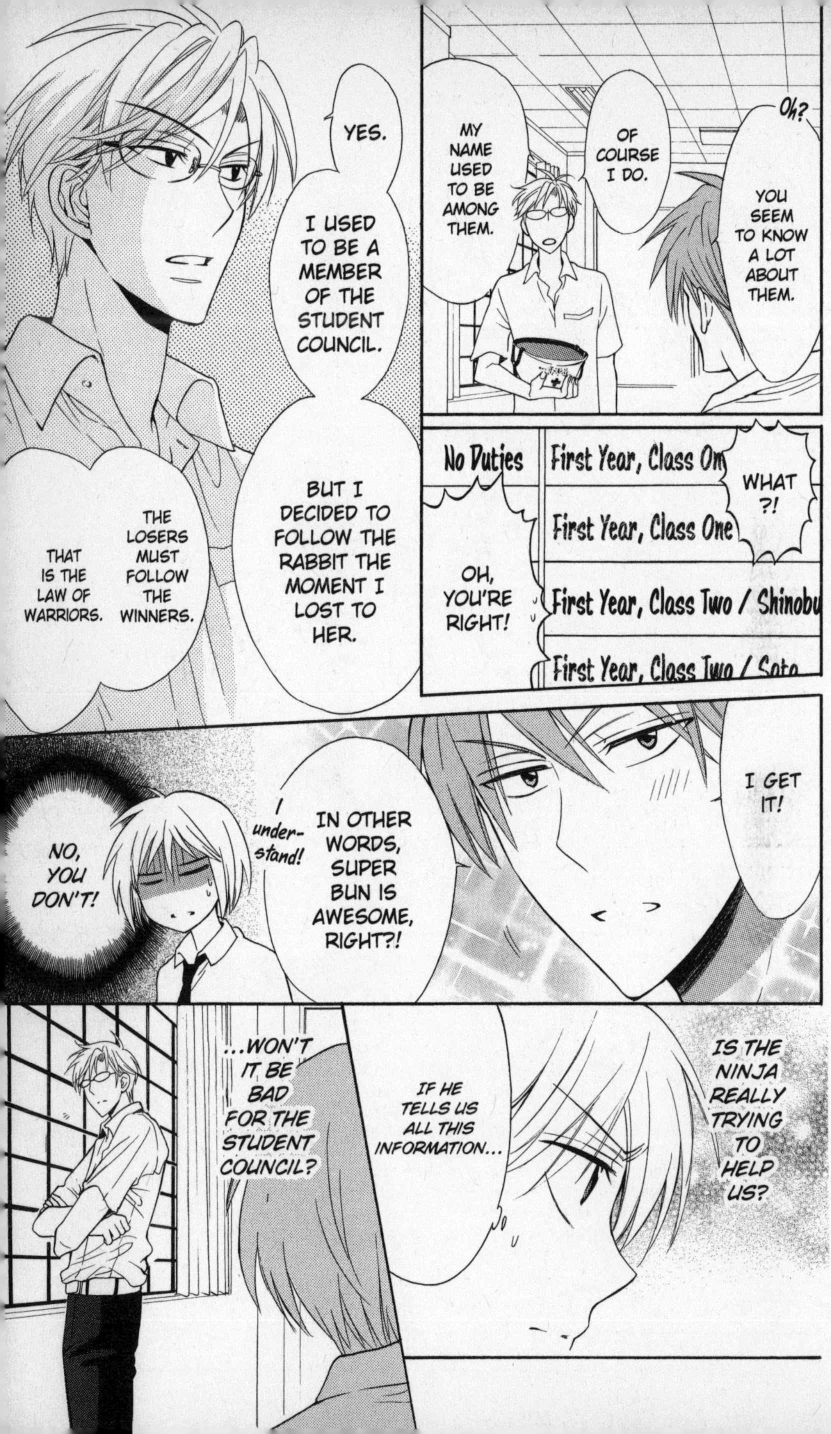
Oh?
YOU SEEM TO KNOW A LOT ABOUT THEM.
OF COURSE I DO.
MY NAME USED TO BE AMONG THEM.
WHAT?!
No Duties
First Year, Class On
First Year, Class One
First Year, Class Two / Shinobu
First Year, Class Two / Sato
OH, YOU'RE RIGHT!
YES.
I USED TO BE A MEMBER OF THE STUDENT COUNCIL.
BUT I DECIDED TO FOLLOW THE RABBIT THE MOMENT I LOST TO HER.
THE LOSERS MUST FOLLOW THE WINNERS.
THAT IS THE LAW OF WARRIORS.
I GET IT!
IN OTHER WORDS, SUPER BUN IS AWESOME, RIGHT?!
I understand!
NO, YOU DON'T!
IS THE NINJA REALLY TRYING TO HELP US?
IF HE TELLS US ALL THIS INFORMATION...
...WON'T IT BE BAD FOR THE STUDENT COUNCIL?

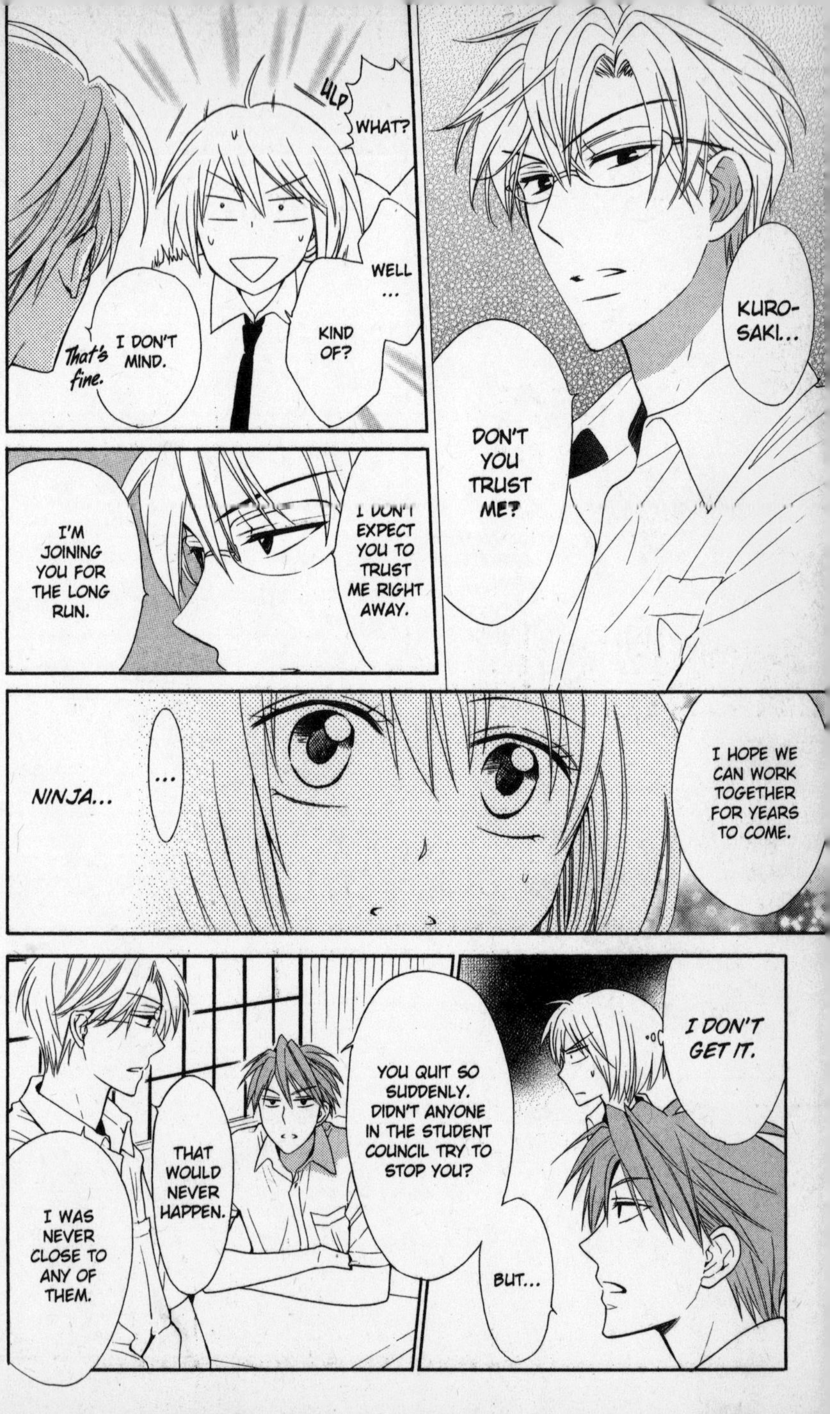
KURO-SAKI...
DON'T YOU TRUST ME?
ULP
WHAT?
WELL...
KIND OF?
I DON'T MIND.
That's fine.
I DON'T EXPECT YOU TO TRUST ME RIGHT AWAY.
I'M JOINING YOU FOR THE LONG RUN.
I HOPE WE CAN WORK TOGETHER FOR YEARS TO COME.
...
NINJA...
I DON'T GET IT.
YOU QUIT SO SUDDENLY. DIDN'T ANYONE IN THE STUDENT COUNCIL TRY TO STOP YOU?
BUT...
THAT WOULD NEVER HAPPEN.
I WAS NEVER CLOSE TO ANY OF THEM.

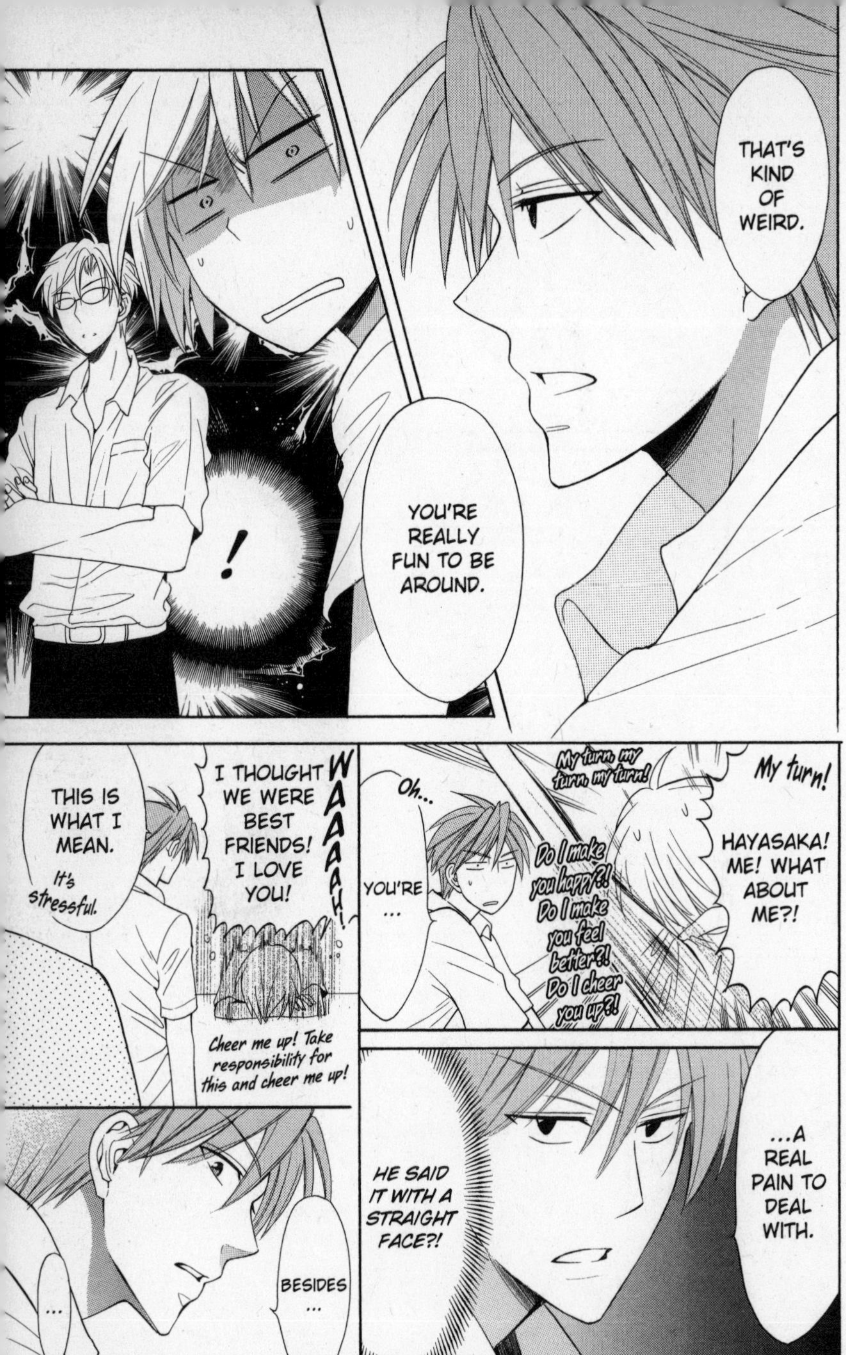
THAT'S KIND OF WEIRD.
YOU'RE REALLY FUN TO BE AROUND.
!
My turn!
HAYASAKA! ME! WHAT ABOUT ME?!
My turn, my turn, my turn!
Do I make you happy?! Do I make you feel better?! Do I cheer you up?!
Oh...
YOU'RE ...
I THOUGHT WE WERE BEST FRIENDS! I LOVE YOU!
WAAAAAH!
Cheer me up! Take responsibility for this and cheer me up!
THIS IS WHAT I MEAN.
It's stressful.
...A REAL PAIN TO DEAL WITH.
HE SAID IT WITH A STRAIGHT FACE?!
BESIDES ...
...

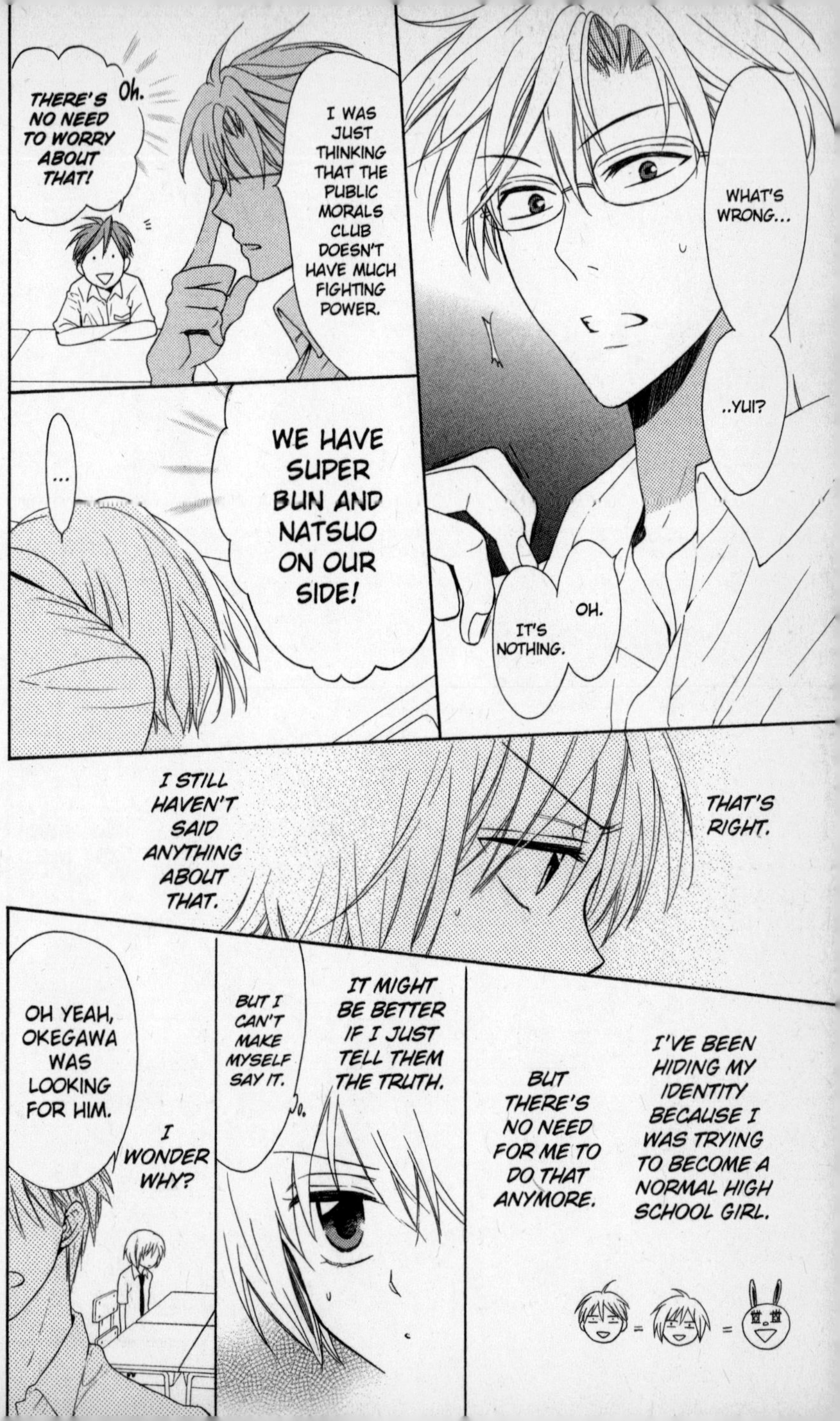
WHAT'S WRONG…
..YUI?
OH.
IT'S NOTHING.
I WAS JUST THINKING THAT THE PUBLIC MORALS CLUB DOESN'T HAVE MUCH FIGHTING POWER.
Oh.
THERE'S NO NEED TO WORRY ABOUT THAT!
WE HAVE SUPER BUN AND NATSUO ON OUR SIDE!
...
THAT'S RIGHT.
I STILL HAVEN'T SAID ANYTHING ABOUT THAT.
I'VE BEEN HIDING MY IDENTITY BECAUSE I WAS TRYING TO BECOME A NORMAL HIGH SCHOOL GIRL.
BUT THERE'S NO NEED FOR ME TO DO THAT ANYMORE.
IT MIGHT BE BETTER IF I JUST TELL THEM THE TRUTH.
BUT I CAN'T MAKE MYSELF SAY IT.
OH YEAH, OKEGAWA WAS LOOKING FOR HIM.
I WONDER WHY?

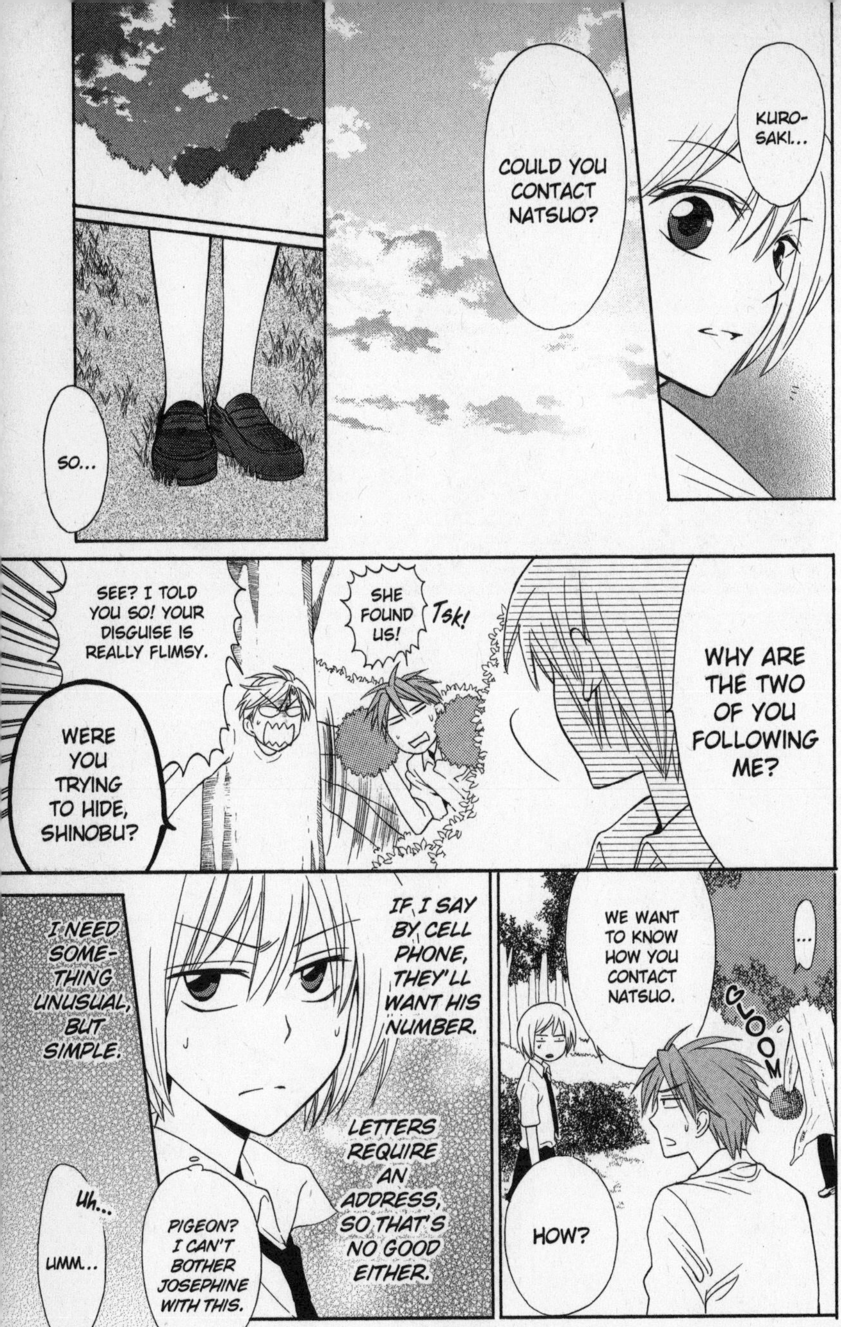
KURO-SAKI...
COULD YOU CONTACT NATSUO?
SO...
WHY ARE THE TWO OF YOU FOLLOWING ME?
SHE FOUND US!
Tsk!
SEE? I TOLD YOU SO! YOUR DISGUISE IS REALLY FLIMSY.
WERE YOU TRYING TO HIDE, SHINOBU?
...
WE WANT TO KNOW HOW YOU CONTACT NATSUO.
GLOOM
HOW?
IF I SAY BY CELL PHONE, THEY'LL WANT HIS NUMBER.
I NEED SOMETHING UNUSUAL, BUT SIMPLE.
LETTERS REQUIRE AN ADDRESS, SO THAT'S NO GOOD EITHER.
PIGEON? I CAN'T BOTHER JOSEPHINE WITH THIS.
Uh...
UMM...

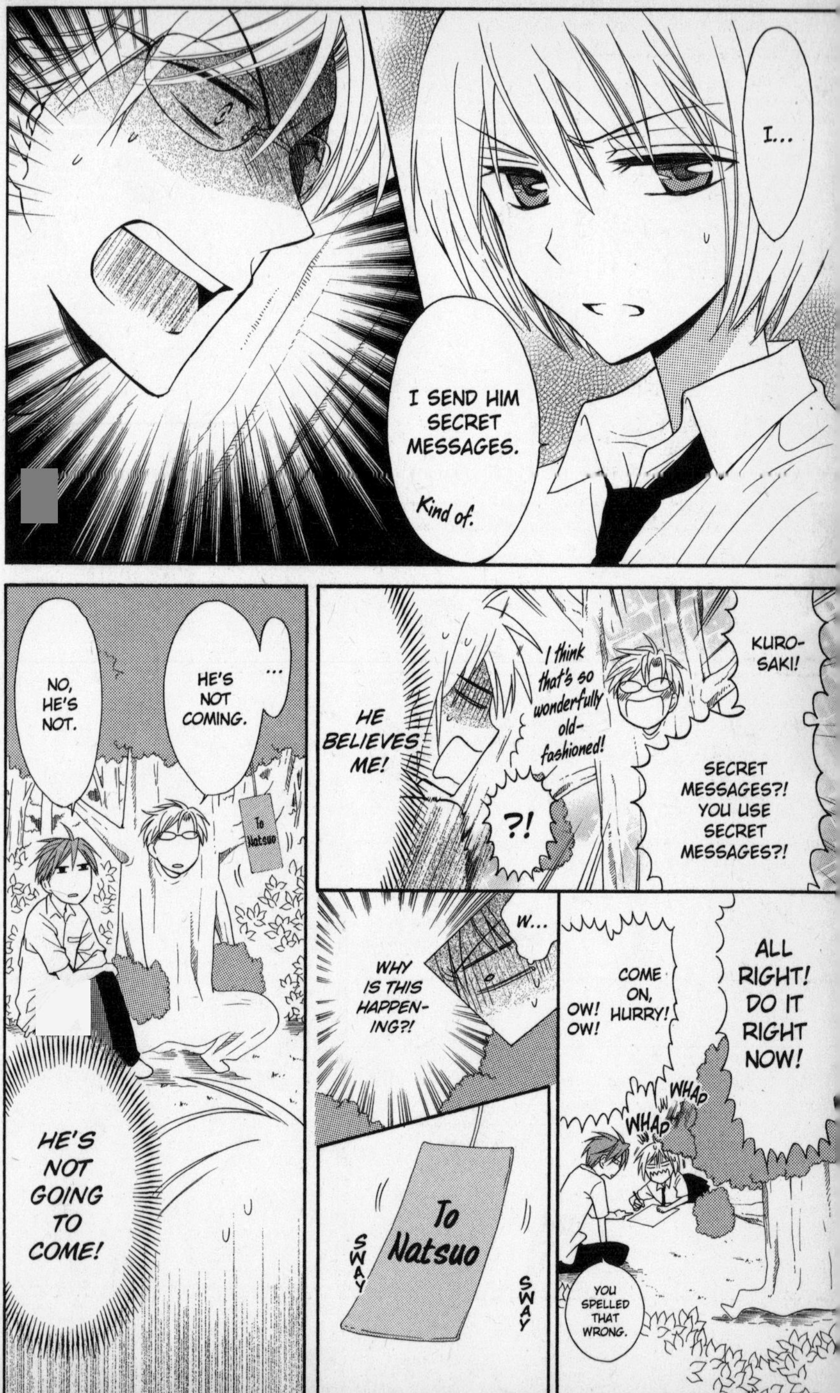
I...
I SEND HIM SECRET MESSAGES.
Kind of.
KURO-SAKI!
SECRET MESSAGES?! YOU USE SECRET MESSAGES?!
I think that's so wonderfully old-fashioned!
?!
HE BELIEVES ME!
ALL RIGHT! DO IT RIGHT NOW!
COME ON, HURRY!
OW! OW!
WHAP
WHAP
YOU SPELLED THAT WRONG.
W...
WHY IS THIS HAPPEN-ING?!
To Natsuo
SWAY
SWAY
...
HE'S NOT COMING.
NO, HE'S NOT.
To Natsuo
HE'S NOT GOING TO COME!

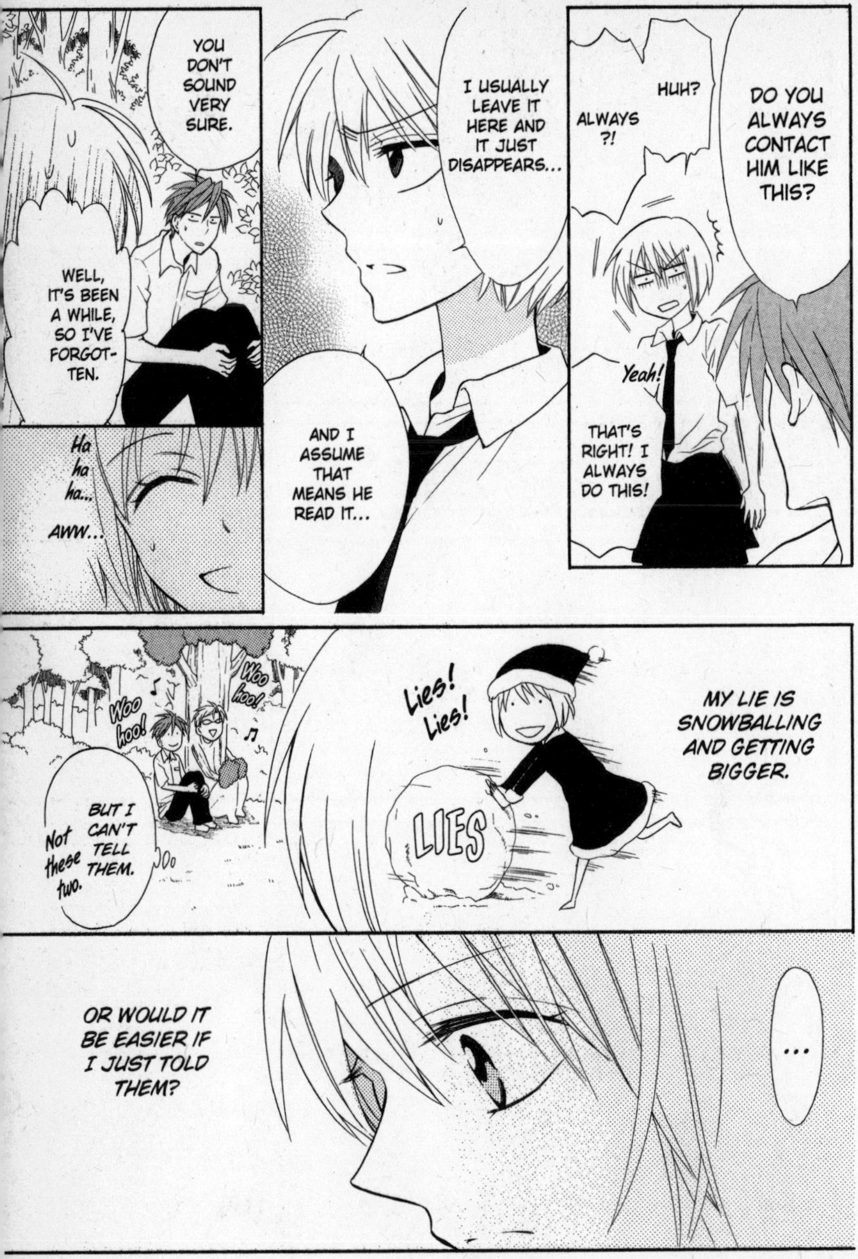
DO YOU ALWAYS CONTACT HIM LIKE THIS?
HUH?
ALWAYS ?!
Yeah!
THAT'S RIGHT! I ALWAYS DO THIS!
I USUALLY LEAVE IT HERE AND IT JUST DISAPPEARS...
AND I ASSUME THAT MEANS HE READ IT...
YOU DON'T SOUND VERY SURE.
WELL, IT'S BEEN A WHILE, SO I'VE FORGOT-TEN.
Ha ha ha...
AWW...
MY LIE IS SNOWBALLING AND GETTING BIGGER.
Lies! Lies!
LIES
Woo hoo!
Woo hoo!
BUT I CAN'T TELL THEM.
Not these two.
...
OR WOULD IT BE EASIER IF I JUST TOLD THEM?

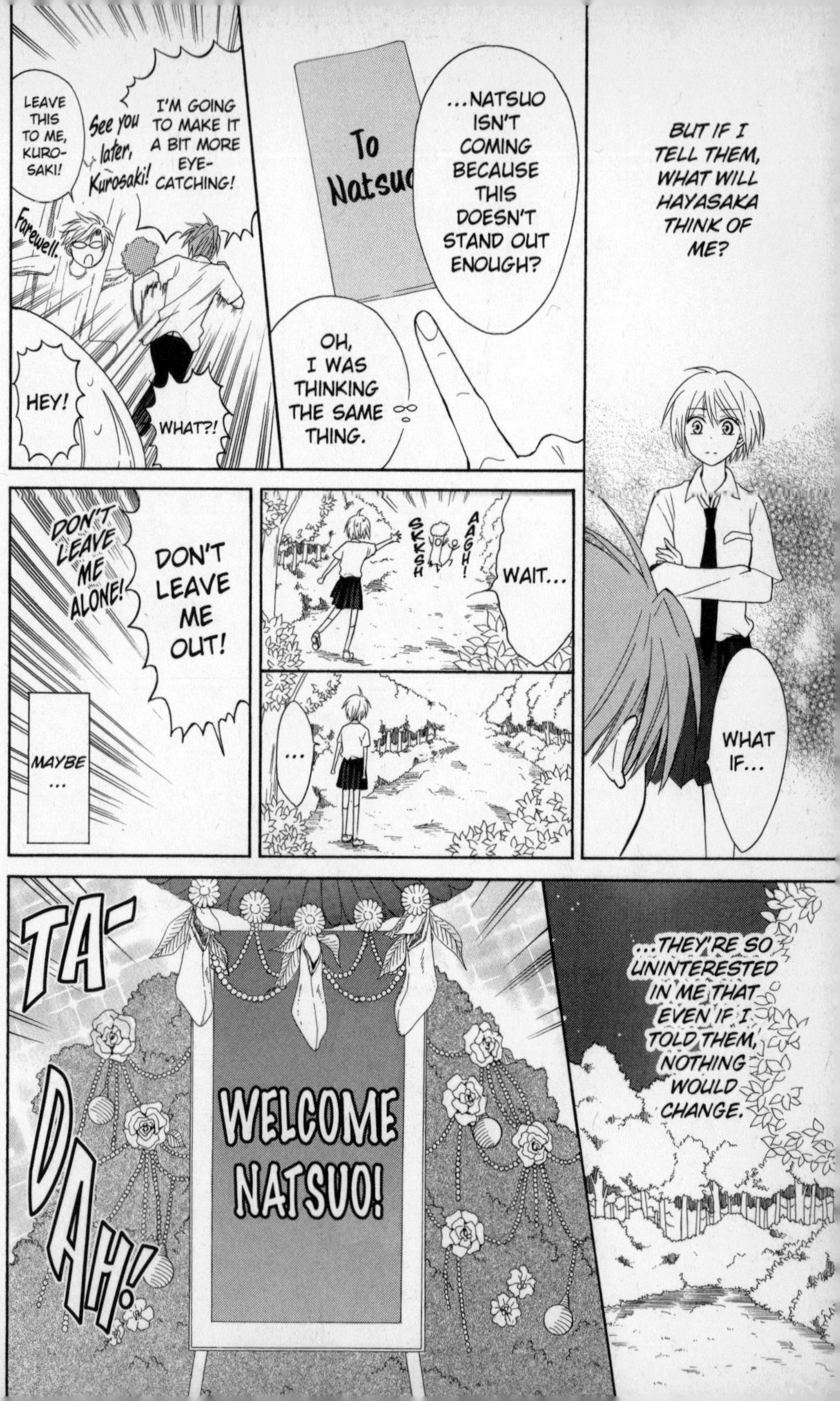
BUT IF I TELL THEM, WHAT WILL HAYASAKA THINK OF ME?
WHAT IF...
To Natsuo
...NATSUO ISN'T COMING BECAUSE THIS DOESN'T STAND OUT ENOUGH?
OH, I WAS THINKING THE SAME THING.
I'M GOING TO MAKE IT A BIT MORE EYE-CATCHING!
See you later, Kurosaki!
LEAVE THIS TO ME, KURO-SAKI!
Farewell.
WHAT?!
HEY!
WAIT...
AAGH!
SKKSH
...
DON'T LEAVE ME OUT!
DON'T LEAVE ME ALONE!
MAYBE...
...THEY'RE SO UNINTERESTED IN ME THAT EVEN IF I TOLD THEM, NOTHING WOULD CHANGE.
TA-DAH!
WELCOME NATSUO!

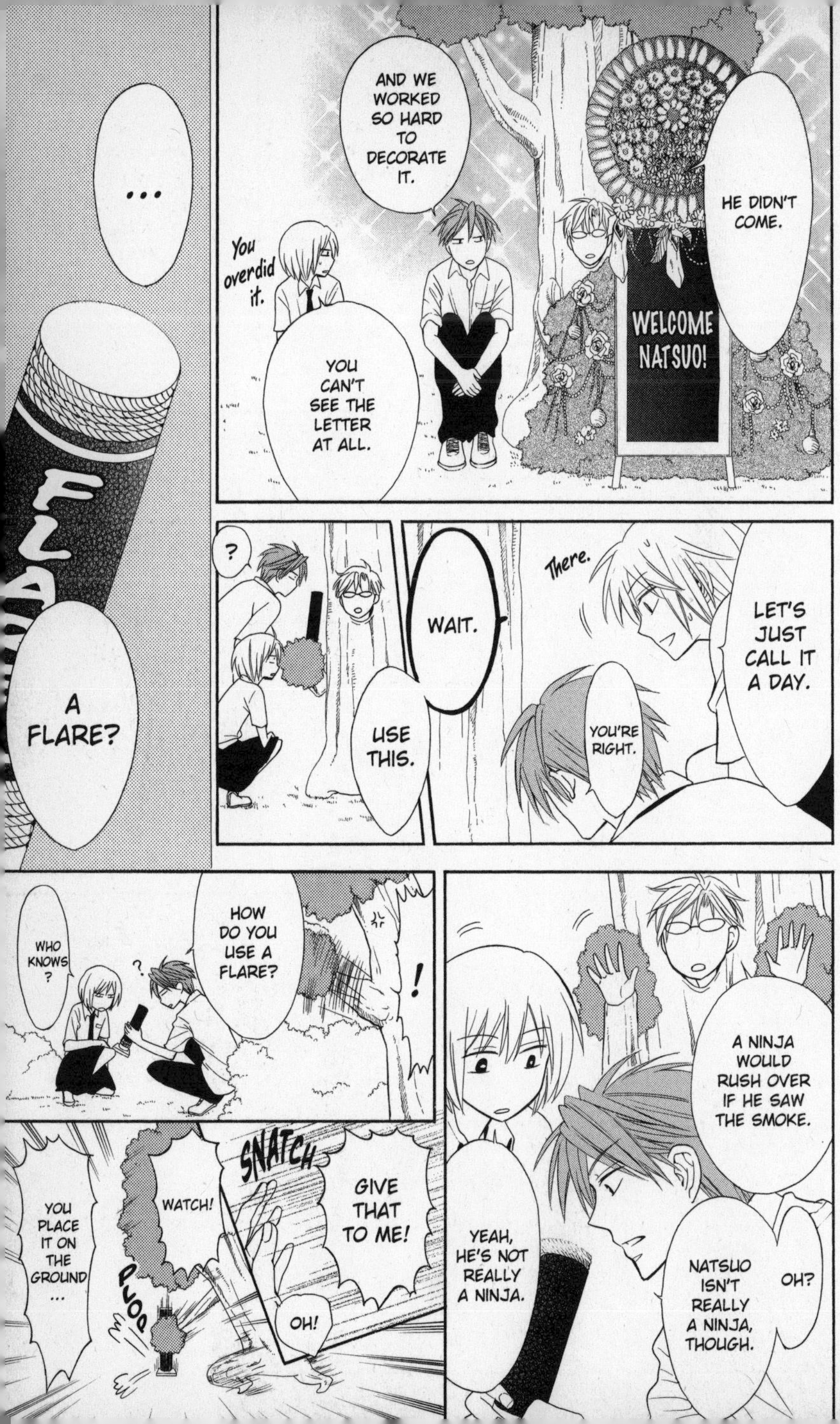
HE DIDN'T COME.
AND WE WORKED SO HARD TO DECORATE IT.
WELCOME NATSUO!
You overdid it.
YOU CAN'T SEE THE LETTER AT ALL.
LET'S JUST CALL IT A DAY.
There.
YOU'RE RIGHT.
WAIT.
USE THIS.
?
...
A FLARE?
A NINJA WOULD RUSH OVER IF HE SAW THE SMOKE.
OH?
NATSUO ISN'T REALLY A NINJA, THOUGH.
YEAH, HE'S NOT REALLY A NINJA.
HOW DO YOU USE A FLARE?
!
?
WHO KNOWS?
GIVE THAT TO ME!
SNATCH
OH!
WATCH!
YOU PLACE IT ON THE GROUND...

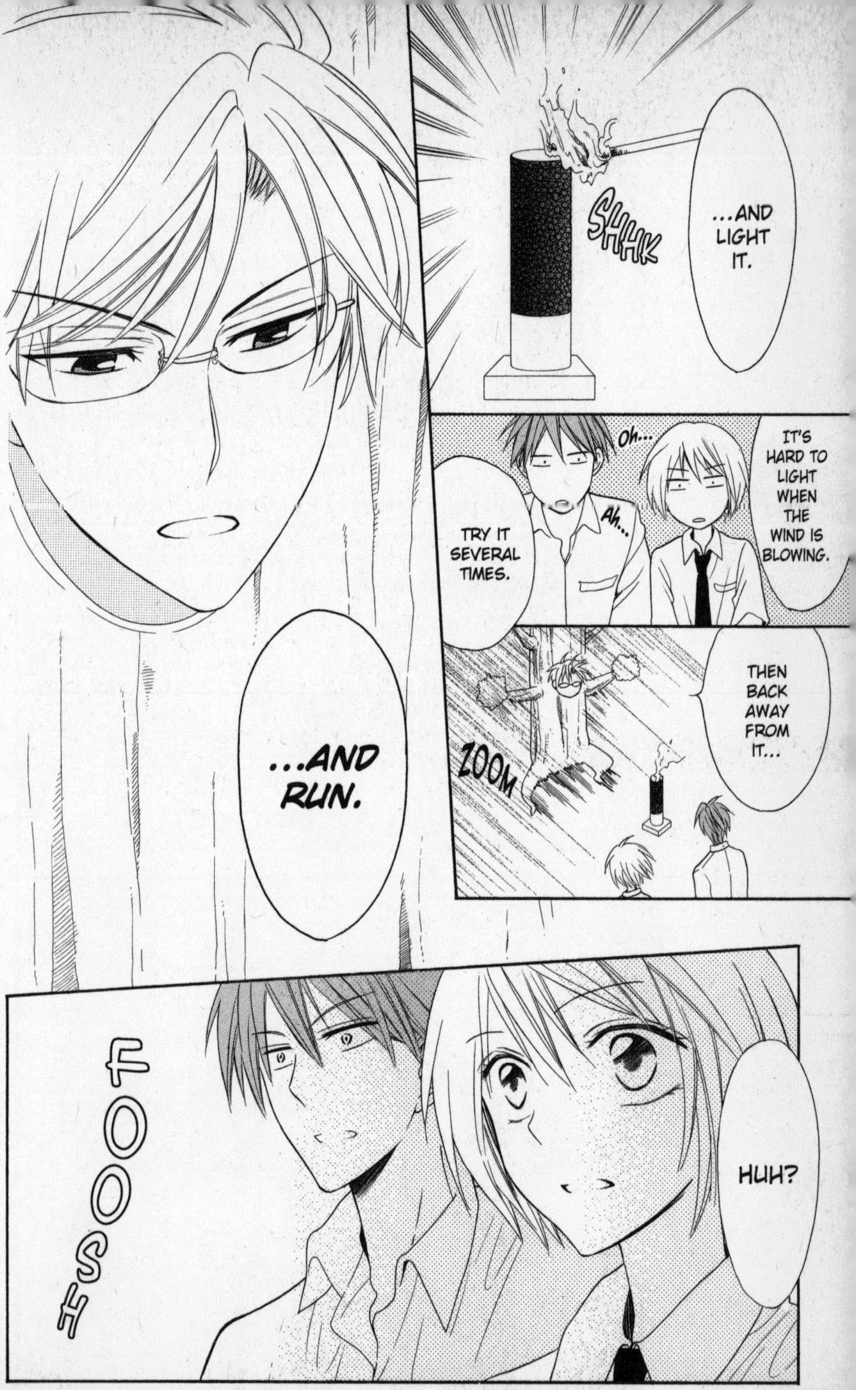
SHHK
...AND LIGHT IT.
IT'S HARD TO LIGHT WHEN THE WIND IS BLOWING.
Oh...
Ah...
TRY IT SEVERAL TIMES.
THEN BACK AWAY FROM IT...
ZOOM
...AND RUN.
HUH?
FOOSH

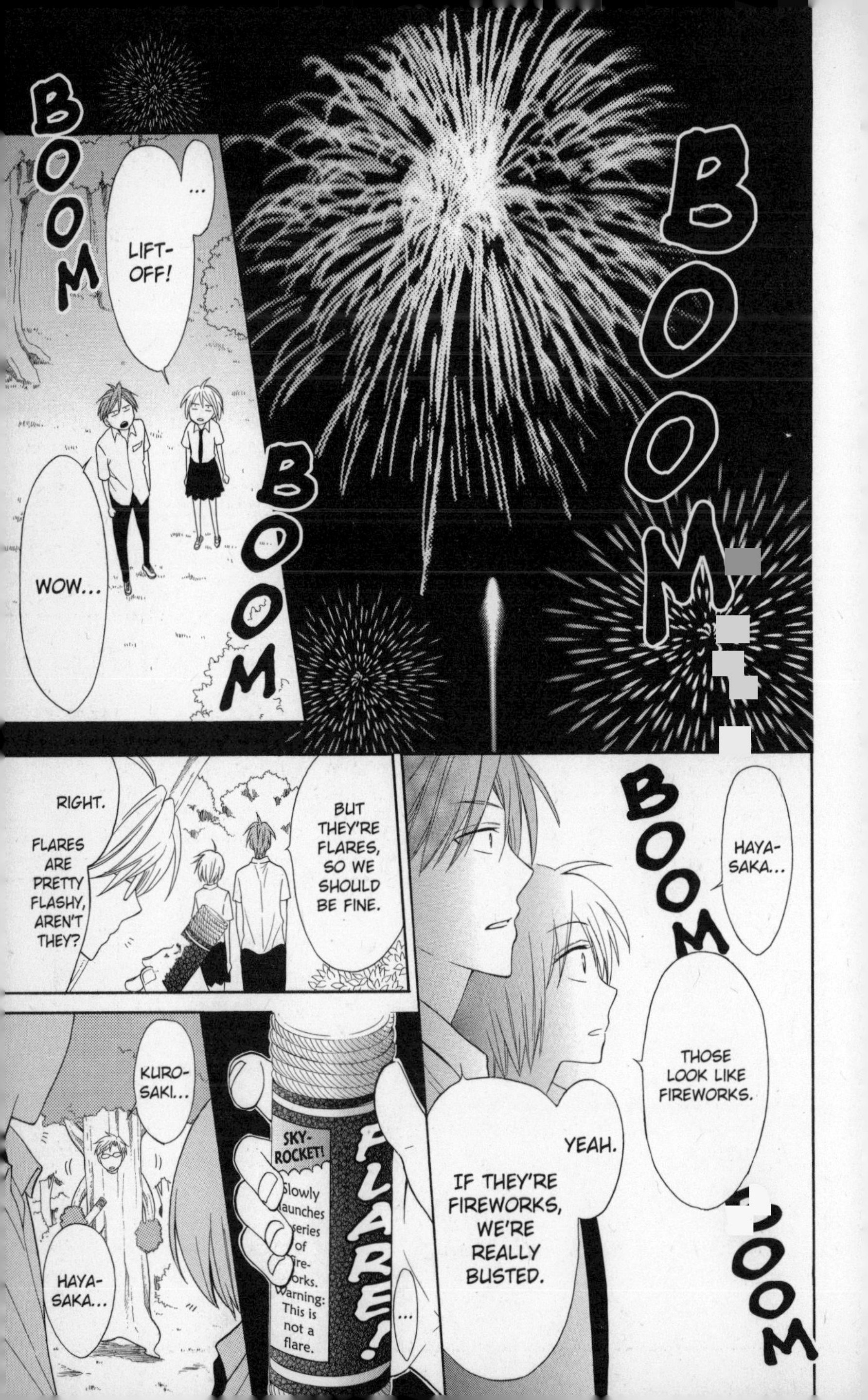
BOOM
BOOM
...
LIFT-OFF!
WOW...
BOOM
BOOM
HAYA-SAKA...
THOSE LOOK LIKE FIREWORKS.
YEAH.
IF THEY'RE FIREWORKS, WE'RE REALLY BUSTED.
BOOM
BOOM
BUT THEY'RE FLARES, SO WE SHOULD BE FINE.
RIGHT.
FLARES ARE PRETTY FLASHY, AREN'T THEY?
KURO-SAKI...
SKY-ROCKET!
Slowly launches a series of fire-works. Warning: This is not a flare.
FLARE!
...
HAYA-SAKA...

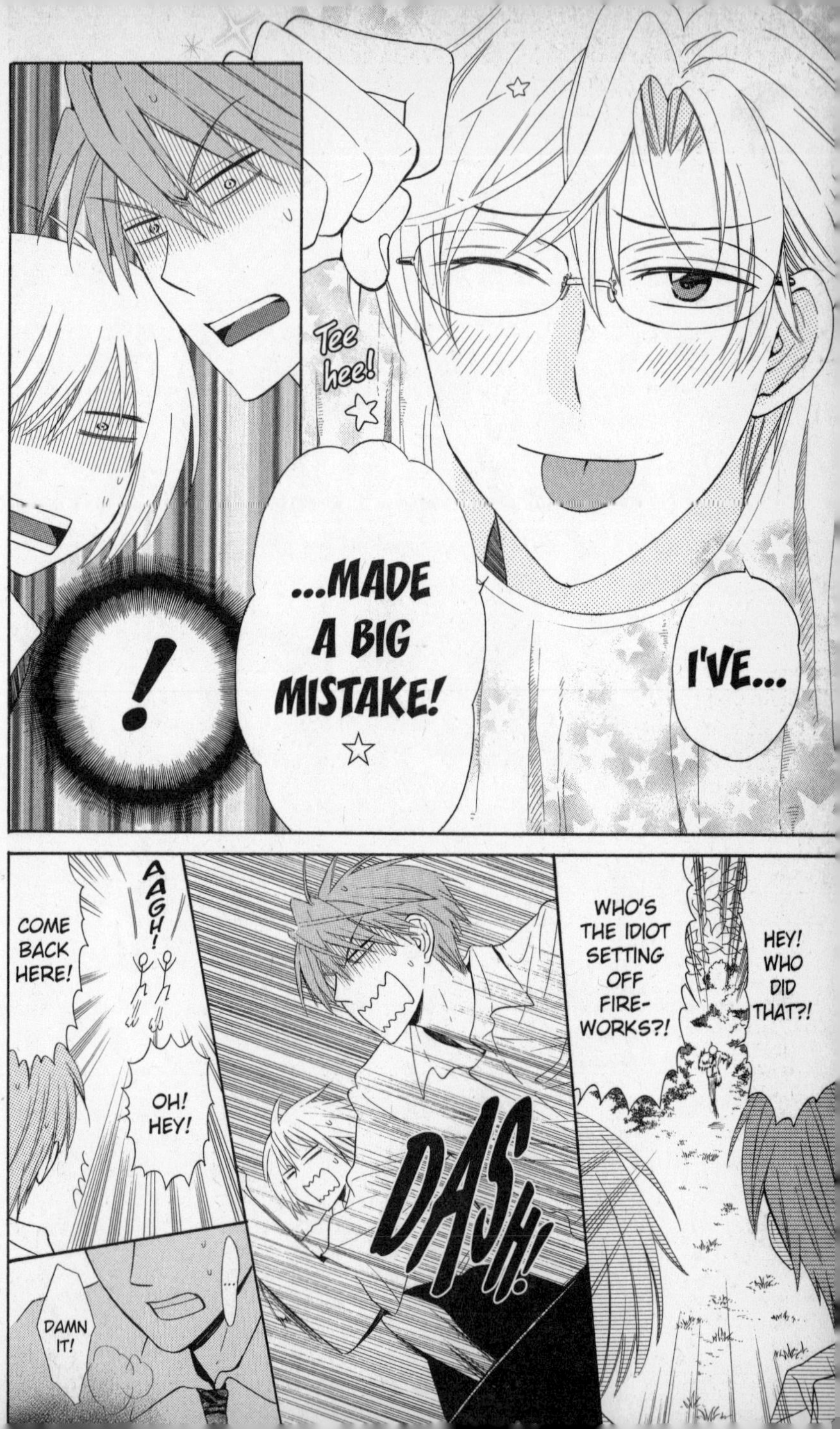
I'VE...
...MADE A BIG MISTAKE! ☆
Tee hee! ☆
!
HEY! WHO DID THAT?!
WHO'S THE IDIOT SETTING OFF FIRE-WORKS?!
DASH!
AAGH!
COME BACK HERE!
OH! HEY!
...
DAMN IT!

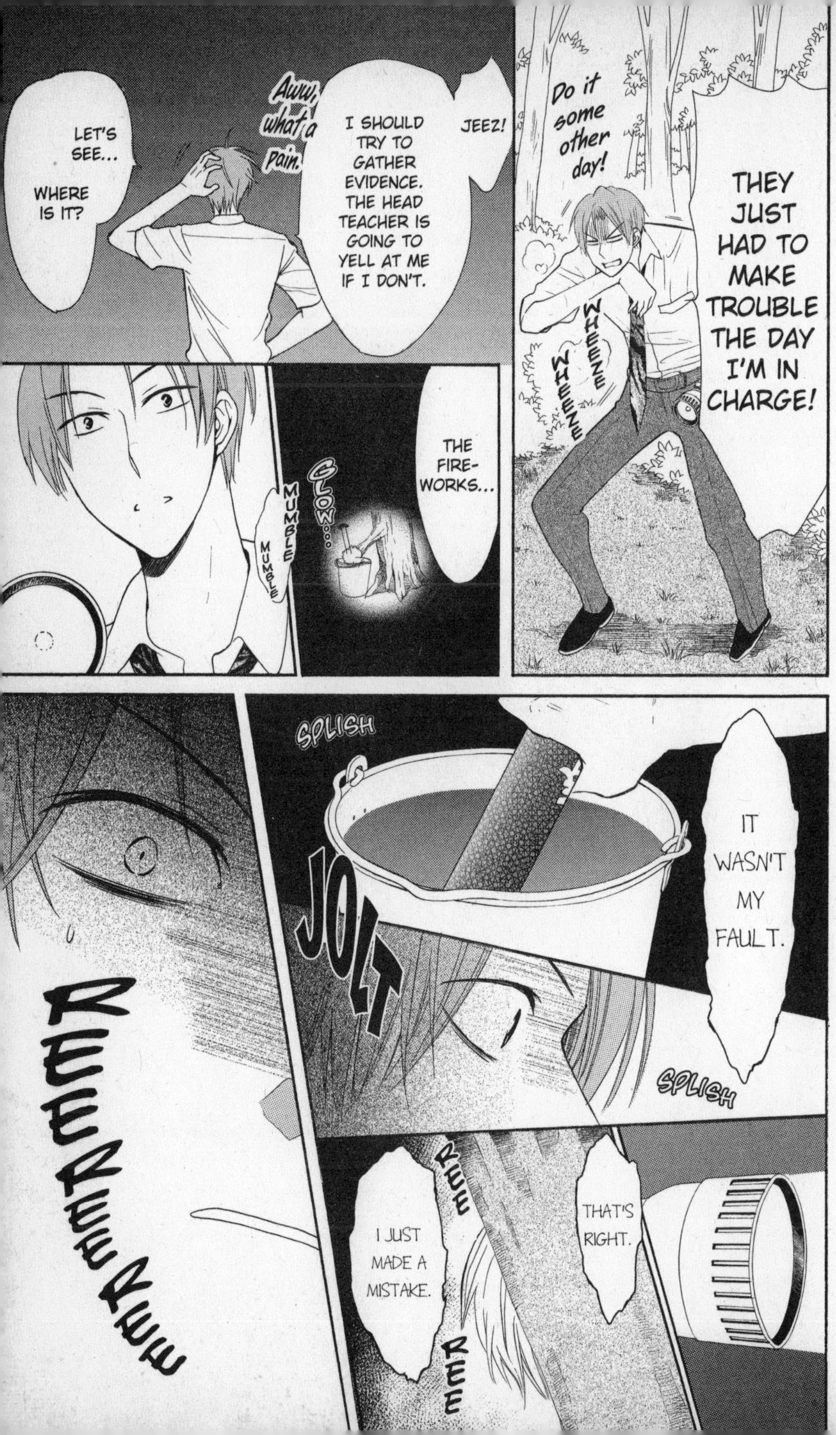
Do it some other day!
THEY JUST HAD TO MAKE TROUBLE THE DAY I'M IN CHARGE!
WHEEZE
WHEEZE
JEEZ!
I SHOULD TRY TO GATHER EVIDENCE. THE HEAD TEACHER IS GOING TO YELL AT ME IF I DON'T.
Aww, what a pain.
LET'S SEE...
WHERE IS IT?
THE FIRE-WORKS...
GLOW...
MUMBLE
MUMBLE
SPLISH
IT WASN'T MY FAULT.
JOLT
SPLISH
THAT'S RIGHT.
REE
I JUST MADE A MISTAKE.
REE
REEREEREEE

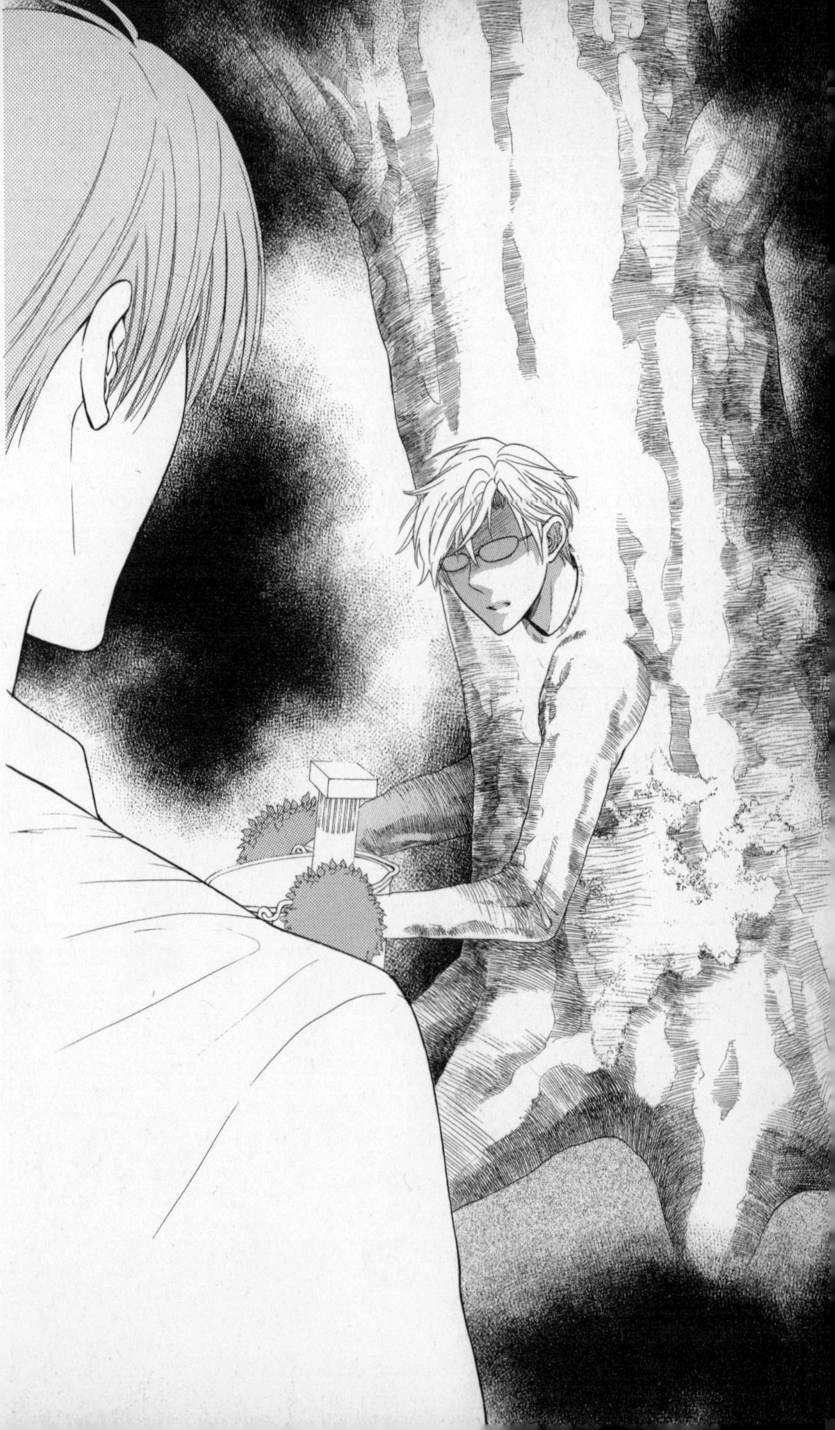

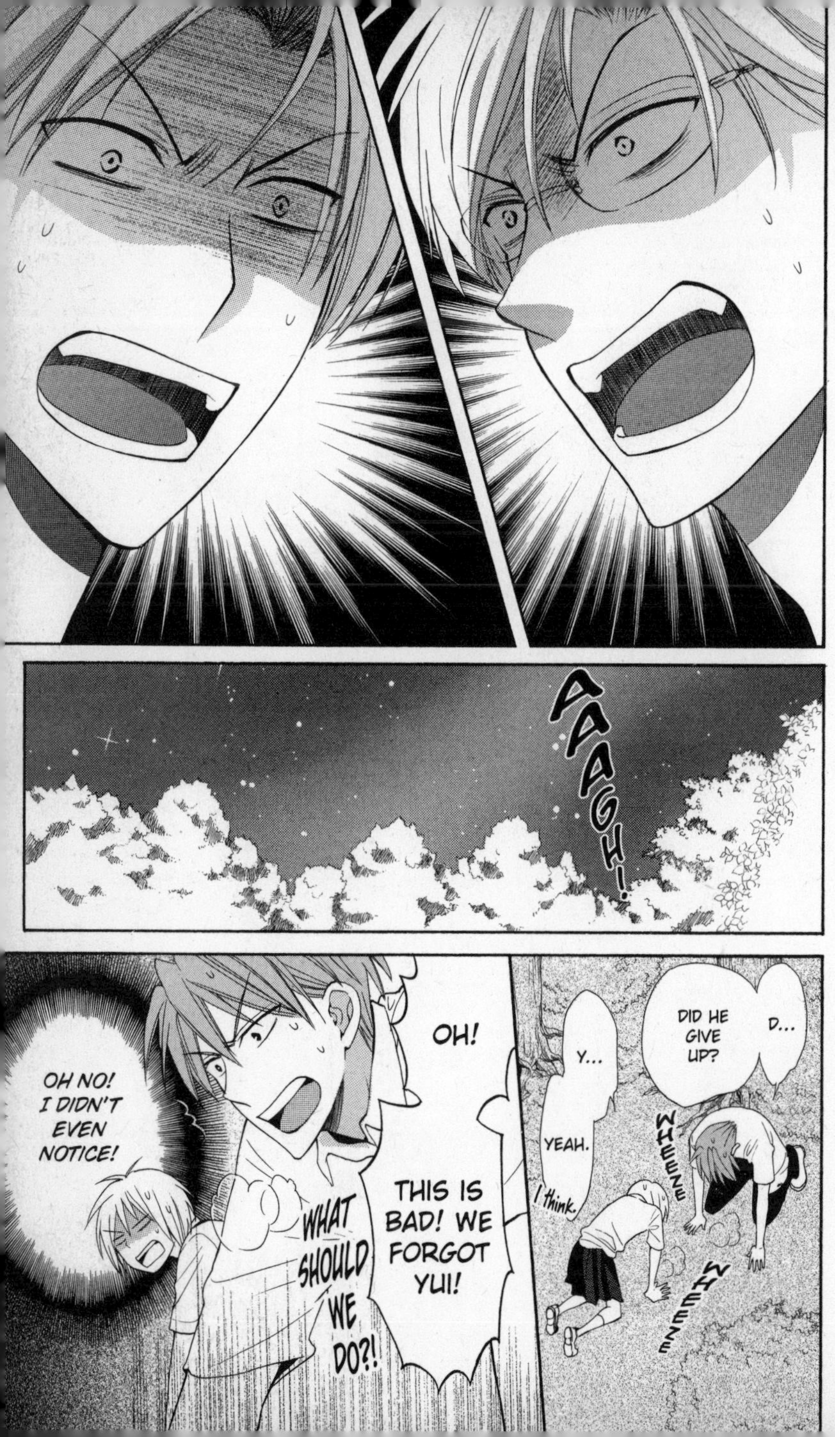
AAAAGH!
D...
DID HE GIVE UP?
Y...
YEAH.
I think.
WHEEZE
WHEEZE
OH!
THIS IS BAD! WE FORGOT YUI!
WHAT SHOULD WE DO?!
OH NO! I DIDN'T EVEN NOTICE!

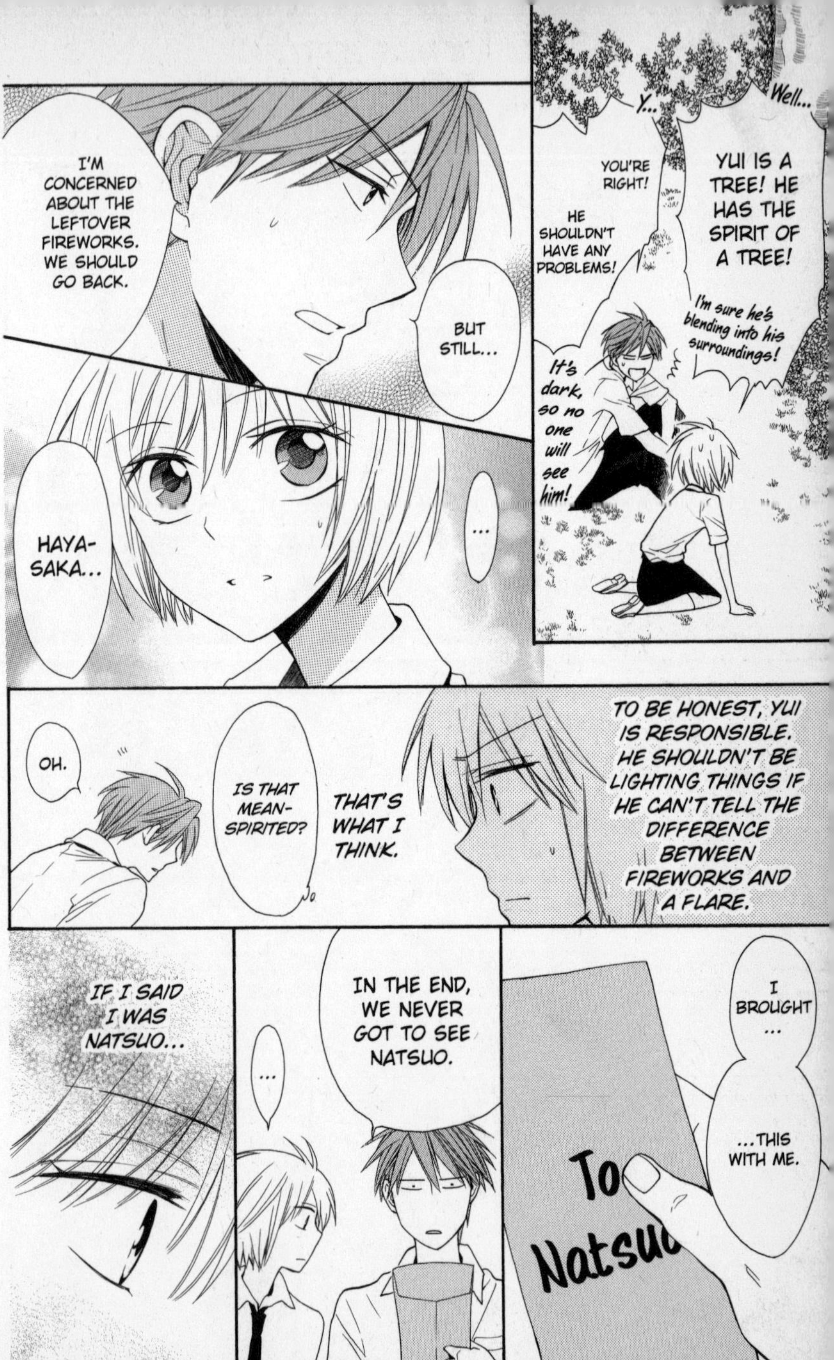

Well...
Y...
YUI IS A TREE! HE HAS THE SPIRIT OF A TREE!
YOU'RE RIGHT!
HE SHOULDN'T HAVE ANY PROBLEMS!
I'm sure he's blending into his surroundings!
It's dark, so no one will see him!
BUT STILL...
I'M CONCERNED ABOUT THE LEFTOVER FIREWORKS. WE SHOULD GO BACK.
...
HAYA-SAKA...
TO BE HONEST, YUI IS RESPONSIBLE. HE SHOULDN'T BE LIGHTING THINGS IF HE CAN'T TELL THE DIFFERENCE BETWEEN FIREWORKS AND A FLARE.
THAT'S WHAT I THINK.
IS THAT MEAN-SPIRITED?
OH.
I BROUGHT...
...THIS WITH ME.
To Natsu
IN THE END, WE NEVER GOT TO SEE NATSUO.
...
IF I SAID I WAS NATSUO...

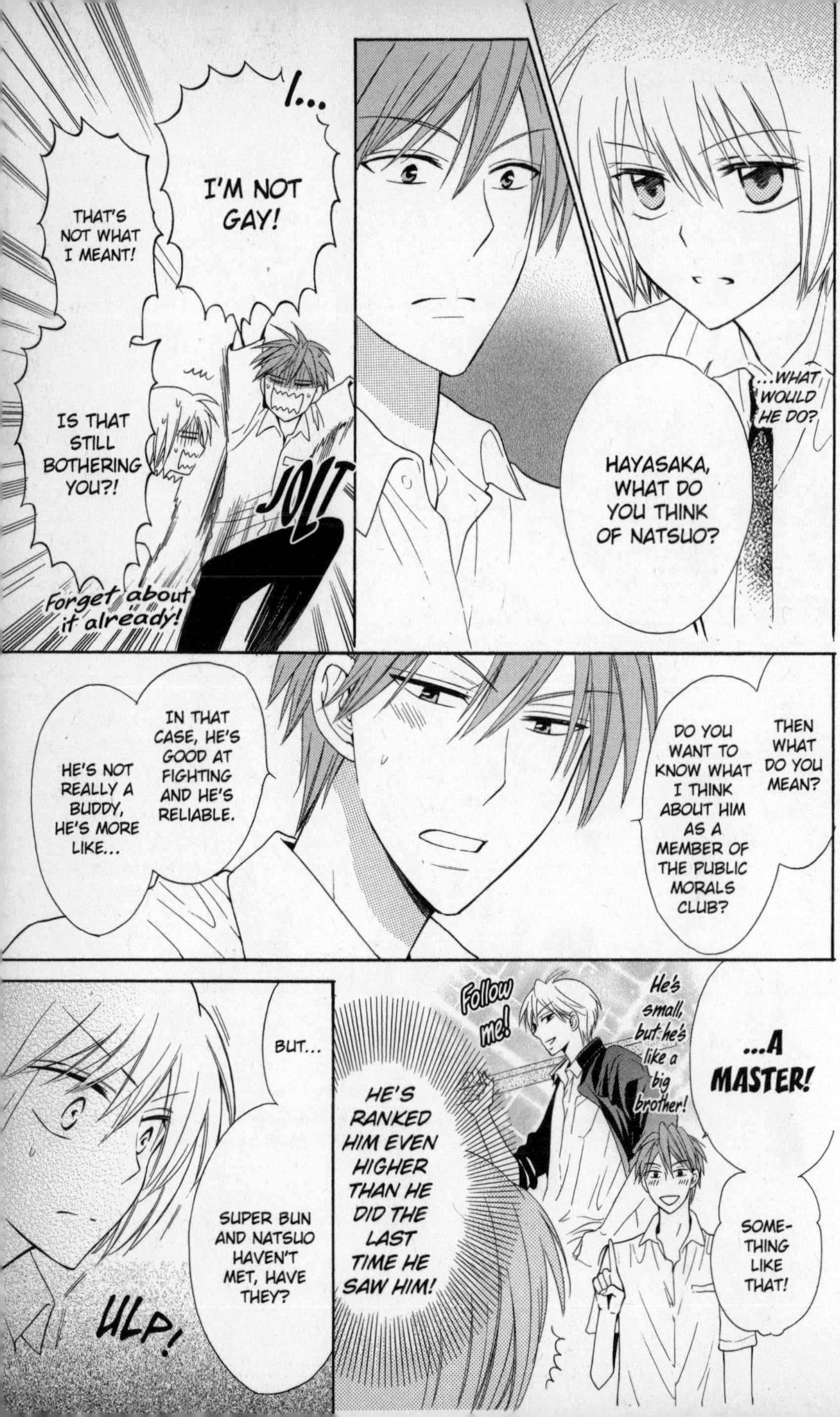
...WHAT WOULD HE DO?
HAYASAKA, WHAT DO YOU THINK OF NATSUO?
I...
I'M NOT GAY!
THAT'S NOT WHAT I MEANT!
IS THAT STILL BOTHERING YOU?!
JOLT
Forget about it already!
THEN WHAT DO YOU MEAN?
DO YOU WANT TO KNOW WHAT I THINK ABOUT HIM AS A MEMBER OF THE PUBLIC MORALS CLUB?
IN THAT CASE, HE'S GOOD AT FIGHTING AND HE'S RELIABLE.
HE'S NOT REALLY A BUDDY, HE'S MORE LIKE...
...A MASTER!
He's small, but he's like a big brother!
Follow me!
SOME-THING LIKE THAT!
HE'S RANKED HIM EVEN HIGHER THAN HE DID THE LAST TIME HE SAW HIM!
BUT...
SUPER BUN AND NATSUO HAVEN'T MET, HAVE THEY?
ULP!

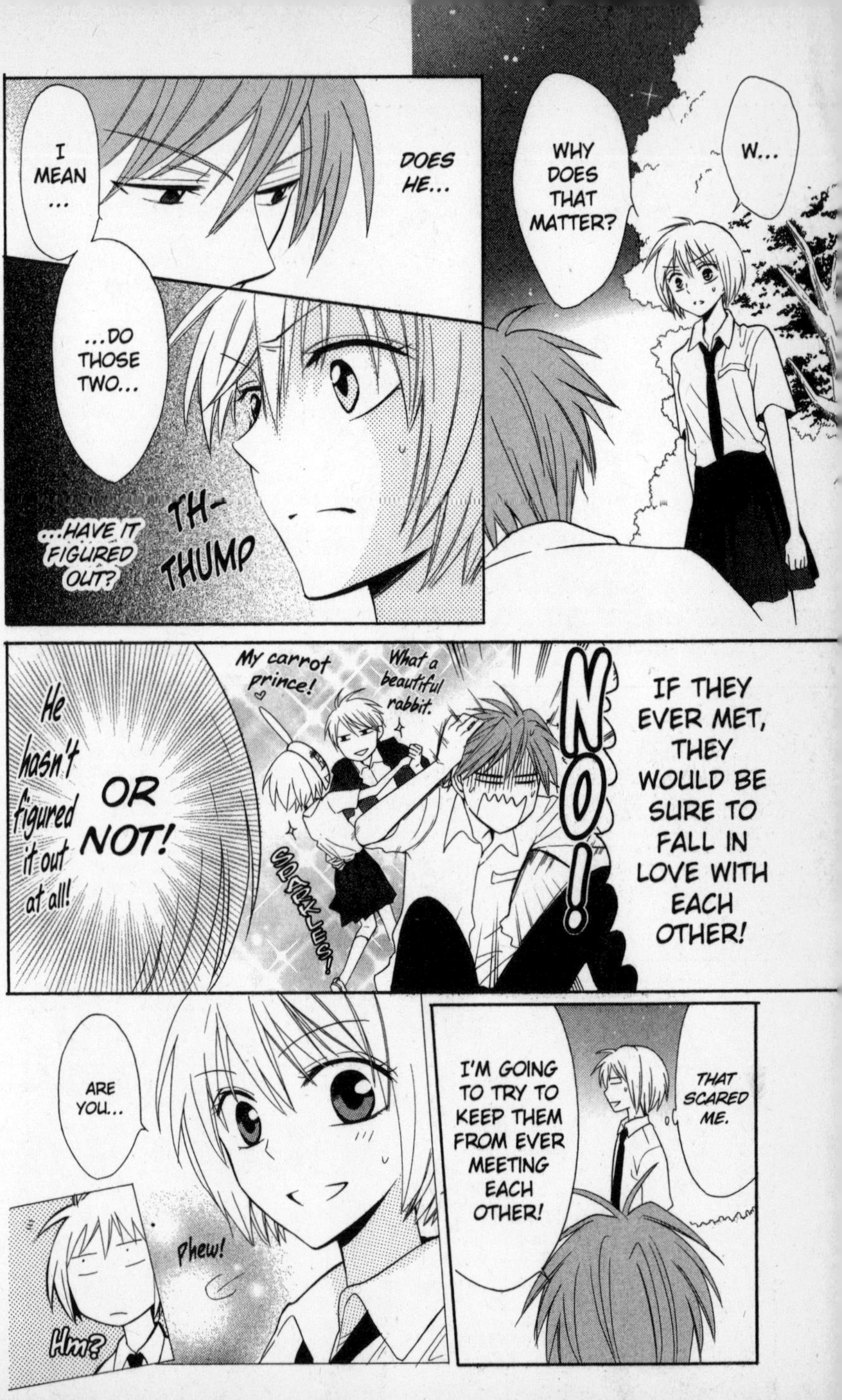
W...
WHY DOES THAT MATTER?
DOES HE...
I MEAN ...
...DO THOSE TWO...
TH-THUMP
...HAVE IT FIGURED OUT?
IF THEY EVER MET, THEY WOULD BE SURE TO FALL IN LOVE WITH EACH OTHER!
NO!
What a beautiful rabbit.
My carrot prince!
OR NOT!
He hasn't figured it out at all!
THAT SCARED ME.
I'M GOING TO TRY TO KEEP THEM FROM EVER MEETING EACH OTHER!
ARE YOU...
Phew!
Hm?

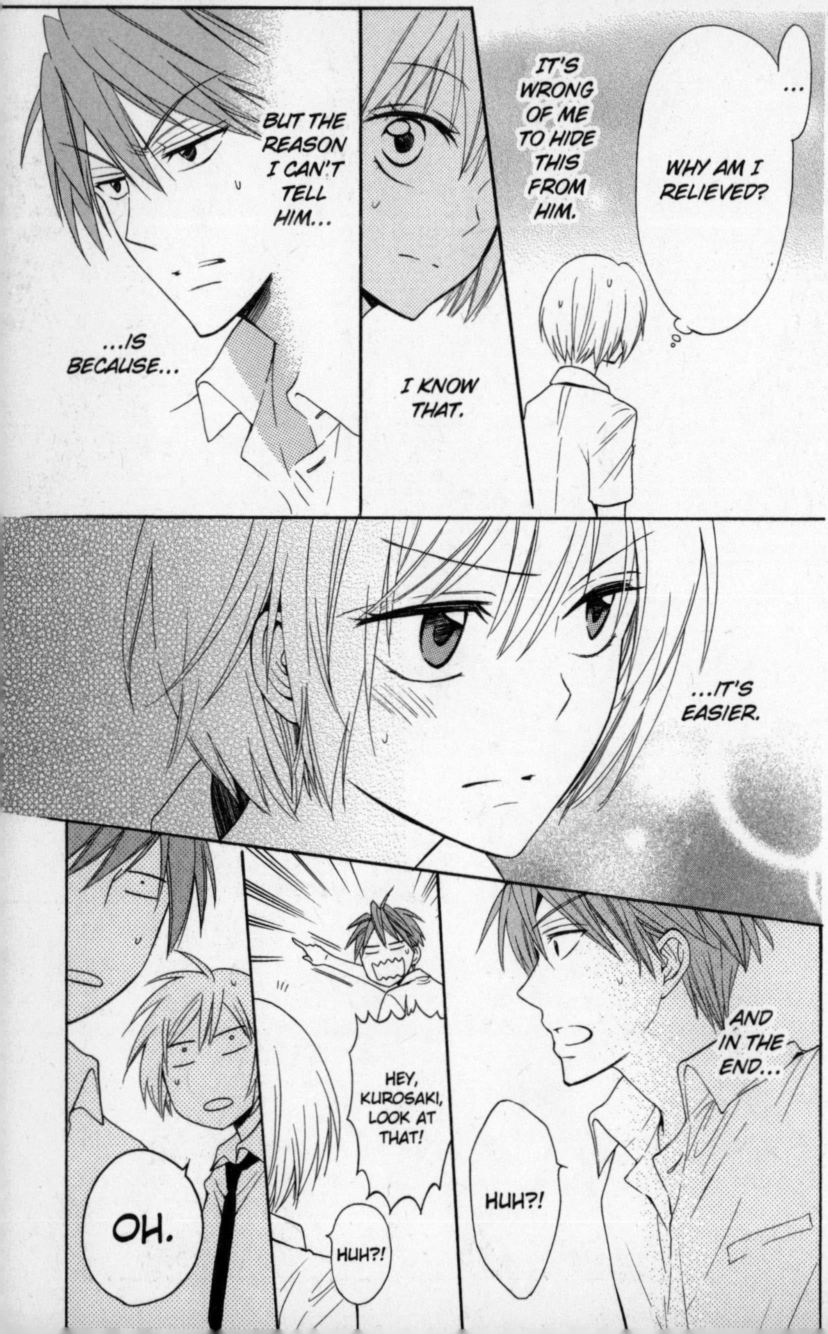
...
WHY AM I RELIEVED?
IT'S WRONG OF ME TO HIDE THIS FROM HIM.
I KNOW THAT.
BUT THE REASON I CAN'T TELL HIM...
...IS BECAUSE...
...IT'S EASIER.
AND IN THE END...
HUH?!
HEY, KUROSAKI, LOOK AT THAT!
HUH?!
OH.

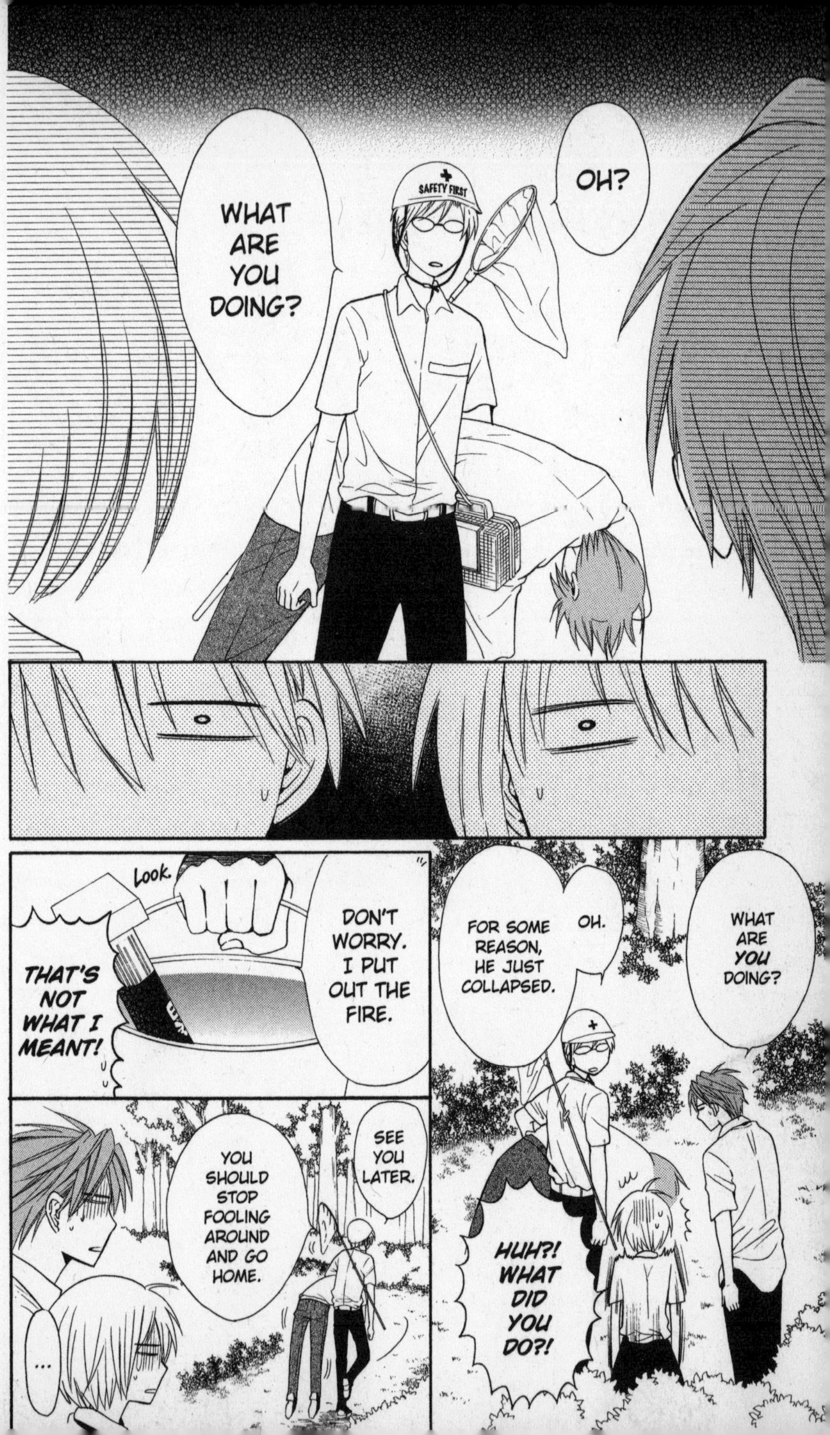
OH?
WHAT ARE YOU DOING?
WHAT ARE YOU DOING?
OH.
FOR SOME REASON, HE JUST COLLAPSED.
HUH?! WHAT DID YOU DO?!
DON'T WORRY. I PUT OUT THE FIRE.
Look.
THAT'S NOT WHAT I MEANT!
SEE YOU LATER.
YOU SHOULD STOP FOOLING AROUND AND GO HOME.
...

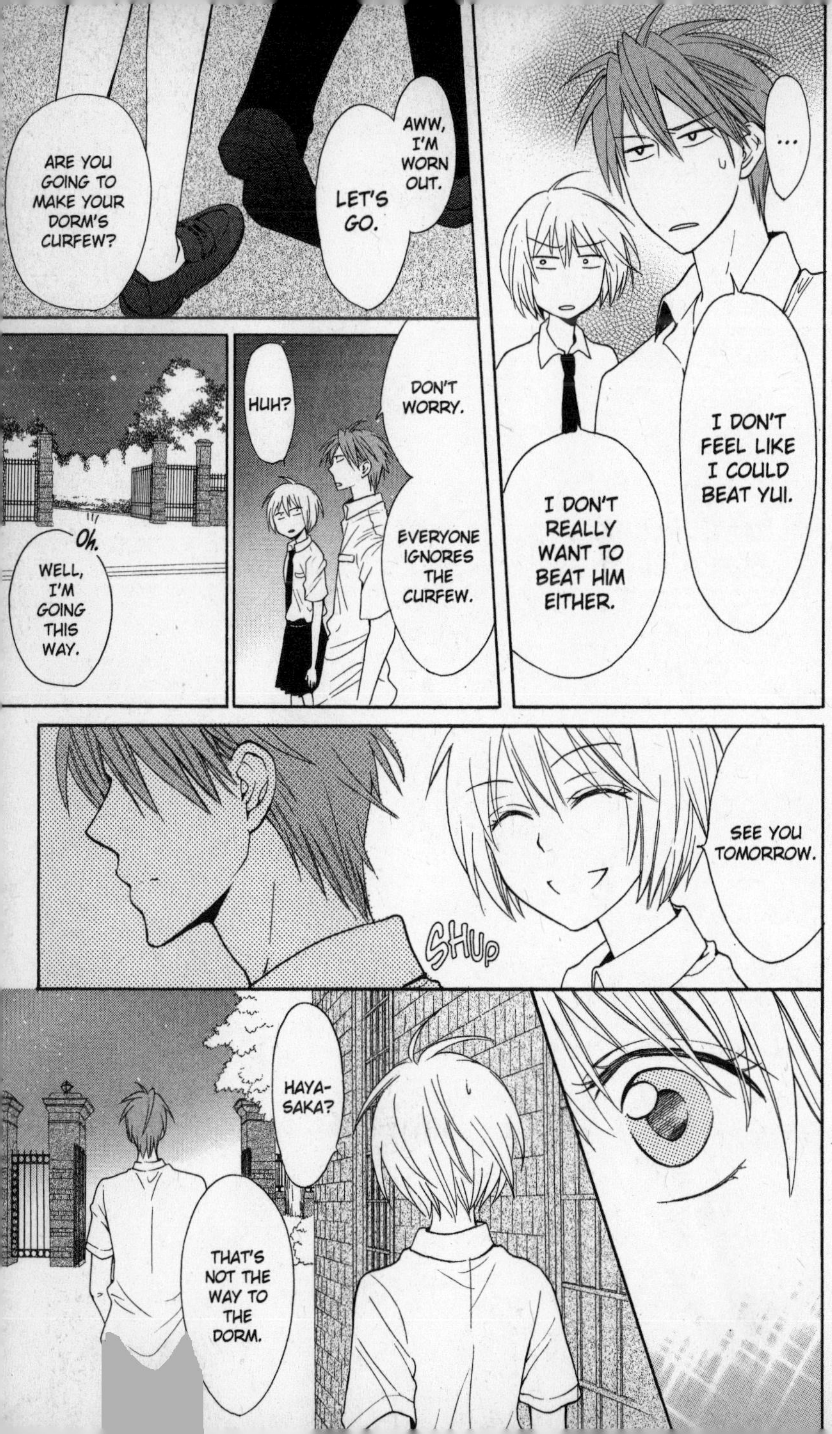
...
I DON'T FEEL LIKE I COULD BEAT YUI.
I DON'T REALLY WANT TO BEAT HIM EITHER.
AWW, I'M WORN OUT.
LET'S GO.
ARE YOU GOING TO MAKE YOUR DORM'S CURFEW?
DON'T WORRY.
EVERYONE IGNORES THE CURFEW.
HUH?
Oh.
WELL, I'M GOING THIS WAY.
SEE YOU TOMORROW.
SHUP
HAYA-SAKA?
THAT'S NOT THE WAY TO THE DORM.

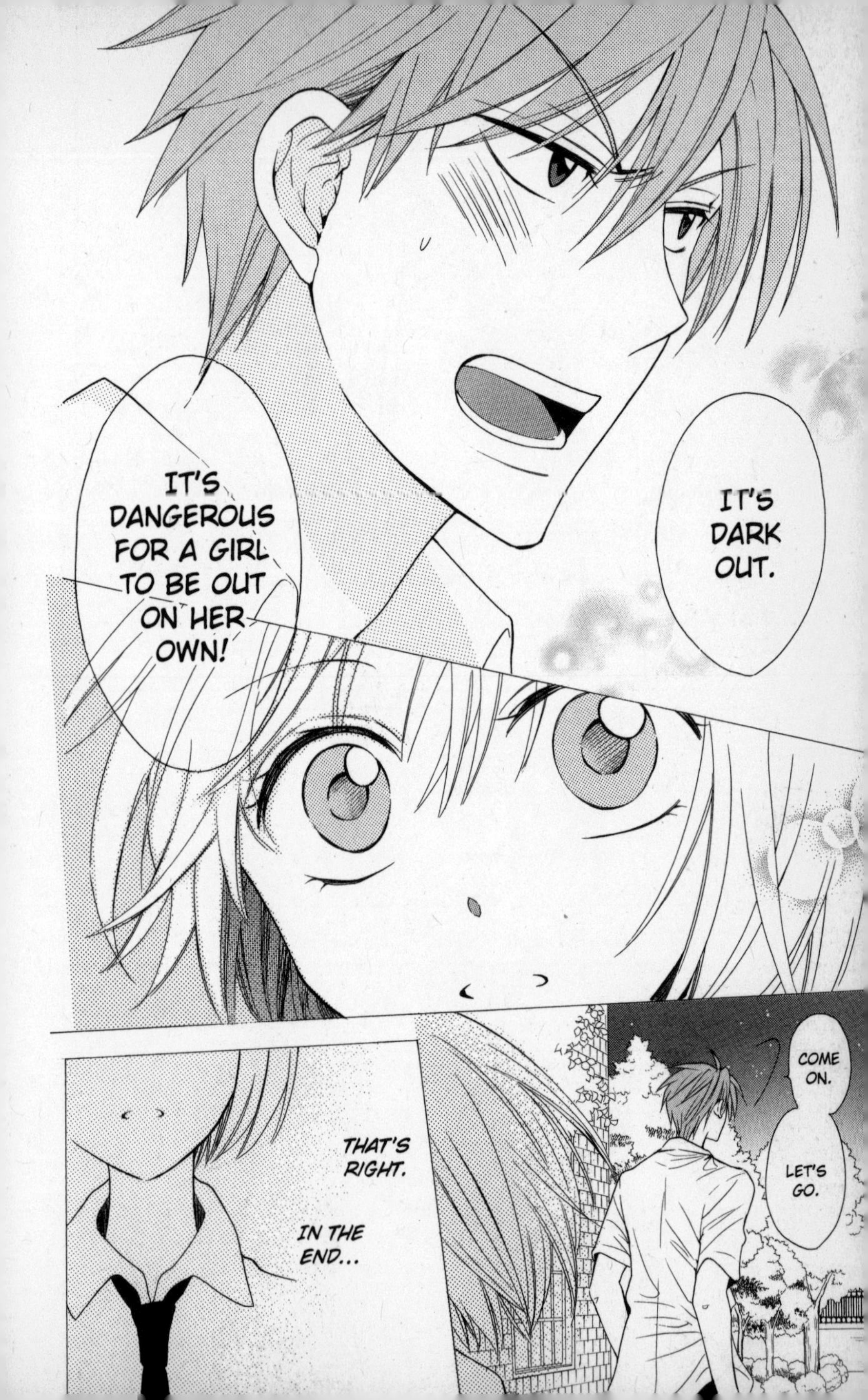
IT'S DARK OUT.
IT'S DANGEROUS FOR A GIRL TO BE OUT ON HER OWN!
COME ON.
LET'S GO.
THAT'S RIGHT.
IN THE END...

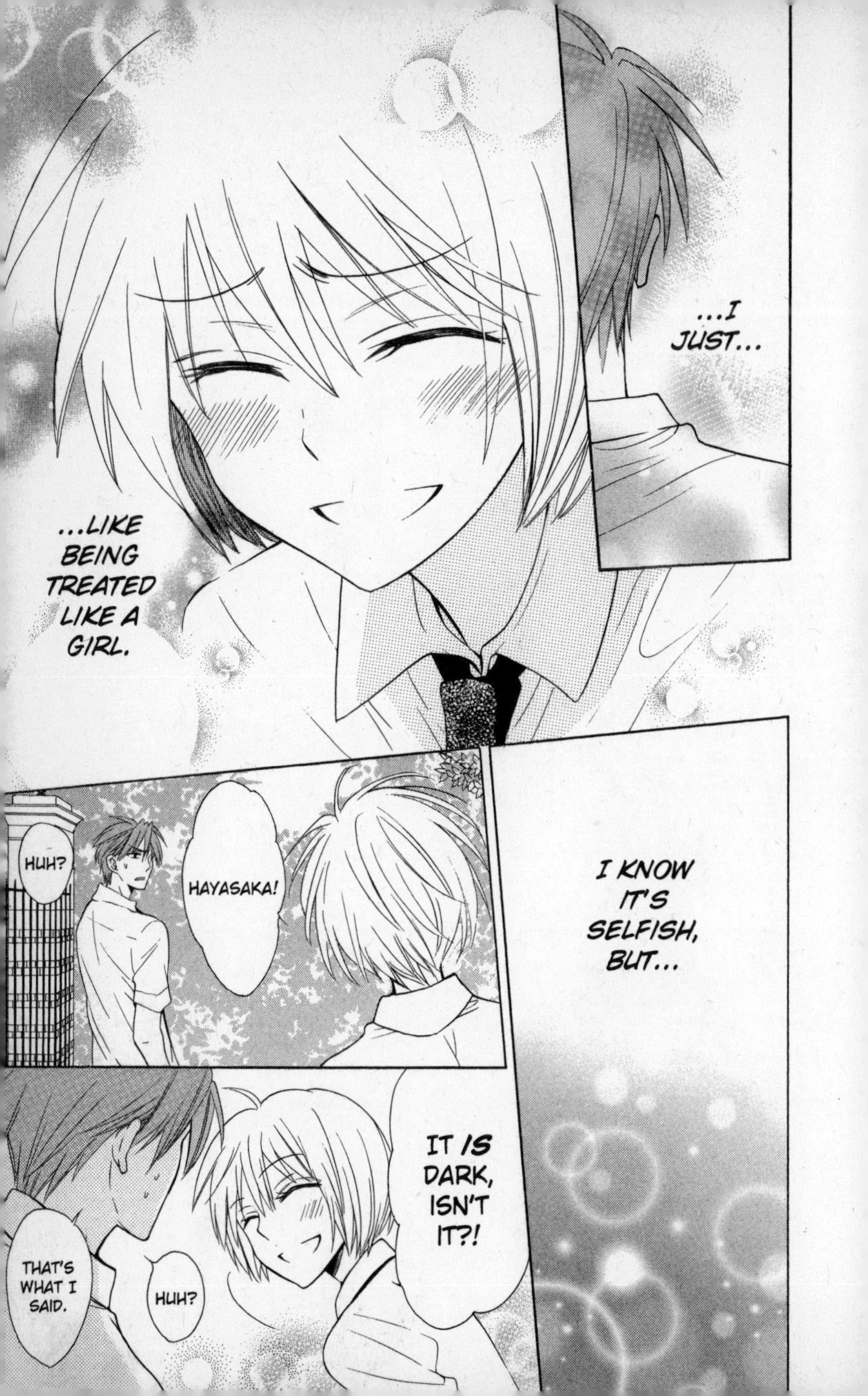
...I JUST...
...LIKE BEING TREATED LIKE A GIRL.
I KNOW IT'S SELFISH, BUT...
HAYASAKA!
HUH?
IT *IS* DARK, ISN'T IT?!
HUH?
THAT'S WHAT I SAID.

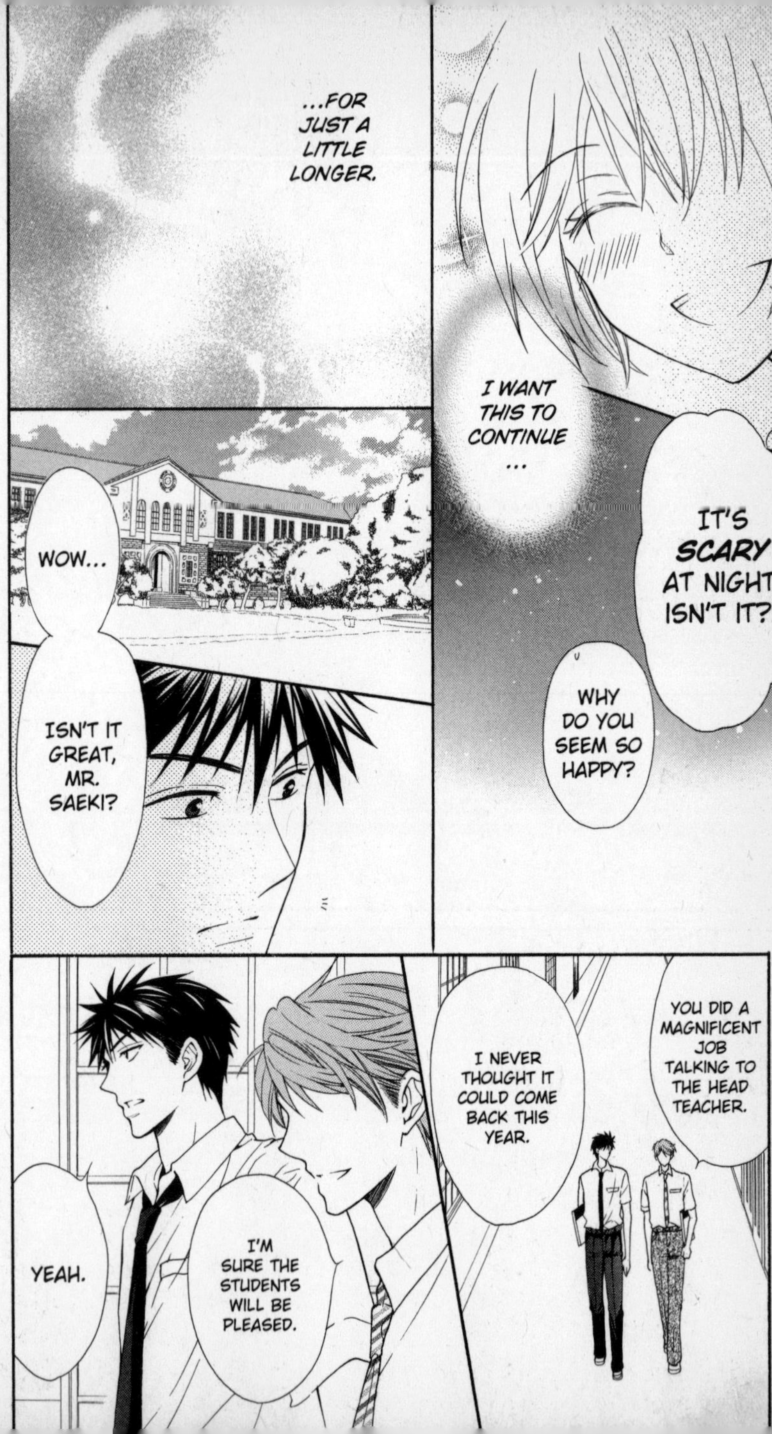
I WANT THIS TO CONTINUE ...
IT'S SCARY AT NIGHT, ISN'T IT?!
WHY DO YOU SEEM SO HAPPY?
...FOR JUST A LITTLE LONGER.
WOW...
ISN'T IT GREAT, MR. SAEKI?
YOU DID A MAGNIFICENT JOB TALKING TO THE HEAD TEACHER.
I NEVER THOUGHT IT COULD COME BACK THIS YEAR.
I'M SURE THE STUDENTS WILL BE PLEASED.
YEAH.

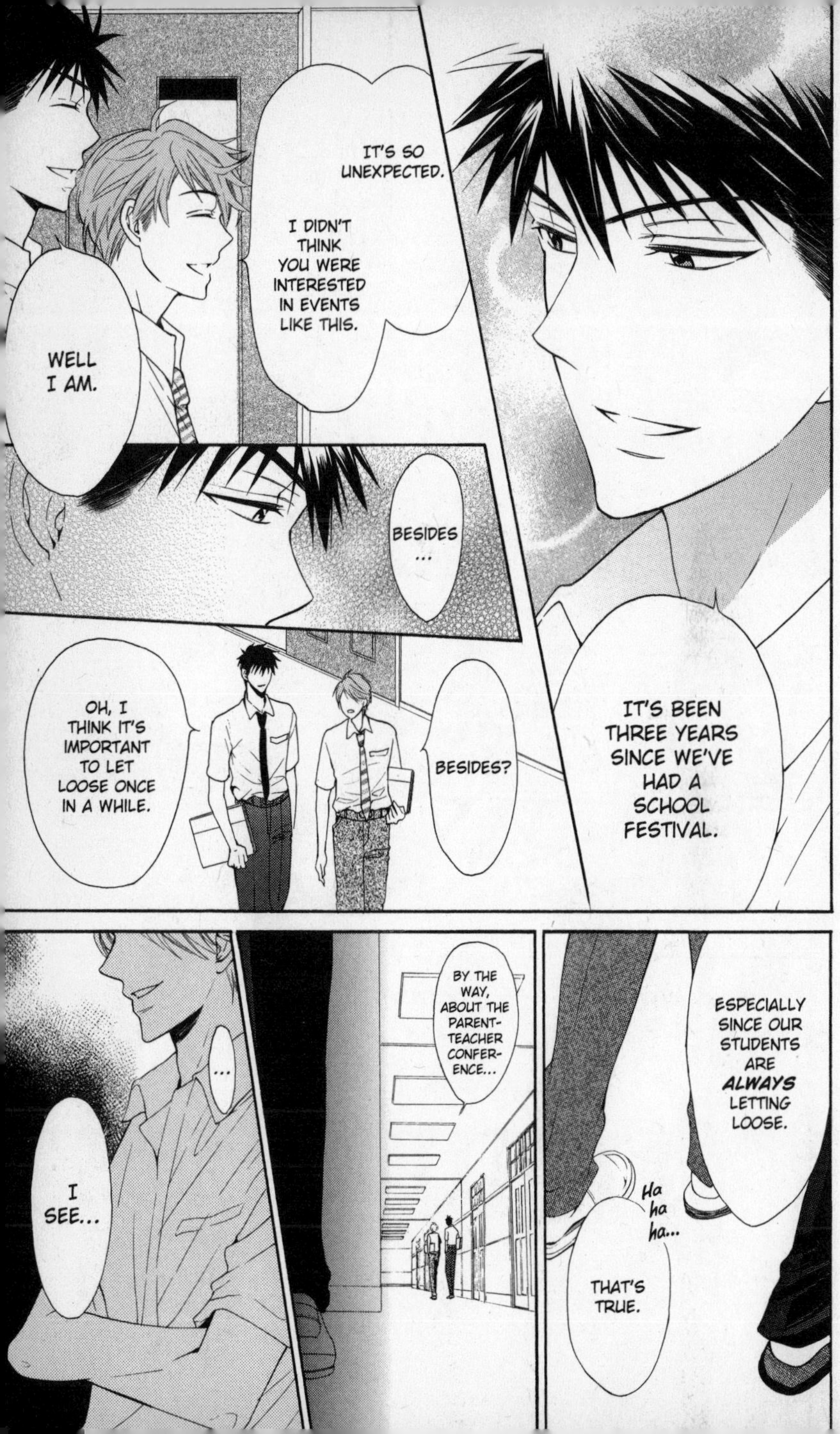
IT'S SO UNEXPECTED.
I DIDN'T THINK YOU WERE INTERESTED IN EVENTS LIKE THIS.
WELL I AM.
BESIDES...
BESIDES?
OH, I THINK IT'S IMPORTANT TO LET LOOSE ONCE IN A WHILE.
IT'S BEEN THREE YEARS SINCE WE'VE HAD A SCHOOL FESTIVAL.
ESPECIALLY SINCE OUR STUDENTS ARE ***ALWAYS*** LETTING LOOSE.
Ha ha ha...
THAT'S TRUE.
BY THE WAY, ABOUT THE PARENT-TEACHER CONFERENCE...
...
I SEE...

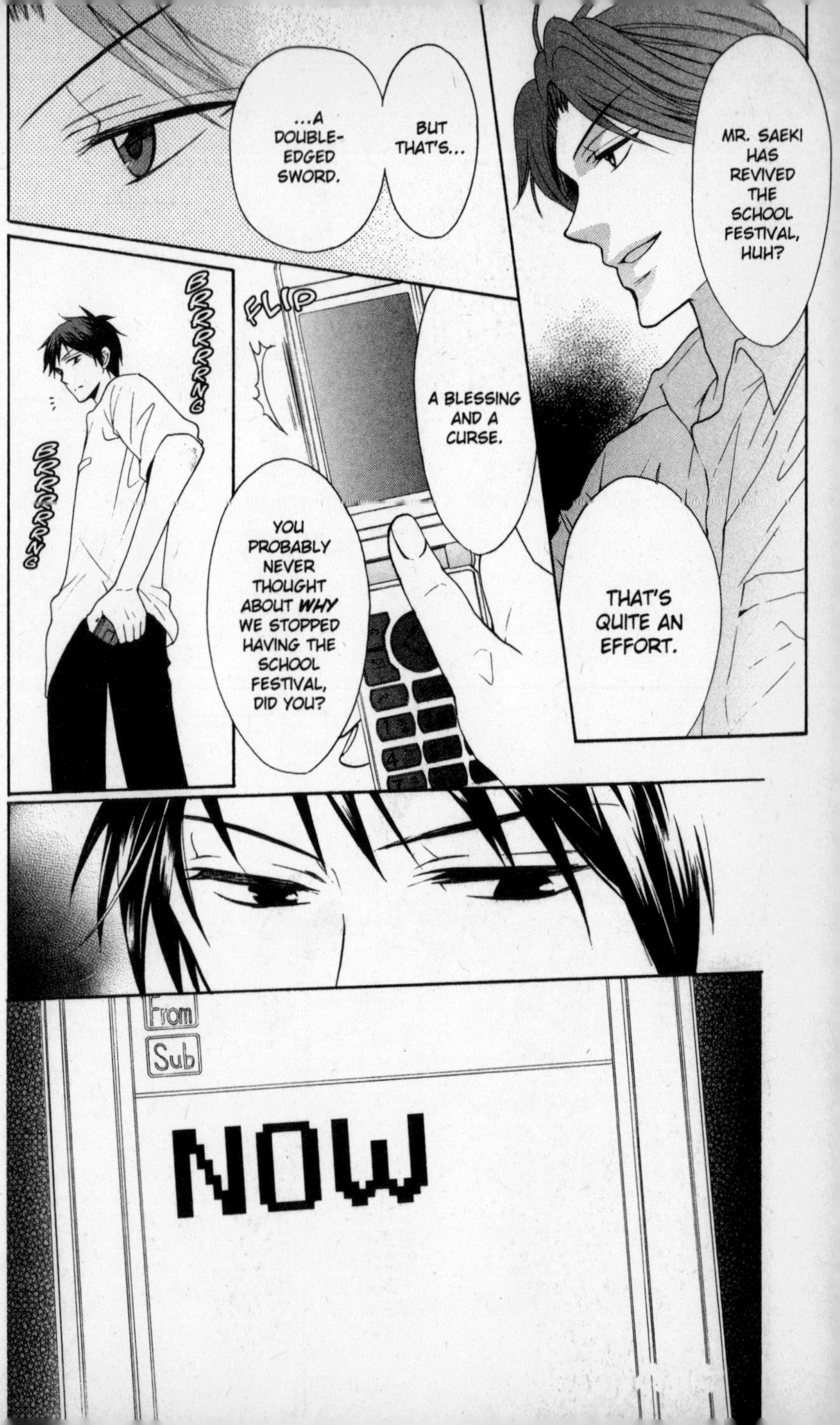
MR. SAEKI HAS REVIVED THE SCHOOL FESTIVAL, HUH?
THAT'S QUITE AN EFFORT.
BUT THAT'S...
...A DOUBLE-EDGED SWORD.
FLIP
A BLESSING AND A CURSE.
YOU PROBABLY NEVER THOUGHT ABOUT WHY WE STOPPED HAVING THE SCHOOL FESTIVAL, DID YOU?
BRRRRRRNG
BRRRRRRNG
From
Sub
NOW

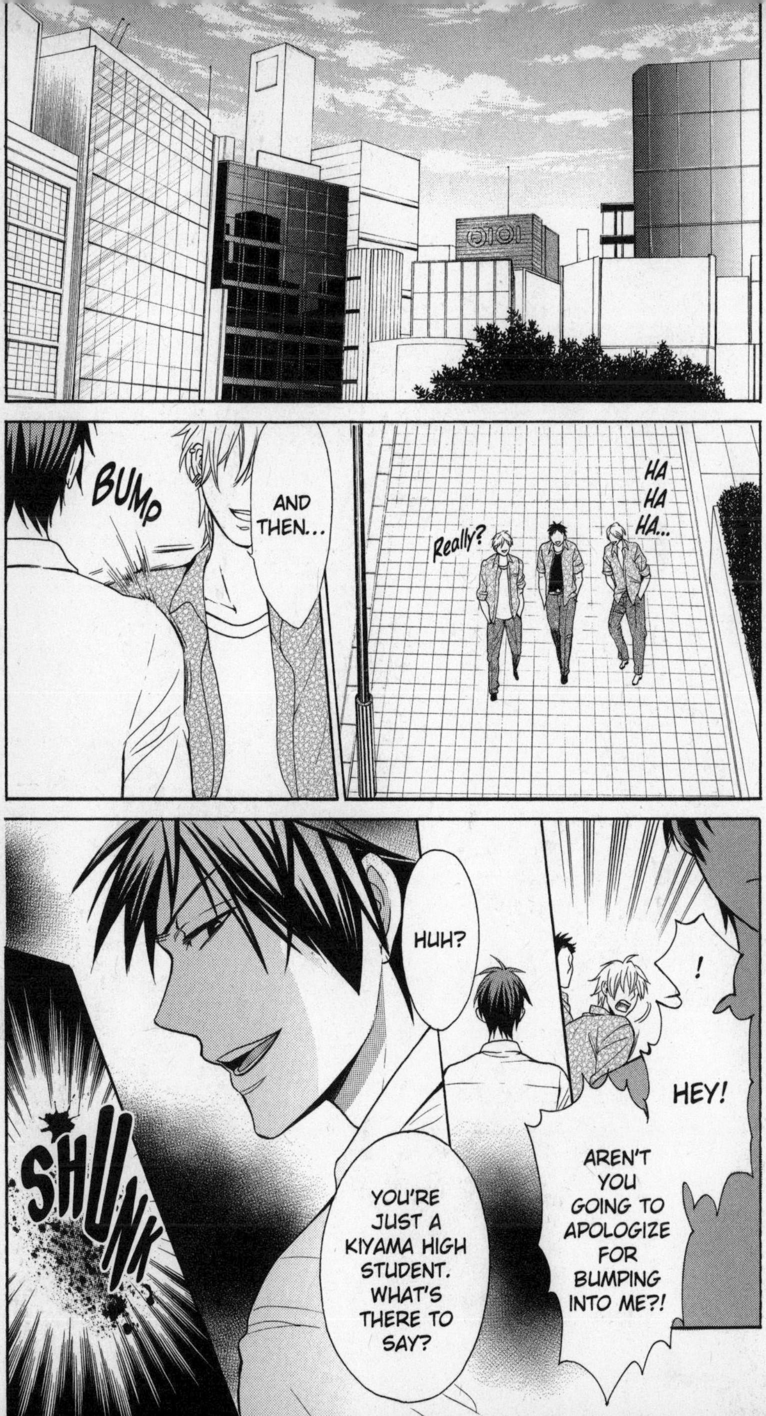
HA HA HA...
Really?
AND THEN...
BUMP
!
HEY!
AREN'T YOU GOING TO APOLOGIZE FOR BUMPING INTO ME?!
HUH?
YOU'RE JUST A KIYAMA HIGH STUDENT. WHAT'S THERE TO SAY?
SHUNK

Chapter 45

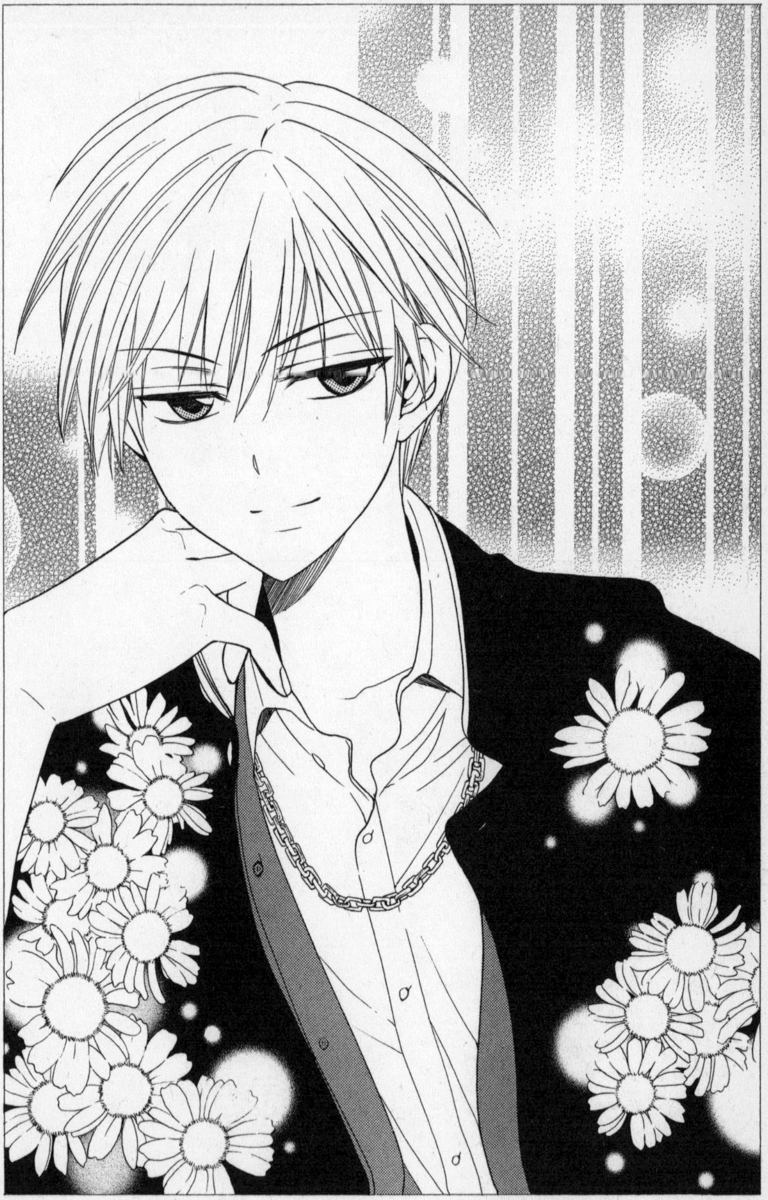

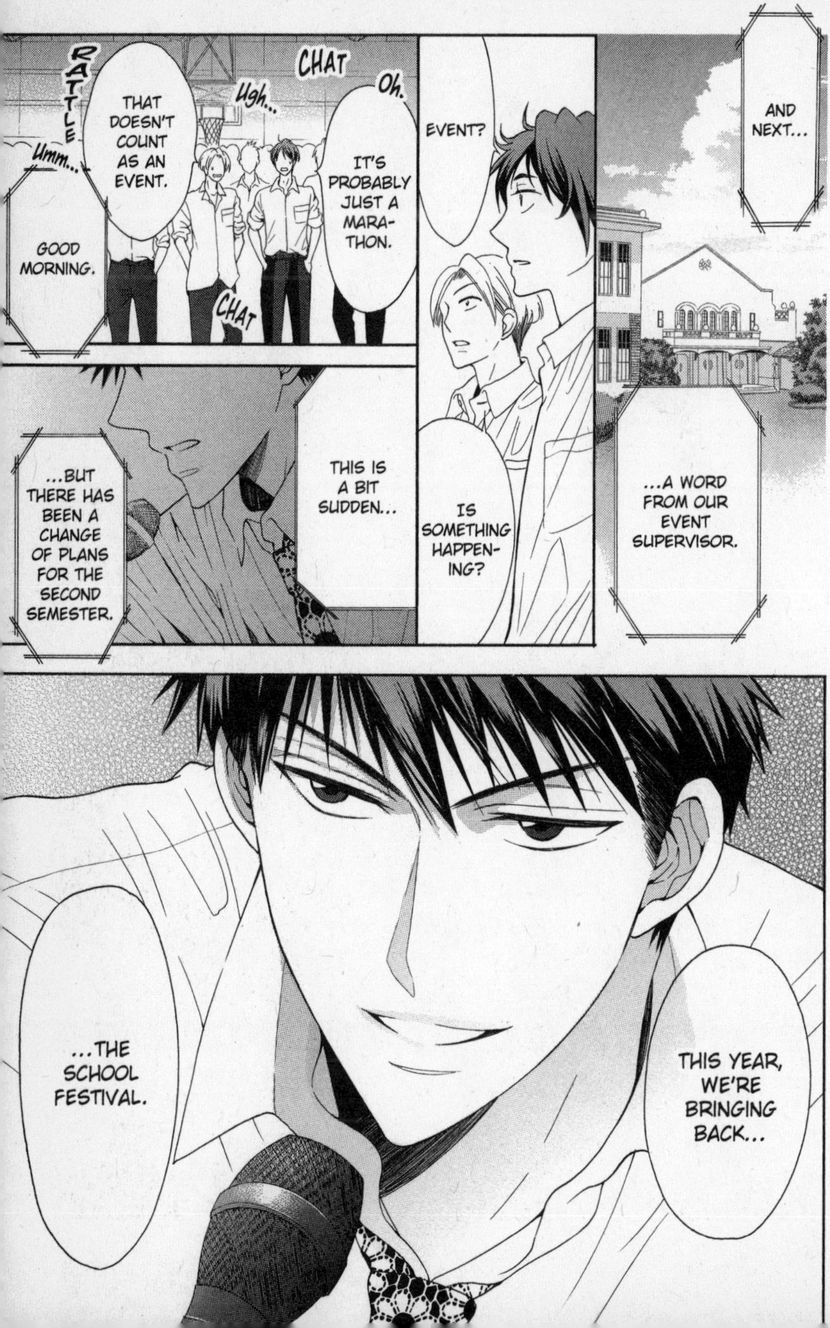
AND NEXT...
...A WORD FROM OUR EVENT SUPERVISOR.
EVENT?
IS SOMETHING HAPPENING?
CHAT
Oh.
IT'S PROBABLY JUST A MARATHON.
Ugh...
THAT DOESN'T COUNT AS AN EVENT.
RATTLE
Umm...
GOOD MORNING.
CHAT
THIS IS A BIT SUDDEN...
...BUT THERE HAS BEEN A CHANGE OF PLANS FOR THE SECOND SEMESTER.
THIS YEAR, WE'RE BRINGING BACK...
...THE SCHOOL FESTIVAL.

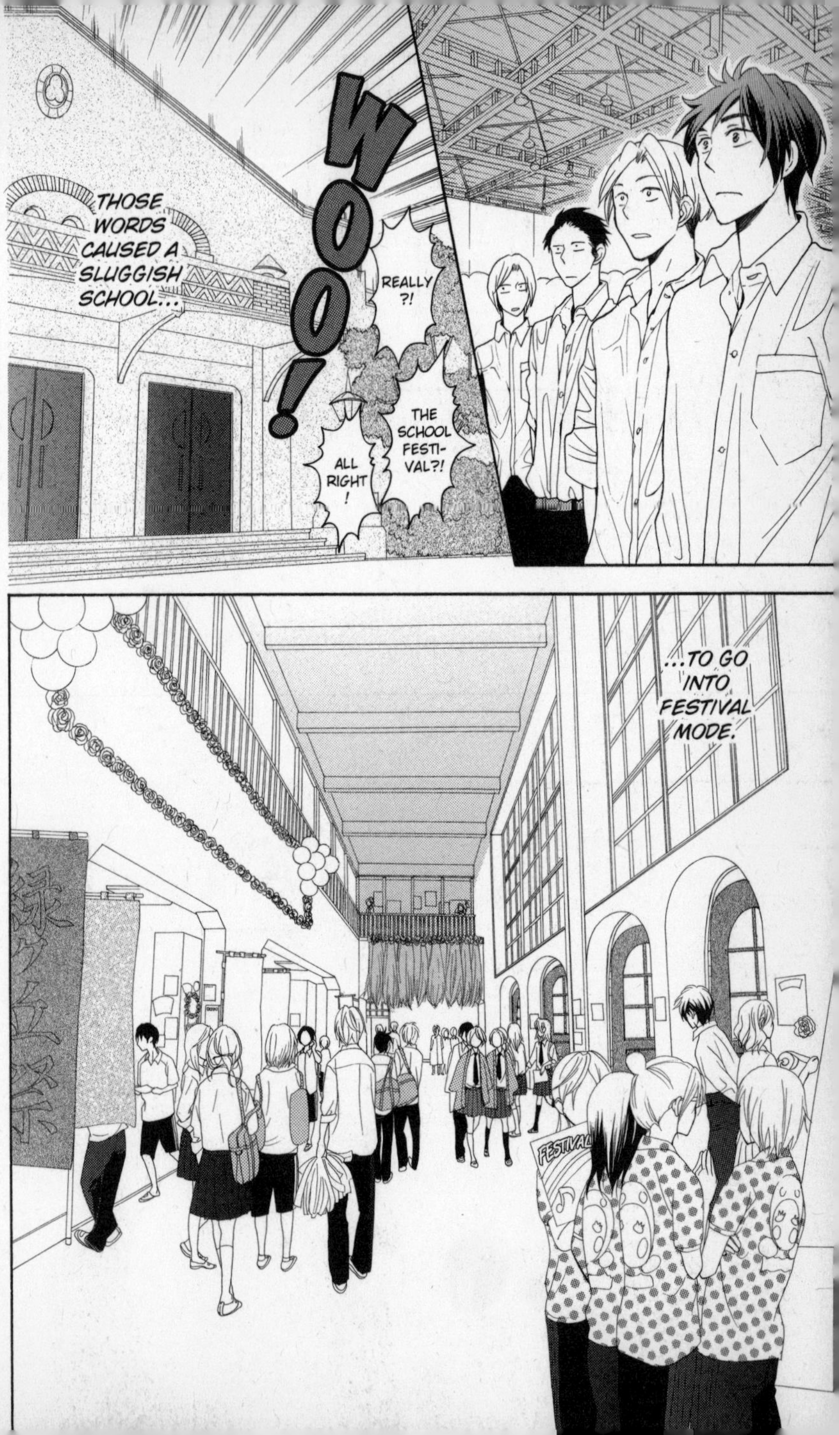
WOO!
REALLY?!
THE SCHOOL FESTI-VAL?!
ALL RIGHT!
THOSE WORDS CAUSED A SLUGGISH SCHOOL...
...TO GO INTO FESTIVAL MODE.

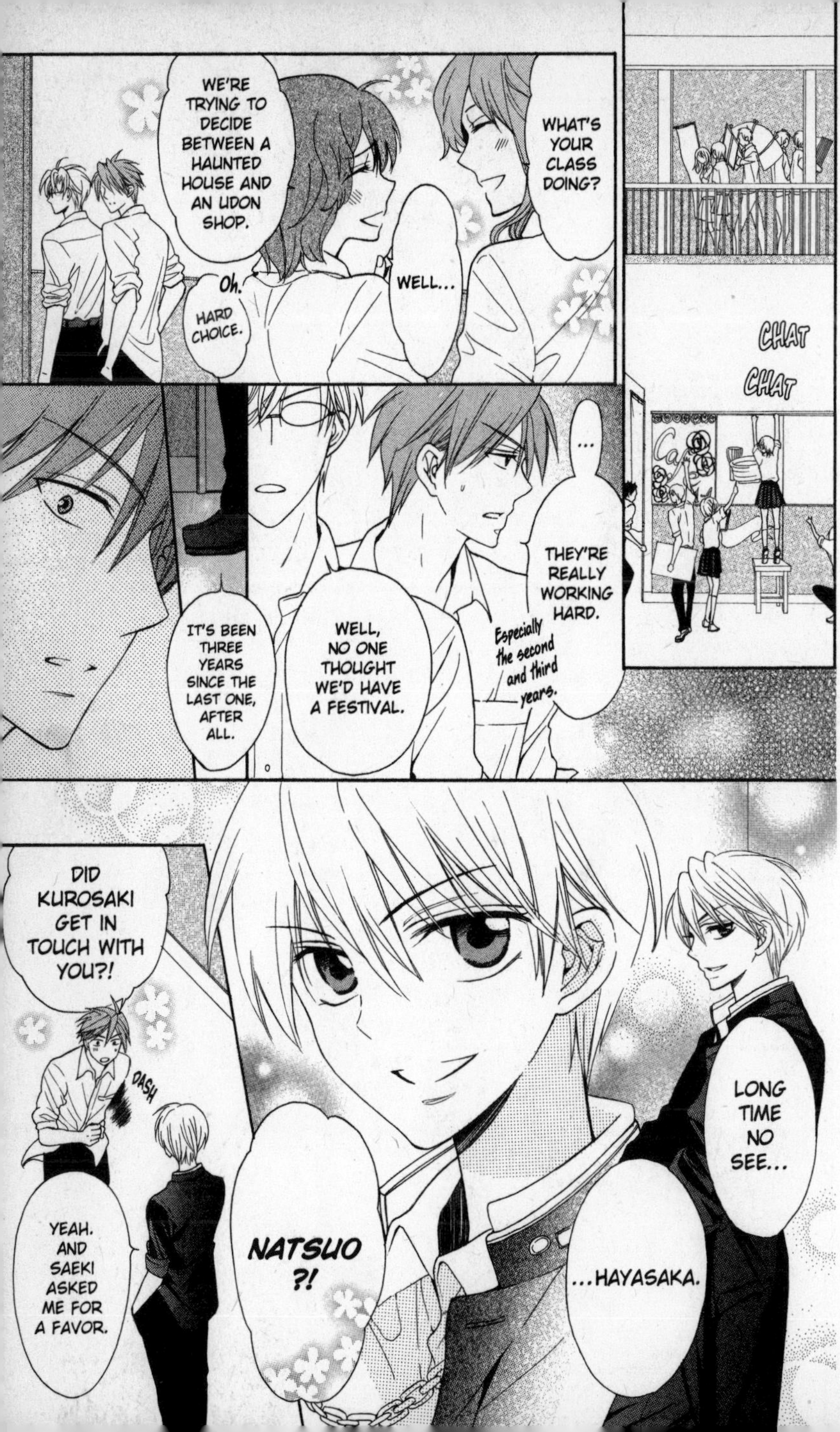
CHAT
CHAT
WHAT'S YOUR CLASS DOING?
WELL...
WE'RE TRYING TO DECIDE BETWEEN A HAUNTED HOUSE AND AN UDON SHOP.
Oh. HARD CHOICE.
...
THEY'RE REALLY WORKING HARD.
Especially the second and third years.
WELL, NO ONE THOUGHT WE'D HAVE A FESTIVAL.
IT'S BEEN THREE YEARS SINCE THE LAST ONE, AFTER ALL.
LONG TIME NO SEE...
...HAYASAKA.
NATSUO ?!
DID KUROSAKI GET IN TOUCH WITH YOU?!
DASH
YEAH. AND SAEKI ASKED ME FOR A FAVOR.

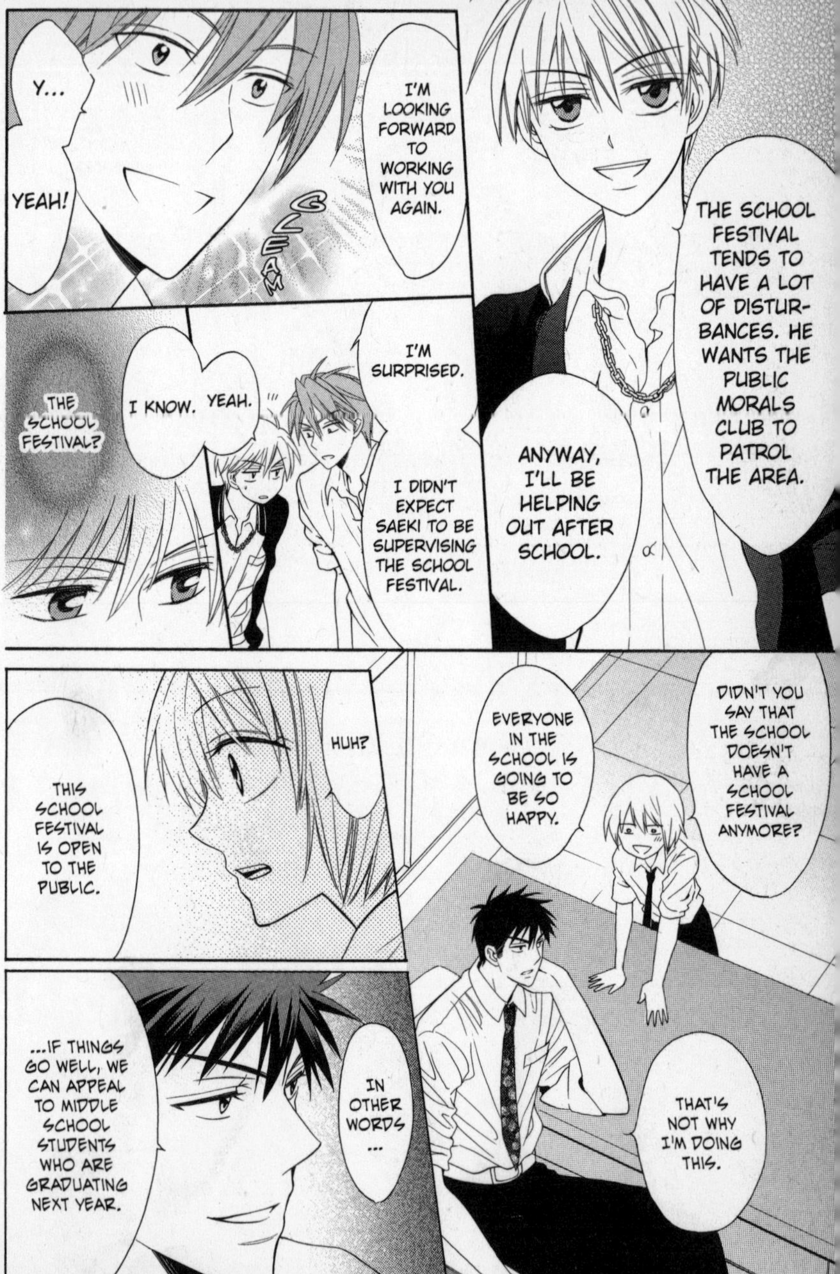
THE SCHOOL FESTIVAL TENDS TO HAVE A LOT OF DISTURBANCES. HE WANTS THE PUBLIC MORALS CLUB TO PATROL THE AREA.
ANYWAY, I'LL BE HELPING OUT AFTER SCHOOL.
I'M LOOKING FORWARD TO WORKING WITH YOU AGAIN.
GLEAM
Y...
YEAH!
I'M SURPRISED.
I DIDN'T EXPECT SAEKI TO BE SUPERVISING THE SCHOOL FESTIVAL.
YEAH.
I KNOW.
THE SCHOOL FESTIVAL?
DIDN'T YOU SAY THAT THE SCHOOL DOESN'T HAVE A SCHOOL FESTIVAL ANYMORE?
EVERYONE IN THE SCHOOL IS GOING TO BE SO HAPPY.
THAT'S NOT WHY I'M DOING THIS.
HUH?
THIS SCHOOL FESTIVAL IS OPEN TO THE PUBLIC.
IN OTHER WORDS...
...IF THINGS GO WELL, WE CAN APPEAL TO MIDDLE SCHOOL STUDENTS WHO ARE GRADUATING NEXT YEAR.

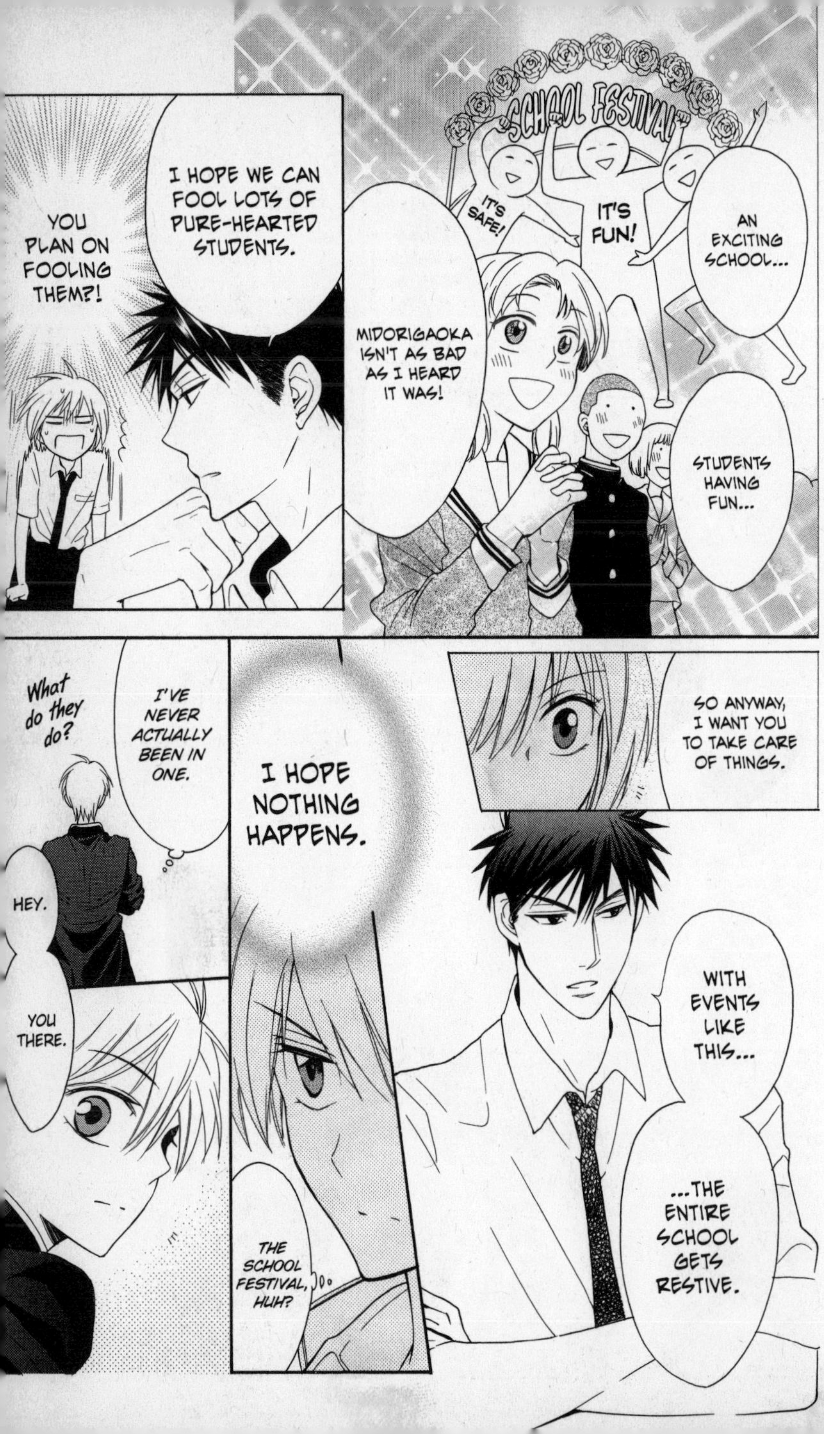
SCHOOL FESTIVAL
AN EXCITING SCHOOL...
IT'S FUN!
IT'S SAFE!
STUDENTS HAVING FUN...
MIDORIGAOKA ISN'T AS BAD AS I HEARD IT WAS!
I HOPE WE CAN FOOL LOTS OF PURE-HEARTED STUDENTS.
YOU PLAN ON FOOLING THEM?!
SO ANYWAY, I WANT YOU TO TAKE CARE OF THINGS.
WITH EVENTS LIKE THIS...
...THE ENTIRE SCHOOL GETS RESTIVE.
I HOPE NOTHING HAPPENS.
THE SCHOOL FESTIVAL, HUH?
I'VE NEVER ACTUALLY BEEN IN ONE.
What do they do?
HEY.
YOU THERE.

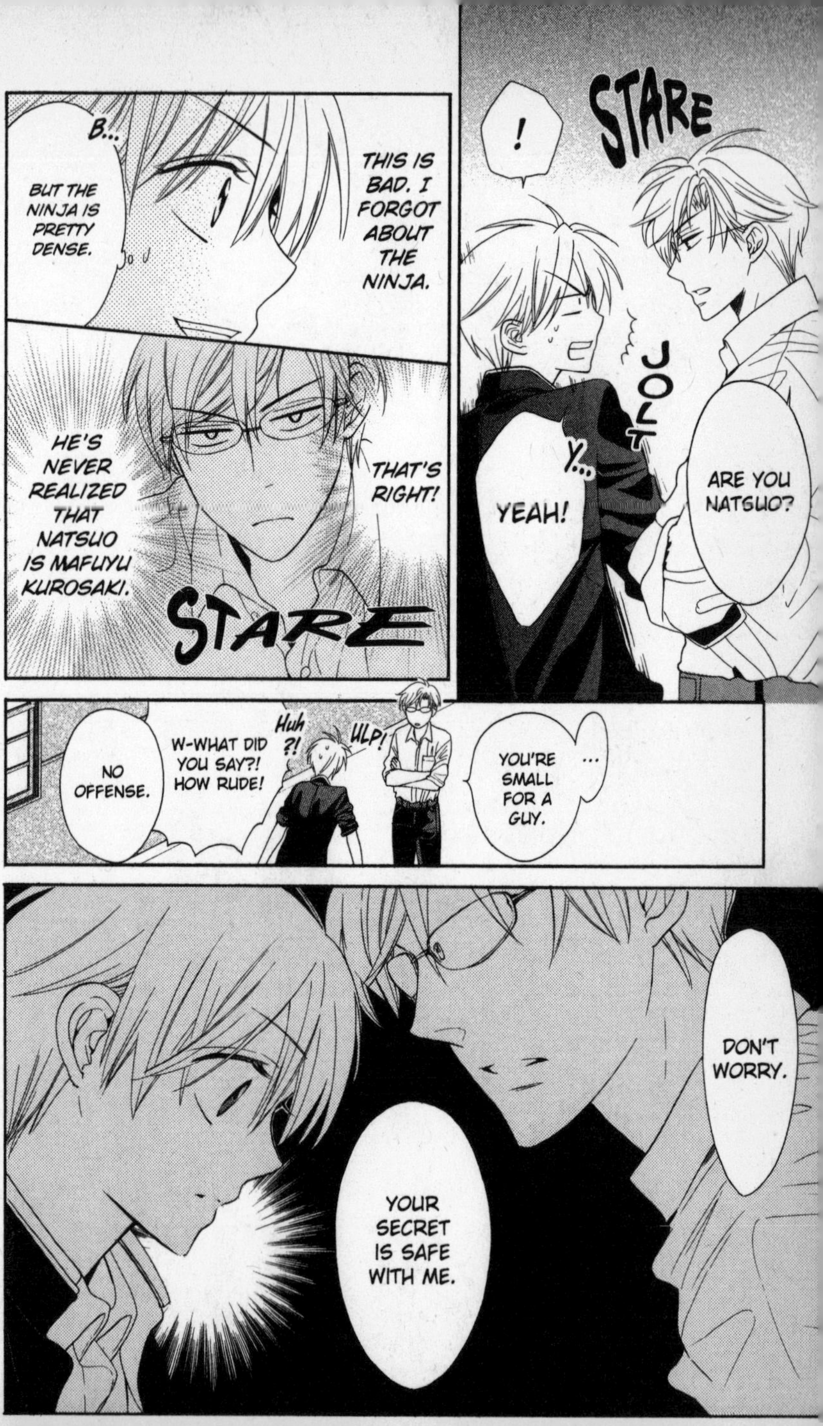
STARE
!
ARE YOU NATSUO?
JOLT
Y...
YEAH!
THIS IS BAD. I FORGOT ABOUT THE NINJA.
B...
BUT THE NINJA IS PRETTY DENSE.
THAT'S RIGHT!
HE'S NEVER REALIZED THAT NATSUO IS MAFUYU KUROSAKI.
STARE
...
YOU'RE SMALL FOR A GUY.
ULP!
Huh ?!
W-WHAT DID YOU SAY?! HOW RUDE!
NO OFFENSE.
DON'T WORRY.
YOUR SECRET IS SAFE WITH ME.

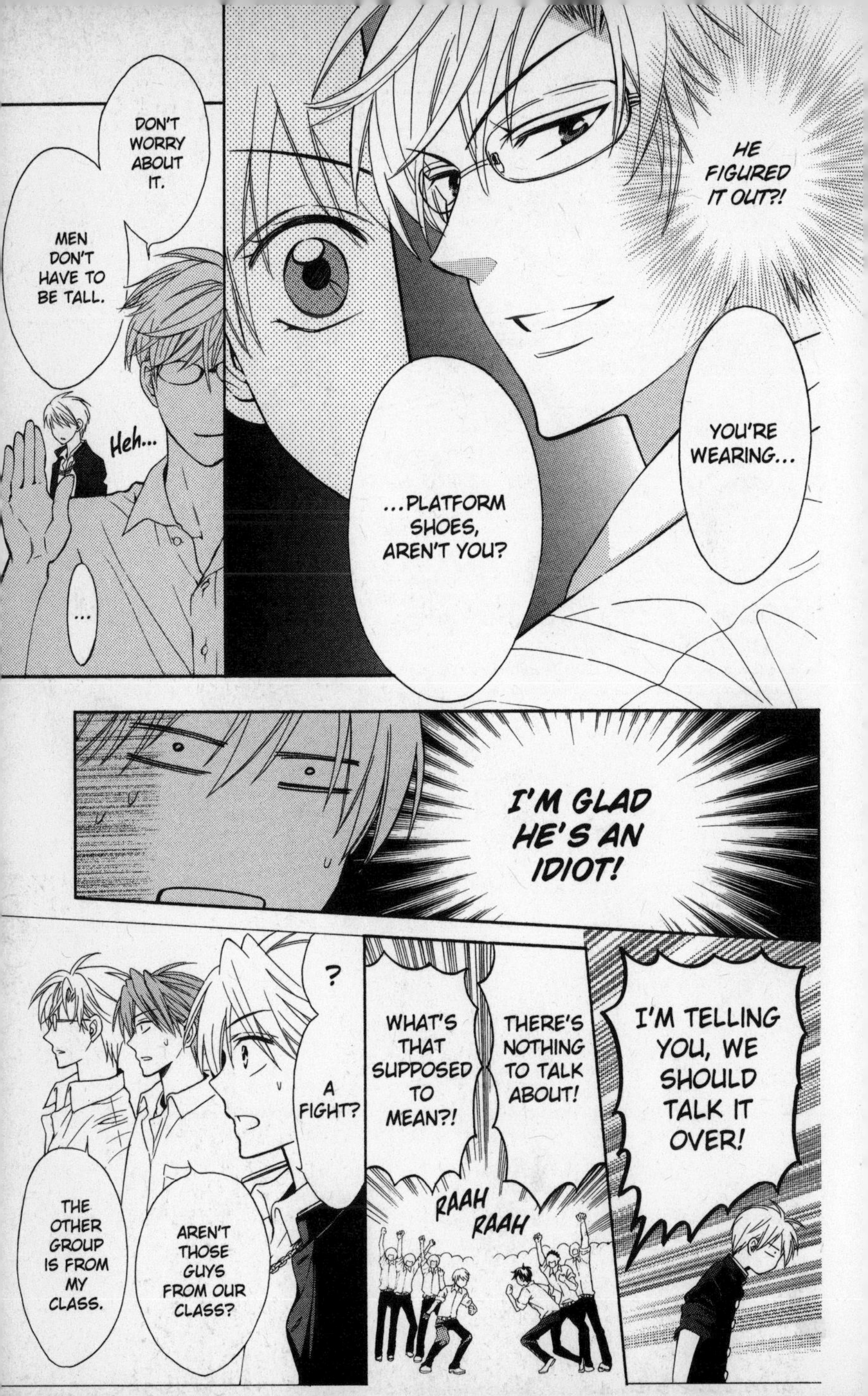
HE FIGURED IT OUT?!
YOU'RE WEARING...
...PLATFORM SHOES, AREN'T YOU?
DON'T WORRY ABOUT IT.
MEN DON'T HAVE TO BE TALL.
Heh...
...
I'M GLAD HE'S AN IDIOT!
I'M TELLING YOU, WE SHOULD TALK IT OVER!
THERE'S NOTHING TO TALK ABOUT!
WHAT'S THAT SUPPOSED TO MEAN?!
RAAH RAAH
?
A FIGHT?
AREN'T THOSE GUYS FROM OUR CLASS?
THE OTHER GROUP IS FROM MY CLASS.

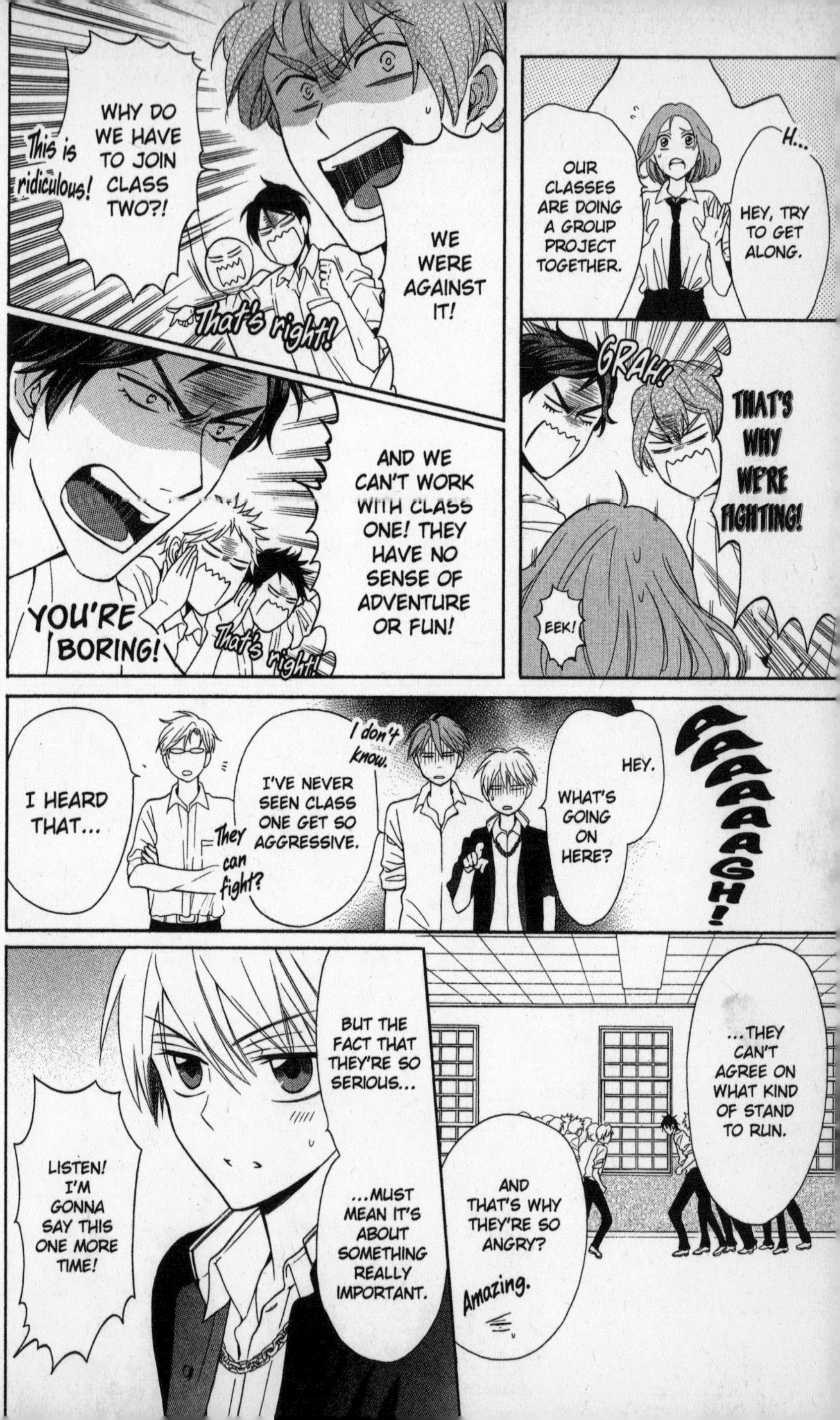
H... HEY, TRY TO GET ALONG.
OUR CLASSES ARE DOING A GROUP PROJECT TOGETHER.
GRAH!
THAT'S WHY WE'RE FIGHTING!
EEK!
WE WERE AGAINST IT!
WHY DO WE HAVE TO JOIN CLASS TWO?!
This is ridiculous!
That's right!
AND WE CAN'T WORK WITH CLASS ONE! THEY HAVE NO SENSE OF ADVENTURE OR FUN!
That's right!
YOU'RE BORING!
AAAAAAGH!
HEY. WHAT'S GOING ON HERE?
I don't know.
I'VE NEVER SEEN CLASS ONE GET SO AGGRESSIVE.
They can fight?
I HEARD THAT...
...THEY CAN'T AGREE ON WHAT KIND OF STAND TO RUN.
AND THAT'S WHY THEY'RE SO ANGRY?
Amazing.
BUT THE FACT THAT THEY'RE SO SERIOUS...
...MUST MEAN IT'S ABOUT SOMETHING REALLY IMPORTANT.
LISTEN! I'M GONNA SAY THIS ONE MORE TIME!

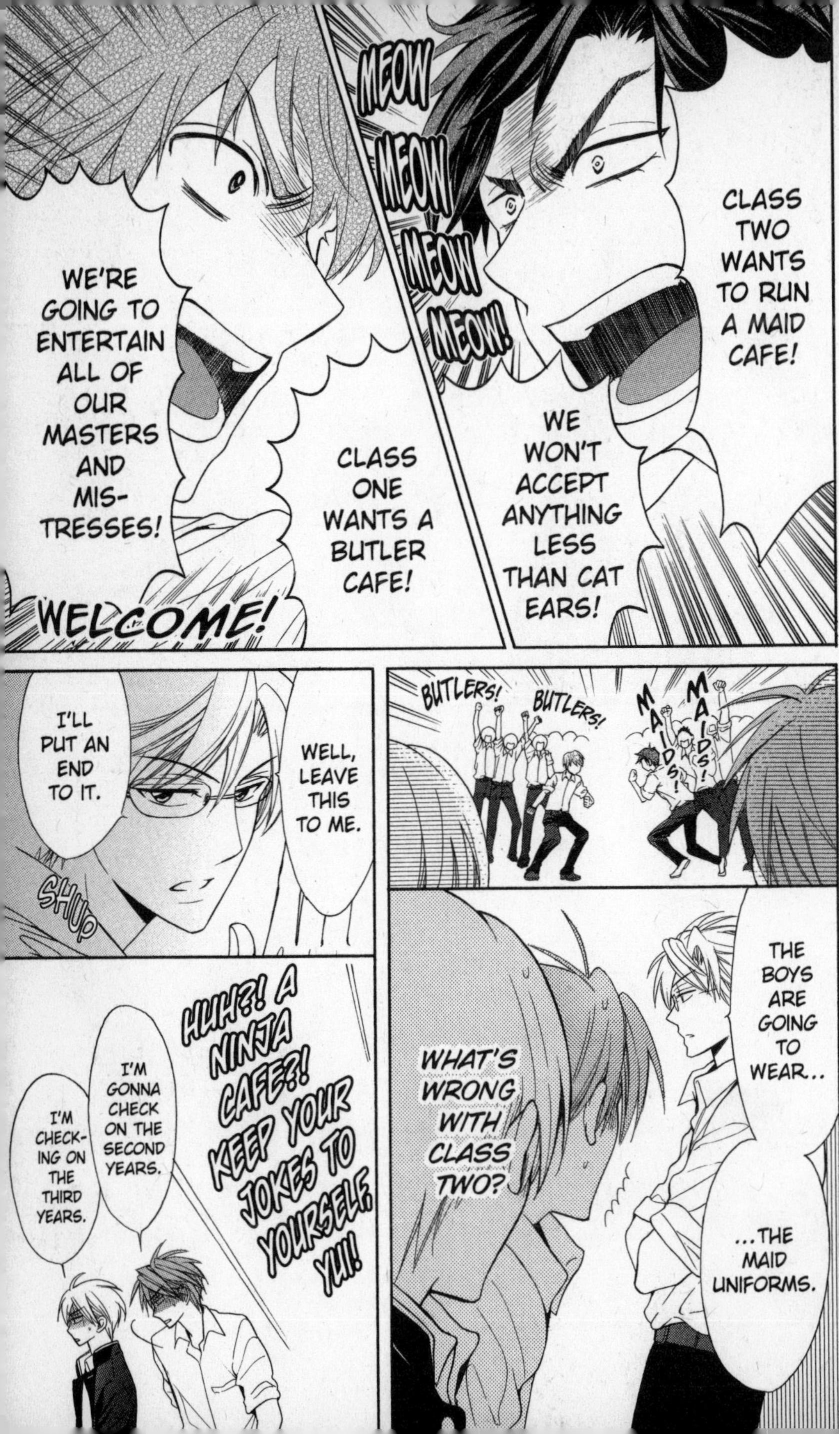
CLASS TWO WANTS TO RUN A MAID CAFE!
MEOW MEOW MEOW MEOW!
WE WON'T ACCEPT ANYTHING LESS THAN CAT EARS!
CLASS ONE WANTS A BUTLER CAFE!
WE'RE GOING TO ENTERTAIN ALL OF OUR MASTERS AND MIS-TRESSES!
WELCOME!
MAIDS! MAIDS!
BUTLERS! BUTLERS!
THE BOYS ARE GOING TO WEAR...
...THE MAID UNIFORMS.
WHAT'S WRONG WITH CLASS TWO?
WELL, LEAVE THIS TO ME.
I'LL PUT AN END TO IT.
SHUP
HUH?! A NINJA CAFE?! KEEP YOUR JOKES TO YOURSELF, YUI!
I'M GONNA CHECK ON THE SECOND YEARS.
I'M CHECK-ING ON THE THIRD YEARS.

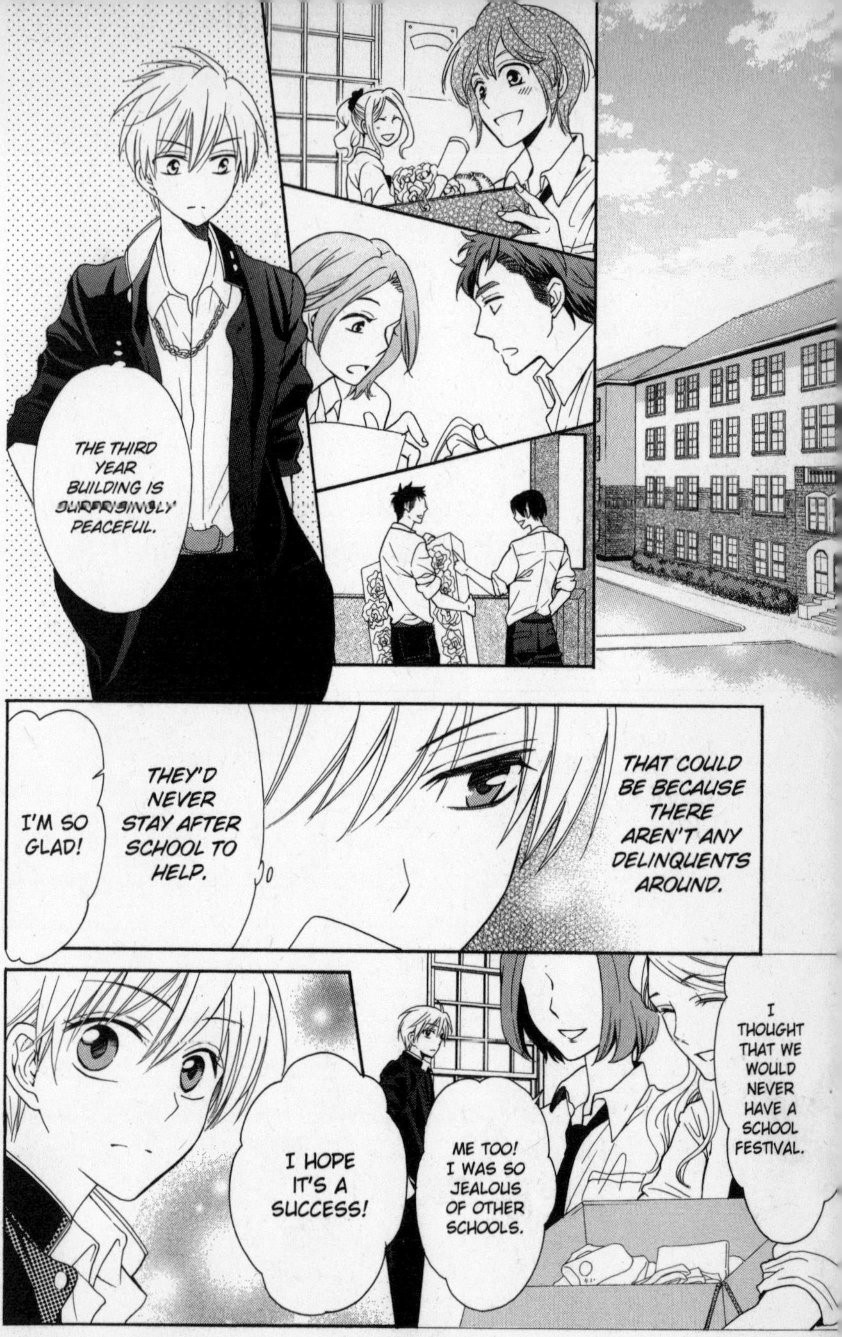
THE THIRD YEAR BUILDING IS SURPRISINGLY PEACEFUL.
THAT COULD BE BECAUSE THERE AREN'T ANY DELINQUENTS AROUND.
THEY'D NEVER STAY AFTER SCHOOL TO HELP.
I'M SO GLAD!
I THOUGHT THAT WE WOULD NEVER HAVE A SCHOOL FESTIVAL.
ME TOO! I WAS SO JEALOUS OF OTHER SCHOOLS.
I HOPE IT'S A SUCCESS!

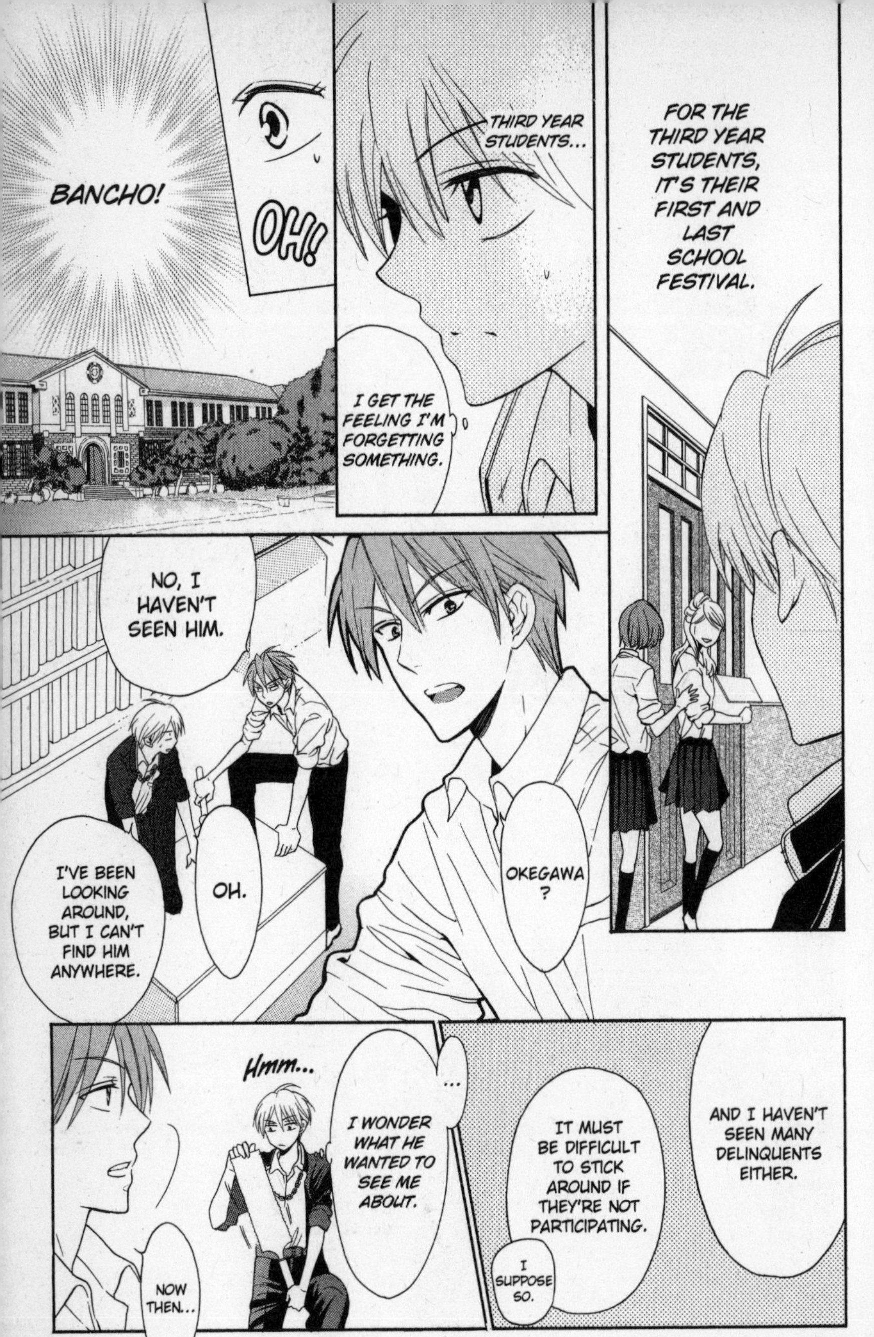
FOR THE THIRD YEAR STUDENTS, IT'S THEIR FIRST AND LAST SCHOOL FESTIVAL.
THIRD YEAR STUDENTS...
I GET THE FEELING I'M FORGETTING SOMETHING.
OH!
BANCHO!
OKEGAWA?
OH.
I'VE BEEN LOOKING AROUND, BUT I CAN'T FIND HIM ANYWHERE.
NO, I HAVEN'T SEEN HIM.
AND I HAVEN'T SEEN MANY DELINQUENTS EITHER.
IT MUST BE DIFFICULT TO STICK AROUND IF THEY'RE NOT PARTICIPATING.
I SUPPOSE SO.
...
I WONDER WHAT HE WANTED TO SEE ME ABOUT.
Hmm...
NOW THEN...

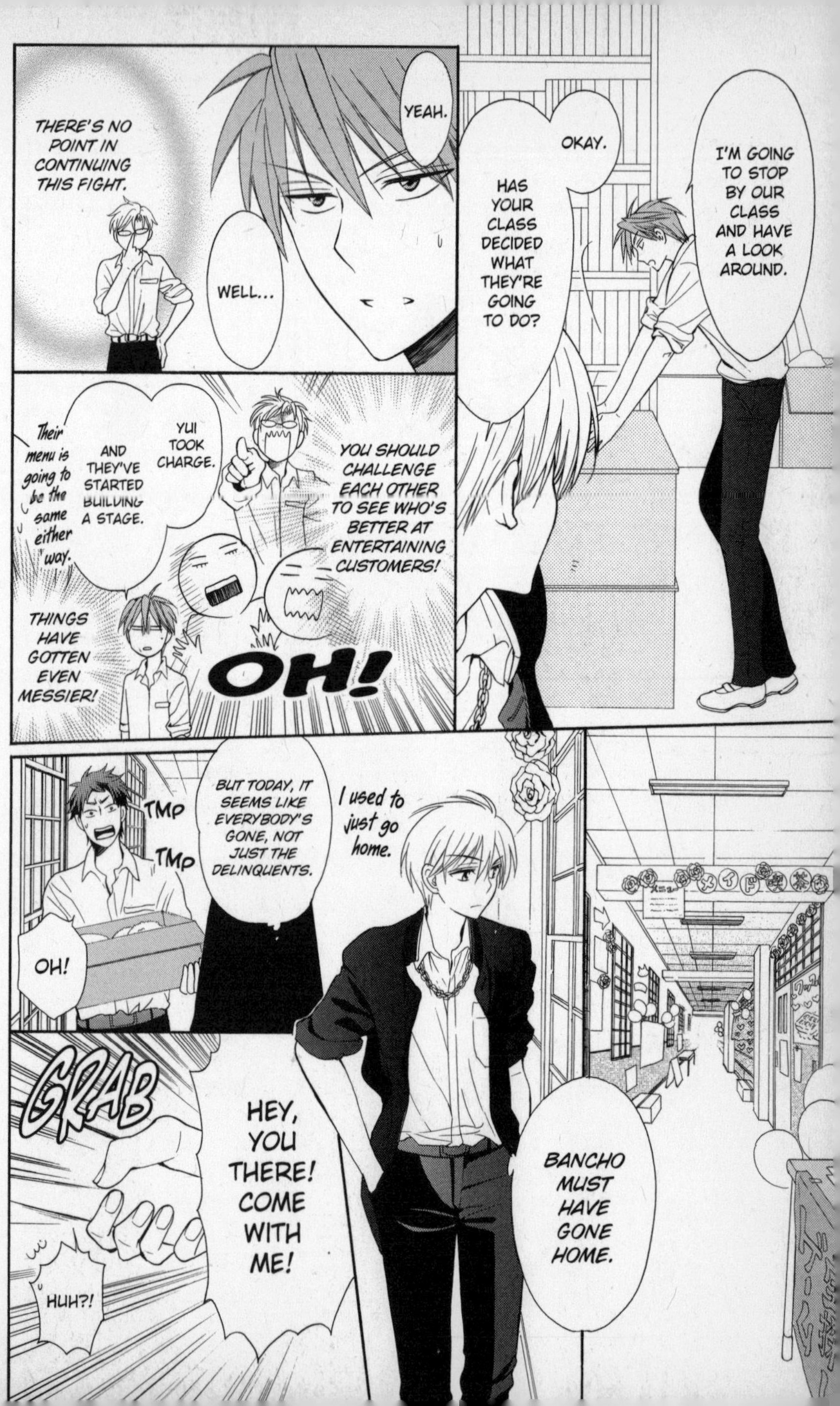
I'M GOING TO STOP BY OUR CLASS AND HAVE A LOOK AROUND.
OKAY.
HAS YOUR CLASS DECIDED WHAT THEY'RE GOING TO DO?
YEAH.
WELL...
THERE'S NO POINT IN CONTINUING THIS FIGHT.
YUI TOOK CHARGE.
AND THEY'VE STARTED BUILDING A STAGE.
Their menu is going to be the same either way.
YOU SHOULD CHALLENGE EACH OTHER TO SEE WHO'S BETTER AT ENTERTAINING CUSTOMERS!
OH!
THINGS HAVE GOTTEN EVEN MESSIER!
BANCHO MUST HAVE GONE HOME.
I used to just go home.
BUT TODAY, IT SEEMS LIKE EVERYBODY'S GONE, NOT JUST THE DELINQUENTS.
TMP
TMP
OH!
GRAB
HEY, YOU THERE! COME WITH ME!
HUH?!

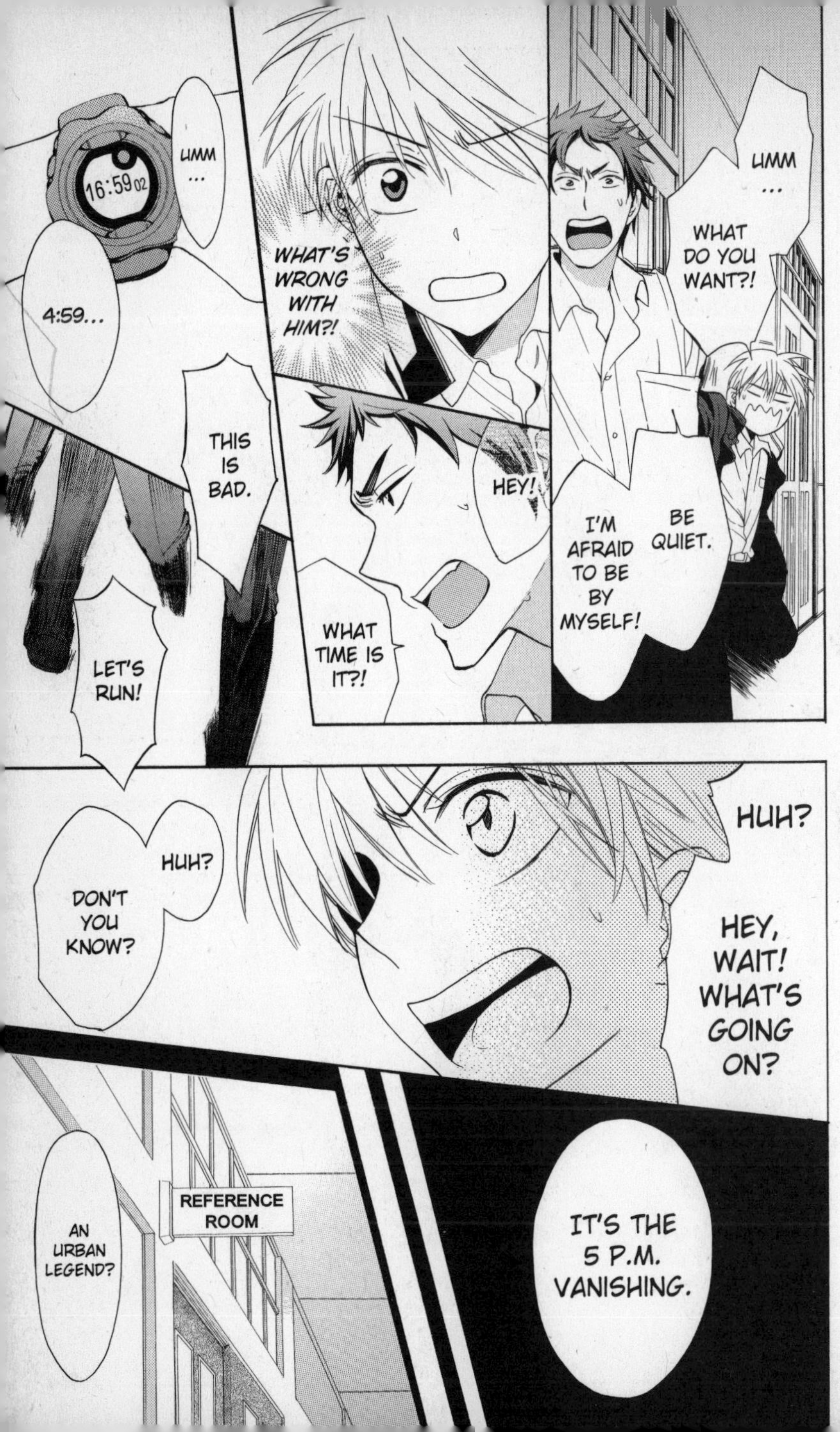
UMM ...
WHAT DO YOU WANT?!
BE QUIET.
I'M AFRAID TO BE BY MYSELF!
WHAT'S WRONG WITH HIM?!
HEY!
WHAT TIME IS IT?!
16:59 02
UMM ...
4:59...
THIS IS BAD.
LET'S RUN!
HUH?
HEY, WAIT! WHAT'S GOING ON?
HUH?
DON'T YOU KNOW?
IT'S THE 5 P.M. VANISHING.
REFERENCE ROOM
AN URBAN LEGEND?

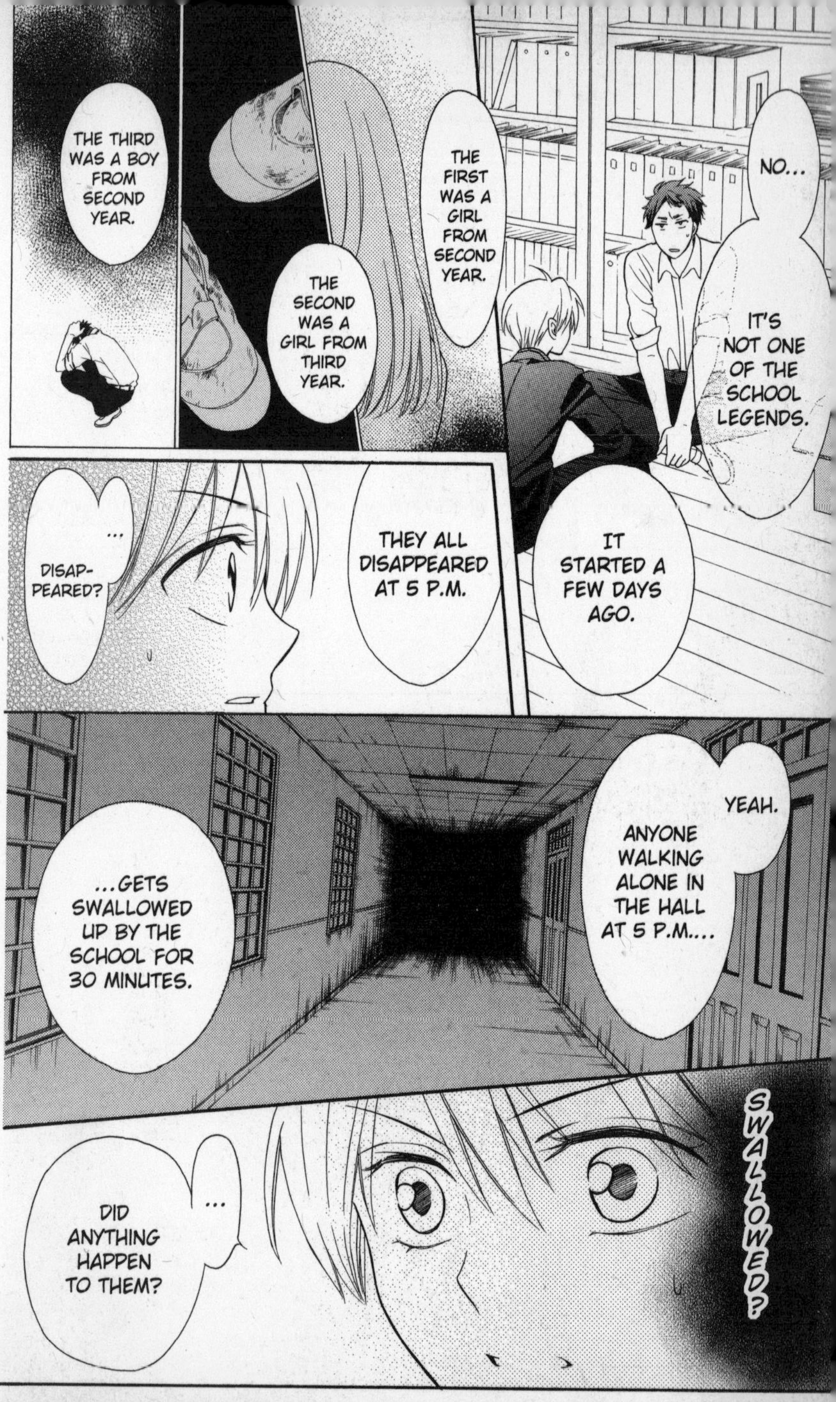
NO... IT'S NOT ONE OF THE SCHOOL LEGENDS.
IT STARTED A FEW DAYS AGO.
THE FIRST WAS A GIRL FROM SECOND YEAR.
THE SECOND WAS A GIRL FROM THIRD YEAR.
THE THIRD WAS A BOY FROM SECOND YEAR.
THEY ALL DISAPPEARED AT 5 P.M.
... DISAP-PEARED?
YEAH. ANYONE WALKING ALONE IN THE HALL AT 5 P.M....
...GETS SWALLOWED UP BY THE SCHOOL FOR 30 MINUTES.
SWALLOWED?
... DID ANYTHING HAPPEN TO THEM?

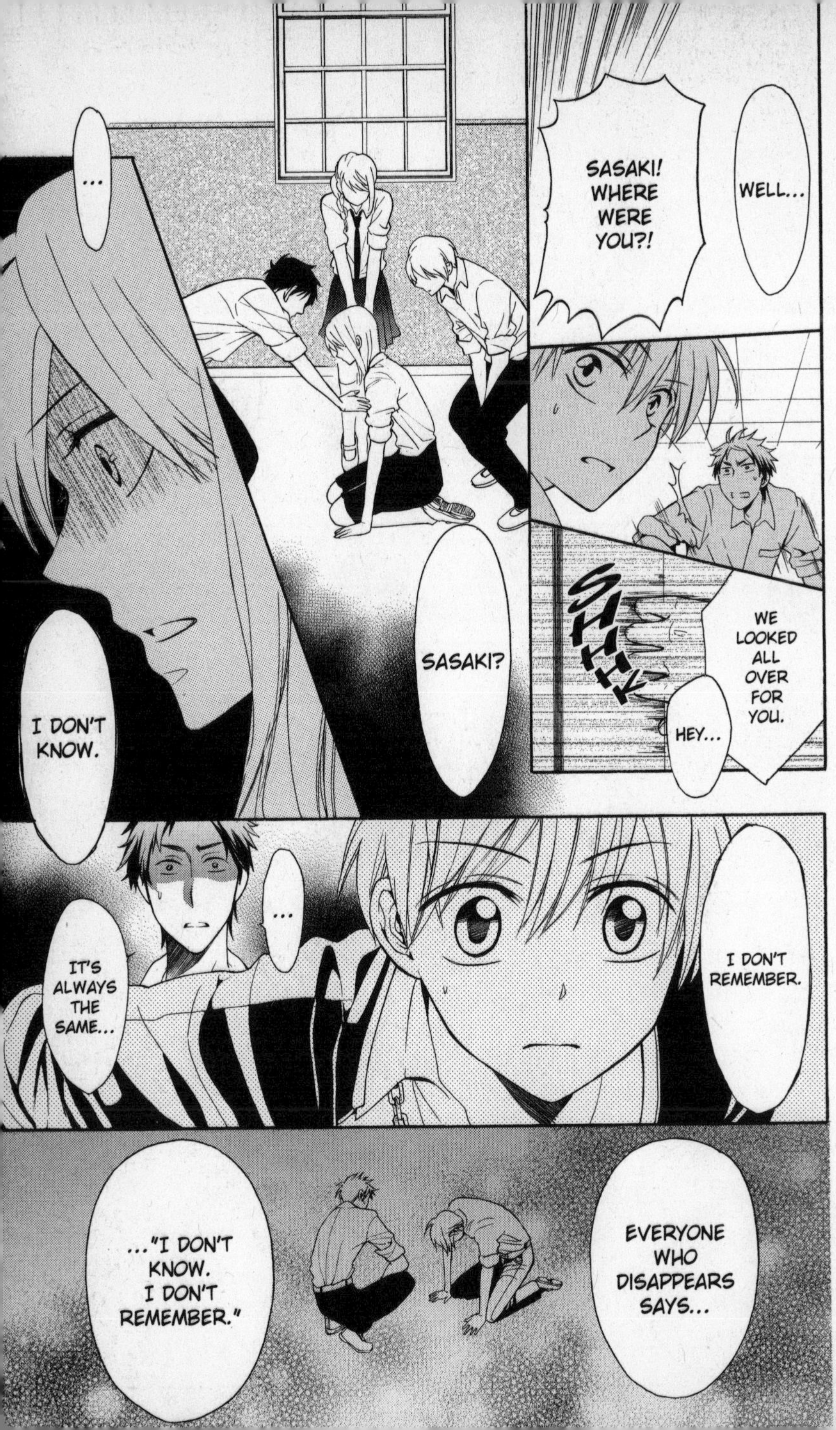
WELL...
SASAKI! WHERE WERE YOU?!
WE LOOKED ALL OVER FOR YOU.
SHHHK
HEY...
SASAKI?
...
I DON'T KNOW.
I DON'T REMEMBER.
...
IT'S ALWAYS THE SAME...
EVERYONE WHO DISAPPEARS SAYS...
..."I DON'T KNOW. I DON'T REMEMBER."

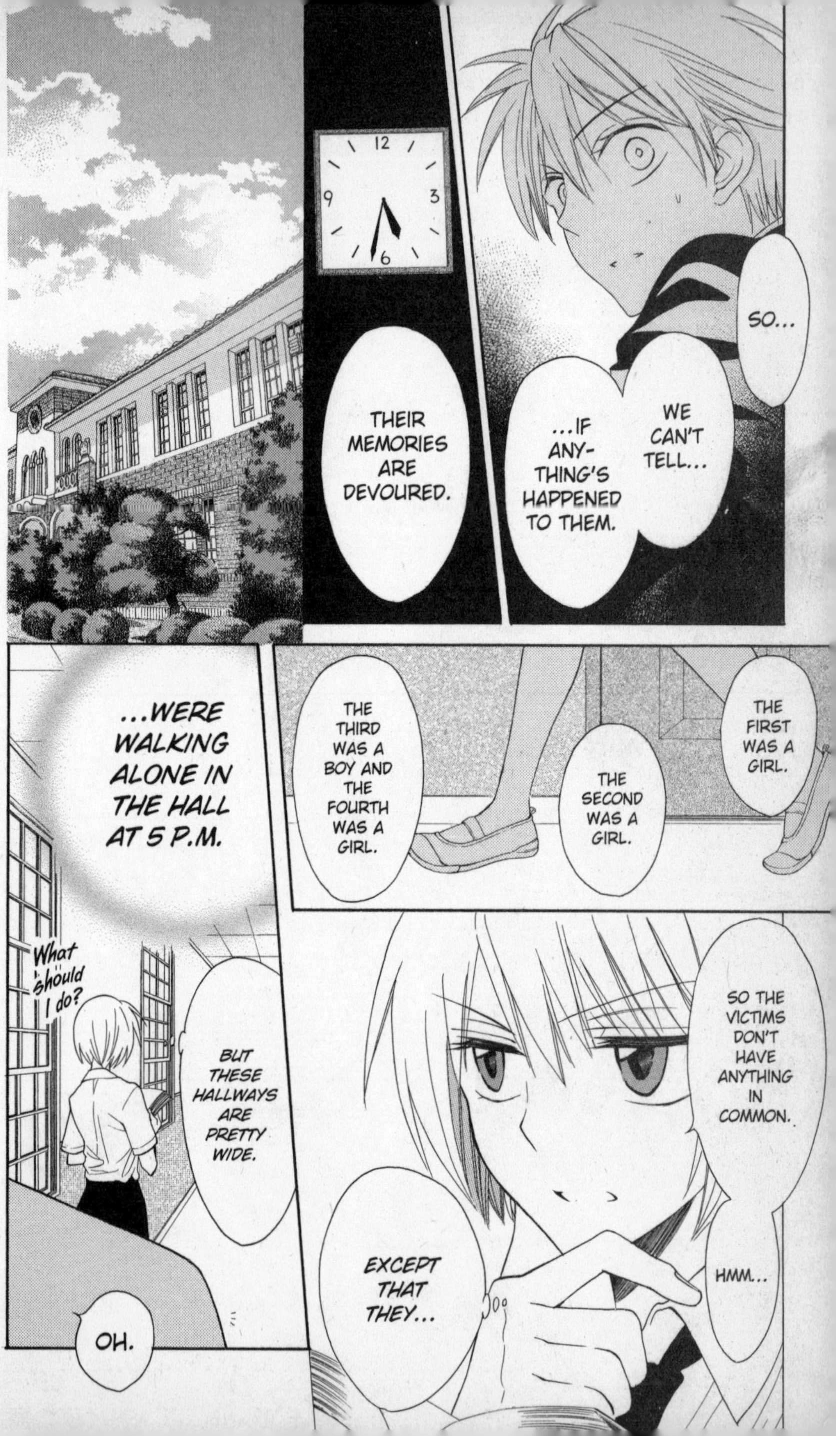
SO...
WE CAN'T TELL...
...IF ANYTHING'S HAPPENED TO THEM.
THEIR MEMORIES ARE DEVOURED.
THE FIRST WAS A GIRL.
THE SECOND WAS A GIRL.
THE THIRD WAS A BOY AND THE FOURTH WAS A GIRL.
SO THE VICTIMS DON'T HAVE ANYTHING IN COMMON.
HMM...
EXCEPT THAT THEY...
...WERE WALKING ALONE IN THE HALL AT 5 P.M.
BUT THESE HALLWAYS ARE PRETTY WIDE.
What should I do?
OH.

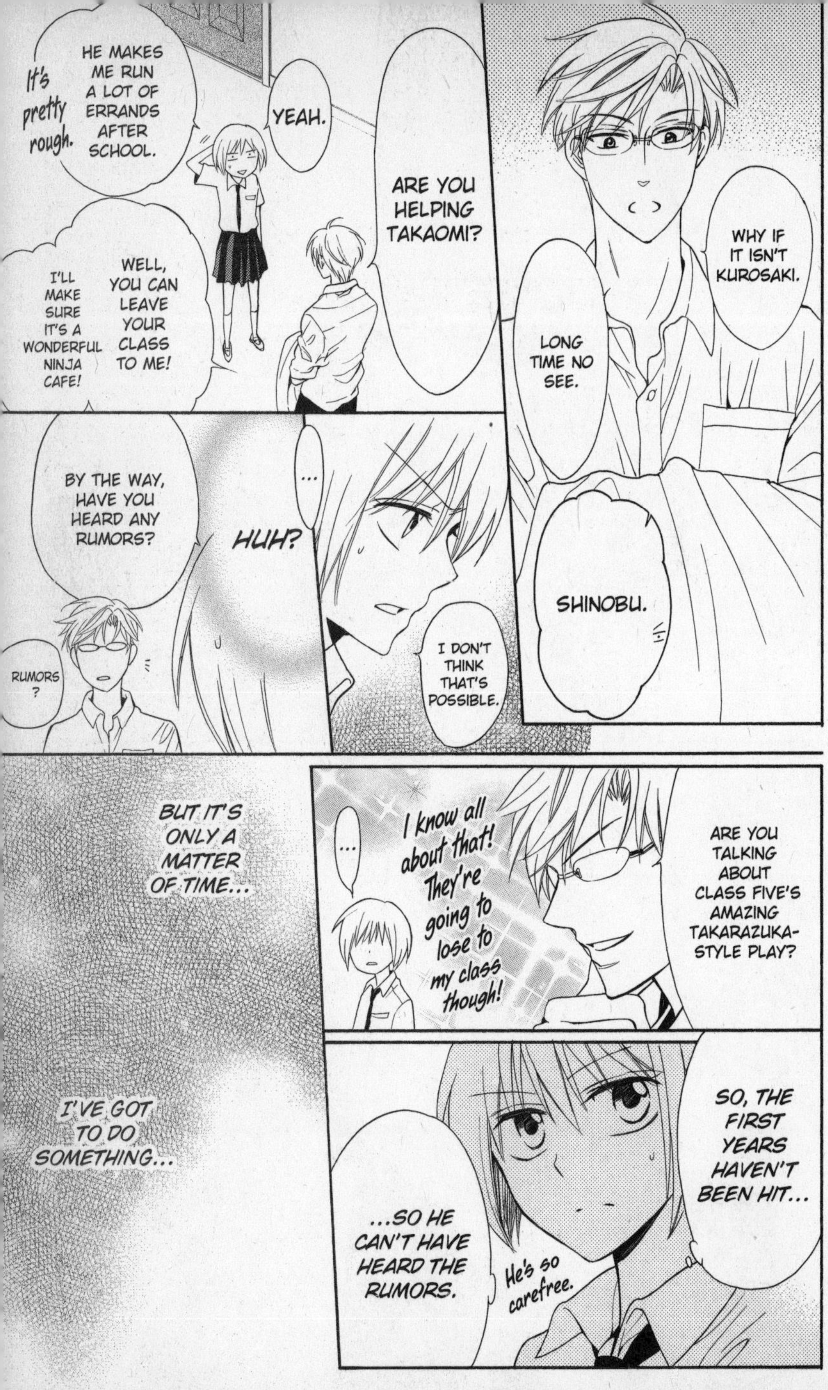

WHY IF IT ISN'T KUROSAKI.
LONG TIME NO SEE.
SHINOBU.
ARE YOU HELPING TAKAOMI?
YEAH.
HE MAKES ME RUN A LOT OF ERRANDS AFTER SCHOOL.
It's pretty rough.
WELL, YOU CAN LEAVE YOUR CLASS TO ME!
I'LL MAKE SURE IT'S A WONDERFUL NINJA CAFE!
...
BY THE WAY, HAVE YOU HEARD ANY RUMORS?
HUH?
I DON'T THINK THAT'S POSSIBLE.
RUMORS?
ARE YOU TALKING ABOUT CLASS FIVE'S AMAZING TAKARAZUKA-STYLE PLAY?
I know all about that! They're going to lose to my class though!
...
SO, THE FIRST YEARS HAVEN'T BEEN HIT...
He's so carefree.
...SO HE CAN'T HAVE HEARD THE RUMORS.
BUT IT'S ONLY A MATTER OF TIME...
I'VE GOT TO DO SOMETHING...

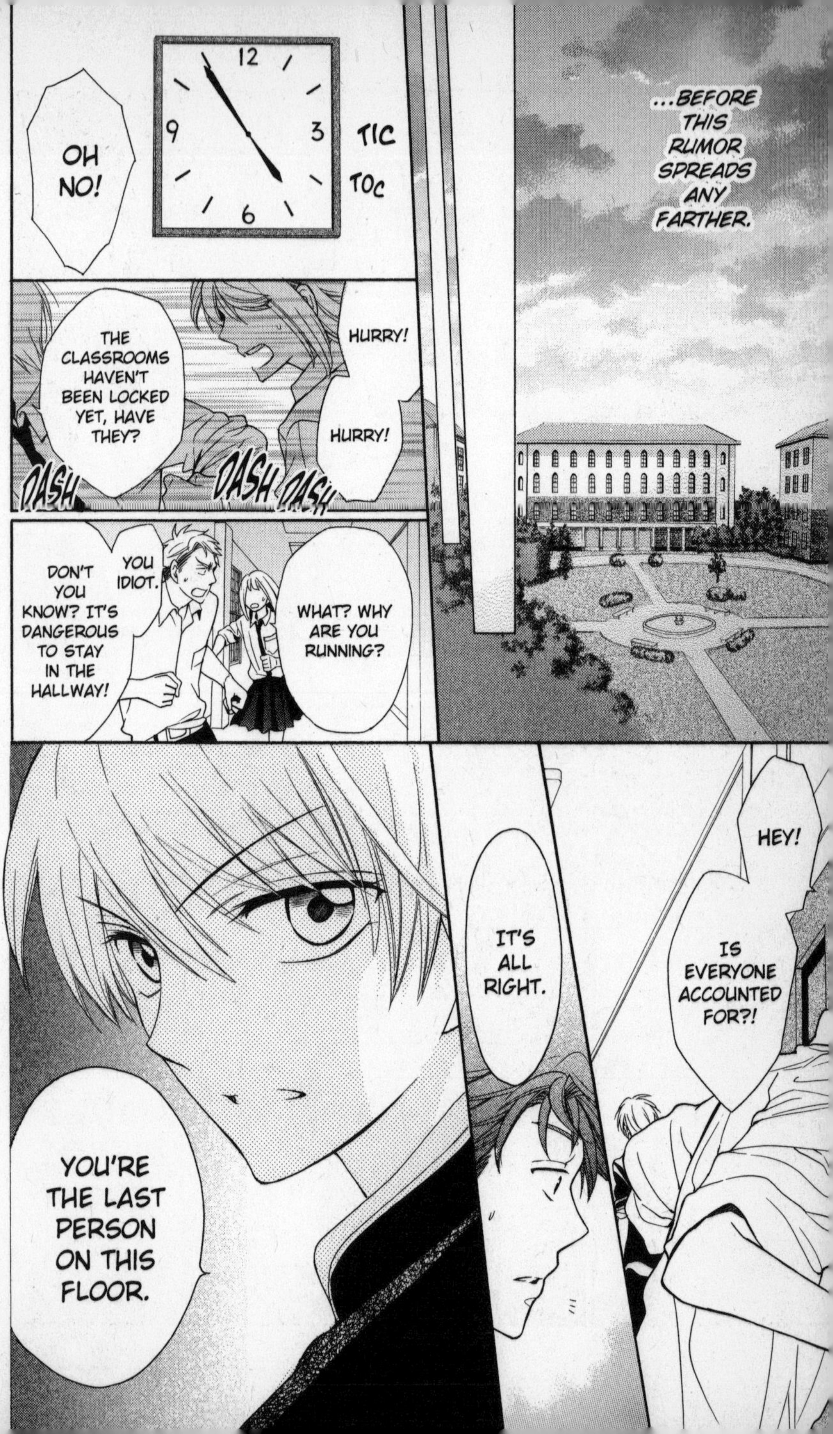
...BEFORE THIS RUMOR SPREADS ANY FARTHER.
TIC
TOC
OH NO!
HURRY!
HURRY!
THE CLASSROOMS HAVEN'T BEEN LOCKED YET, HAVE THEY?
DASH
DASH
DASH
WHAT? WHY ARE YOU RUNNING?
YOU IDIOT.
DON'T YOU KNOW? IT'S DANGEROUS TO STAY IN THE HALLWAY!
HEY!
IS EVERYONE ACCOUNTED FOR?!
IT'S ALL RIGHT.
YOU'RE THE LAST PERSON ON THIS FLOOR.

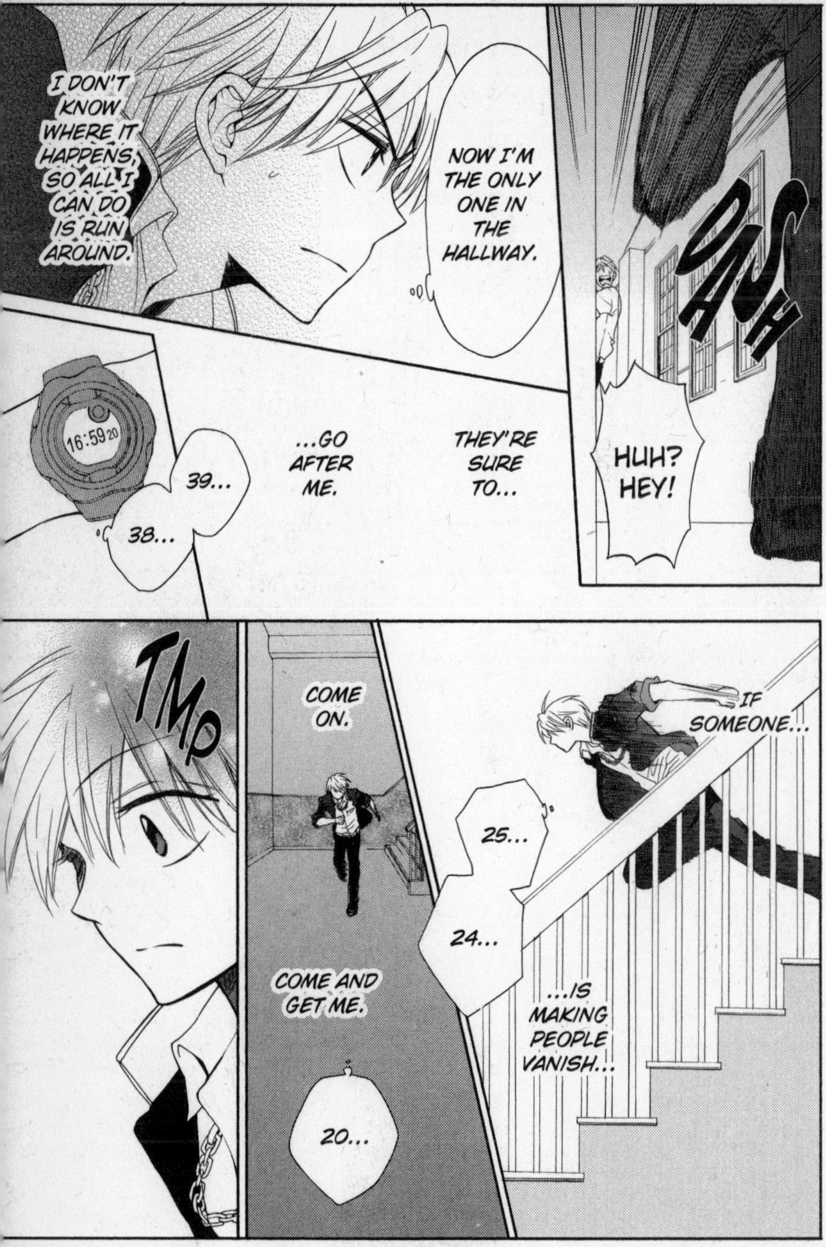
SAH
HUH? HEY!
NOW I'M THE ONLY ONE IN THE HALLWAY.
I DON'T KNOW WHERE IT HAPPENS, SO ALL I CAN DO IS RUN AROUND.
THEY'RE SURE TO...
...GO AFTER ME.
16:59 20
39...
38...
IF SOMEONE...
25...
24...
...IS MAKING PEOPLE VANISH...
COME ON.
COME AND GET ME.
20...
TMP

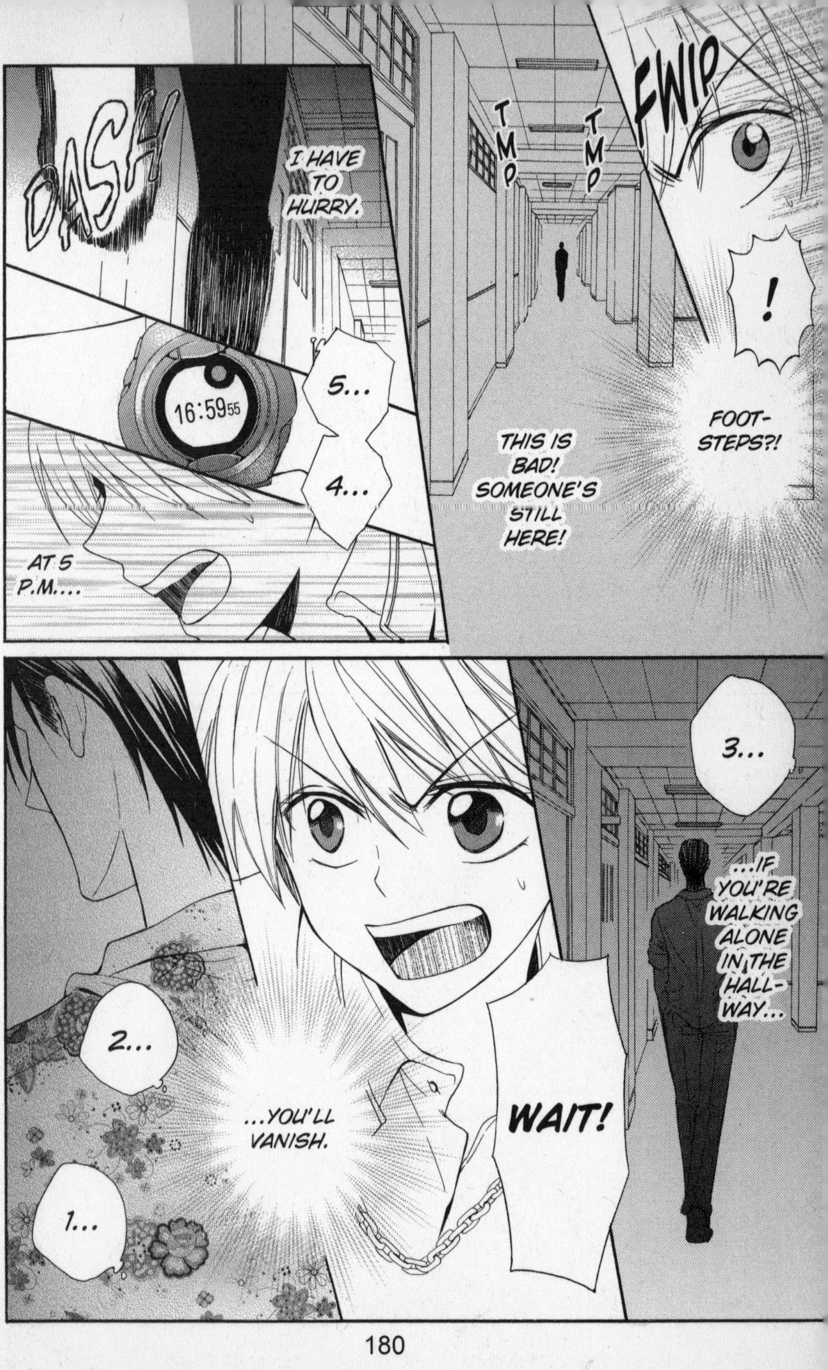
FWIP
!
FOOT-STEPS?!
TMP TMP
THIS IS BAD! SOMEONE'S STILL HERE!
DASH
I HAVE TO HURRY.
16:59 55
5...
4...
AT 5 P.M....
3...
...IF YOU'RE WALKING ALONE IN THE HALL-WAY...
WAIT!
...YOU'LL VANISH.
2...
1...

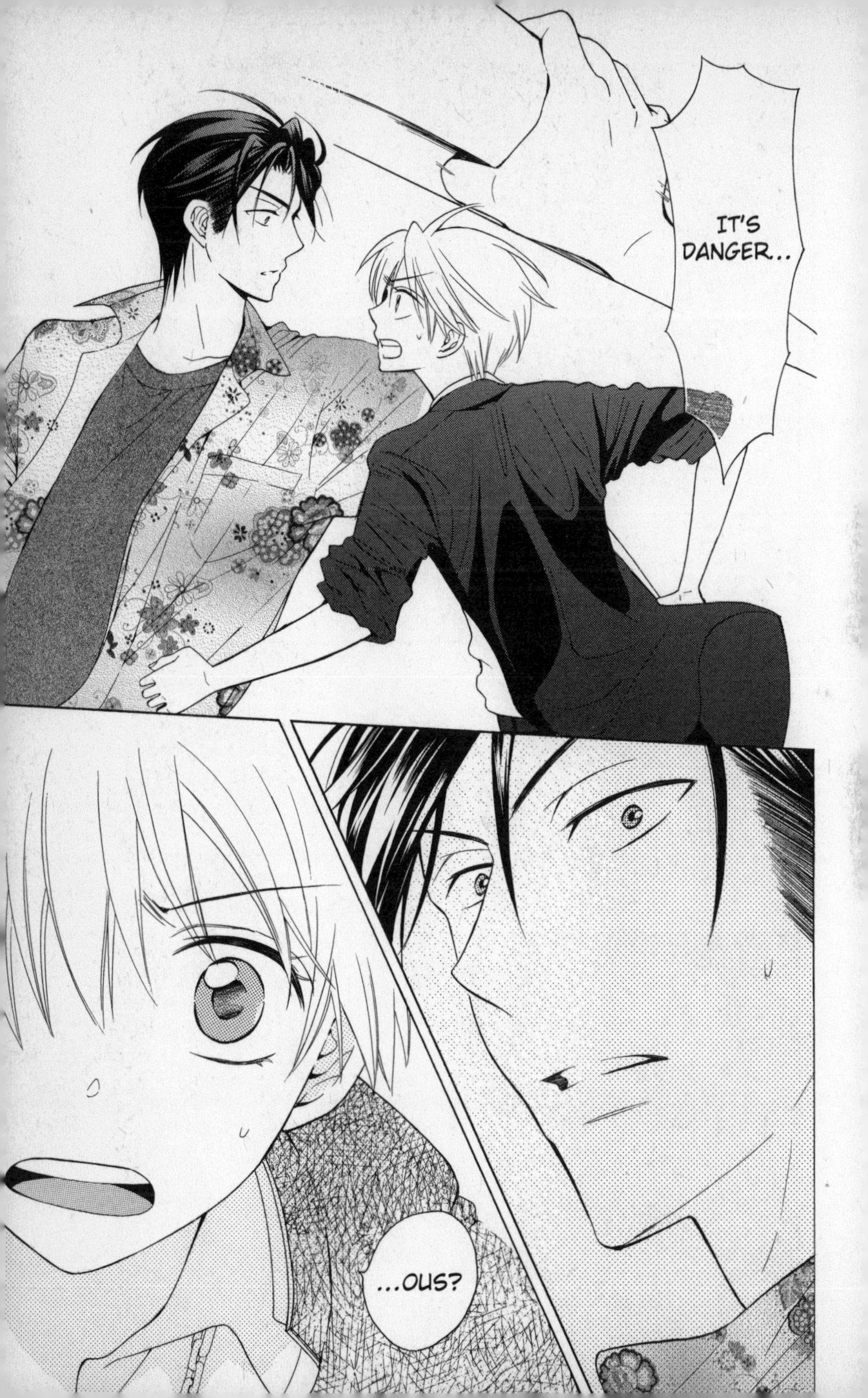
IT'S DANGER...
...OUS?

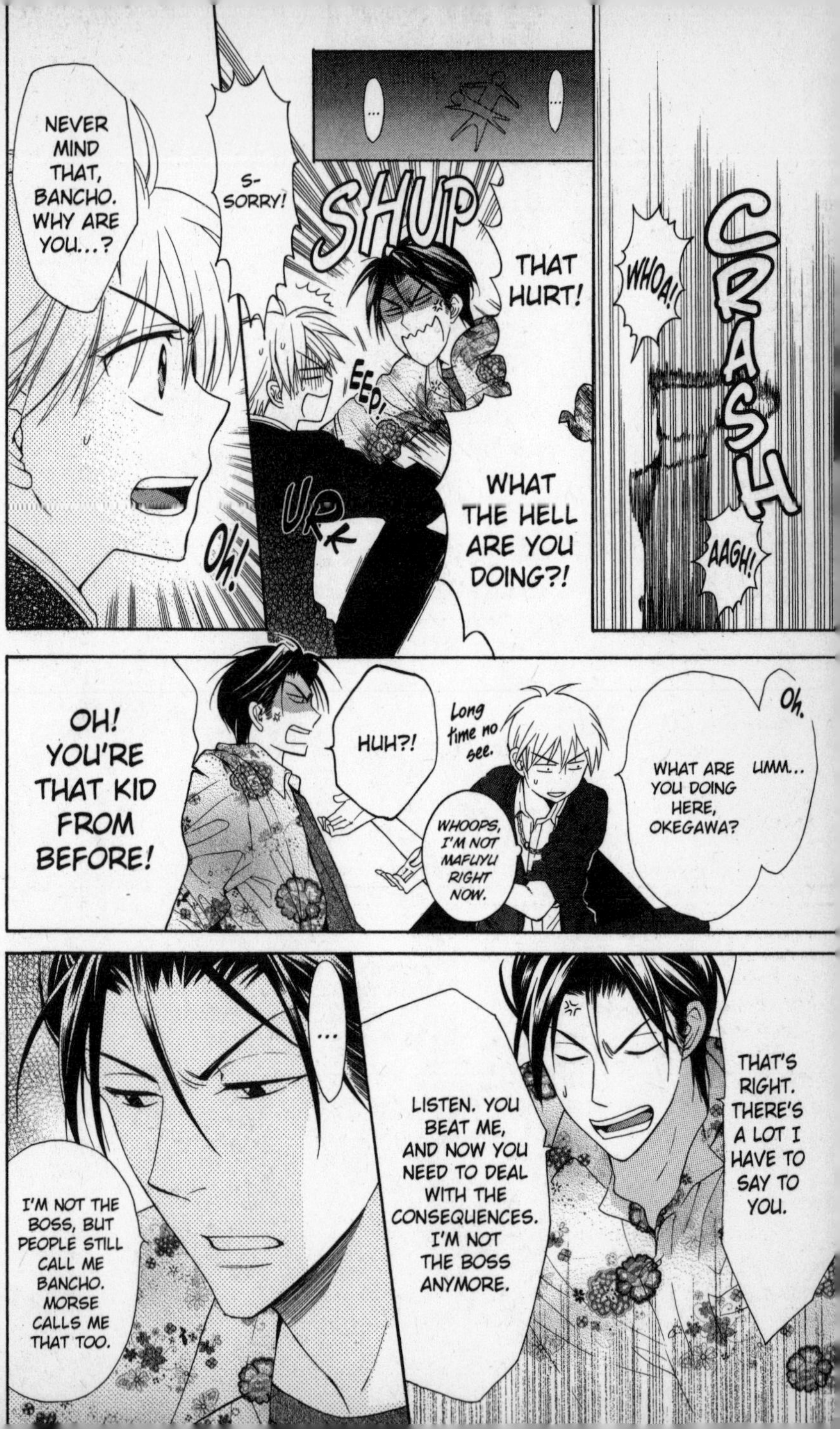
CRASH
WHOA!
AAGH!
...
...
SHUP
THAT HURT!
S-SORRY!
EEP!
WHAT THE HELL ARE YOU DOING?!
URK
Oh!
NEVER MIND THAT, BANCHO. WHY ARE YOU...?
Oh.
UMM...
WHAT ARE YOU DOING HERE, OKEGAWA?
Long time no see.
WHOOPS, I'M NOT MAFUYU RIGHT NOW.
HUH?!
OH! YOU'RE THAT KID FROM BEFORE!
THAT'S RIGHT. THERE'S A LOT I HAVE TO SAY TO YOU.
LISTEN. YOU BEAT ME, AND NOW YOU NEED TO DEAL WITH THE CONSEQUENCES. I'M NOT THE BOSS ANYMORE.
...
I'M NOT THE BOSS, BUT PEOPLE STILL CALL ME BANCHO. MORSE CALLS ME THAT TOO.

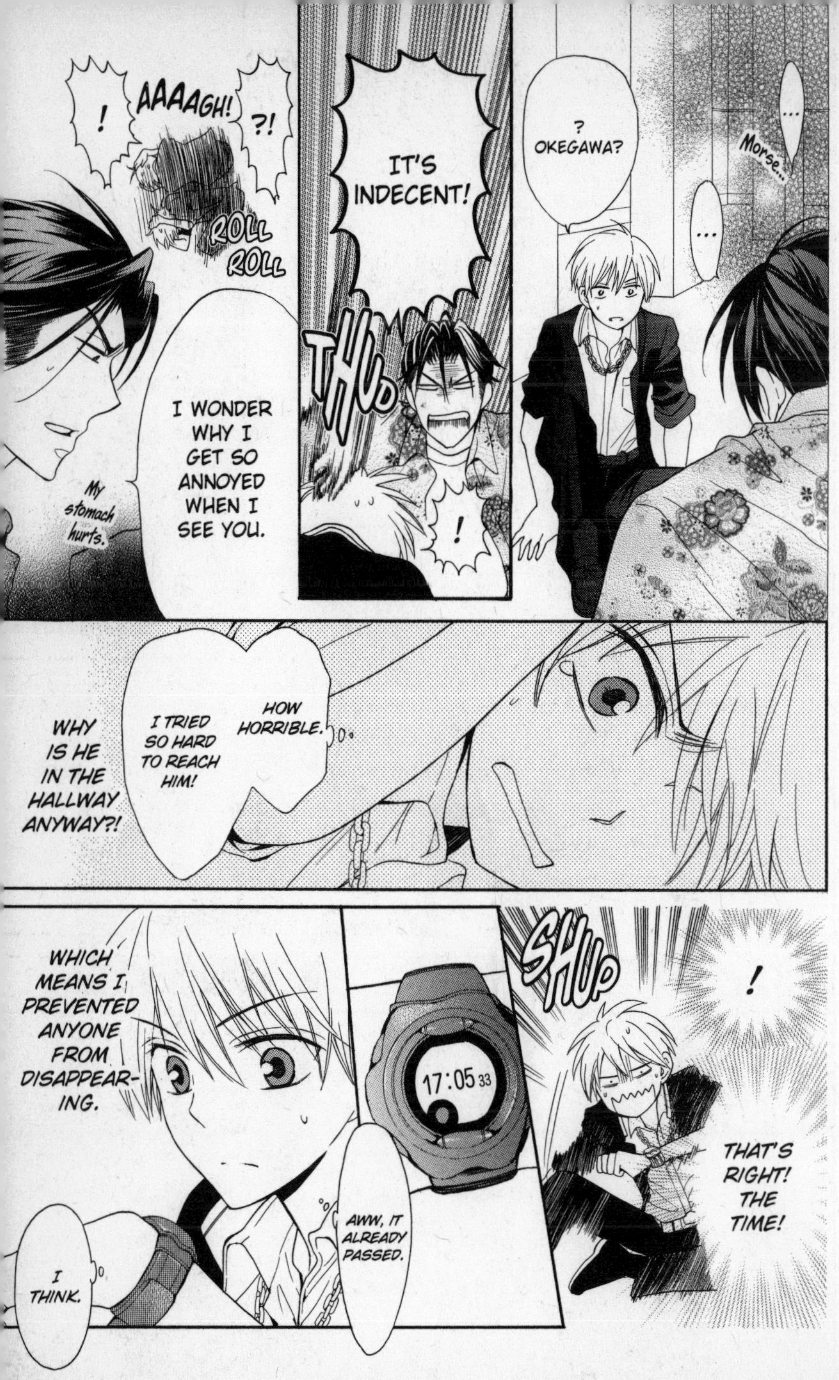
…
Morse…
? OKEGAWA?
…
IT'S INDECENT!
THUD
!
AAAAGH!
!
?!
ROLL ROLL
I WONDER WHY I GET SO ANNOYED WHEN I SEE YOU.
My stomach hurts.
HOW HORRIBLE.
I TRIED SO HARD TO REACH HIM!
WHY IS HE IN THE HALLWAY ANYWAY?!
SHUP
!
THAT'S RIGHT! THE TIME!
17:05 33
AWW, IT ALREADY PASSED.
WHICH MEANS I PREVENTED ANYONE FROM DISAPPEARING.
I THINK.

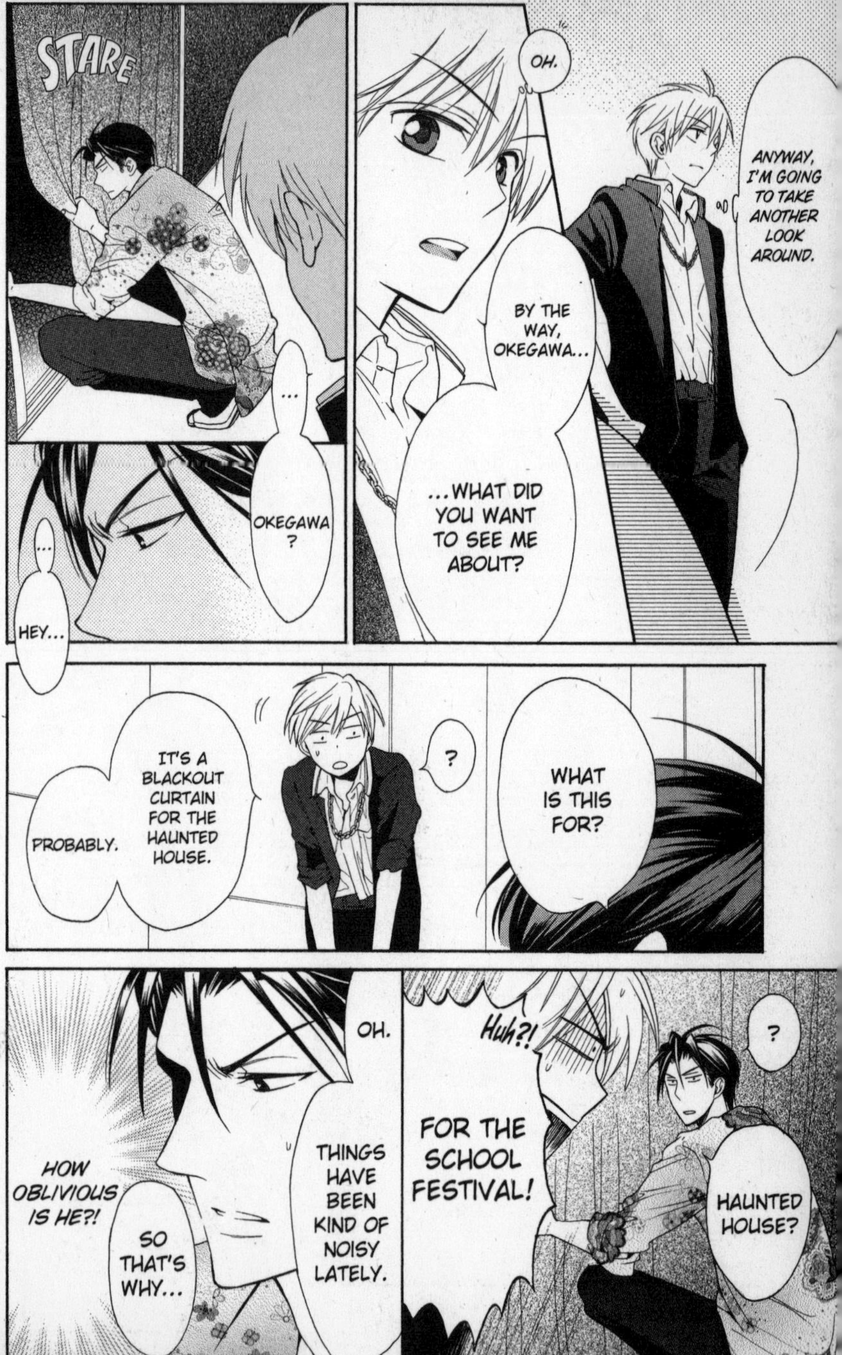
ANYWAY, I'M GOING TO TAKE ANOTHER LOOK AROUND.
OH.
BY THE WAY, OKEGAWA...
...WHAT DID YOU WANT TO SEE ME ABOUT?
STARE
...
OKEGAWA?
...
HEY...
WHAT IS THIS FOR?
?
IT'S A BLACKOUT CURTAIN FOR THE HAUNTED HOUSE.
PROBABLY.
?
HAUNTED HOUSE?
Huh?!
FOR THE SCHOOL FESTIVAL!
OH.
THINGS HAVE BEEN KIND OF NOISY LATELY.
SO THAT'S WHY...
HOW OBLIVIOUS IS HE?!

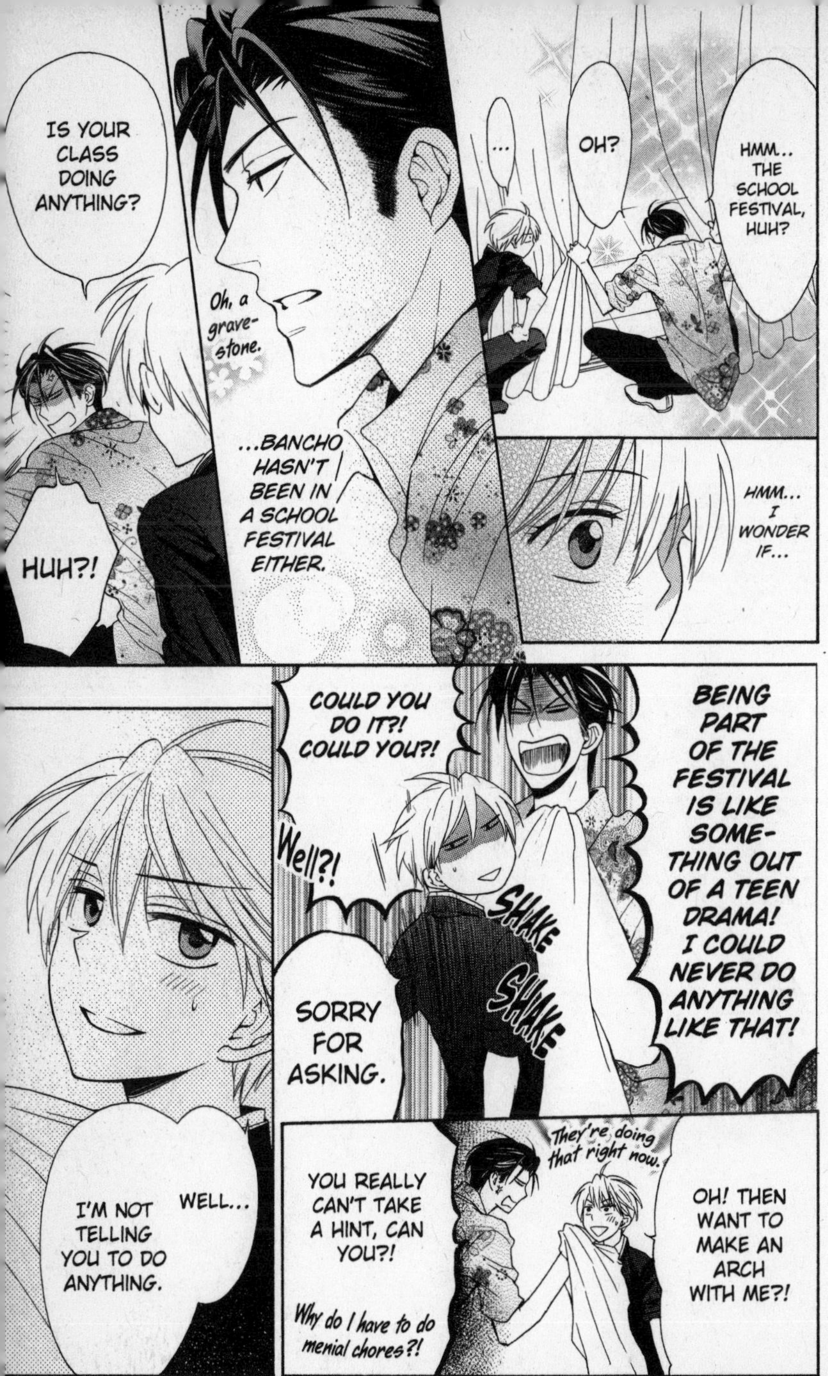
HMM.. THE SCHOOL FESTIVAL, HUH?
OH?
...
HMM... I WONDER IF...
...BANCHO HASN'T BEEN IN A SCHOOL FESTIVAL EITHER.
Oh, a gravestone.
IS YOUR CLASS DOING ANYTHING?
HUH?!
BEING PART OF THE FESTIVAL IS LIKE SOMETHING OUT OF A TEEN DRAMA! I COULD NEVER DO ANYTHING LIKE THAT!
COULD YOU DO IT?! COULD YOU?!
Well?!
SHAKE
SHAKE
SORRY FOR ASKING.
OH! THEN WANT TO MAKE AN ARCH WITH ME?!
They're doing that right now.
YOU REALLY CAN'T TAKE A HINT, CAN YOU?!
Why do I have to do menial chores?!
WELL...
I'M NOT TELLING YOU TO DO ANYTHING.

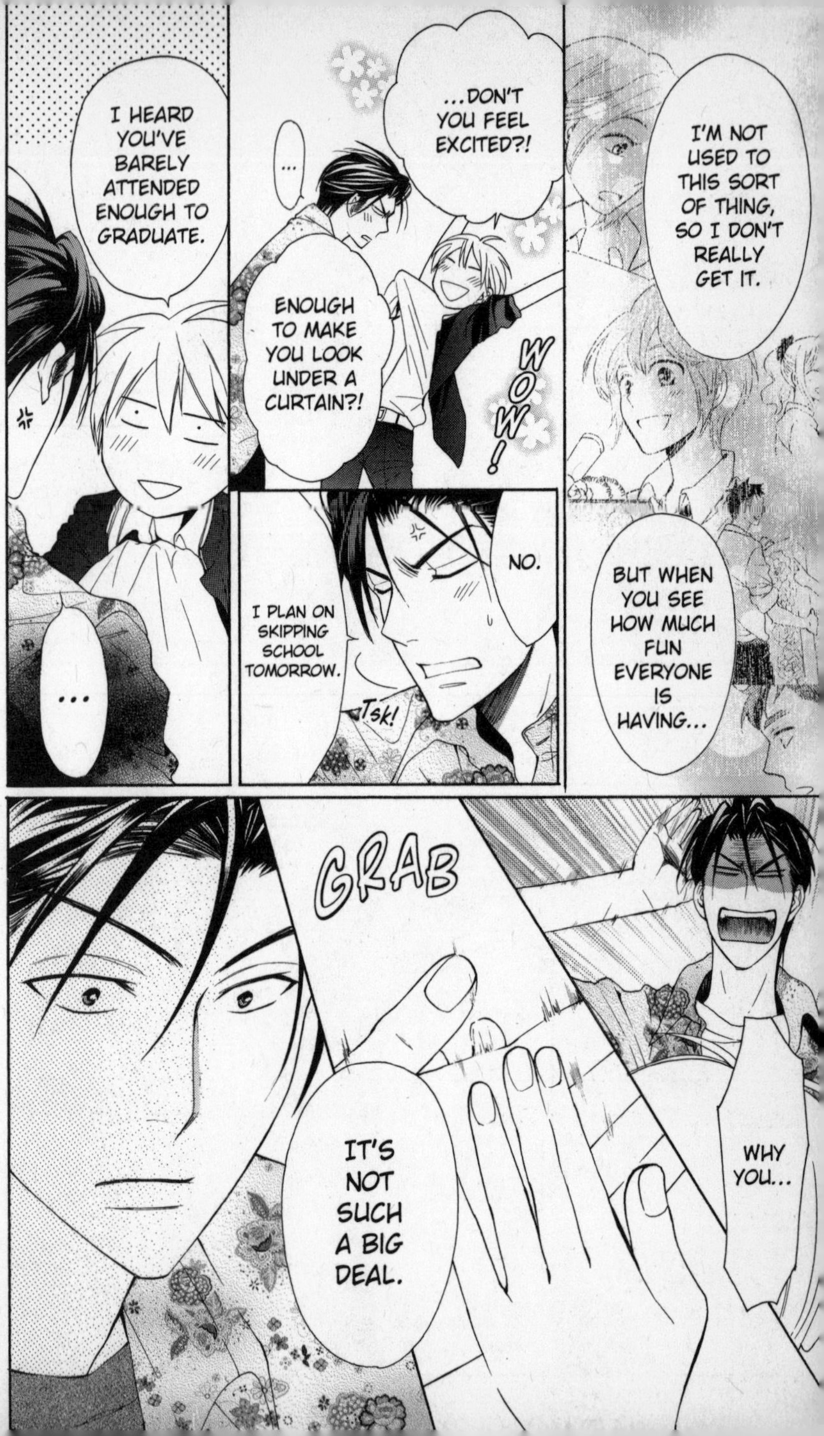
I'M NOT USED TO THIS SORT OF THING, SO I DON'T REALLY GET IT.
BUT WHEN YOU SEE HOW MUCH FUN EVERYONE IS HAVING...
...DON'T YOU FEEL EXCITED?!
...
WOW!
ENOUGH TO MAKE YOU LOOK UNDER A CURTAIN?!
NO.
I PLAN ON SKIPPING SCHOOL TOMORROW.
Tsk!
I HEARD YOU'VE BARELY ATTENDED ENOUGH TO GRADUATE.
...
GRAB
WHY YOU...
IT'S NOT SUCH A BIG DEAL.

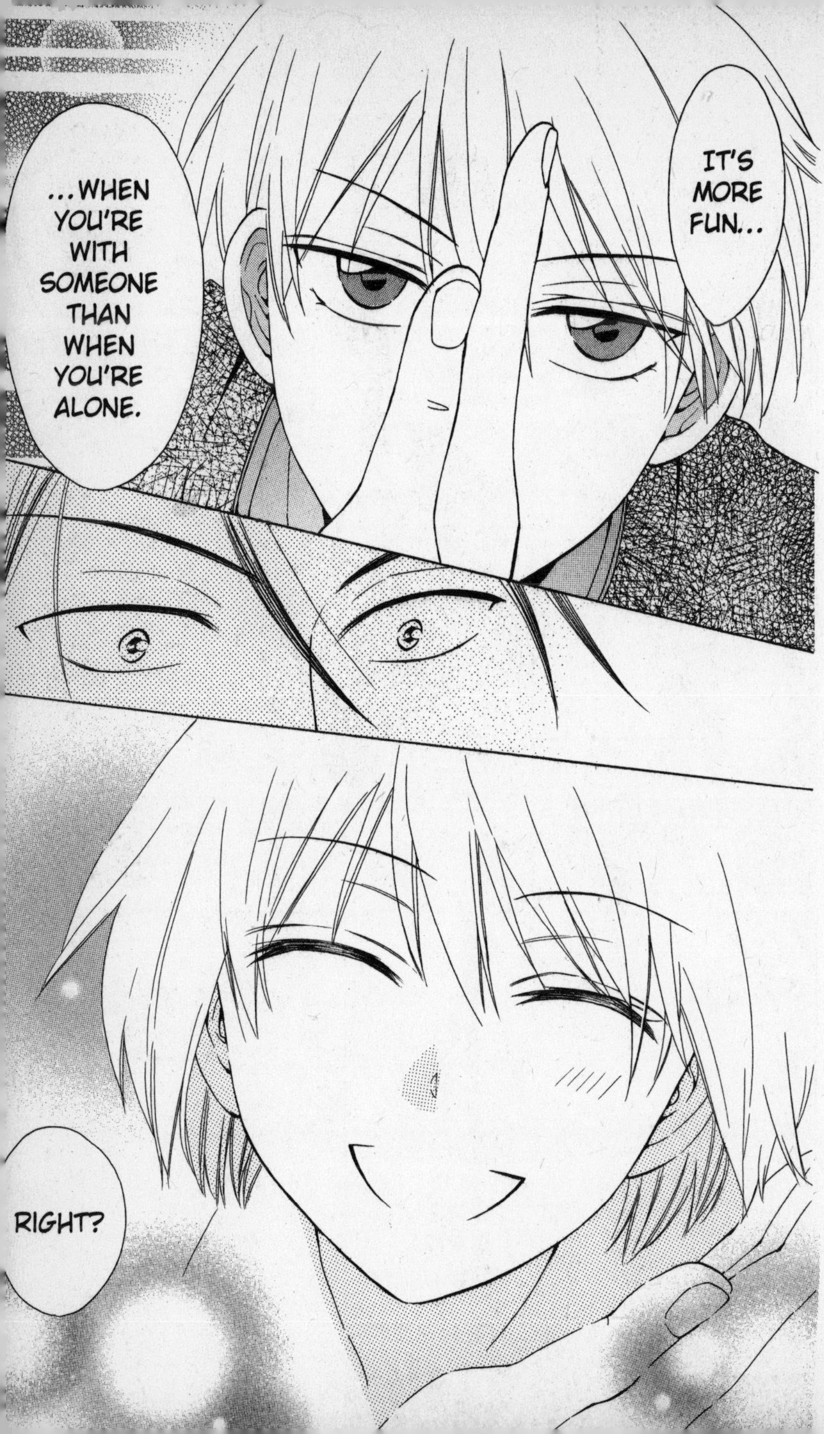
IT'S MORE FUN...
...WHEN YOU'RE WITH SOMEONE THAN WHEN YOU'RE ALONE.
RIGHT?

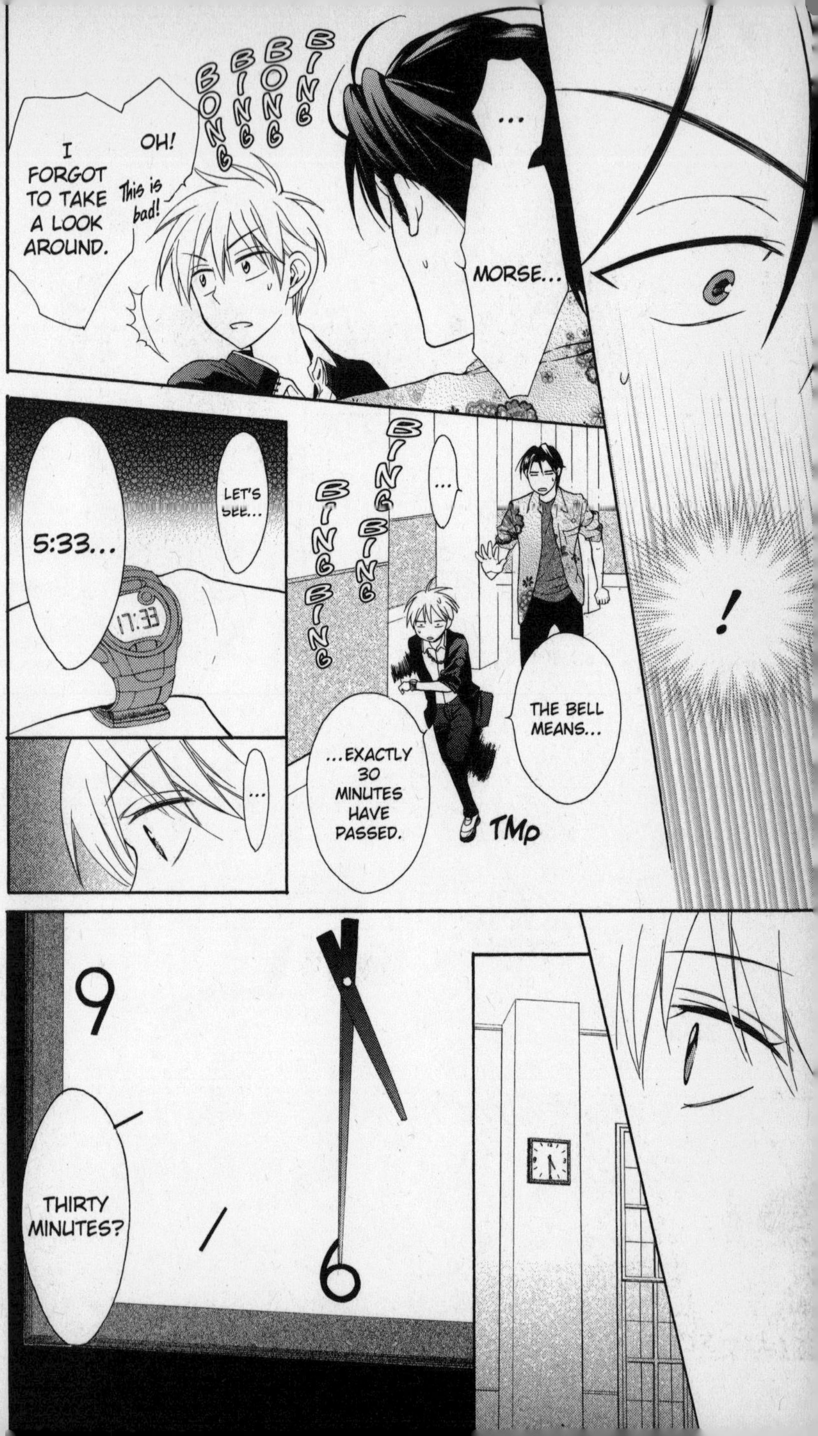
BING
BONG
BING
BONG
...
MORSE...
OH!
This is bad!
I FORGOT TO TAKE A LOOK AROUND.
!
BING BING
BING BING
...
THE BELL MEANS...
...EXACTLY 30 MINUTES HAVE PASSED.
TMP
LET'S SEE...
5:33...
17:33
...
THIRTY MINUTES?

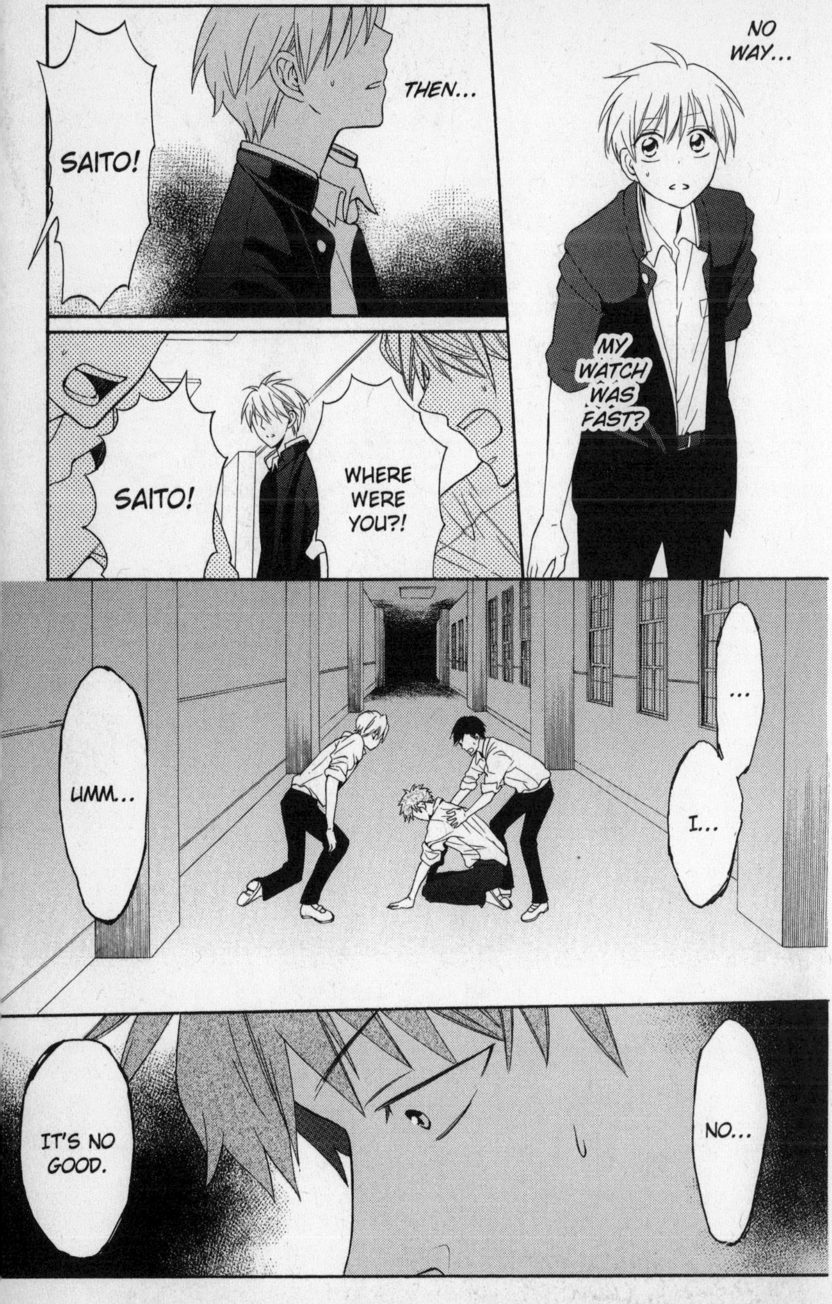
NO WAY...
MY WATCH WAS FAST?
THEN...
SAITO!
WHERE WERE YOU?!
SAITO!
...
I...
UMM...
NO...
IT'S NO GOOD.

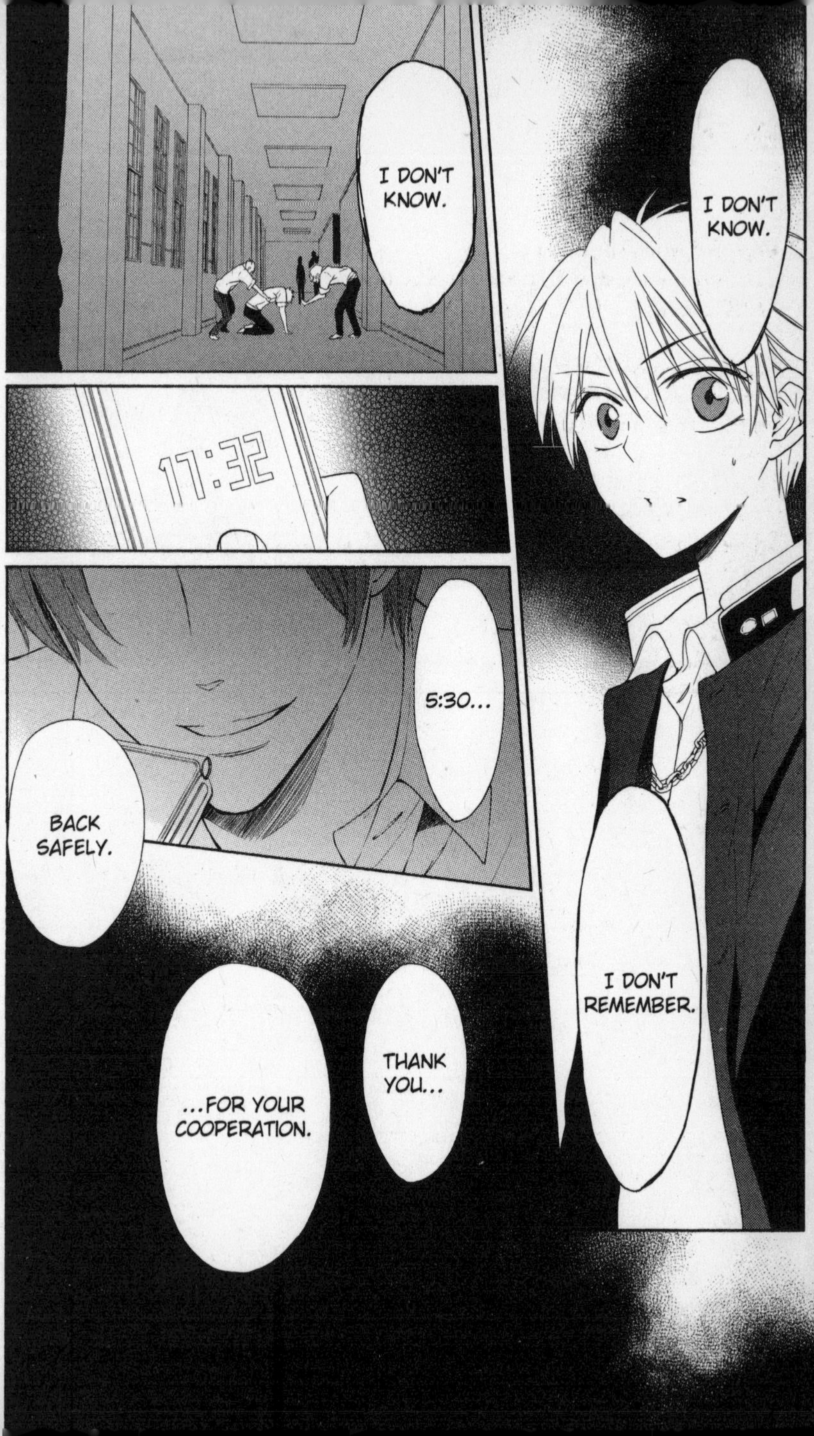
I DON'T KNOW.
I DON'T REMEMBER.
I DON'T KNOW.
17:32
5:30...
BACK SAFELY.
THANK YOU...
...FOR YOUR COOPERATION.

End Notes

Page 75, panel 3: Bancho
The leader of a unit, in this case the head of a gang of delinquents.

Page 95, panel 1: Garnish
Katsuramuki, a method of slicing daikon radishes or carrots into thin sheets.

Page 157, panel 1: School festival
Most Japanese schools hold a yearly cultural festival where each class creates a booth, such as a café or rummage sale.

Page 177, panel 5: Takarazuka
Takarazuka is a famous theater troupe made up solely of women.

Izumi Tsubaki began drawing manga in her first year of high school. She was soon selected to be in the top ten of *Hana to Yume's* HMC (*Hana to Yume* Mangaka Course), and subsequently won *Hana to Yume's* Big Challenge contest. Her debut title, *Chijimete Distance* (Shrink the Distance), ran in 2002 in *Hana to Yume* magazine, issue 17. Her other works include *The Magic Touch* (*Oyayubi kara Romance*) and *Oresama Teacher*, which she is currently working on.

ORESAMA TEACHER
Vol. 8
Shojo Beat Edition

STORY AND ART BY
Izumi Tsubaki

English Translation & Adaptation/JN Productions
Touch-up Art & Lettering/Eric Erbes
Design/Yukiko Whitley
Editor/Pancha Diaz

Printed in the U.S.A.

Published by VIZ Media, LLC
P.O. Box 77010
San Francisco, CA 94107

10 9 8 7 6 5 4 3 2 1
First printing, May 2012

www.viz.com   www.shojobeat.com

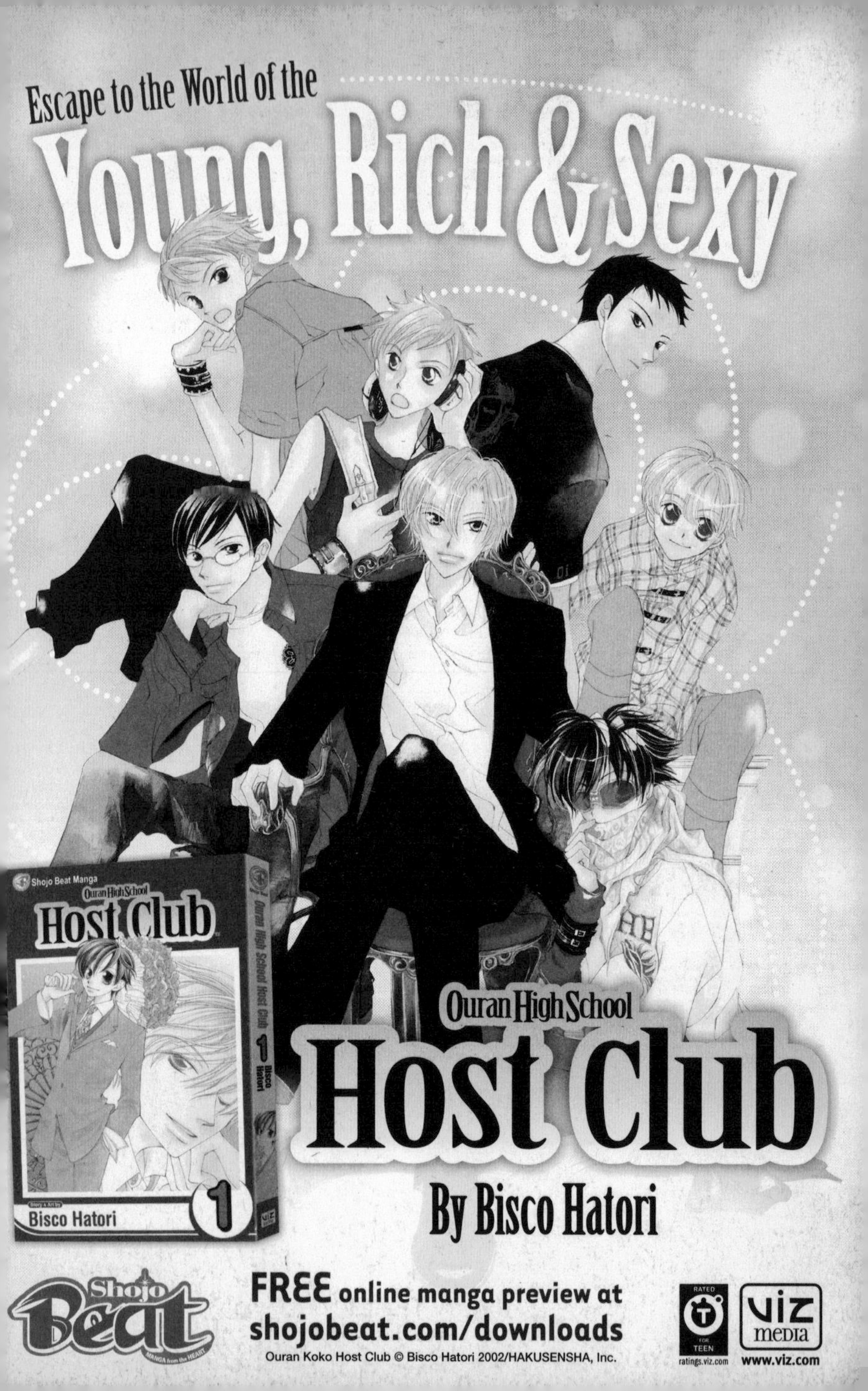

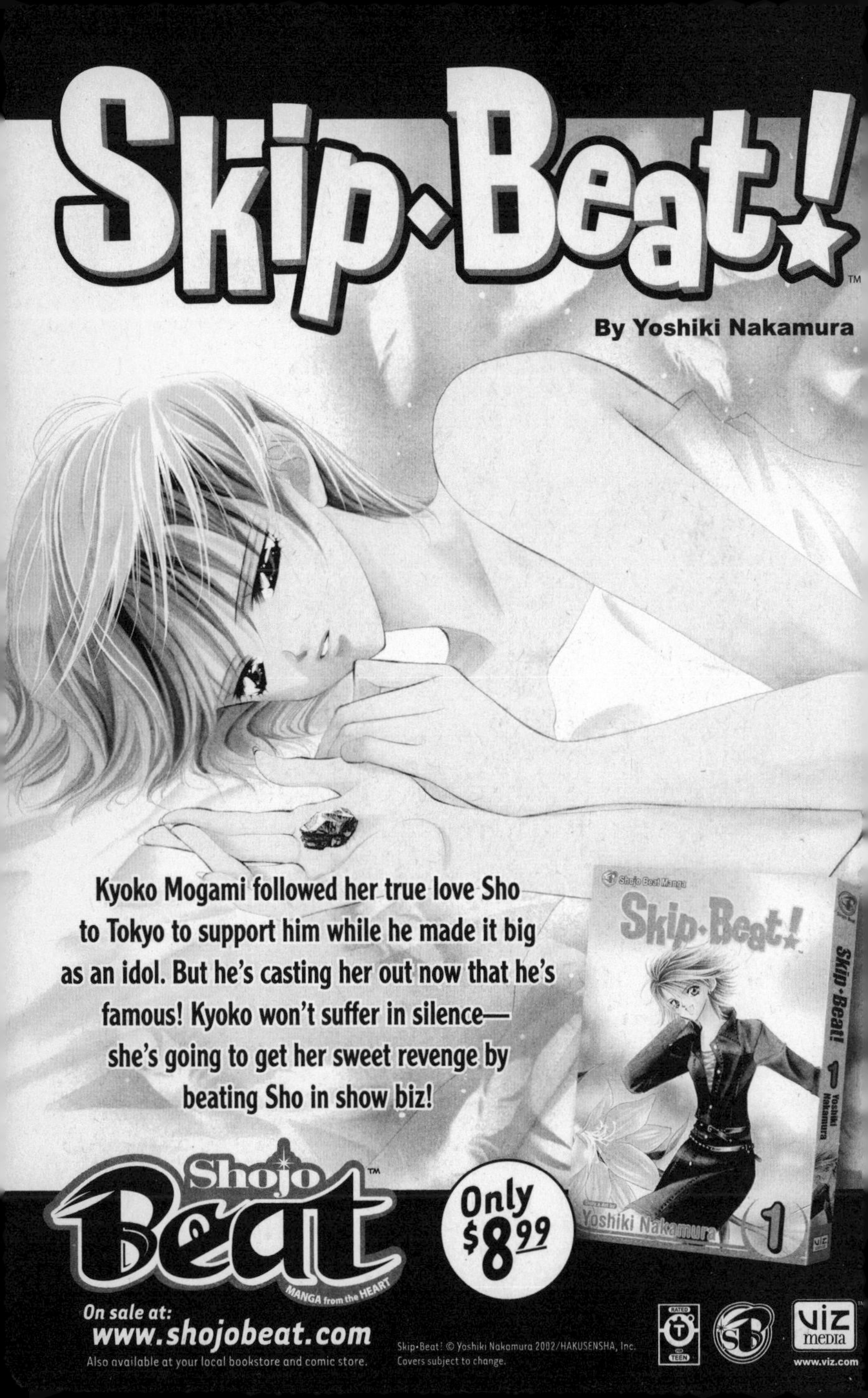
Skip·Beat!™
By Yoshiki Nakamura
Kyoko Mogami followed her true love Sho to Tokyo to support him while he made it big as an idol. But he's casting her out now that he's famous! Kyoko won't suffer in silence— she's going to get her sweet revenge by beating Sho in show biz!
Shojo Beat™
MANGA from the HEART
Only $8.99
Shojo Beat Manga
Skip·Beat!
1
Yoshiki Nakamura
On sale at:
www.shojobeat.com
Also available at your local bookstore and comic store.
Skip·Beat! © Yoshiki Nakamura 2002/HAKUSENSHA, Inc.
Covers subject to change.
RATED T TEEN
VIZ media
www.viz.com

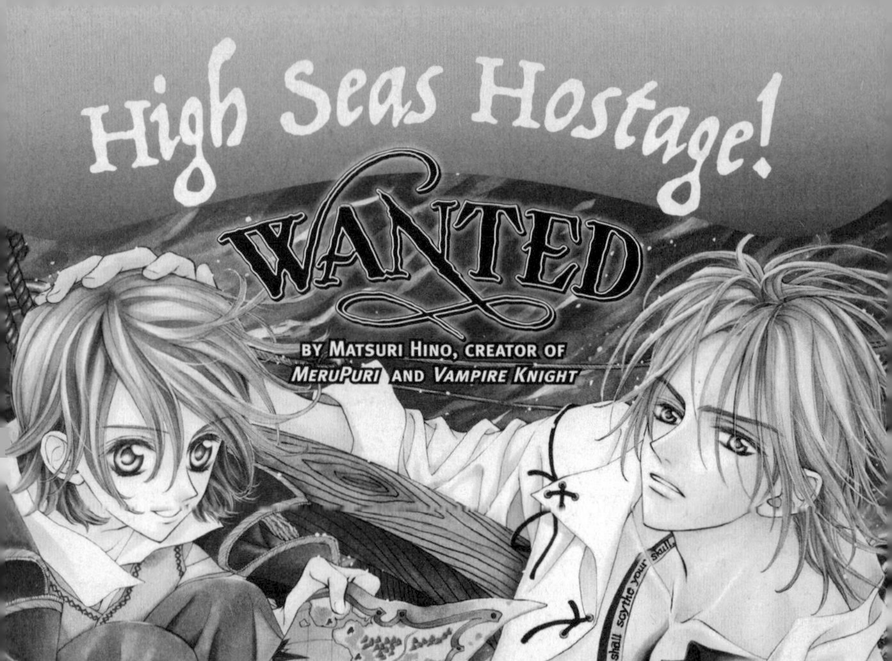
High Seas Hostage!
WANTED
BY MATSURI HINO, CREATOR OF
MERUPURI AND VAMPIRE KNIGHT
Death shall scythe your skull
a real treasure

In search of her kidnapped first love, Armeria disguises herself as a boy to join the crew of the pirate ship that abducted him. What will happen when the former songstress' cross-dressing cover is blown?

FIND OUT IN *WANTED*—MANGA ON SALE NOW!

On sale at **www.shojobeat.com**
Also available at your local bookstore and comic store

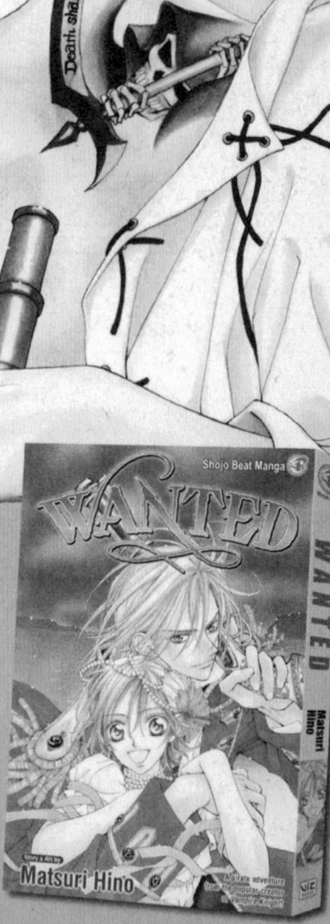
Shojo Beat Manga
WANTED
WANTED
Matsuri Hino
Matsuri Hino

viz media
www.viz.com
RATED T+ FOR OLDER TEEN
ratings.viz.com
Shojo Beat

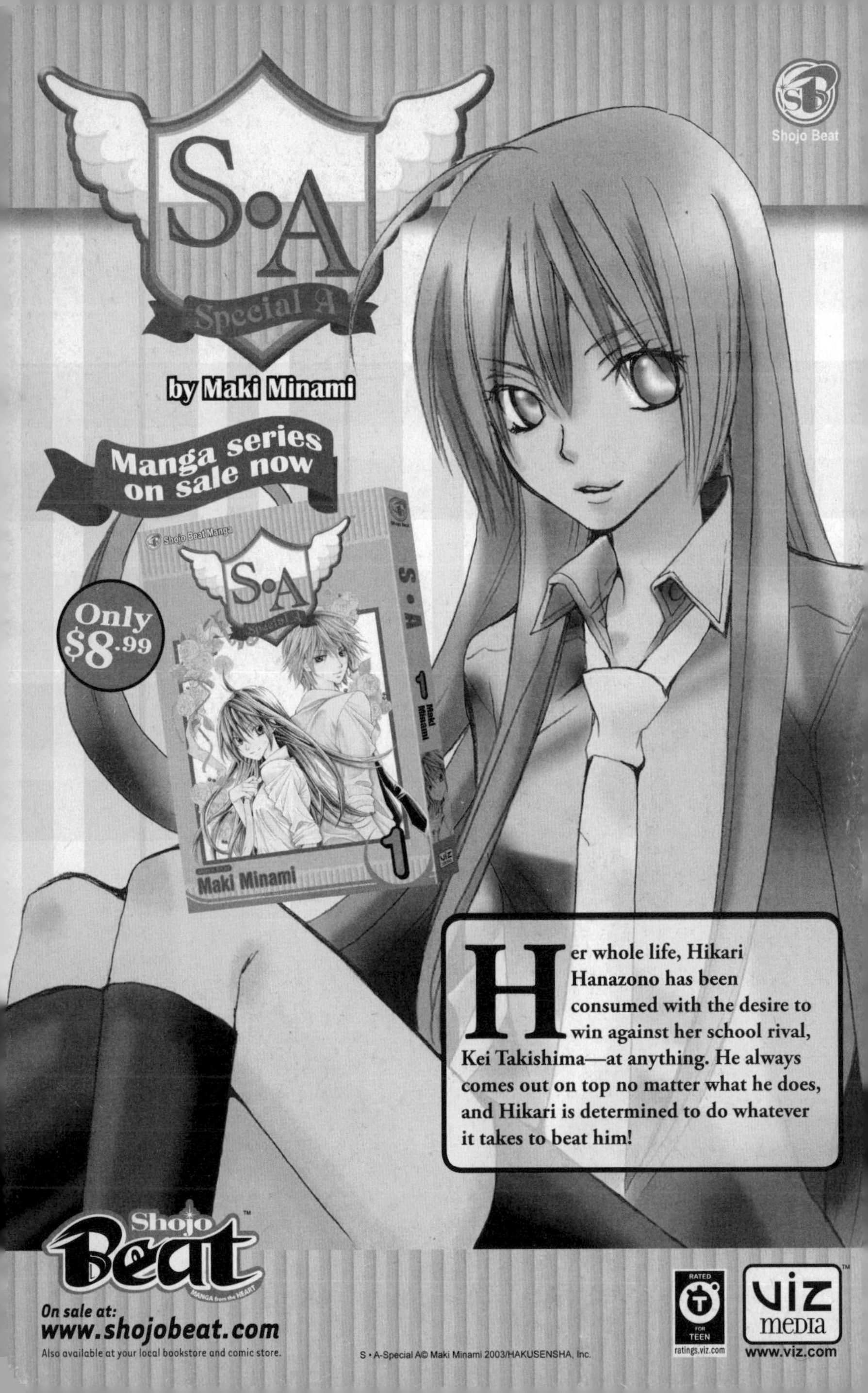
Shojo Beat
S•A
Special A
by Maki Minami
Manga series on sale now
Only $8.99
Shojo Beat Manga
S•A
1
Maki Minami
Her whole life, Hikari Hanazono has been consumed with the desire to win against her school rival, Kei Takishima—at anything. He always comes out on top no matter what he does, and Hikari is determined to do whatever it takes to beat him!
Shojo Beat™
MANGA from the HEART
On sale at:
www.shojobeat.com
Also available at your local bookstore and comic store.
S • A-Special A© Maki Minami 2003/HAKUSENSHA, Inc.
RATED T FOR TEEN
ratings.viz.com
VIZ media
www.viz.com

Don't Hide What's *Inside*

OTOMEN

by **AYA KANNO**

Despite his tough jock exterior, Asuka Masamune harbors a secret love for sewing, shojo manga, and all things girly. But when he finds himself drawn to his domestically inept classmate Ryo, his carefully crafted persona is put to the test. Can Asuka ever show his true self to anyone, much less to the girl he's falling for?

Find out in the *Otomen* manga—buy yours today!